THE PSYCHOLOGY
OF RELIGION

THE MACMILLAN COMPANY
NEW YORK · CHICAGO
DALLAS · ATLANTA · SAN FRANCISCO
LONDON · MANILA

IN CANADA
BRETT-MACMILLAN LTD.
GALT, ONTARIO

THE PSYCHOLOGY
OF RELIGION

*An Introduction to Religious
Experience and Behavior*

WALTER HOUSTON CLARK
DEAN AND PROFESSOR OF PSYCHOLOGY
HARTFORD SCHOOL OF RELIGIOUS EDUCATION
HARTFORD SEMINARY FOUNDATION

New York
THE MACMILLAN COMPANY

Printed in the United States of America

Second Printing 1959

Library of Congress catalog card number: 58-5210

TO

GORDON W. ALLPORT

Teacher, Critic, Friend

PREFACE

This book has been written in response to a need for an up-to-date, comprehensive treatment of the field of the psychology of religion. Recently there has been much work done in the area of religion and mental health, but other areas of the general field have been neglected. I have not omitted the important subject of religion and mental health, but I have tried to make my coverage full and inclusive. Consequently the reader will find something said about nearly all the important areas, though obviously none could be treated exhaustively in a survey volume.

In my subtitle I have called my work an "introduction." The intent has been not so much to present a study of high creativity or originality as to define and describe the field. Hence the reader will find that I have leaned heavily on the works of others in my search for ideas that will help to conceptualize the subject. A further aim has been to introduce students and readers to the important works and theorists of the psychology of religion. The book is up-to-date in the sense that I have preferred the contemporary wherever it seems to represent a real advance over an older psychology. But rather than be merely up-to-date, I have preferred to use studies and concepts that seem useful and significant. Hence recent neglect of the psychology of religion has sometimes forced me as far back as the turn of the century to that incomparable volume, *The Varieties of Religious Experience* by William James, and to other studies of the time. I want my book to be modern but durable as well. Above all I want it to make sense.

The reader will find here the elements of a consistent theory of the place of religion in personality. But in the eclecticism of my approach a final consistency will not appear. The psychology of religion has not advanced to that place where the materials are at hand for such a consistent theory, and I have been unwilling to impose this on my subject matter prematurely. Yet I hope that my book may help to bring this desirable result a bit closer. I have tried to point out significance in the field wherever I could find it. Others will have to separate the dross in the book from what appears to them the gold, and so further refine its psychological concepts. I am merely guiding along the way as far as I can the psychological traveler who wishes to explore religion. I trust that for most it will be a little farther than they have been before.

Finally, I have tried to write as well as I could, to be clear without simplifying too much, to isolate and yet show the relationship of the isolated material to neighboring fields. Furthermore, having suffered from that affliction of the conventional scholar, dullness, I have been at some pains to try to escape here and there from the owlish solemnity of the possessor of a Ph.D. This is partly because I do not wish students to find my work an excellent substitute for a sleeping pill, and partly because I hope the general reader may be beguiled into spending some time among my pages. Of course I know that an author cannot transcend himself, but I shall be disappointed if there should be any reader who at least once during his perusal of the book does not find his labor of comprehension quickening into interest. I look on the psychology of religion not merely as a technology but also as a liberal study with an attraction of its own.

The reader will find the structure of the book suggested in the Table of Contents. The first chapter, "Orientation," is by way of getting things started for those unacquainted with the field. Chapter 2 is important, for in it I try to define what I mean by the term "religion." Chapter 3 on "Methods of Study" can be omitted by the general reader, though not by serious students unless they are already possessed of competence in the field. Part 2 deals with various aspects of religious growth, culminating in a discussion of that toward which one hopes this growth is progressing, namely mature religion. In this section I have tried to pay some attention to psychological dynamics, and to suggest some of those psychological forces and conditions that for good or evil shape the religious life. Part 3 is more thoroughly descriptive and of necessity less well structured in that it deals with various aspects of the religious life. Any religious worker, or others interested in religion, should be acquainted with the chief ways in which religion expresses itself, and here I have described and discussed them psychologically. The last section, "Conclusions," is very brief. Here I have simply called attention to some of the emphases that recur in the main body of the text, some of which were present in my mind before I started to write, while others seemed to grow of themselves as I developed my materials.

I have written of religion with as catholic a purpose as I could summon. By this I mean that I have meant my treatment to apply to religion in general and not to any particular or parochial form of it. I would hope that my generalizations might apply not only to Christianity but to Judaism, Mohammedanism, Hinduism, Buddhism, and other religious faiths as well. But at the same time I must acknowledge my limitations and confess that my first-hand contacts have been mainly with the various forms of Protestant Christianity as they exhibit themselves in the American scene. The reader is hereby warned that he must keep this in mind in reading my book.

The acknowledging of indebtedness is always a pleasant task. Tennyson's Ulysses declares that he is a part of all that he has met. The reverse certainly is true, so that properly I should append a list of names that would be almost as long as the book itself. My earliest conscious memory of an experience to be identified as religious is that of my mother's telling me how Abraham was led out by God to count the stars. If she had not first introduced me to a religious life, this book would never have been written. My wife, by her example, has increased my understanding of Roman Catholic Christianity at its best. Mr. J. G. Case of the Macmillan Company has been a sympathetic editorial consultant during much of the time of composition. My students, past and present, have contributed their portion, especially such as have refused to be so supine as to accept my prejudices without protest. Special thanks are due to Marjorie Cramer who typed the final draft of the manuscript for the publisher and helped with many stylistic suggestions. Dr. Ernest Harms went to much trouble to supply me with suitable drawings to illustrate his theories. Others who have made a contribution either of a clerical or critical nature include Viola B. Angier, Elma M. Baldrick, Winifred Bartunek, Katharine A. Birge, Margareta Brasel, Elizabeth P. Burns,

Walter Houston Clark, Jr., Marjorie L. Davis, Charlotte Devol,
Ambellur N. D. Frederick, Caroline Howard, Eleanor Hope Johnson,
Carole Macklin, and Christine Skelton.

WALTER HOUSTON CLARK

West Hartford, Connecticut

CONTENTS

ACKNOWLEDGMENTS

Grateful acknowledgment is made to the following for permission to quote from copyrighted material:

American Psychological Association for material quoted from "The Cultural Background of the Patient as Part of the Physician's Armamentarium" by H. A. Savitz, which appeared in the *Journal of Abnormal and Social Psychology*, 47, April, 1952.

Association Press: *The Religious Beliefs of Youth*, by Murray G. Ross; copyright 1950.

Bookman Associates; *The Oxford Group: Its History and Significance* by Walter Houston Clark; copyright 1951.

The Macmillan Company; *The Religious Consciousness* by James Bissett Pratt; copyright 1920; and *The Individual and His Religion* by Gordon W. Allport; copyright 1950.

Meridian Books, Inc.; *Mysticism: A Study in the Nature and Development of Man's Spiritual Consciousness* by Evelyn Underhill; copyright 1955.

Paul R. Reynolds & Son; *The Varieties of Religious Experience*; copyright 1902 by William James.

The University of Chicago Press; *Psychotherapy and Personality Change* by Carl R. Rogers and R. F. Dymond; copyright 1954.

John Wiley and Sons, Inc.; *Adolescent Character and Personality* by R. J. Havighurst and H. Taba, copyright 1949.

Part 1

APPROACH TO
THE PSYCHOLOGY
OF RELIGION

Chapter 1

ORIENTATION

It will be a source of delight to many persons, and of regret to others, that the attempt is at last made to study the facts of religion by scientific methods.

—Edwin Diller Starbuck

A young man in law school, with more interest in excitement than in law, is wasting his life in riotous living, generally dissipating the fine talents with which he is endowed. Somehow finding his way to a conference led by a competent college evangelist, he experiences a sudden and cataclysmic conversion that completely changes his aims in life. As a result, twenty years after the event, we find him a priest and member of a religious order, doing a kind of work and finding a satisfaction in life that he never dreamed of before his conversion.

An organization for alcoholics welcomes those who have given up all hope of being able to control their lives, and through a program basically religious rehabilitates more than two thirds of those who seek its help, despite the fact that many of these have resorted to psychiatrists and cures to no avail.

A philosopher, theologian, and musician, against the advice of his friends and colleagues, deserts a brilliant career to bury himself in medical work in Africa because the secret of his faith seems to have escaped the searchings of even his fine mind, and he feels compelled to discover this secret through the direct experience of service.

A young British worker is seared in the crucible of an industrial system that he has seen consume the lives of his parents. It prevents

3

him from supplying for his own wife and family any but a pitifully small share of that abundance which he helps make possible for his employers. He finds an answer to this injustice in the Communist program, and devotes many years of service to the Party cause. The injustice is patent; the weapons he is taught to use are violence, defiance, deception, and hate. Then a religious movement teaches him another solution. The injustice he still recognizes, and the fight still goes on. But now he has replaced the weapons of Communism with a religious way of life which transforms not only his loyalties but his personality as well.

All the foregoing are examples of what happens when religion becomes what William James called "an acute fever."

Yet alongside these examples we can set the long lines of docile, obedient citizens, dressed in their Sunday finery to attend church and synagogue on the Sabbath day. No fever here, but merely the dull habit of the more or less comforting and pleasant performance of conventional religious duties. Sociologists examine the lives of these excellent, respectable churchgoers, and with a fair degree of consistency they come to the same conclusions. So far as the difference in everyday conduct is concerned these church people cannot be distinguished from their neighbors who spend Sunday morning on the golf links or who substitute the ritual of some lodge hall for the ritual prescribed by an ecclesiastical organization.

How are we to reconcile such inconsistent observations? All these examples pass for religious behavior, yet how diverse are the forces that urge and motivate them! Some seem to penetrate to the very springs of personality, transforming and changing the complete person. Others merely touch the surface, creating no more than a kind of outer garment of behavior. It is such paradoxes with which the student of religion has to wrestle. The existence of these contradictions explains how on the one hand religion is looked upon as the one force that may transform and save our tottering civilization, while on the other it is regarded as an empty convention rooted in superstition and expressed as respectability.

In part this book will deal with some of these cultural conundrums, for the psychology of religion will at least throw light on them and bring their solutions closer. At the same time it will help to illuminate some of the dark recesses of the human personality to aid us in understanding why people behave as they do, and how, rightly understood, religion may really perform for us those saving functions that in so many languages of creed and of ritual and of tongue we are promised that it will perform.

Status of the psychology of religion. Unlike other branches of psychology, the psychology of religion has never enjoyed a wholly respectable academic status. It belongs partly to religion and partly to psychology, and more often than not it has fallen between these two stools.

The modern psychologist thinks of himself as a scientist and tries to adapt scientific method to the study of human behavior. But there is no aspect of this behavior more complex than the religious life. Aware of the fact that natural scientists are often scornful of the ambiguity of his conclusions in less complex areas, the psychologist becomes even more wary when approaching religion. Though he can be quite an unorthodox fellow, with the courage of his convictions in certain ways, he cannot ignore the criticism of colleagues that he has been unscientific. The risk of this has too often kept him from studying religion.

On the other hand, the religious scholar is not equipped with the social-scientific tools necessary for a thorough study of religious psychology. Fertile as he may be in theoretical speculation, he is not trained in the more direct methods of empirical observation. He is skilled in the manipulation of verbal symbols or the handling of ancient documents and manuscripts. From the conscious pride in the centuries of academic tradition that lie behind him, he is apt to regard psychology as an upstart hardly worthy of being taken very seriously. It seems to him to lack a depth commensurate with the subject that he loves so well. Furthermore he finds "no speculation" in the cold eye which, it seems to him, the psychologist "glares with." He thinks that studies that may concern such subtle matters as spiritual truth should not be treated with such terrifying objectivity.

A third consideration has hampered many scholars, regardless of their disciplines, who have attempted to study the psychology of religion. Whether because of ecclesiastical vested interests or the natural feeling of the individual that his religious life is intimate and private, many people have voiced strong objections to the study of the personal religious life. Not so long ago a bishop denounced a professor at a university for having the temerity to circulate a questionnaire among his students asking them about their religious lives. Then, it is well known that active religious movements are not hospitable to attempts by scholars to study them unless the group is assured beforehand that the conclusions will be wholly favorable.[1]

These are a few of the reasons why the psychology of religion has not received the attention to which its importance entitles it. They help to explain why much that has been written about the subject seems elementary or thin. These considerations must be kept in mind as we approach a brief historical survey of religious psychology.

HISTORY OF THE PSYCHOLOGY OF RELIGION

Theoretical studies. To select a date or an event with which the history of the psychology of religion began would be as artificial as dating the beginning of history. The Bible is full of psychological comments on religion, and no century, country, or culture which has become self-conscious about religion is without its psychologists who have had something to say, more or less systematically, about this fascinating subject. Just as the modern study of psychology had its roots in philosophy, so does the psychology of religion. Buddha, Socrates, Plato, Jeremiah, Plotinus, and Augustine are typical of some of the ancients who looked inward and reported the processes that they observed there. In New England before the American Revolution Jonathan Edwards showed a strong intuitive sense of psychological factors in A *Treatise Concerning Religious Affections,* while in a later generation the German philosopher Schleiermacher was another student of religious experience whose views and interests were in some ways similar to those of Edwards. The more modern approach to the psychological study of religion dates from about 1881 when G. Stanley Hall, one of the great figures of his day in the field of psychology and eventually President of Clark University, studied conversion in connection with his central interest in adolescence. Also before the turn of the century, articles in the general field were pub-

[1] See for example the studies of Jehovah's Witnesses by M. S. Czatt or T. W. Sprague. The author ran into similar resistance in his study of the Oxford Group (Moral Re-Armament).

lished by several scholars including Hall, W. H. Burnham, A. H. Daniels, James H. Leuba, and George Albert Coe. But if the beginning of the modern American movement in the study of the psychology of religion must be given one date rather than another, it should be set at 1899, when Edwin Diller Starbuck published his volume entitled *The Psychology of Religion*.

Starbuck had been a student of William James at a time before James' own interest in the field had flowered. Indeed James' interest owed considerably more to Starbuck than *vice versa*. Always hospitable to new ideas, James had allowed his brilliant student to pursue empirical research in the field of religious growth and conversion. Starbuck eventually transferred to Clark University and continued his work there with the encouragement of G. Stanley Hall. His volume summarized his findings and was the first systematic work in the field. The modern reader of Starbuck finds that conversion seems to be overemphasized, but since that was the fashion of the day in most Protestant evangelical circles the book simply reflects the interests of the times. Yet it is well written and still repays study. It not only stirred up much interest and stimulated research among American students, but achieved international recognition as well, and was translated into German.

At the same time, George Albert Coe had been carrying on researches in the field of religious psychology, in part with the use of hypnosis, in an attempt to link the religious reactions of people to their temperaments. His book *The Spiritual Life* came out in 1900. In this work Coe reacted somewhat against the contemporary emphasis on conversion. He stressed the religious nurture of youth, and pointed out that for many the playing down of conflict and religious storm and stress leads to a more normal and fruitful type of religious development. Coe remained throughout his life a vigorous advocate of empirical methods in psychological study and religious education. This earlier volume, together with his own *The Psychology of Religion* published in 1916, made Coe an influence that can still be identified in the field.

But the most celebrated of all modern works on the psychology of religion is William James' *The Varieties of Religious Experience*. The occasion for this work was the invitation to the distinguished American to deliver the Gifford Lectures on Natural Religion at Edinburgh in 1900–1901. But the previous summer, during a holiday in the Adirondack Mountains, he had gone out for a ramble and had become lost in the woods. The resulting strain and exposure damaged his heart, with the result that he was forced to postpone his lectures for a year. This mishap, so unfortunate for him, was a happy accident for the psychology of religion, for the consequent rest ordered by his physician gave him the leisure of over a year's time to read and reflect on his subject and to compose the famous lectures that form the basis for the work.

A feature of the book is the profuse use of concrete illustrations, for which he was indebted in some measure to Starbuck. Almost exclusively these are in the form of case material, as often as possible in the words of the subjects. The book also is marked by James' deliberate selection for study of extreme and highly individualized forms of the religious life. This represents at once his feeling that religion is basically an individual rather than a social phenomenon and his conviction that religion shows itself more clearly in extremes. James nowhere illustrates better the central tenets of his pragmatic philosophy, for which he is so well known. He insists that it is neither the origins nor the processes of the religious life that justify it so much as the results. No matter how disreputable the genesis of a religious impulse or how psychopathic the founders of a religious movement, if the consequent religious activities are beneficial to the individual or to society the religion is thereby justified.

However, it is not so much the concrete psychological matter of the book nor even James' conclusions that constitute its true greatness. The terminology is that of the time and many of the conclusions may be questioned. It is rather the expression of the man himself that communicates itself in large part through a grace of expression and a liveliness of style seldom found in religious writing and never matched among psychologists. There are those who may object that this describes a work whose worth is literary and not psychological, and in part this may be true. But the chief value of the book lies in its keen insights into the human mind, its bold speculations concerning the springs of the spiritual life, and its stimulating conclusions pregnant with suggestive leads for psychological investigation. If the words of the wise are as goads, here we have the wise psychologist at his best. All of this, together with the author's broad and humane powers of sympathy, make the reading of the book a liberal education. No psychologist of religion can afford to neglect *Varieties*; it has towered over the other works on the subject for over half a century. It does not seem too daring a forecast to speculate that it may prove to be the most durable of all the works of this engaging and stimulating philosopher.

Stimulated by such pioneer works, interest in the psychology of religion grew during the next fifteen years. *The Journal of Religious Psychology* started publication in 1904, as *The American Journal of Religious Psychology and Education,* and continued until 1915. In 1910, *The Psychology of Religious Experience* by E. S. Ames was published. Ames was influenced by Harold Höffding's *The Philosophy of Religion,* published in 1906, and makes the point that religion has its origin in the attempt to conserve social values. Another book with considerable influence on psychologies of religion, which also emphasized the social roots of religion, was made available to English readers about nine years later. This was *The Elementary Forms of the Religious Life* by the French sociologist, Emile Durkheim.

A very different approach is to be found in George M. Stratton's *Psychology of the Religious Life,* published in 1911, which sets forth the stimulating thesis that religion has its source in conflict within the individual. Still another important name during the heyday of the psychology of religion is that of James H. Leuba, who taught for many years at Bryn Mawr College. More than most, Leuba tended toward naturalistic explanations of religious phenomena, pointing out, for example, the similarity of the reports of mystics to those of people who have been under the influence of drugs. He published *A Psychological Study of Religion* in 1912. This had been preceded by numerous journal articles and was followed by other books and articles, of which one was *The Psychology of Religious Mysticism* in 1925.

In 1920 there appeared the book which perhaps is second only to James' *Varieties* in this field. This was James B. Pratt's *The Religious Consciousness.* Pratt was a graduate of Williams College, and spent almost the whole of his teaching career there as a much respected professor of philosophy. Though primarily a philosopher, he had done empirical research while a graduate student at Harvard in the field of the psychology of religious belief, and had published a book on it in 1907. As a deeply religious man himself, Pratt wrote with the authority of one who knew something of his subject at first hand. His sympathies, like those of James, were broad, and to his own Protestant convictions he brought an understanding of the values of Catholicism and considerable first-hand knowledge of the religions of India. The two high points of the book are his chapters on objective and subjective worship and the five chapters on mysticism which close the volume. While not as brilliant as James', Pratt's style is clear, with the addition of occasional quiet humor. His work is profound and thoroughly scholarly.

Since 1920 books on the psychology of religion, though there have been a considerable number, tend to be either slighter or more restricted in scope than the works of Pratt and James. There are many, however, that are worthy of note. In 1923 Rudolf Otto's *The Idea of the Holy* ("Das Heilige") was translated from the German. This is an attempt by Otto to define the psychological experience of the apprehension of the holy, which he takes to be the central element in worship. This work is intuitive rather than empirical in its approach, and its insights are profound and stimulating. Popular in its own day, it deserves to be read more than it is. In the same year appeared *An Introduction to the Psychology of Religion* by Robert H. Thouless of Cambridge University. C. C. Josey, a lifelong student of religious psychology, brought out a brief volume on the psychology of religion in 1927, while Elmer T. Clark reported extensive research on conversion in 1929 in *The Psychology of Religious Awakening*. In this he compares conversion experiences of his day with those reported a generation or two before. Another interesting work on conversion had been translated from the Italian two years before this, *Religious Conversion* by Sante de Sanctis. In 1929 there appeared a book on religion by a psychologist thoroughly trained and respected in his field, *The Psychology of Religious Adjustment* by Edmund S. Conklin.

In 1935 appeared *Normative Psychology of Religion* by H. N. and R. W. Wieman; the next year, *The Psychology of Christian Personality*, by Ernest M. Ligon. The latter is an attempt to derive a definition of the religious life from a study of the Gospels, and is of interest chiefly as the foundation on which the Character Research Project at Union College is built. Karl R. Stolz, late Dean of the

Hartford School of Religious Education, was primarily a religious scholar, but he became one of the pioneers in the field of pastoral psychology; his *The Psychology of Religious Living*, published in 1937, is a competent and scholarly piece of work, though weak in empirical illustration. One of the most recent systematic books on the psychology of religion is Paul E. Johnson's *Psychology of Religion*, published in 1945. This is a brief work, more appreciative of the positive values of religion than some. It attempts to present the psychology of religion in its full scope, but simply and clearly. Dr. Johnson has recently published another title in the field, *Personality and Religion*, in which he attempts to integrate religion and modern personality theory.

Another book, even briefer, but more influential in calling the attention of both psychologists and religious scholars to the common ground between them, is Gordon W. Allport's *The Individual and His Religion*, which appeared in 1950. Coming from a Harvard professor and former president of the American Psychological Association, it served to lend to religion much needed respectability as a proper subject for the psychologist's attention. Based on the Lowell Lectures delivered by the author in Boston, and in the tradition of James' work, the book is stimulating reading for the general educated reader. Like James, Allport emphasizes the individuality of religious experience, but he specializes in describing the systematically developed and reasoned type of religion that has more appeal for the intellect than do the passionate and extreme forms of religious experience that James describes. Though the book forms a coherent whole, it does not pretend to be a complete treatise on the subject, but is, rather, a series of brilliant essays on psychology and religion.

Perhaps one other work should be mentioned, though it does not belong principally in this field. This is Eduard Spranger's *Lebensformen*, published in German in 1924, then translated into English under the title *Types of Men* in 1928. It is an intuitive study of what Spranger considers the six fundamental value systems of mankind, of which religion is one. This has proved to be germinative reading for many psychologists. Based on this is the much used Allport-Vernon *Study of Values*, a questionnaire which has thrown light on religious motives. Spranger has not only helped to define religion, but has also served to put the desire to know God into perspective beside other motives such as the striving for knowledge, beauty, power, riches, and the urge to serve other people.

Religion and mental health. Left out of account up to this point is a movement that is a very definite and important part of the psychology of religion, and yet it has a distinctive character and literature of its own. This is the field of religion and health, particularly mental health. Whereas the works we have been describing have approached religion in the tradition of speculative philosophy crossed with the quantitative-empirical methods of psychological science, the subject of religion and health is more closely allied with medicine, psychotherapy, and the practical concerns of pastoral counseling. This emphasis in religious psychology is anticipated in James' *Varieties* in the chapter entitled "Religion and neurology" as well as in the chapter on "The religion of healthy-mindedness" at the point at which James discusses Christian Science and the mind-cure movement.

So many books have been published in this field that there is space to mention only a few representative ones. Currently there is much more interest and activity here than in traditional religious psychology, and when people talk about the approach between psychology and religion they are usually thinking of the recent flags of truce that more and more have been exchanged between psychiatrists and the clergy. Traditionally, people in search of health have sought it through religion and magic even more than they have had recourse to medicine. The Bible, and particularly the New Testament, is full of accounts of healing miracles, while Frazer's *The Golden Bough* gives numerous instances of contemporary magical formulas for healing that suggest a very large recourse to superstition in the past.

The outstanding modern religious movement to emphasize health is of course Christian Science which, despite its name, has little use for science as that term is understood by modern medicine. The Roman Catholic church recognizes healing miracles, and the shrine at Lourdes, France, best represents this aspect of her teaching. While the cures are looked on as supernatural in essence, the Church, unlike Christian Science, not only admits of the ministrations of physicians but even calls on medicine to certify and so to assist at the pronouncement of cures. Though the Church does not emphasize psychological factors, the psychologist sees psychology operating strongly in many ways to help effect these cures.[2] An important pioneer attempt to link religion and medicine was the Emanuel Movement which had its center at Emanuel Episcopal Church in Boston and dates from 1905. The book *Religion and Medicine* by Worcester, McComb, and Coriat, two clergymen and a doctor, who were leaders in the movement, was published in 1908 and describes the principles of the work. The Guild of Health, a contemporary English organization with similar aims, was started about this same time and still functions. Yet these early movements were generalized attempts to reconcile religion and healing. They did not specialize in psychological ills nor in combining religious values and psychological methods in an approach to personal problems. The latter emphasis derived chiefly from other sources.

In 1920 a churchworker in the prime of life, with degrees in various fields, suffered a mental breakdown so serious that he had to be hospitalized, while his family was informed that he was unlikely to recover. Because of the gravity of the diagnosis he was not promptly released when recovery actually did ensue, and so he had an opportunity as a sane person to look about him in the hospital. In doing this and talking to his fellow patients, particularly about religion, he found several cases besides his own where religion either was or could have been a factor in recovery. The man was Anton T. Boisen, and the experience was to be the beginning of the ministry to the insane in mental hospitals throughout America.

Five years later, after study at Harvard and Andover Newton Theological Seminary, and by dint of a persevering search and much persuasion, Boisen managed to carve out for himself the post of Chaplain on the staff of Worcester State Hospital in Worcester, Massachusetts; he was the first to hold such a post at a public mental hospital. At about the same time he received permission to arrange for some clinical training for a few theological students at the hospital, a work that was expanded at the Chicago Theological Seminary. Today such work is sponsored by many theological schools and is carried on nationally under the auspices of the Council for Clinical Training and the Institute for Clinical Pastoral Care.

[2] For a discussion of the foregoing as well as a review of many other movements in the field, see Weatherhead's *Psychology, Religion, and Healing.*

In 1936 Boisen published an account of his work and his studies under the title *The Exploration of the Inner World*. This is a most important book for psychology as well as for religion, and is as significant for its theoretical suggestions for the dynamics of mental disease as for its practical suggestions for the cooperation of psychiatry and religion. Furthermore, Boisen gives many insights into the psychology of famous religious figures, such as the prophet George Fox, founder of the Quaker movement, whose life history gives many evidences of psychotic episodes. He shows how little understanding the typical modern physician would have of the man who gave so much of religious value to the world. The book even makes the bold yet reverent speculation that the knowledge of psychotic experience may help us in the understanding of Jesus himself, particularly with regard to his Messianic consciousness, even though Boisen does not believe that Jesus was unbalanced.

But Boisen was not the only, nor even necessarily the first, worker in this field. John Rathbone Oliver, who was both a psychiatrist and a clergyman, published *Pastoral Psychiatry and Mental Health* in 1932, and in 1934 *Fear*, an "autobiography" of a breakdown. Well known is the respect for religion that characterizes the writings of C. G. Jung, whose *Modern Man in Search of a Soul* appeared in 1933. Jung had been a former close associate of Freud in the development of the psychoanalytic movement, and his attitude concerning religion was one of the points on which the two differed. The general reader is apt to find the books of Jung rather murky, though flashes of meaning may be revealed through persevering study. Freud's own comments on religion are uncomplimentary, since he felt that most of his patients were using it as an escape from reality. Such comments are most conveniently found in *Totem and Taboo* and *The Future of an Illusion*. A very readable book which shows how religious values may be combined with psychoanalytic theory, *Ways to Psychic Health*, by the Swiss psychiatrist Maeder, was translated and published in 1953, while another psychoanalyst interested in religion has been Erich Fromm, for example, in *Psychoanalysis and Religion*.

Additional impetus to the respect for religion among psychiatrists was contributed by the growing achievement of Alcoholics Anonymous, which had its genesis in the early 1930's. The Salvation Army and other missions to the "down-and-outs" had long demonstrated the therapeutic value of religion in reclaiming drunkards,[3] but psychiatrists seldom see down-and-outs except in a perfunctory way. Alcoholics Anonymous introduced what is essentially a religious therapy to drinkers from all strata of society. As a result, many psychiatrists began to re-evaluate their attitude toward religion and the effect of religious experience in the therapeutic situation.[4] The book *Alcoholics Anonymous*, describing the movement with many case illustrations, was first published in 1942.

As these other events were developing, clergymen, who for some time had been digesting psychoanalysis and other psychological ideas, for their part began to wonder actively how they could cooperate with what in some respects seemed to be the "wave of the future." The first reactions to Freud had included many outraged denunciations of what seemed a counsel of irreligion and license. But by the 1940's these had subsided mostly to occasional mutterings, and the clergy, particularly the liberal Protestants, had decided not only to bend with the wind but to adapt it to their own purposes. Something of a pioneer in the field was *Pastoral Psychology* by Stolz, while Cabot and Dicks' *The Art of Ministering to the Sick*, published in 1936, made free use of psychological principles. Another writer who has written extensively and well in the field of counseling and adjustment with reference to religion is Rollo May. But the counseling technique that has made the greatest impact on religious counselors, with the possible exception of psychoanalysis, is a method which itself owes much to psychoanalysis. This is the so-called "non-directive" or "client-centered" method, which first saw the light of day in published form in 1942 in the book *Counseling and Psychotherapy* by Carl R. Rogers, the originator of the technique. This has been followed up by those who have adapted his methods to the pastoral field, notably Seward Hiltner and Carol Wise, each of whom has used the title *Pastoral Counseling* for a book. Father Curran has adapted Rogers' techniques for Catholicism in *Counseling in Catholic Life and Education*.

Nor have the theologians been unaware of the development in this field, as is witnessed by Roberts' *Psychotherapy and a Christian View*

[3] For a good journalistic account of some cases, see Harold Begbie's *Twice-Born Men*.

[4] For example, see H. M. Tiebout, "Therapeutic Mechanism of Alcoholics Anonymous" in *American Journal of Psychiatry* for 1944.

of Man and Tillich's *The Courage to Be*. The popularity of pastoral psychology is attested by two periodicals, *The Journal of Pastoral Care* and *Pastoral Psychology*, as well as by the Pastoral Psychology Book Club. The wider field of the psychology of religion has been represented by no periodical since the demise of the *Journal of Religious Psychology* in 1915, though several associations that serve the general cause have been founded. The Society for the Scientific Study of Religion, for example, which holds regular meetings in both the Boston and New York areas and has branches elsewhere, was founded to stimulate the study of religion by social scientists. The Academy of Religion and Mental Health specializes in the promotion of intercommunication between ministers and psychiatrists.

This sketch of the development of the psychology of religion has been all too brief, and many important names and books have had to be omitted.[5] But it will serve to indicate where the present volume stands in the tradition.[6] Rather than specializing on the practical field of religion and mental health, it belongs with those books that describe more generally religious behavior and the religious personality.

[5] For further details, see Chap. 1 in Johnson's *Psychology of Religion*, or Chap. 8 in Stolz's *The Psychology of Religious Living*.

[6] The serious student of religious psychology should make himself well acquainted with current psychological schools and movements. Heidbreder's *Seven Psychologies* is a readable and still useful resource, while Woodworth's *Contemporary Schools of Psychology* (*Revised*) is more up-to-date.

Chapter 2

WHAT IS RELIGION?

I speak not now of your ordinary religious believer, who follows the conventional observances of his country, whether it be Buddhist, Christian, or Mohammedan. His religion has been made for him by others, communicated to him by tradition, determined to fixed forms by imitation, and retained by habit. It would profit us little to study this second-hand religious life. We must make search rather for the original experiences which were the pattern-setters to all this mass of suggested feeling and imitated conduct. These experiences we can only find in individuals for whom religion exists not as a dull habit, but as an acute fever rather.

—William James

There is no more difficult word to define than "religion." There are at least three reasons for this. In the first place and chiefly, religious experience is an inward and subjective thing. Furthermore it is highly individualized. Each person reads into the word his own experience, or what he takes for religious experience, in such a way that no two people who exchange views about religion are ever talking about quite the same thing.

The second reason is that there is nothing about which people are capable of feeling more strongly than their religion. "Religion" is, at least to the average man, a "virtue word." A virtue word is one like "democracy," with such favorable connotations that almost everyone tends to want to be identified with it, as opposed to "smear words" like "atheist" or "Communist" which almost everyone eschews. In one of his essays Stephen Leacock points out that you can accuse a person of almost any deficiency other than the lack of a sense of

17

humor; at that point he will probably get red in the face and explode. Leacock might well have included religion with his statement. There are very few people who can stand being called irreligious. In general, people will readily admit that they don't go to church, or that they don't believe in God (though they will not like to be called atheists), or that they look on all kinds of religious practices as silly, but as soon as one accuses them of being irreligious their blood pressures immediately begin to climb and they become violently defensive. Perhaps an exception to these statements is a certain type of scientist for whom religion is a "smear" word; but he will react just as emotionally in the opposite way. Hence there is always a potential emotional charge lurking in the background in any discussion of the meaning of religion. This will tend to distort any attempt to define the term.

Finally, a concept of religion will be influenced by the purposes of the person making the definition. The parson with a dwindling congregation is apt to have a fond spot in his heart for the view that identifies religion with churchgoing; the mystic is bound to emphasize inwardness; while the anthropologist studying religion is prone to define it in terms of observable activities and customs. Each scholar naturally will define religion for his own purpose. Of course, this is a problem encountered in defining all terms, but the difficulties are sufficiently magnified in the case of religion to explain why social scientists tend to become exceedingly evasive when asked to define the term.[1] Nevertheless, even though we are in a field where no one, or perhaps everyone, may set himself up as an authority on what religion is, it is none the less important that anyone who sets out to discuss it feel the obligation to try to make as clear as possible just what he is describing. This will be our task in the next few paragraphs.

Definitions or conceptions of religion as applied to the psychological field may be divided into three types. First, there are those that refuse to mark off religion from other aspects of psychic life.

And an old priest said, Speak to us of religion.
And he said:

---

[1] For the variety of definitions of religion found among social scientists, see pp. 45–46 in Chap. 3.

Have I spoken this day of aught else?
Is not religion all deeds and all reflections
And that which is neither deed nor reflection, but
a wonder and a surprise ever springing from the soul,
even while the hands hew the stone or tend the loom.
Who can separate his faith from his actions, or
his belief from his occupations?
Who can spread his hours before him, saying, "This
for God and this for myself; This for my soul and this
other for my body"? . . .
Your daily life is your temple and your religion
Whenever you enter into it take with it your all.[2]

This concept has in it elements of profound truth, and is particularly well adapted to the ends of those who are distressed over the sterile bickerings between creedal interests, or of religious educators concerned over the failure of church-school teachings to carry beyond the churches' walls. It is noteworthy that George Albert Coe is one of the few psychologists of religion who, though refusing to define religion, leans toward this type of definition, and that he also exhibited a lifelong interest in religious education.[3] Yet, while appreciating the values in this type of definition, we must discard it for our purposes as too broad to be useful. If the point be raised that in rejecting such a large canvas we are rejecting reality itself, then we must plead guilty to the charge. Yet all analysis of so wonderful a phenomenon as the human mind must involve some oversimplification if we are not to become lost in the infinitely tangled web of its complexity. Some focus is essential if we are to think about the mind at all.

A second group of definitions emphasizes the *social* aspect of religion and tends to see religion as arising from the give-and-take between human beings. As we would expect, this is the view taken by the typical sociologist or social psychologist, for it serves the purposes of his particular emphasis and interest. Durkheim, for example, holds that religion is a completely social phenomenon, while Talcott Par-

[2] Kahlil Gibran, *The Prophet*, pp. 87–88.
[3] See, for example, his *Psychology of Religion*, pp. 9–10: ". . . no observed separation between religious and other mental processes has been pointed out . . ."; see also Note, p. 13.

sons, the sociologist, largely agrees with him. "A religion we will define as a set of beliefs, practices, and institutions which men have evolved in various societies," says Parsons in giving his definition of religion.[4] Ames belongs with this same general group, for he defines religion as "the consciousness of the highest social values,"[5] though he arrives at his definition through the somewhat different emphasis of one who is interested in ethics and morality. Manifestly, since the question of ethics cannot arise unless there are two or more people involved, if religion is to be identified with ethics, there must first be a "society." It is obvious that this emphasis in the study of religion will lead to important insights and conclusions which no psychologist can afford to neglect, but a sociological concern is not to be the central interest in our own study.

The third category of definitions stresses the individual and his experiences. Indeed, some psychologists are so impressed with the highly personal and individualized character of religious experience that on this account they hesitate to define it at all. Thus in Allport's *The Individual and His Religion* we find no definition of religion. Though there is a definition of the religious sentiment, we feel that even this is given with reluctance, for it does not appear until nearly the middle of the book and is confined to the religion of maturity. Here the mature religious sentiment is defined as "a disposition, built up through experience, to respond favorably, and in certain habitual ways, to conceptual objects and principles that the *individual* [italics ours] regards as of ultimate importance in his own life, and as having to do with what he regards as permanent or central in the nature of things."[6] This is quite like the definition that James gives of religion, though James goes even further in divorcing himself from the sociological viewpoint by defining it as "the feelings, acts, and experiences of individual men in their solitude, so far as they apprehend themselves to stand in relation to whatever they may consider the divine."[7] However, some psychologists find room for both the sociological and the personal definitions of religion. Thus Pratt conceives of it as "the

---

[4] See his Hazen Foundation pamphlet, *Religious Perspectives in College Teaching in Sociology and Social Psychology*, p. 7.

[5] *The Psychology of Religious Experience*, p. vii; see also pp. 168–169 and elsewhere.

[6] P. 56.

[7] *Varieties*, pp. 31–32.

serious and social attitude of *individuals or communities* [italics ours] toward the power or powers which they conceive as having ultimate control over their interests and destinies." [8]

It should be noted here that the word "social" may be used by psychologists of religion in two senses. In the usual sense it designates the relationships between human beings, but it may be thought of as describing the experience that the religious person feels that he is having in his relationship to what he conceives of as the divine. It is in this sense that Pratt uses the term, his sociological emphasis coming out in his use of the term "communities." Though he does not use the term "social," the idea comprised in this meaning of the term appears in Johnson's definition of religion as "personal cooperation with a trusted Creator of Values." [9]

It should be noted that many of these definitions, as we would expect, make reference to "higher powers" or God. But the reader must understand that the psychologist, *as a psychologist,* has no business in assuming the existence of God as a fact, or in trying to prove His existence or to disprove it. This is the function of the theologians. This conviction explains why some psychologists, like Allport, strive to omit references to the divine in their definitions. When the psychologist does refer to God, or an equivalent idea, it simply reflects the fact that the idea of the divine or of some supersensible power usually, though not always, is found among those who are self-consciously religious. Consequently, any reference to God by the psychologist of religion is simply by way of describing the consciousness of the individual, or what the person reports it to be.

With this brief review of what other psychologists have thought of as religion, we will go on to our own ideas. In the space we have allotted to the foregoing we have hardly been able to present an exhaustive discussion, for there are many other aspects of the problem that deserve attention. But it will serve as an introduction, and the interested reader may find fuller statements elsewhere.[10]

With the full recognition that we are on ground where the experts

---

[8] *The Religious Consciousness,* p. 2.

[9] *Psychology of Religion,* p. 30.

[10] E.g. Pratt, *op. cit.,* Chap. 1; James, *op. cit.,* Lecture 2; Coe, *The Psychology of Religion,* first four chapters, *passim.* An earlier treatment of the ideas about to be developed will be found in the author's article "The Psychology of Religious Values," in *Personality,* Symposium No. 1.

disagree, and thus well aware of the hazards involved, we will venture our own definition. It is our feeling that religion can be *most characteristically* described as *the inner experience of the individual when he senses a Beyond, especially as evidenced by the effect of this experience on his behavior when he actively attempts to harmonize his life with the Beyond.* This is not proposed as a definition to end all discussion, but is simply by way of informing the reader what the author has in mind, or rather in the back of his mind, when he discusses religion. For religion is too large and inclusive a term to be stringently confined within any definition suitable for the use of a psychologist, and we may be using the term occasionally in a less rigorous sense, as will be explained later on in the discussion.

It will be noted that religion is first of all described as something inward, and secondly in such terms as to suggest that the essential experience partakes of mystical qualities; for the term *Beyond* stands for what is felt to be a supernatural or supersensible force, most probably personal in nature, apprehended by a psychological process of which the individual can give no very adequate account. The definition might have stopped there, but if so, it would have been of small use to the social scientist, who requires something more concrete for his study. Indeed, it is not only the social scientist, but also religious people who might be said to have something of a prejudice in favor of a religion that has concrete results. Christians might reflect on the fact that it was Jesus who said, "by their fruits ye shall know them." Hence it is not only the social-scientific demand but a real conviction that genuine inwardness of experience brings something in the way of results that suggests this facet of our definition. Where there are no results we can well suspect that often supposed inward experience is little more than a matter of verbalization. At the same time we must grant that in true religion the inward experience always must come first, and its fruits may not appear immediately.

Actually I suspect that we shall find much less disagreement on this point if we allow people to define for themselves what they mean by the behavior alluded to in the definition. For there will always be *some* influence of inner experience on behavior, even though it might be nothing more overt than a slight quickening of the pulse or a moment of abstraction. But for our purposes we can think of the inner experience, however it may arise, as the mental process that sooner or later will activate the behavior that the psychologist observes.

One more feature of the definition worthy of note is represented by the last phrase, *actively attempts to harmonize his life with the Beyond*. The most characteristic reaction to inner religious experience is to please, by appropriate actions, the divine person with whom one feels he has been in contact during the experience, or at least to bring one's life into harmony with the essential reality apprehended through the experience. This serves to differentiate the religious attitude from the merely superstitious or magical. Much that passes for religion in practice is the attempt to coerce or at least influence the deity through adherence to the proper ritual, creed, or form of prayer. There is a tendency in each religion or denomination to represent as fact the assertion that it has a corner on the market in such efficacious practices. But the characteristic religious attitude is not so much an attempt to persuade God to regulate His activities according to the wishes of the worshiper, as it is a striving to know Him to the end that the believer may come into closer harmony with the divine Will.

But the definition we have proposed, be it remembered, simply represents the *most characteristic* type of religious experience and behavior. There is much activity associated with it, in varying degrees of closeness, that passes for religion and in a certain sense is. For convenience we might divide religious behavior into three categories according to its association with what we have described in our definition. Accordingly we may term essential religious experience and behavior as *Primary religious behavior,* meaning an authentic inner experience of the divine combined with whatever efforts the individual may make to harmonize his life with the divine, as described in our definition. Obviously we are going to run into much difficulty in determining what we mean by an "authentic" inner experience. Only the subject himself can tell, and frequently he himself may not recognize the difference between deep and quite superficial religious experience. Even the saints have had difficulty with this distinction. This is why we need to call on the outwardly observable behavior of the individual to help us validate the experience.

Of course, this approach is a very unsatisfactory one for a social scientist, but it points out a dilemma hard to escape. For if we rely on behavior alone, wholly apart from any subjective testimony, we may identify actions as religious that really are not so at all. Two women may go to church, the one to worship God and the other so that the neighbors may get a look at her new hat. The problem is very much like telling when a person is really in love. Nobody really knows, including the lover himself, though only he has direct access to his state of mind. Yet no one doubts that there is a reality represented by the expression "in love." Whether the youth who says he is in love is really so or merely indulging in a thin, romanticized approximation of love we determine partly by what he says and partly by how he acts, especially over a period of time. It is by a similar process that we recognize primary religion. While we may have to do some violence to it in devising "operational definitions" for the purpose of scientific study, we must try not to lose sight of the essential whole, that is so much better apprehended by the poet, the prophet, the saint, and even by that sometimes despised but always sturdy friend in time of trouble, common sense.

Yet it is quite obvious that not everything that passes for religious behavior, and in some sense deserves the term, could meet the test of what we have described as primary behavior. Many people have exhibited the latter, or some pale approximation to it, at some time during their lives, as the result of which they have acquired certain habits or assumed certain obligations which impinge on and modify their usual everyday behavior. This latter we will call *Secondary religious behavior*. For instance, a vivid conversion experience may fit the category of primary behavior. As the result of this the individual may join a church and punctiliously present himself for worship every Sunday for the rest of his days. But most of those Sundays may represent a very routine and uninspired carrying out of what he considers an obligation undertaken under very solemn circumstances. We do not necessarily have to hold that such is useless. There is a function for secondary religious behavior to perform, and it certainly is much more common than the primary type. But there is a quite obvious distinction between the two, at least in theory, which will help the student of religion to be clearer about what he is studying.

Then there is a kind of religious behavior even farther removed from the primary, which we will call *Tertiary religious behavior*. This has nothing of the primary about it, nor is it the result of any first-hand experience, but is simply a matter of religious routine or convention accepted on the authority of someone else. The religious behavior of children making their early acquaintance with religious customs and ideas is mainly of this kind, though this need not always be the case. It may grow into the primary type and from there on to the secondary type, but religious observance is usually first learned by some more or less mechanical process of conditioning or imitation. And we get the impression that a rather considerable number of repectable churchgoers have never felt the remotest approach to a spiritual experience, however thorough their performance of all the literal duties that their churches enjoin. That they have no conception of what religion is at first hand, they have no more idea than the youth who, having learned to make love out of a book, thinks of himself as the Great Lover. Like him the tertiary religious personality has learned by rote. Again we cannot exactly say that these people have nothing to contribute to religion, though certainly they do much to bring discredit on it and to confuse those who are studying it. Frequently they are the very pillars of the institution and may hold the positions of deacon, vestryman, chief worker for the ladies' aid, money collector, Sunday School superintendent, and occasionally, we regret to say, even pastor of the flock.

It is perhaps too much to say that these people are incapable of a real spiritual experience, for often, much to their own surprise, they become converted, or mystically moved, or have visions of truths they never dreamed existed. These happenings partially explain the impact of some revivals. But in the case of some people we wonder whether, for all practical purposes, a primary religious experience is not completely beyond their capacities. Any teacher of literature has known students to whom he despairs of teaching an appreciation of good reading, while there are others who will never hear music except as noise. The Roman Catholic Church makes use of the concept of "invincible ignorance." Perhaps the spiritual capacities of some are just invincibly absent. But obviously this is mere speculation, for we can never know what a shift in environment may do for a given individual. All we can say is that, so far as is *outwardly observable*, there seem to be many persons of this kind both in and out of religious bodies.

A puzzling special case of our threefold characterization is the intensely emotional but narrow religious life of the strongly partisan believer and the bigot. Strangely, it would seem that this type of individual may properly belong at times to the primary religious-behavior category, while at other times he may demonstrate secondary or tertiary behavior. Endowed with keen spiritual sensitivity joined with a limited intellectual imagination, this type of individual should properly be classified as demonstrating primary religious behavior.

But frequently one senses an element, in what otherwise might seem a most intense expression of pure religion, that suggests defensiveness. The narrow believer may strike us as protesting too much. He is just a little too afraid of living and letting live; of tolerating opinions opposed to his own. This leads one to suspect that often he represents a religious conviction, once warm, that is growing cold, and that he is unwilling to admit to others, and especially to himself, that such is the case. Even more often he has never experienced anything more than the forms of religion. Many sturdy sons of the Church are of this type. They are the people who vigorously defend her interests and lay about them with lusty strokes to see that others are coerced by the letter of Church law, just as they themselves are coerced by forms the substance of which they have never experienced and cannot understand. Yet in a paradoxical way some of these people, partly bigoted and partly sincere, may at various times demonstrate all three kinds of religious behavior.

Perhaps more should be said of the religious bigot. While it is doubtless hard to find him in his pure form, for we can never be sure that a given bigot has no admixture in his nature of some portion of a sincere desire "to harmonize his life with the Beyond," nevertheless this unlovely type of personality does not commend himself as the epitome of primary religious behavior at its best. On the contrary, there is something distinctly anti-religious about him which most of his friends—and all his enemies—cannot always specifically recognize but do sense quite strongly. We have already suggested that the narrow, coercing zeal of the religious bigot conceals an inward fear that his faith may be hollow. His behavior is a cover-up.

But, more actively, his religion may be the means of his expressing a will-to-power, or his way of asserting his own particular vested interest. G. W. Allport discusses a study of differing values among two groups, one high in anti-Semitism and another low in it.[11] The anti-Semites were highest in indicating their preference for power values, and economic values. Conversely, these values were lowest for the group low in anti-Semitism. It is quite likely that the same power drives motivate many religious bigots, and we can understand that their support of religion may be merely a convention enabling them unconsciously to satisfy other urges. Thus religious bigotry can become a particularly subtle and hence virulent form of tertiary religious behavior.

William James speaks of individuals "for whom religion exists not as a dull habit but as an acute fever," and it is about this latter kind, but not its bigoted form, that his *Varieties* was written. This type, which interested him, comes close to being identical with our primary religious group. People in this group are very much in the minority but exert an influence far out of all proportion to their numbers. These are the people to whom Jesus referred as the salt of the earth and the leaven in the loaf. They may be Jew or Gentile, Catholic or Protestant, Christian or non-Christian. But the student must get used to seeing this man of primary religious experience as a member of a minority often exceedingly small, the hard but luminous core of the whole amorphous enterprise that we call religion.

And it is most important that the scholar distinguish between this luminous core and its pale outer fringes. For it is the failure of scholars in all fields, but particularly of the social scientists, to make the important distinction between these categories that has led to many invalid or at least confused conclusions about religion. If one could take a census, the result would show that the members of the secondary and tertiary groups far outnumber those in the primary, not only in the population in general but even in the churches—one is almost tempted to say *especially* in the churches. Most social scientists who have studied the churches have not painted a very flattering picture. As careful an investigator as Edward L. Thorndike concluded that the churches are no more than clubs of estimable people, interested in preserving traditional rites and ceremonies, rather than forces for human betterment.[12]

[11] *The Nature of Prejudice*, p. 439.
[12] See for example his book *Your City*, p. 99. One feels that Thorndike sensed this distinction even though he was not very explicit about it.

A more careful analysis of just what is being studied, and more discrimination in defining religion would disclose that conclusions proper to one form of religion are inappropriate to another. The secondary and tertiary types may be very flat and sterile and well deserve the aspersions of Thorndike and others like him. But with primary religious behavior it is a very different matter. Quantitative methods of investigation may miss the point unless we are very careful about how we apply them. While we do not intend in our volume to address ourselves as completely as James to religious extremes, we want the reader to know that throughout our book we will have in mind, as the most characteristic form of religion, the personal, primary religious behavior as we have tried to define it.

Chapter 3

METHODS OF STUDY

Today, however, a scientific study of religion seems to combine two concepts that contradict each other in structure, method, and goals. Science is man-centered—religion is God-centered. Science deals with the world from the point of view of sensory experience acting upon man from without—religion deals with the world as an internal experience. Science has its origin in reason—religion in faith. Science is based upon methods—religion upon revelation. The objects of science are facts—the objects of religion are values. The aim of science is to give us the good life for our bodies—the aim of religion is to give us the good life for our souls. . . .

However, if we deal with religion not as theology but as a phenomenon of man's attitudes, of his beliefs, his expressions and his inner experiences, then religion becomes a subject of study for the social sciences.

—Werner Wolff

The psychology of religion is a science to the extent that it uses scientific methods. It is true that it cannot exclude the insights of intuition and the use of subjectivism, whatever the strictures of the behaviorists. But luckily for the psychology of religion, doctrinaire behaviorism, having long since lost its "first fine careless rapture," has yielded its earlier strong hold on the loyalties of psychologists. A more catholic spirit among them not only acknowledges an access to the psyche through subjectivism but also is hard at work devising scientific methods of studying the subjective consciousness of even the individual case, as will shortly be demonstrated. The psychologist of religion must explore man's inner consciousness and never slacken in his search for scientific means of doing so.

Yet he must also welcome the philosopher's spirit, which is the

29

habit of looking on the mind not only in its wholeness but also in its relationships with all of life. This characterizes particularly the writing of James and of Pratt, both of whom exemplify the ability to give vitality to the psychology of religion. At the same time the religious psychologist demonstrates his basically scientific orientation in his refusal to accept guesswork and speculative surmise, no matter how plausible, when an exact technique is available for settling the question. For example, it would seem to involve no great hazard for one to conclude without any special need for proof that women are more religious than men, yet the scientific student of the problem will start to answer the question by counting the relative attendance of the sexes at church services, administering tests and questionnaires bearing on the subject, or in other ways investigating whatever aspects of the problem can fruitfully be pursued by precise and quantitative methods. No scientist is jusified in making easy assumptions, no matter how arduous the scientific alternative.

The faith of the scientist holds that all knowledge will some day be capable of scientific demonstration and proof. This is the essential article of his "religious creed," the idealistic correlate of which he demonstrates in his devotion to the thorny and difficult pursuit of exact knowledge through experiment, precise investigation, and ever-vigilant emotional restraint. This belief of the scientist is like a religious faith, since it cannot be proved; obviously all knowledge has not been scientifically demonstrated. The scientist's faith is further like religion in that it calls forth a discipline of the human spirit that is in no wise inferior to the discipline of the most zealous religious ascetic. This circumstance should remind the scientist to beware of that most characteristic weakness of all religious people, the sin of intolerance and spiritual pride.

But it is quite obvious that our picture of duty in the scientific study of religion is a counsel of perfection. If no speculations were to be allowed, most writing in the psychological field could hardly exist. Discussion and speculation are the mortar put between what bricks of fact we can find, the whole of which composes the edifice we are building. It is in his application of speculative data that what philosophical competence the psychologist has must play its part. At the very least, he must be keenly aware of the point at which he stops being a scientist, lest he confuse fact and fancy, and confusing them should evaluate them alike. His first duty is to strive for this clearness of sight, and an essential step in this process is to become well acquainted with the ways of psychological science.

In reviewing methods that have been used, and in casting about for those new ones that are necessary if the study of the psychology of religion is to become at the same time more scientific and more profound, we should remind ourselves of our concept of religion. Both the secondary and tertiary forms should be included along with the primary. But the latter is to come nearer the focus of our study, and we should remember that, according to our definition, it consists both of inner experience and outer expression. Some methods will be better adapted to the study of experience and others to expression. But our enterprise as a whole must do justice to both.

We have not the space to give the subject of methods the full attention it deserves, but at least we will try to indicate some of the more important approaches.[1] It is not possible to separate them in a strict way, for it is inevitable and desirable that a problem be approached by a combination of methods, and often there is overlapping between them; but for the purpose of exposition each of these will be described under a separate head.

The personal document. "One of the most subjective of all areas of experience is the religious life. It is safe to say that it has never been studied with even partial adequacy by any means other than the personal document." So declares Gordon W. Allport in *The Use of Personal Documents in Psychological Science*,[2] a searching and indispensable reference for all psychologists concerned with this approach to personality, on which the following discussion is largely based.

[1] For a philosophical discussion of methods in the psychological study of religion, see Pratt, *op. cit.*, Chap. 2; for other discussions, see Johnson, *op. cit.*, Chap. 1; Stolz, *op. cit.*, Chap. 9. For general discussions of methods of studying personality, see McClelland, *Personality*, Part I; Allport, *Personality*, Part IV; or nearly any textbook on the psychology of personality. *The Study of Personality*, edited by Brand, is a book of readings for the advanced student. L. W. Ferguson's *Personality Measurement* is another title in the field, while R. B. Cattell's *Personality and Motivation Structure and Measurement* is advanced and recent.

[2] P. 38. Another important publication in this field is Dollard's *Criteria for the Life History*. Though it is narrower in scope than Allport's monograph and heavily Freudian in its approach, Dollard demonstrated that his criteria could elicit excellent case histories in *Children of Bondage*, a study of Negro adolescents written in collaboration with Allison Davis. P. E. Johnson's *Personality and Religion* makes effective use of case material.

While some might contend that Allport's remark is an overstatement, nevertheless it underlines the importance of the personal document in the study of religious experience and helps to explain why we have mentioned it first. Of course, the personal document is not strictly speaking a method, but rather represents an essential means by which the religious life is approached. Furthermore, it is the traditional way, in which William James was the most important pioneer. *Varieties* abounds in quotations both from classical descriptions of religious experience and from more commonplace and private sources. If, as we have contended, religion is "the inner experience of the individual when he senses a Beyond," then the psychologist wants to get as close to this inner experience as he can. Outside of being himself one who has had such an experience or intimately known such people, his most available and most nearly first-hand means of getting at the inwardness of the experience is through written documents of various types, such as autobiographies, diaries, descriptions in response to open-end questionnaires, memoirs, confessions, and the recorded protocols of interviews. Occasionally also a work of the imagination is transparently autobiographical and can be used as such a source. This is the case with Carlyle's *Sartor Resartus*, to which we intend to make illustrative reference from time to time during our discussions in later chapters. Diogenes Teufelsdröckh, the protagonist of the work, is simply an alias for Thomas Carlyle so far as the account of his inward spiritual experiences is concerned.

Crucial to the problem of how to study the personal document is the question whether it can profitably be studied by scientific means. If science can do no better than any shrewd peruser of the document without recourse to scientific discipline, then we had better leave alone the pretense that the personal document can be of much use to science. Allport lists the three aims of science as *understanding, prediction,* and *control,* beyond that which man can achieve "through his own unaided common sense." [3] Thus if we can study the personal document by some systematic process, which helps us to accomplish our aims, then we can utilize the personal document as a source of scientific data.

Of Allport's three aims, that which will concern us more immediately in this work is understanding. Prediction and control,

[3] *The Use of Personal Documents,* p. 148.

partly as validation, tend to appertain more to the latter stages of science, for they presuppose a certain amount of understanding. The psychology of religion, as a scientific discipline, is hardly out of its swaddling clothes. Hence we must not expect too much precision in any of these areas. But ultimately, it is the *method* which is the criterion of distinction, and to be scientific this method should impose on the student some systematic discipline instrumental in achieving one or more of the three aims.

As we have indicated, Allport feels that the scientist should fulfill these aims "beyond that which he can achieve through his unaided common sense." By "common sense" presumably Allport would include the intuitive and speculative processes so usual in the religious field. We take it that by "beyond" he means, not necessarily "better," but "different." For example, scientific conclusions are much more dependable than the pronouncements of the religious prophet, but it does not follow that they are profounder or even more valuable. There are indeed many religious assumptions that are capable of being superseded or refined through scientific exactitude, and it is here that religion may profit from the ministrations of the religious psychologist. In areas such as theology and religious value, it is unlikely that science will or should have the last word.[4]

In further pursuing the problem of the scientific use of personal documents, Allport distinguishes what he terms the "nomothetic" and the "idiographic" approaches. In nomothetic science we study many cases in order to discover universal generalizations. Personal documents can be used nomothetically if there are enough of them, and often there are. But very often the psychologist is interested in an intensive study of only *one* document. Particularly in religion this may be an account of a high order of uniqueness, with even salient features occurring only once in all of history, for example, the *Confessions* of St. Augustine. It is obvious that any generalization supposed to have validity for other people made on the basis of the inspection of one case would be extremely hazardous, and there are many social scientists who deny scientific significance to the study of any one document.

[4] For evidence that even the vigorous proponent of science finds the problem of value a thorny one, see Chap. 28, "Designing a Culture," in B. F. Skinner's *Science and Human Behavior*.

Allport disagrees, however, and contends that the intensive study of a single document may uncover scientific generalizations so specialized that they may be illustrated only within the context of that one case.[5] This is the "idiographic" approach, and provided this kind of study can be carried out with due regard for such considerations as checks from independent sources, internal consistency, and the predictive success of interpretations, this variety of investigation can be accredited as scientific. The idiographic concept is of high importance for the psychology of religion. Naturally, the nomothetic approach is very useful, particularly in the study of the secondary and tertiary forms of religious behavior. Yet primary religion is much more individualized. Furthermore, its significance often increases in proportion to its individuality, and there is no area of human experience where the insights of the individual are of more importance or of more influence than they are in religion. Indeed, it has been the insistence by most scientific students of religion on the nomothetic approach which has caused them to concentrate on religion's more common secondary and tertiary forms, and which has given them a bad name with sensitive religious minds who somehow feel that there is "something more" that has been left out. It is this "something more" that immediately becomes available to the psychologist who gives his mind to the techniques of the idiographic study of personal documents.

By way of illustration, let us present two studies in which psychologists have developed techniques for studying personal documents that have suggestive value for the study of religion, though neither was designed for the express purpose of studying religion.

The first of these techniques was developed by R. K. White and is called "value-analysis." [6] This involves analyzing a document by counting words with value connotations and classifying them in such a way as to arrive at the pattern of the value system of the individual under study. White illustrates this by a value-analysis of Richard Wright's *Black Boy*. One of his value categories includes religion, and while the concept of religion in this case is extremely elementary and would have to be considerably refined before it

[5] *Op cit.*, pp. 147–148.
[6] *Journal of Social Psychology*, 19, 1944, pp. 351–358; *Journal of Abnormal and Social Psychology*, 42, 1947, pp. 440–461.

would be useful for the religious psychologist, nevertheless the technique has promise.

Another study, considerably richer in its approach, and correspondingly less "scientific" in the rigor of its conclusions, is reported in an article by L. W. Ferguson, "The evaluative attitudes of Jonathan Swift." [7] This involved a thorough study of biographical records, writings, and documents relating to the life of Swift, then filling out the Allport-Vernon *Study of Values*, a questionnaire designed to analyze the value system of the individual, as the investigator felt that Swift would have done. This indicated that, contrary to a contemporary biography of Swift, he was much more social and religious in his emphases than the biography suggests. Of course, there is a large element of the subjective that obviously would creep into a study like this, despite careful preparation, in the considerable task of weighing the evidence. Furthermore, it would be hard to check, even if a second person were to go through a similar arduous process in the same way. Nevertheless, it might be possible to get several students of the life of the same individual to fill out the questionnaire. To the extent that there might be found agreement, there could be assumed some scientific confirmation of conclusions, while the systematic nature of the process might well add something to the insights into the value system of a personality, a concern always of moment to the religious psychologist. It is unfortunate that neither Ferguson nor others seem to have followed up this promising technique.[8]

Questionnaire and interview. Closely allied to the personal document is the questionnaire, which may be regarded as a special kind of personal document. However, its typical form, in which the subject is simply asked to answer *yes* or *no* or to indicate a choice among a list of alternatives, is used as a measurement device and lacks the freedom and opportunity for spontaneity of response that characterizes the personal document. Of course, the wise designer of a questionnaire will provide an opportunity for the subject to answer with more freedom if he so desires; or perhaps the questions simply pose

[7] *Psychological Record*, 3, 1939, pp. 26–44.

[8] For further discussion of other recent developments in the study of personal documents, see McClelland, *op. cit.*, pp. 30–38.

general topics on which the respondent is asked to write. To the extent that this is true the product becomes more like the documents we have discussed in the previous section. Starbuck and Pratt made extensive use of this open-ended feature in their questionnaires. However, in our discussion here, we will have in mind the more restricted type.

The usefulness of the questionnaire is most obvious in the field of nomothetic research. It is a ready means of collecting answers on a number of topics from a large group, and of getting this information in a tabulation that can be quantified and manipulated statistically. Usually the questionnaire refers to the person filling it out, though occasionally it may have reference to someone else. The questionnaire enjoys its chief usefulness when it seeks information of an external nature such as "To what denomination do you belong?" but if it is critically and cautiously used it may give the psychologist access to deeper levels of consciousness and provide useful information. A very large portion of research in the field of the psychology of religion makes use of the questionnaire.

The defects of the questionnaire, on the other hand, are pretty well known among psychologists. In the first place, this method presupposes cooperation by the respondent, as well as insight and intelligence. If, for example, to the question "In what state were you previous to your conversion?" one should find the answer "New Jersey," one might wonder whether it represented a touch of dullness, or just a burst of facetiousness from one of those popular guinea pigs for so many psychological studies, an undergraduate. In either case, the response would be useless or misleading, and yet answers of only slightly smaller enormity often find their way into the statistical hopper and so influence conclusions.

Then the phrasing of questionnaire items requires a high degree of skill. Otherwise they may confuse or, what is worse, mean one thing to the investigator and another to the respondent. Again, the question may suggest the answer and so provide the investigator with the answer he expects. Or the categories set up by the questionnaire may so constrain answers that experience is distorted.

Finally, a most important consideration is the question of how representative the questionnaire sample may be. For example, a questionnaire on religion will doubtless appeal more to those who have an interest in religion, so that the less religious may not bother to answer. If the investigator assumes that his responding population is a simple cross section of all persons, his conclusions quite likely will be dubious or distorted. He must face the fact that questionnaires are not extremely welcome among all sections of the general public. A very wholesome practice is to run a pilot study with a representative but restricted group to whom the investigator has closer access. This will enable him to anticipate and so to provide against at least some of the pitfalls of which we have spoken.

An example of the use of the questionnaire in religious research is to be found in the author's study of Moral Re-Armament.[9] Reasoning that it would be hopeless to expect much objectivity from those who had recently participated in the movement, he sent out questionnaires only to those whose first contact with it had been at least ten years previous. Such questions as "Were you active in the movement?" concerned simple matters of fact, while "Did you feel its influence on you to have been beneficial? If so, in what specific ways?" involved more subjectivity. Some questions called for extended comment, while others such as "Did the experience increase your sense of religious certainty?," required a simple *yes* or *no* answer or merely a check mark. At the other extreme respondents were encouraged to respond to an open-ended invitation to express themselves in any pertinent way not suggested by the questions. Some of the responses were augmented by a personal interview in order to extend understanding of the case and confirm the replies.

However, it must be said that many careful investigators are skeptical of the value of most questionnaires. Ernest M. Ligon of the Character Research Project at Union College, Schenectady, N.Y., states that he has found the questionnaire the most difficult measuring instrument to construct.[10]

As illustrated in the study of Moral Re-Armament, a means of supplementing a questionnaire investigation is *the interview*. This may be for the purpose of checking the questionnaire or of gaining more intimate insights into certain aspects of the study. While such are very expensive in terms of time required, they are well worth it, and even when a large number of respondents might desirably be

[9] See *The Oxford Group*, Part III and Appendix.
[10] See his *Dimensions of Character*, pp. 335, 368.

polled, interviews may well replace written questionnaires, for they usually make up in quality what they lack in quantity. Interviews are dependent on satisfactory *rapport* between interviewer and interviewee, and this is a skill that differs in different people. But interviewers may be trained and the skill can be learned at least in part. Depending on the purpose of the investigation, interviews may be *standardized*. This means that the same questions will be asked each individual. Or it may be more *open* or *non-directive*. This means that the interviewee will be left free to talk about what seems significant to him with a minimum of prompting. The practice is growing among psychologists to preserve such interviews verbatim, sometimes stenographically, more often by recording machine. This provides a record that can be studied later on. Of course the interview is often used independently of a questionnaire study.

The *public opinion poll* is a specialized adaptation of both the questionnaire and the interview, designed to sample ideas of the general public. This is sometimes used to elicit information about religious subjects. One of the chief hazards is the problem of proper sampling. For example, the Seventh Day Adventist "Voice of Prophecy" radio program conducted a survey to determine the most popular religious song in North America.[11] This was reported to be "The Old Rugged Cross." One might very properly question whether the "public" was not confined largely to the audience of the program. A more impressive poll was conducted by Lincoln Barnett based on interviews with "a cross section of Americans from coast to coast," which showed that 95 per cent believed in God, 2 per cent were agnostic, 2 per cent atheistic, while 1 per cent declined to reply. Other information on the religious habits and beliefs of Americans were included.[12]

Scales. A scale is a measurement device that seeks to indicate the amount of a fairly specific personality variable or its place along a continuum. In this way, one person can be compared with another, say in the liberalism or conservatism of his religious beliefs. Very

[11] Reported in *The Witness* (Episcopal) for Sept. 24, 1953.
[12] "God and the American People," in *Ladies Home Journal*, Sept., 1948, pp. 37, 230–240.

often questionnaires are used for this purpose. E. J. Chave has devised a number of such scales to indicate religious attitudes such as the attitude toward God and the Church. It is also quite common practice, particularly in the newer type of church school program, to use rating scales to indicate growth and progress in religious education. Professor Ligon makes extensive use of rating scales which he has devised. One of his scales, for example, indicates ratings on an individual's philosophy of life. Approximately 16 per cent of those he has studied are designated as "Highly developed philosophy of life for age," 34 per cent as "Rational outlook on life," 34 per cent as "Somewhat irrational outlook on life," and 16 per cent as "Total lack of philosophy of life."

In most of these cases the scores are not obtained from questionnaires but represent the estimates and observations of some third person. They usually involve the checking of categories along a graduated scale, called a "rating scale," perhaps with the addition of concrete descriptive material to support the rating. Naturally, such ratings are highly subjective and may be very unreliable. The literature on personality appraisal indicates refinements which will improve ratings.[13]

Tests. Perhaps the psychologist's best way to measure behavior is to devise a test for it, standardized if possible, but so far this has proved difficult in the field of religion. It is relatively easy to put a task to an individual under controlled conditions that will elicit intelligent behavior and so serve as a measure of his intelligence. Yet how is one to do so with religion and feel sure he has a valid measure of it? Furthermore, prejudices and attitudes about religion being what they are, the religious psychologist has need of being either a very great diplomat or a very courageous investigator if he is to risk the criticism that may fall to his lot if in cold blood he uses religious stimuli for scientific purposes.

However, successful tests have been constructed in fields very close to religion, even if not in that of the essential religious process as we have defined it. Some of these have been "behavioral tests," utilizing not so much pencil and paper as actual behavior elicited as part of the everyday life of children, controlled and observed. Perhaps the

[13] See bibliography for books in this field by Cattell and Ferguson.

most satisfactory examples of these are still those devised by Hartshorne and May for their studies in the Character Education Inquiry at Columbia University in the 1920's. Very ingenious tests of honesty and cooperativeness were among the most successful of these. For example, familiar games were set up and the amount of cheating was unobtrusively observed and recorded. An elaborate study was made of the relationship of this type of behavior among children to various community influences, including that of the Church. The conclusions were not very flattering to religion, or what was taken as such, and there have been many criticisms of the interpretations. But there would seem to be little doubt that the techniques for testing behavior itself are models that should be studied by other students interested in the field.[14]

Experimentation. Probably the pioneer in the field of experimentation in the religious field was George Albert Coe who, about the turn of the century, used hypnosis to determine certain temperamental traits, particularly suggestibility, which he tried to relate to religious states such as mysticism.[15] Of course experimentation in the field of religion, which often involves testing, runs into some of the same difficulties as the latter; and this may help to explain why there has been so little of it. However, it is strange that the modern religious-education movement in Protestantism, which has been touched by the scientific movement and is hospitable to it, has not made more use of experimentation in evaluating its techniques. Probably the Character Education Project, mentioned above, is one of the few exceptions. Evaluation in religious education tends to rest on the pronouncements of experts in the field, or on the subjective impressions of workers only more or less systematically trained. It would seem that there is much room for rigorous experiment in this and other religious fields.

[14] The Psychological Corporation, 522 Fifth Ave., New York City 18, sells tests of many publishers and will also give advice as to appropriate tests and their use. The *Mental Measurements Yearbook*, edited by O. K. Buros and published from time to time by Rutgers Univ. Press gives lists and comments on tests as they come out. Freeman's *Theory and Practice of Psychological Testing* is helpful for principles and comments on the commoner tests. Other references already mentioned in this chapter will also be found useful.

[15] See *The Spiritual Life.*

A full discussion of the technique of the psychological experiment is outside our scope, but at least one feature should be mentioned; that is the importance of *control*. This means that when a factor is under study great care must be taken to exclude the influence of other variables that may very easily be overlooked. It is, of course, much simpler to control conditions when one is studying a rat, or a simple reaction among human beings, than it is to control a study of religion. But this may be done with reasonable effectiveness through a *control group*. In its simplest form this is a group closely similar to the experimental group and subjected to the same conditions except for the crucial factor under study. For instance, a church school might institute a program for reducing prejudice. Yet even if prejudice was actually demonstrated to have diminished in the course of the program, the careful social scientist could not conclude that this *resulted from* the program. Due to some other influence, this might have occurred anyway without benefit of the program. Only if a control group in the same church school or a very similar one showed a real difference in the amount of its prejudice could this difference be conceived as the result of the program. The psychologist of religion who wishes to do effective experimental research must make himself the master of this and other features of the art of experimental design.[16]

A simple example of the use of experimentation in religion may be found in Ligon's *Dimensions of Character*.[17] Two similar Christian church schools with different curricula, one constructed by the Character Research Project (CRP) and another called Curriculum X (Cur X), were compared on the basis of how well each school was meeting the aims of its curriculum. This was done by asking children to write essays on their ideas about Jesus. Without knowing their source, judges from both churches ranked fifty-six essays as to whether they suggested that the objectives of the curriculum of each judge's particular church were being achieved. In this case each church school served as a control or comparison group for the other. By

[16] For a brief introduction to experimentation and further references, see Munn, *Psychology*, Chap. 2, also Goode and Hatt, *Methods in Social Research*, Chaps. 7–8. Ligon's book cited is a generalized discussion of research methods in the field of character and religious education; Chaps. 10–12 deal especially with experimentation.

[17] Pp. 269–272, 289 ff.

a statistical device it was shown that the CRP judges had ranked CRP essays on the whole as indicating better realization of CRP objectives than Cur X essays. On the other hand, Cur X judges did not, with significant consistency, rank Cur X essays as coming closer to Cur X objectives than CRP essays. It was concluded that the Character Research Project curriculum was making positive progress in achieving its objectives, while the evidence did not clearly show that this was true of Curriculum X. In such ways may psychological experimentation be useful in the field of religion.

Sociological and anthropological observations. The line between sociology and social anthropology is considerably blurred, and scholars in both fields continually poach on each other's preserve, with or without the landlord's consent. In general, social anthropology is more concerned with the distinction of cultures and subcultures, whereas sociology is interested in the behavior of people in groups with no special consideration for cultural differences. In both cases religion may be a concern of the student, who is a psychologist to the extent that he is concerned with what light these disciplines can throw on the reactions of the individual in his psychological aspect.

The most obvious way to gather such data is by the simple method of observation. Yet it must be something more than the naive observation the ordinary person is carrying on during most of his waking moments. It must be disciplined and systematic. Experimentation can be thought of as the ultimate in the way of disciplined observation. What we are talking about here, however, is simply observation of groups in the natural pursuance of their affairs with the minimum of interference. This reduces the consequent self-consciousness that comes when people are aware that others are looking at them with a cold and appraising eye. Systematic considerations include a preliminary review of the problem so that the investigator knows just what he wishes to observe, and the preparation of some sort of log or diary to preserve the data until the time when it is to be reviewed and written up in final form.[18]

But probably the most serious objection to be brought against the ordinary type of scientific observation is that, like Mr. Pickwick

[18] See Goode and Hatt, *op. cit.*, Chap. 10.

in his encounter with the cabman, the outsider busily at work in filling a notebook with exact and learned observations may record only surface manifestations and entirely miss the feelings and the meanings underneath. The devout worshiper, prostrate before the high altar, is having a very different experience from the eager man with a pencil in the back row. Unless the latter has had a similar experience himself or has extraordinary powers of empathy, his notes on the proceedings may amount to little more than psychological gibberish. Sad though this situation may be for the scientific stickler, the cause of understanding will best be served if the investigator can find some way of entering into the experience of those he is observing. This has led social scientists to join or otherwise identify themselves with groups that they may be observing. This method has come to be known as *participant observation*, which probably first became a well-defined and self-conscious technique in 1940 through an article by the anthropologist Florence Kluckhohn in the *American Journal of Sociology*.[19] There are obvious dangers in this technique, for the investigator may do so thorough a job of identification that perspective is lost. Indeed, there have been cases where, with scientific zeal, social scientists have joined a culture or a movement, and then have refused to write it up in scientific form, so thoroughly have their feelings been enlisted. Nevertheless, it would seem that such dangers are the lesser evil, particularly in describing an experience as inward as religion, and that this is a most promising technique for the psychology of religion.

A very successful piece of sociological research into religious experience using this method was demonstrated by Dr. T. W. Sprague of Cambridge, Massachusetts, who made a study of Jehovah's Witnesses.[20] Dr. Sprague identified himself with the sect and participated in some of its activities; this enabled him to give a much more sympathetic and informed account of the movement than would have been possible had he merely viewed it from the outside. At the same time he retained sufficient perspective not to abrogate the critical objectivity that should characterize the scholar.

In connection with anthropological studies, mention should be

[19] Vol. 46, 1940, pp. 331–343.
[20] *Some Problems in the Integration of Social Groups with Special Reference to Jehovah's Witnesses.*

made of the *comparative* method. *Comparative* psychology is usually thought of as the study of analogies between animal and human psychology, but it is quite obvious that one cannot generate religion in animals; though it is true that B. F. Skinner is reported to have trained pigeons to perform sundry bowings and scrapings which have been likened to religious ritual. Cultural anthropological studies of religion, however, give a means of comparing differing religious practices and their psychological correlatives. Frazer's *The Golden Bough,* for example, while principally concerned with external custom, nevertheless contains psychological speculations, as in the chapter on magic and religion, which perform this comparative function.

Statistics. Data in quantitative form can be manipulated by statistical treatment so as further to refine their precision. Some religious people reject such maneuvers with scorn and indignation feeling that they are calculated to profane the sacred, or at the very least to apply a yardstick to the immeasurable. It must be admitted that statisticians, being mere human beings, sometimes press their methods too warmly on psychologists. Statistics is a fascinating study, and the statistician, after mastering a new method for refining data, very naturally is eager to see it used. In view of the crudity which of necessity characterizes most of the instruments used to collect data, statistical refinement to the fourth decimal place may be like putting a razor edge on a hoe, or calculating to the exact second the ending of the Mesozoic era of geological time. It is also possible for psychological sense to be lost in a welter of statistical manipulation. There is no area of psychology where common sense is more needful.

But there still remains an area of usefulness for statistical tools in the psychology of religion. The reactions of large numbers of people cannot adequately be described without summarizing devices; most populations cannot be studied in their entirety but must be sampled; while comparisons frequently have to be made with mathematical help. So the psychologist has to know something of the science of constructing charts and tables, ways of knowing that his population has been sampled in sufficient numbers to justify his conclusions, or expressions of correlation that serve to summarize unwieldy comparisons. As long as his knowledge of them does not go to his head, the psychologist of religion will find that such concepts as the proper way to round decimal points, the standard deviation, partial correlation, and the chi-square method of measuring statistical probability are good servants to him in the solution of many problems.

Perhaps special mention should be made of *factor-analysis,* a rather complicated statistical technique for breaking down personality concepts into component parts, which has recently come into prominence. As we will see increasingly as we go on, religion is complicated by many diverse elements, and it would seem that factor-analysis should be useful in its study. While there have been some studies of religion (mixed with other variables) by this method, there have not been too many as yet that seem very convincing or enlightening. Probably more than with any other statistical device, data are likely to be turned into the factor-analytical grinder with meaning and to come out with none, or at least to leave the psychologist somewhat more confused than when he started the process. Yet it must be remembered that the technique is a new one, that it has some successes to its credit, and that it should provide a good supplementary device for the study of just such a complex personality variable as the religious sentiment. It should be given further trials by psychologists interested in religion.

An example of factor-analysis is A *Factor-Analytic Study of Chicago Protestant Ministers' Conceptions of What it Means to be Religious,* a doctoral dissertation at the University of Chicago by A. D. Shand. This was based on interviews yielding 2,400 items reduced to 180 subgroups. Factor-analysis showed these subgroups to arrange themselves mainly into four inter-correlating "clusters" or factors, two of which were fundamentalist and two non-fundamentalist. In other words, to be religious was defined by some non-fundamentalists as (1) "theistic brotherliness" with the emphasis on general altruistic concern, and by others as (2) "theistic-Christian" with the emphasis on specifically Christian doctrine; by fundamentalists as (3) "righteous-formalistic" or somewhat ecclesiastical, and on the other hand as (4) "practical" with religion expressed in everyday life. These divisions seem to make sense, and doubtless are sufficiently refined to be useful in further precise study.

On the other hand, with much less trouble the author of this book sent out a questionnaire and secured responses from 68 students of social science giving their definition of religion.[21] The replies were then analyzed by inspection, and yielded six categories: concepts of (1) the supernatural, (2) ultimate values, (3) the group, (4) institutions and creeds, (5) theology, (6) the interaction between the inner and outer aspects of life. The latter study was not nearly so precise but was sufficient for its purpose, namely to demonstrate the wide diversity in defining religion among those who may suppose that since they all use the term "religion" they are studying the same thing. For this purpose factor-analysis would have been a waste of time and energy. This contrast will illustrate the point that not only with regard to factor-analysis but also in the use of other methods and statistical tools the psychologist of religion must be guided by a consideration of his aims and by common sense.

The developmental approach. Psychologists are often interested in the origins of the various aspects of man's psychic life and how these aspects develop. This is the developmental approach. Though it is not exactly a method, it seems wise to include it here. Religious psychologists and religious educators have a particular concern about origins, while every religiously-minded person has his moments of interest in such things.

One of the means of such study is biographical accounts, particularly autobiographies or diaries—in other words, personal documents, as already noted. Augustine's *Confessions*, Carlyle's *Sartor Resartus*, and Edmund Gosse's *Father and Son* are diverse examples of autobiographical material that throws light on the origins of religious attitudes.

Personality theory also sometimes touches on the origins of religious impulses. Thus Freud's psychoanalytical theory, which is basically developmental in its emphasis, explains religion as deriving from guilt impulses originating in childhood, and belief in God as the search for a "father image."

In the early days of the scientific study of religious psychology, around 1900 and before, there was considerable interest in the religious life of children and adolescents, and this interest still continues, though more under the auspices of religious educators, where rigorous controls unfortunately have not been observed as strictly

[21] "How Do Social Scientists Define Religion?"

as might be desired. Modern ways of pursuing developmental studies include the direct observation of the behavior of children and the careful recording of their conversation. Characteristic reactions of the different age groups can be noted, and by means of these, deductions can be made about the development of the impulses under study. Much more satisfactory but correspondingly more difficult is the longitudinal study, where the same individual or individuals are followed over a period of years, ideally from infancy to maturity. Because of the time and expense involved, such studies have tended to be scarce in the general psychological field, but even more scarce in religion. It is obviously a pasture that greatly needs to be cropped by the religious psychologist.[22]

The clinical method and projective techniques. The clinical method is characterized chiefly by the concern with personality adjustment and therapy for the sick soul. Since both psychiatry and religion have a common interest in increasing the effectiveness of the individual life, there has been an increasing tendency to join forces, as has already been mentioned in the previous chapter. Confession, for example, is utilized both by the psychiatrist and the priest, and like Molière's character who was surprised to find that he had been speaking prose all his life, so psychiatrists are undergoing a similar awakening in finding that their therapies are often little more than the "hearing of confessions." The clinical method is focused on the individual, and, while the therapeutic aim is usually present, the technique may also incidentally be of use as a research or teaching instrument. Any means of gathering data about the individual that shows promise may be and is used, depending on the abilities and predilections of the therapist; but essential to the method is some form of interview. Naturally the success or failure of the method is only partly dependent on scientific procedure, for the personality and skill of the therapist is of rather crucial importance. Hence it must be acknowledged that the clinical method is at least as much of an art as it is a science.

One of the chief diagnostic instruments in the armory of the therapist is the *projective test.* This perhaps should have been

[22] Professor Ligon, *op. cit.*, p. 411, promises some longitudinal studies of religious growth in the near future.

treated under the section on tests, but it is so closely associated with the work of the clinician that it has been allotted to this section. Strictly speaking, projective techniques have not enjoyed wide use by the psychologist of religion, at least in his academic character, but much material elicited by the tests is religious in nature, and it is quite likely that there will be more use made of them in the future. Moreover, religious agencies, through their commerce with psychiatrists, are beginning to gain some appreciation of the practical uses of these devices, chiefly in the appraisal of the stability of personnel.

The general method of the projective test is to present the subject with some more or less ambiguous but standardized stimuli and then leave him free to react, with a minimum of interference. The theory is that he will disclose underlying personality urges the more freely for being unconscious that he is doing so. The best known projective test is the *Rorschach,* which uses ink-blots as stimuli. Another is the *Thematic Apperception Test,* first developed in studies of young men, which uses vaguely drawn pictures of people with whom the subject may identify himself. With children, doll figures are used which the child may use to represent persons in his family, including himself. In the free doll play the child will disclose his attitudes and distresses. The Character Research Project has used projective techniques in evaluating religious and character training. Young people are asked to write on topics such as "three wishes," "the kind of person I would like to be like," or "my heroes." Responses are then analyzed for evidences of the influence of the training.[23] In such tests religious material may be an incidental part of the disclosures. In all of these tests, despite the attempts of the test devisers to make them scientific and train administrators, interpreters will differ about their meaning so that interpretation continues to be something of an art. But since of all standardized tests they seem to tap the deepest layers of personality, they should be of interest to the psychologist of religion and the therapist.[24]

The case study.   The case study has been put near the end of the list because it is to a large degree a synthetic method. It may make

[23] Ligon, *ibid.,* pp. 367–368.
[24] For an account of projective tests, see John Bell, *Projective Techniques.*

primary use of personal documents, but it may also use data derived from interviews, tests, observation, or any other of the methods discussed in this chapter. Any piece of information that may throw light on the psychology of the individual in accordance with the purpose of the investigator may be included in the case study. The case study may be undertaken for the purpose of therapy for the individual under study, or to facilitate the understanding of the individual for the mere sake of understanding, or because he represents a type so that an understanding of his psychology will throw light on the psychology of other people like him, or for the purpose of illustrating a point the psychologist has in mind, or when studies are made of individuals in a group in order to derive general laws. Quite often the case study is in the form of a *case history*, which is simply a name for the method when it is approached longitudinally or genetically. In this case as much and as reliable information is obtained as is available about the early history of the individual under study. It is always well for the social scientist who contemplates making a case study to consult references that will give him guidance in his methods in terms of the aims he has in mind.[25]

The survey. Another synthetic method is the survey, which is the most comprehensive of all since it includes the case study. Strictly speaking, it is a sociological rather than a psychological type of study since it is used to review large groups of people, such as make up an organization or a community. But usually the survey has its psychological aspect, and as a person who may be asked to participate in a survey or who may want to use information that a survey may give, the psychologist should be familiar with the procedure. Among the best-known surveys were those of the Lynds of an American Midwestern city, published under the titles *Middletown* and *Middletown in Transition*. The religious life of the community was one aspect covered. More specific psychological information, particularly in the area of the effect of religious affiliation on reputation for character, is to be found in the more recent studies of the youth in a smaller Midwestern community, by Havighurst and Taba, reported in *Ado-*

[25] See, for example, Gee, *Social Science Research Methods*, Chap. 7, or Allport, *Use of Personal Documents*, Chap. 2, for discussion and further references.

lescent Character and Personality, and Hollingshead's *Elmtown's Youth.* The Character Education Inquiry by Hartshorne and May, mentioned above, might also be considered a survey.

As with the case method, the form of a survey is somewhat loose and depends on what the problem under study may happen to be. Some surveys have been so loose that social scientists have accorded them little homage. On the other hand, others are tightly organized and convincing in their conclusions. As with other branches of social-scientific study, the more comprehensive the problem the more difficult it is to be clear and explicit in one's methodology; the more restricted the problem the more highly gratifying the procedure is likely to be to the scientific conscience. To be able to determine his plan with intelligence, the investigator must be acquainted with the general principles of the survey, as well as with particular surveys that have been made previously in the field of his interest.[26]

These then are the chief methods available to the psychologist of religion in pursuing his scientific way toward understanding some of the most cunning secrets of the human mind and heart, the ways of a man with his God, and the effect of those transactions on his behavior. But the psychologist must remember that methods are merely instruments and that the possession of instruments does not guarantee their effective use. Is ownership of a surgeon's kit a sufficient recommendation of the surgeon? Not only must the instruments be proved through use, but also there must be added to them judgment, insight, sympathy, sensitivity, and all those other nameless and subtle characteristics that go to make up intuition. Allport has called the human mind "the most sensitive recording machine ever devised," and it is this machine that must gather up the clues from the totality of experience, scientific and otherwise, in order to create meaning. We will not get very far in our study of religion if we do not make use of the scientific instruments available to us; on the other hand, we will merely stultify our conclusions if we do not know when to abandon methodology and scientific rigor in order to go beyond them. But the psychologist of religion must always be as scientific as he can, considering the complexity and difficulty of the task that falls to his lot.

[26] See Gee, *op. cit.,* Chap. 10, for a general discussion of the survey.

SUMMARY

The psychologist of religion must master the psychological methods of study already devised. At the same time he must be resourceful and continually alert to devise and discover new ways of precise and objective investigation in this most difficult field.

Chief among his skills should be his capacity to treat systematically the *personal document* as his most important path to understanding the intimate core and uniqueness of individual religious experience. Frequently used in the study of religion is the *questionnaire*, a deceptively obvious method in which the unwary psychologist will encounter many pitfalls. Often used as a check on questionnaire results are *interviews*, both "standardized" and "open-ended." The interview is often used as a method sufficient unto itself, while the *public opinion poll* is a specialized adaptation of the questionnaire or interview designed to sample the ideas of the general public. Often religious or character traits are evaluated by requesting an acquaintance to describe or rate an individual. Whenever a psychological device produces scores that can be distributed along a continuum, we call this a *scale*, so that when ratings are scaled they are called *rating scales*. On the other hand when religious behavior or achievement is systematically appraised under standardized conditions we call this a *test*.

Experimentation is particularly difficult in the field of religion, but it has been used. The development of *statistical devices* such as *factor-analysis* and *chi-square* help us when we attempt to make psychological measurements in the religious field. *Sociological* or *anthropological observation* is the method often used when we are interested in the religious behavior of groups, where *participant observation* is a special type particularly adapted to religion. Anthropologists especially are likely to use the *comparative method* in which one religious group is compared with another. Religious growth is best studied through the *genetic approach*, either of the individual or of groups. The *clinical method* is applicable to problems of religious adjustment or the role of religion as it relates to mental health. Particularly in this connection, *projective techniques* along with the *case study* may yield diagnostic information of interest to the psychologist of religion. The latter method involves the systematic gathering of data relative to a single individual. The *survey* uses a composite of methods and is useful when the social psychologist or sociologist wishes to secure a religious appraisal of a community.

But despite all these methods it is impossible to be merely scientific in studying religion. The psychologist in such a rich and complex area requires a sound methodology and something more as well if he is to give meaning to his data. But first he must not shrink from extending his more certain knowledge as far as his scientific equipment will allow him.[27]

[27] A critic of this chapter suggests that too much emphasis has been placed on methods in themselves, and that the issue would be better stated as follows: (a) any science is a disinterested study of phenomena; (b) the methods are a consequence of the disinterest and the nature of the subject matter; (c) therefore, other and established methods may or may not work for the psychology of religion. If they do, use them; if not, devise new ones. Any demonstration and proof to commend itself to a disinterested person is scientific. Otherwise it is not.
While there is something to be said for this point of view, it would seem to us that something more than disinterest should be required of the investigator. If he is a psychologist he should be equipped with the tools of psychology. Hence the psychologist of religion must have rather exact knowledge of the methods of psychology even though he will also have to be resourceful in devising new techniques.

Part 2

RELIGIOUS GROWTH

Chapter 4

THE PSYCHOLOGICAL
SOURCES OF RELIGION

Know that, by nature, every creature seeks to become like God. Nature's intent is neither food nor drink nor clothing nor comfort, nor anything else in which God is left out. Whether you like it or not, secretly nature seeks, hunts, tries to ferret out the track on which God may be found.
                                                                    —Meister Eckhart

Continued observations . . . especially in clinical practice, leads almost inevitably to the conclusion that deeper and more fundamental than sexuality, deeper than the craving for social power, deeper even than the desire for possessions, there is a still more generalized and more universal craving in the human make-up. *It is the craving for knowledge of the right direction—for orientation.*
                                                                    —William H. Sheldon

The sources of religion are intricate, and intertwined with all other aspects of man's psychic life. Furthermore their roots are so enshrouded in the mists that lie about the dark recesses of the personality that no scientist has yet clearly identified them, let alone unraveled these complicated and elusive strands. Some of the questions that we should bear in mind in our quest for origins would include the following:

Can we trace religious experiences, however complex, back to some single tap root without which they could not exist? If so what would that root be? On the other hand, if we find that the sources are many, which of these sources serve as psychological impulsions

55

and so can be thought of as real sources of religious experience, and which are simply modifying factors that influence the form and the manner of expression? Similarly, which of these sources act as impelling drives and which are to be thought of as capacities whose presence is indeed necessary to a religious experience but which may or may not be exercised, depending on whether the drives stimulate their use? Dante's capacity for song was in a different sense a source of his poetry than was his sight of Beatrice which called much of it forth. This latter consideration suggests that religion may be *instrumental* or *intrinsic*.[1] That is, its function may be to serve some other psychological urge, or it may provide its own satisfaction and reason for being. To what extent do the instrumental and intrinsic functions of religion play their psychological parts in personality?

Obviously any answers we can get to questions such as these will enhance our understanding of religion and its psychological meaning. However, we must be careful of certain errors into which it is particularly easy for us to fall. The first is that of judging the value of religion according to its psychological roots. In *Varieties* William James argues against this error with special eloquence. With particular reference to the pathological background of certain religious leaders he states:

To plead the organic causation of a religious state of mind, then, in refutation of its claim to possess superior religious value, is quite illogical and arbitrary. . . . When we think certain states of mind superior to others, is it ever because of what we know concerning their organic antecedents? No! it is always for two entirely different reasons. It is either because we take an immediate delight in them; or else it is because we believe them to bring us good consequential fruits for life.[2]

In other words, it is results, not origins, that determine value. Judging by origins is a fallacy that not only the psychologist, but also, and more often, the ordinary man is tempted to commit. For example, the worth of a man's religion is often judged by the social class from which the religion originated. Furthermore we must remember that in our study the question of the value of religion is not properly our concern nor within the range of our competence.

[1] See Johnson's *Psychology of Religion,* p. 45.
[2] Pp. 15–16.

Yet it is inevitable that our findings will have a bearing on the question of religious value and worth. Practically, this will be the interest of many who read our volume. Consequently we will occasionally refer to the subject of value, at the same time that we point out its partially extraneous nature in warning against judging religious value by origin.

Another kindred fallacy against which the reader must be warned is that of assuming that because certain less worthy elements may be detected in the religious consciousness there is nothing more to it. This is sometimes called the "nothing but" fallacy. As Freud points out, religion may be an escape from reality and the search for a father image.[3] But it does not follow that religion is *nothing but* an escape. We can detect elements of superstition in the practices of many religious bodies, but it does not follow that these practices are *nothing but* superstition. Religious visions can often be shown to be pathological manifestations, but it does not follow that religious visions are invariably *nothing but* hallucinations.[4] Though we attempt to reduce religion to an understandable collection of elements, we must remember that the totality of the religious life presents a picture too large for our canvas. In trying to delimit our discussion of religion in order to make it comprehensible, we still sense a bewildering complex of elements and forces beyond our scope. Consequently it is even less likely that such oversimplifications as the "nothing but" conceptions do any more than pinpoint tiny sections of the vast area of man's psychic life which we call religion.

Monistic views. But in spite of our great respect for the complexity of the human spirit we must review the ideas of a few scholars which, even though we may regard them as too simple and only partial and tentative, nevertheless help to throw some light on our problem.

There have been many who conceive of religion as emanating from a single spring. In the Middle Ages as well as in succeeding years, particularly in the time of the Enlightenment, religion was thought by some to be a particular expression of the life of reason.

[3] See *Totem and Taboo* and *The Future of an Illusion*.
[4] James deals with the general problem of religious pathology and its significance in Chap. 1 of *Varieties*.

Thomas Aquinas in his great work the *Summa Theologica* held that
the existence of God can be proved logically. This view is still held
by the Jesuits and other modern exponents of scholasticism, though
reason is not thought by them to be the sole source of religion. The
philosopher Hegel maintained that "religion is absolutely true knowledge" and "the region of eternal truth." [5]

Partly in opposition to concepts such as these, one of the early
thinkers to represent a really psychological point of view nevertheless espoused a one-sided theory of his own. Friedrich Schleiermacher [6] insisted that religion proper is characterized by neither
thinking nor acting, but comes from the sense of absolute dependence. From this is derived the concept of God and the moral force
that accompanies it. Despite the exclusiveness of both of these
points of view, we should not shut our eyes to the truths they contain. Though it may well be doubted that there are very many individuals who owe their religious life exclusively to acts of reason,
yet rational thoughts play some part even in the religion of the
humblest, while men can be found who, like Hegel, conceive of religion almost wholly in intellectual terms. Much more universal and
strong is the feeling of dependence discussed by Schleiermacher.
Writing in this humanistic age we would lay less emphasis on his
adjective "absolute," but that dependence to some amount is there
is evident in many Christian hymns and speaks out in many prayers:

O Lord, our heavenly father, Almighty and everlasting God, who hast
safely brought us to the beginning of this day; Defend us in the same
with thy mighty power; and grant that this day we fall into no sin, neither
run into any kind of danger; but that all our doings, being ordered by thy
governance, may be righteous in thy sight.[7]

There are also modern writers who have offered restricted explanations of the origins of religion. Rudolf Otto ascribes religion to a
direct apprehension of what he calls the "Wholly Other." The mental state induced he calls the "numinous," an experience of great
awe or "amazement absolute" in the presence of a divine object.
Furthermore he says, "This mental state is perfectly *sui generis* and

---

[5] *Philosophy of Religion*, Vol. I, p. 90.
[6] See his *On Religion*; also Stolz, *op. cit.*, p. 124.
[7] *Book of Common Prayer*.

irreducible to any other." [8] This implies a specialized capacity, a kind of "sixth sense" which enables man to come into contact with the divine. It is not that Otto would deny other concomitants, such as reason, which may blend with the numinous, but he insists that the numinous is fundamentally unique and apart from other psychological functions. Psychologically speaking, therefore, Otto would trace religious experience to man's possession of this capacity.

We must confess to a certain fondness for Otto's theory. It would fit neatly into that part of our concept of religion where we define it as "the inner experience of the individual when he senses a Beyond." Furthermore, the reading of Otto has a certain convincing quality, and the reception accorded *The Idea of the Holy* in certain quarters on both sides of the Atlantic suggests that he speaks for many others besides himself. His hypothesis certainly deserves consideration. Yet our psychological conscience constrains us to note that what he has to say is little more than a descriptive hypothesis. So far as we are aware, there are no systematic empirical studies that would either support or refute it. Perhaps, through a kind of Copernican *tour de force*, Otto has brought simplicity out of complexity and put his finger on the essence of the religious life. We are not in the position to state with finality that he has not. But whether we are still blinded by a superfluity of data which draws a mist before our eyes, or simply beset by such a cloud of scientific witnesses, we feel constrained to note that Otto's theory is almost wholly an intuitive one. The hypothesis deserves consideration and further study. It may come close to disclosing the secret of the religious life, but science has not as yet validated it, and in any case it still seems too simple to do justice to the full complexity of the religious life.

Another modern who would seem to entertain a too simple conception of the source of religion is the great Sigmund Freud. Because of his preoccupation with neuroses, and perhaps also because of his own personal religious views, Freud tended to see religion in its more infantile aspects. But while religious people may justly complain of the distortions in his point of view, we are not justified in passing over the ideas of one who towered over his contemporaries in the field of psychology by virtue of having been the founder of psychoanalysis. His views are in sharp contrast with those of Rudolf

[8] *Idea of the Holy*, p. 7.

Otto. Indeed it is doubtful that the two were talking about the same psychological experience when they used the term "religion"; a possible exception to this disparity occurs in Freud's allusion to the "oceanic feeling," which he took to be a retreat into infancy. Freud's speculations were based on a much closer observation of actual cases and a more thoroughgoing analysis of man's total personality, and the two men were sensitive to different aspects of the personality, so that they cannot really be compared.

It is a commonplace to say that Freud saw all human drives as ultimately deriving from sex. This is an oversimplification that does not do justice to the complexities that Freud reported in his keen observations of human nature. In the first place, his definition of sex was much wider and more inclusive than popular billboard conceptions of the term. In the second, his later writings, such as *Beyond the Pleasure Principle*, speculate on the existence of other urges, such as the so-called "death instinct," a kind of biological drive of the organism to return to an inorganic state, which would seem to have little relation to the sex urge or *libido*.

In terms of cultural development, Freud makes much of the theory that religion developed from totemism and magic, in which he leans heavily on the researches and speculations of Sir James Frazer.[9] In discussing cultural research he naturally finds support for his psychoanalytical theories in the behavior of primitives, and likens the development of the individual to the development of the race. Religion, as he views it, can indeed be linked with sex, for he sees a sense of guilt as a problem with which all religions attempt to cope. This guilt is conceived of as deriving at least in part from the *Oedipus complex*. Freud explains this complex as the situation in which the little boy "falls in love" with the mother, deriving from a rebellion against the father. Then in expiation for this act of rebellion and as an expression of tender feelings toward the father, the son attempts a reconciliation with the father which involves trying to appropriate the father's good qualities and to do his will. This leads to the search for the "father image." It is out of this

---

[9] See Freud, *Totem and Taboo*. For a concise presentation of Frazer's theory of the development of religion from magic, see *The Golden Bough*, Chap. 4. For a brief refutation of this general position see Stolz, *op. cit.*, pp. 45–50.

search that the idea of God arises and herein Freud finds the source of religion.[10]

In so brief a discussion we can hardly do justice to Freud's reasoning and observations, many of which are acute and stimulating, and the sort of processes which we have described must not be conceived to manifest themselves too literally or obviously. Freud thought of them as taking place on the unconscious level or perhaps acted out symbolically, as they would be in religious ritual. But when we boil his theory down on the simplest terms, it would seem to maintain that the most essential component of the religious life is the search for the father image, which in turn is derived from a sense of guilt. It is this theory which enables us to classify Freud with those who find the religious life of man flowing from a source that is relatively clear and simple.

Still another monistic view holds that a "religious instinct" solves the problem. This idea was popular in the earlier days of religious psychology when "instinct" psychology tended to explain not only religion but many other forms of human behavior in the same way. Man is incurably religious—so the argument ran; wherever the anthropologist searches, whether among the most primitive peoples or the most sophisticated, he invariably finds religion. *Ergo* there must be planted in human nature a religious urge that makes man seek for God. This is an instinct.

But since those halcyon times for the instinct theory, psychologists and other social scientists have carried on many discussions about it. The more it was discussed the more obvious it became that the discussions led to no conclusions, for the reason that no clear definition of the word "instinct" could be agreed upon. "When I use a word it means exactly what I mean it to mean, neither more nor less." This dictum from *Alice in Wonderland* might properly have been uttered by every psychologist who used the word "instinct." Freud, for example, defined an instinct as "a tendency innate in living organic matter, impelling it toward the reinstatement of an earlier condition." [11] Other definitions were equally individualized, and

---

[10] See *op. cit.* in *Basic Writings of Sigmund Freud*, esp. pp. 914 ff., and *The Future of an Illusion*; also Lee, *Freud and Christianity*, Chap. 9.

[11] *Beyond the Pleasure Principle*, p. 44.

finally social scientists have agreed to limit the concept of instinct to complicated, relatively invariable, inborn and unlearned reactions to certain stimuli. There is a story of a biologist who made a pet of a beaver, which he kept upstairs in his home. One day he was disconcerted to find the beaver chewing down the balustrade in order to build a dam at the top of the stairs. This is a good example of the invariability of a true instinct. Thus if it could be demonstrated, for example, that man, at the sound of a church bell and regardless of where he was or what he was doing, invariably reached for his best clothes, marched to church, said his prayers, dutifully listened to a sermon, and then marched out again at the recessional hymn, we might say that he had a religious instinct. But since there is obviously nothing invariable or rigid in the way that different people express their religious feelings or even have them at all, we must conclude that, as defined, man lacks a religious instinct, or indeed any true instinct. Even the most doughty champion of the instinct theory, William McDougall, could find no specific instinct of religion. Religion, he thought, was a complex of several instincts, and indeed even he finally admitted that the concept of instinctive behavior in human beings had merely led to confusion and controversy, even though he did not give up his theories.[12]

Perhaps a final monistic source for religion, akin to the religious instinct, is inborn temperament. Psychologists have not given the attention to this source of human behavior that they have to environmental influences, largely because there is much more that can be done about the latter. In addition, in recent times, American social scientists have tended to depreciate the importance of inborn inheritance—perhaps as unworthy in a democratic society. Consequently we do not know as much about the psychological influence of heredity as we would like. But it obviously has an important place in the study of personality. The appearance is that some people are temperamentally more disposed to religious experience than others, and that this is at least to some extent independent of upbringing and environment. Mystical sensitivity, for example, would seem to lie in this category. But regardless of how fundamental or special

[12] See his *Outline of Psychology* for a discussion of his theories, his *The Energies of Men* for later views, especially p. 78; for the modern view of instincts see Munn, *Psychology*, p. 272 ff.

this factor is, we can at any rate note that temperament is a strong modifying factor as a source of religious behavior.[13]

Faculty psychology. Aristotle has commented on the inability of man to describe anything without saying that it is like something else. This is nowhere more true than in the case of the psychologists when they discuss the human mind. John Locke compared it to a wax tablet on which experience made impressions; Thorndike thought of it as a kind of vast telephone exchange through which stimuli were connected with appropriate reactions; while Freud likened it to a closed hydraulic system in which an urge was no sooner repressed than it began to exert pressure in some other part of the system. The important thing to remember about all these concepts is that they are all figures of speech which by analogy help to make a little clearer certain aspects of the personality. But they all involve their fallacies as well.

One of the most influential and also most fallacious of these figures of speech was that which likened the human mind to a muscle with several "faculties." This concept has been out of fashion with the psychologists these many years, yet it remains true that, looked at in a certain way, the mind *is* like a muscle in which can be distinguished the faculties of reason, feeling, and will. Studying this concept further will help us to understand some of the features of religion as it expresses itself in human behavior. Perhaps it is too much to say that here we have put our finger on the *sources* of religious life. Rather the faculties influence the *style* of expression through which religion comes to view.

Reason, of course, is the intellectual function of the mind. The theologian is an illustration of religion expressing itself through intellect. Reason is the tempering, ordering, judging, and directing function of the personality. It anticipates absurdities and errors before they come, and saves people from going to extremes. Furthermore, as it directs a theology, or an approximation to it, it supplies that structural undergirding of logical security so necessary to a religious institution as well as to wholesome individual religion. While

[13] For a book on religion written mainly from the hereditary constitutional point of view, see H. Helwig, *Soul Sorrow: The Psychiatrist Speaks to the Minister.*

not a theology, this book is an example of the operation of reason in the field of religion. It is an attempt to order and to make sense out of religion when viewed from the perspective of psychology.

Sophisticated people and sophisticated religions make much of this reasoning function. So respectable is reason in religion that even those who are not very reasonable give it lip service. But reasonable religion can become very cold and very sterile when it is overemphasized, sometimes to the extent that it ceases to be a real religion and is nothing more than an intellectual exercise. Yet there are those for whom reason has been the chief ingredient in that "inner experience of the individual" as he "senses a Beyond," which we had in mind in our definition.

But, however overemphasized the intellect may be, no one's religious life can be purely intellectual. Religion, like all of life, also needs vitality and warmth and passion. It was this that the faculty psychologists had in mind when they defined the faculty of *feeling* or *emotion*. More than the other faculties this has remained as a well-defined object of study for psychologists, and much work has been done in the field.[14] But here we must be content merely with describing it in relation to religion. The importance of emotion in religion has been underestimated by intellectuals, who usually associate emotion with religious *hoi polloi* who dwell in what they regard as religious slums, such as the evangelistic gospel tent and the rescue mission. Often a new religious movement that wishes to appeal to the upper classes has to make a great show of not relying on the emotions. This is the case with the Moral Re-Armament movement, though probably its chief psychological value is that it stirs the emotions and puts life into ideals that have long lain dormant in merely intellectual forms.[15] The practical religious mind in all its forms has seen to it that emotion plays its part in religious expression, whether it be through music, ritual, dancing, or a heavy thumping of the religious drums by the excited evangelist on the rostrum. The question is not whether a religious experience will contain emo-

[14] For an introduction, see Munn, *op. cit.*, Chaps. 14 and 15. The religious psychologist should be informed in this area.

[15] See the author's *The Oxford Group*, Part III, for cases, and especially Chap. 18 for a discussion of the relation of emotion and intellectual elements in this type of religion.

tion, but what the proportions shall be. For there is no doubt that emotional religion, overemphasized, is hardly edifying. An emotional orgy, even though in the name of religion, is not religion at all.

This brings us to the last of the three faculties that we have mentioned, that of the *will*. We need not linger over the problem of whether there is any such thing, a question that has been a matter of as much controversy among the psychologists as among the theologians. We must remember that the concept of the faculties is a mere figure of speech for our convenience, and is no more rigorous or exact than other concepts more popular in psychological circles. What the will represents is the executive functions of the human spirit. A religious experience may be properly intellectualized and characterized by intense emotion, and yet the implications of the experience may never be carried out, or actions may contradict the experience they are supposed to express. In the terms of faculty psychology we say that the person's "will is weak." He has "done those things which he ought not to have done and left undone those things which he ought to have done." It is through the idea of the will and the control which the individual is supposed to have over it that the concept of morality arises.

Scientific study has demonstrated that the idea of the freedom of the will is at least in part an illusion, for we are all so strongly conditioned by past experience that some avenues of action are for practical purposes closed to us. How many of us would leap to our feet at a church service and interrupt the preacher, however much we might feel like it? And can all of us repress a shudder at the sight of a snake? Yet the appearance is that there are in life significant avenues among which we may make our choice, and it would seem wholesome and the better part of wisdom, both religiously and psychologically, to make this assumption. At any rate, it lies at the back of our mind when we speak in our definition of religion of the effect of the individual's inner experience on his behavior "when he actively attempts to harmonize his life with the Beyond." We are not likely to have much respect for a person's faith if it lacks this executive function, a necessary ingredient in the really religious life.

But, like the other functions, it too may be overemphasized. The man whom we call the religious "do-gooder" may simply be someone whose religious activities we misunderstand and dislike, but frequently the dislike may be soundly based on an intuitive comprehension of an individual whose efforts to keep up his religious respectability in the community are without any intellectual or emotional backing. Such people are the bane of every church and synagogue. So efficient are they in serving the Church that they cannot be ignored, and yet they are never liked and gum the wheels of what might otherwise be smoothly running organizations. Fellow worshipers consciously feel that these people *ought* to be approved and liked; they follow all the rules, mouth every creed, with special emphasis on the jot and tittle, and, like Mrs. Jellyby in *Bleak House,* are in the forefront in any movement for the improvement of conditions they know nothing about. Whole movements or organizations may suffer from the same deficiencies and indeed are seldom completely free from them, particularly when early zeal has begun to deteriorate and there is little left to justify a movement except the imitation of the ways supposed to have characterized the founders. In the political area we see the results in one-hundred per cent Americanism and super-nationalism, while in the religious field it has been particularly evident in the decay of Puritanism.

We see then that reason, emotion, and the will all play their parts in the development of a well-rounded and wholesome religious experience. There is much overlapping, and distinctions are not always clear, particularly between the emotional and volitional areas; but that is inevitable when the whole is a blend of several elements.

Thomas' "four wishes."   In place of the concept of instinct so popular among the psychologists of McDougall's time and earlier, modern psychology has developed the idea of *need* or *drive.* In most cases systems designed to explain human behavior in these terms are simply the old instincts dressed up in new names. All that the change in terms signifies is that psychologists wish to distinguish between the drives of animals with their highly stereotyped modes of expression, properly called instincts, and similar drives in human beings with their relatively high degree of generalization and extreme flexibility of expression. Man, in other words, has much more choice in the means he may use to satisfy his drives.

One of the best known and simplest system of such drives is the famous "four wishes" of W. I. Thomas.[16] Thomas was a social psychologist interested in the problems in adjustment of immigrants to American city life. In his studies of these people certain problems appeared again and again, and these he traced to four basic drives or *wishes*. These wishes had no specific reference to religion, and we are making use of them here, first because they appeal to us as comprehensive and basic, second because they are simple and easily kept in mind, and third because they will illustrate how seemingly non-religious elements help to supply the background of drive which creates the religious sentiment and blends with it.[17]

Reasons for accepting drives

The "four wishes" of Thomas are *security, response, recognition,* and *new experience.* The wish for security is the need for the wherewithal to support life, which shows itself most characteristically in the search for food, shelter, and clothing, or the means of obtaining such. The wish for response expresses the need that all people have for affiliation, the desire to love and to be loved which, if unfulfilled, has such devastating consequences for the personality. The wish for recognition is the need that everyone has to be respected and recognized by others as a person of worth and value in the community. The wish for new experience is associated with that eminently human capacity for being bored, from which springs, for example, the "divine discontent" of the poet which everyone harbors in his soul in some form. This urge rebels against too much monotony, and while it may sometimes clash with other wishes, notably the wish for security, along with them it clamors to be expressed. Such were the basic drives that Thomas discovered in the human personality. Provision for satisfying these wishes can be discerned, either explicitly or implicitly, in most if not all religions. We will illustrate mostly through reference to the Judeo-Christian tradition, which will be familiar to most of our readers.

[16] See Thomas and Znaniecki, *The Polish Peasant in Europe and America,* or, for a brief account, the first chapter of Thomas, *The Unadjusted Girl.*

[17] Another system that might be used is that of H. A. Murray's "needs" as developed in *Explorations in Personality.* There are twenty or thirty of these, of which the needs of Achievement, Affiliation, Exhibition, Recognition, Seclusion, and Sex are typical. However, the analysis would be too extensive for the few pages at our disposal.

"Give us this day our daily bread" is the wish for security expressed in the Lord's Prayer, while there is no need to belabor the fact that probably the large majority of all Christian prayers contain this wish in some form. Without stopping at this point to distinguish magic from religion, we might hazard the speculation that most of the ecclesiastical apparatus would fall to the ground, along with the majority of the world's business, were the wish for security by some stroke suddenly abolished from human nature. A friend describes an ocean-crossing during wartime. The night before the first Sunday at sea, submarines were reported and the passengers alerted. The next day, the shipboard communion service was crowded. The following Sunday saw the ship well out of the danger area. The same service on that day was all but deserted. However, this is not meant to imply that religion is necessarily at fault. On the contrary, only a religion that is an authentic expression of the poignant and durable longings of mankind will survive. There is a difference in quality between, on the one hand, the self-centered variety of religious superstition, which attempts to curry divine favor for the exclusive benefit of the worshiper and his immediate interests, and, on the other hand, the loftier kind, which implores the deity out of the same sense of need but in a spirit of humility and with awareness of the radical dependence of all mankind on cosmic processes that no man has created. It is this latter mood that stimulates the essential type of religious experience and leads man to attempt to harmonize his life with the will of the Beyond.

So with the other wishes. They furnish the soil out of which grows all religious life, and yet the harvest yield will differ in both amount and quality. The wish for response is particularly prominent in higher forms of religion. In Christianity the idea that "God is love" is but the quintessence of the recognition of the importance of this need in the individual's spiritual economy, and psychologically represents the projection by man onto his God of that which he senses as the indispensable condition of meaningful human existence. And religion is also concerned with love between man and man. The Christian religion is not the only one whose history is studded with friendships and fellowships that have played a large part in its success. While religion is obviously by no means the only avenue through which the need for response operates, nevertheless there is a quality of response shared in a religious context which at its best is more satisfying than that of any other variety.[18]

But along with the bonds of response on a religious basis among men, there is also the religious experience that involves love between man and God. Regardless of the fact that the realities of this relationship are beyond the scope of psychological science, there is no doubt that the wish for response often sends the religious person to this divine source for his satisfaction, either consequent on a failure of earthly response or because of intrinsic satisfactions. Jesus not only enjoined his followers to love the Lord their God with all their hearts and souls and minds, but also to love their neighbors as themselves. Furthermore God is conceived as a father who loves his children, full of "loving kindness and tender mercy." Full of affiliative conceptions is the ritual and the theology of the ages, while the psychological implications of the worship of the Virgin Mary in Christianity, the various mother-goddesses of antiquity, and the cults of various primitive faiths [19] point to the wish for response as a potent source of drives that lead to religious experience.

The wishes for recognition and new experience are more implicitly involved with the satisfactions that religion offers. Yet the recognition in high religion of the rights and worth of the individual is clearly set forth in the Judeo-Christian tradition, as in the Parable of the Lost Sheep or the Laws of Moses. A particularly effective feature of the Protestant Reformation was the renewal of the confidence of the individual in himself as a result of the emphasis on his value in the sight of God, and the belief in the priesthood of all believers. Psychologically this helps to make the Reformation more understandable as a movement which in part appealed to that wish for recognition which is another of those basic needs described by Thomas. Likewise we can see this need operating at all levels of spiritual depth, wherever religion functions. There are some who chiefly exploit their church or religious organization as an easy means of getting noticed, but, psychologically as well as spiritually, any religious movement must be considered shallow that in some way or other leaves this human craving completely out of account.

[18] Moral Re-Armament is only one of many modern illustrations of this truth. See my *The Oxford Group*, pp. 242–244.
[19] See Frazer's *The Golden Bough* for an account of these.

The wish for new experience is a more subtle and yet an equally important source of the religious life. *God Is My Adventure* is the title of a recent collection of religious biographies, while the account of anyone who has had a genuine religious experience leaves no doubt that religion is no commonplace, pedestrian affair. Witness the wrestling with God by the Patriarch Jacob, the flight from the "Hound of Heaven" in Francis Thompson's poem, or the glorious poetry of the Book of Job, which could be the expression only of a profound and exciting spiritual experience. Even religion in its more superficial aspects offers excitement, as the typical evangelistic meeting indicates. It is said that one of the reasons for the success of evangelistic campaigns in the time of the frontier and early American settlements was that they offered the readiest means for the hardworking pioneers to find an escape from their everyday drudgery into a world of temporary exhilaration.

Symbolically the note of new experience is sounded clearly, albeit often only faintly, in religious ritual. The liturgy of the Christian year provides not only elements of invariability, but also change as the different seasons succeed one another. Naturally the tighter ecclesiastical organizations tend to disapprove of any excess spirit of adventure on the part of the individual, and sound dark warnings against the "love of novelty," as is often the case in the Roman Catholic church; but these same churches are not averse to church fairs and an occasional "mission," the Catholic equivalent of Protestant evangelistic meetings. In addition, many Catholics are no strangers to the kind of inwardness that stirs a man to the depths of his soul, as in the case of Francis Thompson.

Like its satisfaction of the other wishes, religion fulfills this need for new experience with peculiar intensity and fullness. The radical throwing of one's whole self into a wild and sublime speculation, seen only through the eye of faith, most probably in opposition to what others call common sense, is an experience largely to be sustained through a sense of an adventure. As compared with this, the risking of one's fortune on the turn of a wheel at Monte Carlo pales into insignificance. The fact that so many see religion merely as a stuffy affair is simply another proof of our contention that primary religious experience falls to the lot of a small minority.

Thou calledst, and shoutedst, and burstest, my deafness. Thou flashedst, shonest, and scatteredst my blindness. Thou breathedst odours, and I drew in breath and pant for Thee. Thou touchedst me, and I burned for Thy peace. For Thou hast created us for Thyself, and our heart is restless until it find rest in Thee.[20]

Conflict, the life and the death urges.   G. M. Stratton, in *Psychology of the Religious Life,* contends that the basic source of religion is conflict. With rich use of illustration, his whole treatise is an elaboration of this theme. The antithetical pairs, good and evil, activity and passivity, humility and confidence, are examples of some of the indicated dichotomies out of which religion arises.

There is no doubt that conflict is closely associated with religious impulses, as it is with all of man's psychological life. Conflict as a means of accentuating distress is a prime source of learning and therefore of progress. In the conflict between moral standards, or the conflict of religious ideas, there evolve new syntheses and new ideas. Furthermore, as conflict becomes more poignant, man is driven to seek the help and solace of the divine. Particularly in this latter sense can we conceive of conflict as one of the sources of the religious life.

But in another sense this source is secondary, for it depends on the basic urges or the circumstances out of which the conflicts arise. If conflicts arise out of the contending urges to action and passivity, for example, and this leads to religion, we can well pose the query whether the two urges do not precede the conflict. This being obviously so, it would seem that the urges rather than the conflict arising from them are the ultimate, at least more basic, sources of religion. Indeed, sometimes it is predominantly man's passive side, and sometimes his active urges, operating alone and with conflict playing no very prominent role, that lead to religious experience. Conflict doubtless may heighten religion, and in that sense may be looked on as a stimulus, but it would appear to us that it is not a fundamental source of religious impulses.

We have used activity and passivity merely as illustrations, yet here we would like to go on and discuss them further as sources of religion

[20] St. Augustine, *Confessions,* in Phillips, *The Choice Is Always Ours,* p. 491.

in their own right, as well as to continue in a way the theme of conflict. While he made no attempt to explain religion in this connection, we will here again refer to Freud, who made some interesting
speculations with respect to the origin of the biological urges toward
activity and passivity. There is in every organism, he said, an impulse
toward the reinstatement of earlier conditions. Ultimately, this includes a wish to return to the inorganic state, and this he called the
"death instinct." This instinct he came to feel was even more basic
than the sexual urge.[21] The fact that an organism seldom seeks death
by the most obvious path but, on the contrary, attempts to protect its
existence and even to extend it beyond its own individual existence
through reproduction, he explains as a kind of circuitous way of
seeking death. This indirection is due to a contrary impulse which
he calls the "life instinct" or "life instincts," since he thinks of it as
being expressed in various ways. He is not too clear in explaining
the relationship and origins of these two opposed urges, doubtless
because, as he admits, he is not too sure of the soundness of his own
speculations. The important point for us is to note that this keen
and profound observer felt that these urges were fundamental in
their importance for human psychology.

Following R. S. Lee's stimulating chapter, "Life and Death," in
his study of the relationship of psychoanalysis and religion, *Freud
and Christianity*, we will attempt to go beyond Freud in relating
these two "instincts" to religion. The question may be raised as to
why we need all this learned reference to Freud when it is so obvious
that passivity and activity are universal and normal phases of
everyone's life style. We might have left him out, but we wish to
call attention to the fact that there are profound and subtle problems concerned with these two urges, otherwise Freud would not
have spent so many pages on them. Also his terms of "life" and
"death" call dramatic attention to probably the most important im-
plication of the two urges. For the ultimate passivity is death, while
activity is the very essence of life, the inscrutable and mysterious
urge that is responsible for the development of species, including
man.

[21] For his discussion, see the latter parts of *Beyond the Pleasure Principle*,
p. 44 ff. We are not using rigorously the concept of the death instinct as conceived by Freud, who emphasized it largely as a means of accounting for men's
destructive urges.

These two urges are obviously not confined to religion, for they influence all aspects of physical behavior and mental life. We shake off the influence of the death urge as we rise from our beds in the morning, only to succumb to it as we give ourselves up to sleep at night. Perhaps it is too pat to identify everything that goes under the name of "liberalism" with the life urge and "conservatism" with death, for appearances are sometimes misleading. The two sometimes aid one another, sometimes oppose, and so subtle is their relationship that the profoundest things about them must often be spoken in paradox. Yet if we must have a generalization about them this one is best, and for the purposes of our discussion we can think of the life urge as that which impels toward change and progress, while the death urge moves men toward that quiescent conservation of things as they are, which ultimately arrives at the stagnation of death. It is of course important that as scientists we divorce our minds from any emotional preferences that we may have for the terms, "liberal" or "progressive," and "conservative." We must remember that no living organism, including man, can escape expressing both of these urges. They may be relatively stronger or weaker in different individuals, but by the implacable conditions of nature and the human nature by which we live, both are stamped indelibly into the basic structure of every personality. It follows, then, that every considerable expression of man's nature, whatever its dominant character, must give a place to both.

This is eminently true of religion, and we must expect it to be in part an expression of the life wish, and in part of the death urge. In general we can think of the prophet as the spokesman for the life urge and the priest, with his conservative functions, as the representative of the death urge. Indeed, any particular form of religion must strike some sort of balance between the two, and if that balance be too one-sided the religion will be unnatural and will fail. But in actuality all religions express some dominant orientation. Thus Hinduism, with its emphasis on contemplation and the caste system, and Buddhism, with Nirvana as its aim, would both seem to favor the death urge; while Zoroastrianism, Judaism, Mohammedanism, and Christianity would be examples of more active faiths. Taoism would appear to be a balance, with its emphasis on *yin*, the negative principle of the cosmos, and *yang*, the positive. Confucianism would appear to balance the conservative emphasis on ancestor worship with an active emphasis on morality.

But Freud says that the death urge is the stronger of the two and must ultimately win out. This would appear to be supported by the increasing hold that conservatism secures among all religions as time passes, particularly when they become strongly institutionalized. Despite the dynamic character of Western man, it is to be doubted whether Christianity has expressed the predominantly active implications of the teachings of Jesus to the same extent that it has the passive. The Middle Ages were a time when emphasis was laid on preparation not so much for this world as the world to come; the charges of the Marxists that "religion is the opium of the people" has more force than most church people are likely to admit; while wherever one looks in contemporary religious life he sees signs of the predominance of passivity and conservatism.

The question may be raised whether the dynamic character of Western civilization does not argue for the dynamic quality of its dominant religion, Christianity. It is dynamic in certain respects, notably in its missionary movement. But much of the religion of the common man represents either an escape from life or an activity pretty well compartmentalized. In neither case does it strongly influence the ordinary works of our civilization. The popular concept of the future life, for example, with its harps and songs and life of ease, is one which could hardly be enjoyed very long by anyone unless he were to all intents and practical purposes dead. An investigator who analyzed the dominant psychological mood in Christian hymns discovered that fifty-eight per cent dealt with either the wish for a return to a more infantile stage or looked forward to a future state of passive bliss. Only a small percentage of the hymns sounded what could be described as a dominantly active note.[22] Furthermore, we might cite the tendency toward economic and social conservatism among churchgoers, though the implications of Christ's teaching are the direct reverse.[23]

This helps to explain why so many churches have a "youth problem," that is, difficulty in attracting older adolescents and younger

[22] K. Young, "The Psychology of Hymns."
[23] See Britt, *Social Psychology of Modern Life*, Chap. 18, or J. Davis, *Capitalism and its Culture*.

adults.[24] This is the age at which both biologically and intellectually the life urge is strongest; consequently it is this age that is least attracted by a program usually dominated by those in whom the death urge is increasingly operative as the source of religious impulses. This means that ecclesiastical machinery and teaching is devoted disproportionately to comfort and consolation, vested interests, the preparation for a passive life in the next world, and the repetition of what has been in the past. This being the case, it is a wonder that the churches hold the loyalty of as many young people as they do.

The explanation lies partly in the fact that the principal message of the Gospel definitely emphasizes the life urge. Words of comfort there are in abundance, as well as the invitation to cast one's burdens on the Lord. But the essential message is so radical that few have had the courage to take it seriously, and of these by far the greater number have been the young. The protective covering of respectability and quietism which the average pastor throws over the Bible doubtless saves it from criticism in times of extreme reactionary sentiment. This suggests that the youth problem might be considerably aided through a more forthright interpretation of religious truth. The suggestion may seem too strong and to carry dangerous implications to those whose chief concern is with ecclesiastical vested interests. But if so, it would be much better for the Church to give up the expression of the life urge and devote itself exclusively to the service of old ladies and old gentlemen, together with the aim of making such out of the young people in their midst as quickly as possible.

There is one more thing that should be noted before we leave this subject. We have said that the expression of the death urge and the life urge in religion is not always obvious but is frequently paradoxical. Thus the attempt of the individual to preserve his life is not always the expression of the life urge, and may be just the reverse. The wish to preserve one's life for the purpose of repeating

[24] A count by the author at three different services of various Protestant denominations showed 136 attendants clearly over 40, to 52 under that age. A Catholic study by J. H. Fichter, "The Profile of Catholic Religious Life," shows least religious observance in the 30–39 decade, with rising observance as age advances.

an endless succession of supine pleasures owes more to the death urge. One sees this motive catered to in advertisements where insurance companies urge the reader to take out a retirement annuity so that he may retire early and do nothing but enjoy himself the rest of his life. This, of course, is psychologically in the same class as encouraging the worshiper to be good so that on death he may retire to a heavenly sphere in order to indulge his laziness. Jesus, indeed, used the conventional figures concerning the after life, but his conception of life in this world was hardly a prescription to appeal to those whose desire is to enjoy a comfortable respectability: witness the lives of his disciples and his words to the rich young ruler. His own acceptance of death was not the expression of the death urge but of the life urge, and represented that willingness to risk one's life for an ideal that much more often characterizes the young than the old. It was with such considerations in mind that he uttered the paradox, psychologically one of the profound insights of the ages, that "he who seeketh to save his life will lose it."

Religion as a value.   In seeking for the motivational sources of the religious life we have more or less tacitly utilized the concept of "drives" in trying to explain them. In other words, we have thought of these various factors as a kind of "push-from-behind" urging the personality in the general direction of the religious life. Here again we wish to repeat our earlier warning that in speaking of the human mind we are forced to use figures of speech which often gloss over, by the use of plausible analogies, our ignorance of what really is happening.

This is certainly true with respect to our concept of drive, which would seem to be useful only up to a certain point and needs to be supplemented with other concepts. One concept which will aid in this supplementation is that of *value*. We think of a value as something to be desired, and indeed this desirability often derives from a drive. Thus the thirst drive gives water a value for the organism. We can think of the resulting activity of drinking as one of *avoiding* the thirst, or *approaching* the water. But apparently the same general situation will have different results according to whether the avoidance or the approach motive is uppermost in the mind of the behaving organism. This appeals to common sense, and it has considerable experimental support behind it.[25] When we use the term "value" we are implying motivation conceived of in terms of approach rather than avoidance. This in turn implies a situation allowing more freedom for the organism. A drive is conceived of as operating willy-nilly, and needs only to be strong enough to be considered invincible. A value, on the other hand, exerts attraction, and while some objects may be spoken of as "irresistibly attractive," like Cleopatra, one understands that a considerable element of choice is present.

Consequently when religion is spoken of as a "value" the emphasis is on positive approach rather than mere negative avoidance of something else. When this is so, religion is conceived of as more of an intrinsic rather than an instrumental activity; that is, satisfying in its own right rather than a means of fulfilling some other drive. Hence it is not surprising that Spranger in *Types of Men,* in which people are classified according to the values they espouse, defines religion as "the highest and absolutely satisfying value experience." [26] This value experience is described by Spranger under two categories. It is conceived of as mysticism sometimes of a *transcendental,* at other times of an *immanent* type. The "transcendental mystic" enjoys a religion of a much more intrinsic character. The "immanent mystic" lives more in the world and is closer to Spranger's *social* type, for whom the well-being of others is the chief value. With the latter there is more of the instrumental element present, for to some extent religion may be the means of benefiting other people. But in both cases the idea of attraction is important to the concept.

Just as it has been discovered in the laboratory that an animal's performance will differ, depending on whether the motivation underlying its activity is that of relatively free approach or a kind of compulsive push due to anxiety or a drive that has reached an acute pitch of urgency, so we would expect that the quality of religious behavior and experience will differ depending on whether one is attracted to religion or is driven to it. A little reflection tells us that this is so. It would perhaps be convenient if we could neatly dif-

[25] For a review of this experimentation and a discussion of what he terms a "two-factor theory of motivation," see McClelland, *Personality*, Chaps. 12–13. The problem is also discussed, with implications for religion, in G. W. Allport's *Becoming*.

[26] P. 213.

ferentiate these two kinds of religion, to show that one kind is invariably better than the other. Probably this could be done up to a certain point, but doubtless it can be carried too far. Both roads to genuine religion—the inner experience of a Beyond, and the attempt to harmonize one's life with the Beyond—are equally valid. "Man's extremity is God's opportunity," it has been said, and many have been driven to seek God who thereby have discovered a lively religious faith. In part this would seem to have been the case with Martin Luther, who, impelled by the terror of a thunderstorm, promised God he would become a monk.

Nevertheless, for a person to be driven to religion through a sense of urgency in some crisis may mean that the experience will be superficial. The drunkard who feels compelled to join the church with the idea that somehow this will make self-control easier for him may fall away rather quickly when he finds that it is not quite that easy, while pious resolutions made on a sickbed have a way of disintegrating when the sinner miraculously recovers. Other people may be attracted to religion with similar superficiality, but when once religion has been experienced as a genuine and intrinsic value it is apt to have a durability beyond that which characterizes it when it is merely instrumental. "A deeply moving religious experience," declares Allport, "is not readily forgotten, but is likely to remain as a focus of thought and desire." [27] Yet we do not have the precise information that we would like in order to deal with this problem adequately. Here is a fertile field for research, which would give us the information that we need for the psychology of religion at the same time that it would throw important light on personality.

The quest for life's meaning. When we review the foregoing speculations as to the sources of the religious life, we can see that they are various and many, particularly when we reflect that the possible sources have merely been sampled. Others have been so impressed by the complexity of these sources that they have hesitated to postulate any universal and clearly defined points to which religion traces its origins. To quote Allport once again:

The conclusion we come to is that the subjective religious attitude of every individual is, in both its essential and non-essential features, unlike

[27] *Personality*, p. 226.

that of any other individual. The roots of religion are so numerous, the weight of their influence in individual lives so varied, and the forms of rational interpretation so endless, that uniformity of product is impossible. Only in respect to certain basic biological functions do men closely resemble one another. In the higher reaches of personality uniqueness of function becomes more apparent. And since no department of personality is subject to more complex development than the religious sentiment, it is precisely in this area that we must expect to find the ultimate divergences.[28]

Yet nearly every psychologist who has thought about the problem of origins has his own favorite theory as to how religion comes about. The complexity of which Allport has written we cannot gainsay, and we have tried to make clear that each of the sources we have reviewed can play only its own part in explaining the religious life. That no two individuals will be quite alike is clear. Clear also is the fact that since religion is man's most highly developed function we will find more individuality in religious development than in any other aspect of the personality.

But we are inclined to believe that, with respect to the type of religion that we have tried to define as the subject of this book's discussions, *the quest for life's meaning* comes closer to constituting the origin for the religious life than any other single source. This does not exclude other sources nor does it deny uniqueness to the religious life of the individual. Neither does it set up religion as the only path by which people seek for the meaning of life. It is not an original idea, for often it has been proposed by psychologists as well as by others. Many are the Sunday sermons which celebrate religion as the answer to man's search for life's meaning. Furthermore it has at least some empirical support. C. S. Braden of Northwestern University asked over two thousand people why they were religious. Many answers were given, but the answer that "religion gives meaning to life" was the one most frequently offered.[29]

Though we must be careful of *a priori* reasoning, it is to be noted that there is some logic in favor of this answer to our problem. Why should people seek an experience of God and attempt to harmonize their lives with His will? Proponents of temperament would say that

---

[28] *The Individual and His Religion*, pp. 26–27.
[29] "Why People Are Religious—a Study in Religious Motivation."

this is an inherited tendency. Rudolf Otto and St. Augustine would both agree in holding that this is the way people are made, that they are born with an innate capacity of sensing God and cannot help themselves. My hound spends most of his day tied up, listless and uninterested, leading a veritable "dog's life." But once a day he is taken for a walk in the fields. It is then that he comes to life; his eyes are alert and his muscles tense as he tracks down every scent to its source in bush or wood. This results from his being born that way. It is the function for which he has been bred over many generations. He cannot help his responses and he is happy only when exercising them. To the extent that our religious capabilities are intrinsic, this kind of explanation is basic and explains the religious urge. But, though there are exceptions, most people do not seem to exhibit this spontaneous joy in religious experience.

Yet everyone does feel the need for meaning in life, for when meaning is gone energy flags and the individual begins to entertain thoughts of suicide. And even if the experience of the Beyond first resulted from some innate capacity, why should the individual wish to take the time from his other duties to cultivate it? And more particularly, why should he make any attempt to harmonize his life with the Beyond? It would seem not unreasonable to suppose that not only the satisfaction that it might grant in itself but more especially the cosmic significance that it throws over everything that he does would in a larger sense explain its appeal. Even the most thoroughgoing mystic cannot sustain his experiences of vision for more than a short time. It is the hope for these delicious moments that keeps him steadfast through the rest of his existence and governs his behavior. They become, in the words of the poet,

> The anchor of my purest thoughts, the nurse,
> The guide, the guardian of my heart, and soul
> Of all my moral being.

Another question that may legitimately be asked is whether religion should have any pre-eminence over other ways of discovering meaning in life. It would appear that it has. Philosophy attempts to explain the riddle of existence, but philosophy appeals chiefly to the mind. The search for beauty is adequate for the artist, but there are many parts of life that this search does not touch. A devotion to the welfare of one's fellow men is a particularly rewarding way of life, yet in itself it leaves the question of a reason for such activity in abeyance. Religion provides a cosmic explanation at the same time that it may be a quest that has its own reward, like the search for beauty. In the great religions it blends with the life of service to one's fellow men and provides a reason for that life. It involves the three faculties of reason, emotion, and will. There is no activity incapable of being related to it. It is this comprehensive nature of the religious life that makes it such a satisfactory explanation for the journey through life.

In *The Courage to Be,* Paul Tillich distinguishes between "neurotic anxiety" and "existential anxiety." The latter is the normal, ordinary anxiety inherent in human life, such as the anxiety of death, of emptiness or loss of meaning, and of condemnation. Such anxiety is present in all of us, while the neurotic demonstrates anxiety in a twisted form[30] But religion may minister to both kinds of anxiety. In its existential form it is inescapable; hence the function of religion in part as a means of coping with anxiety.

Our conclusions concerning the psychological sources of religion, then are that they are many and complex. The patterns and responses are highly developed and unique in each individual. But, most importantly, we conclude that religion derives its force from the fact that it best supplies the answer to the cry that man utters for something that will give his life significance.

SUMMARY

We must be careful not to evaluate religion with reference to its sources but rather by what it develops into. Furthermore, there is no great unanimity among scholars as to just what its sources are. Some drives or mental functions are seen as the one and only source of religion. These are variously given as reason, dependence, the "numinous," sex, the religious "instinct," and inborn temperament.

Among more generalized and complex sources we note the old "faculty" theory that sees the mind as a muscle, with religion expressed through reason, emotion, and the will. We can also see religion as fulfilling Thomas' four wishes of security, response, recog-

[30] See especially Chaps. 2 and 3.

nition, and new experience. Religion has also been conceived as arising from conflict, one form of which we have noted as an adaptation of Freud's so-called life and death wishes. In this speculation we have suggested that religion must express both the active and passive urges.

But there is a subtle difference in the motivation of those who are driven to religion and those who are attracted to it as a supreme value. For the latter the religious life may be an end in itself. As we look into the religious lives of individuals we find all these sources illustrated in different patterns and with different emphases. Yet it is our speculation that more than anything else, and most universally, it is the fact that religion affords the most satisfying goal in the search for meaning in life that sustains it for the average man.

Chapter 5

THE RELIGION
OF CHILDHOOD

The highest whom I knew on Earth I here saw bowed down, with awe
unspeakable, before a Higher in Heaven: such things, especially in infancy, reach inwards to the very core of your being.

—Carlyle

When a behaviorist, a psychoanalyst, and a Jesuit can all agree
on a certain proposition, it would seem a fairly safe assumption that
there must be some validity in it. The generalization that we have
in mind is that the early years of the individual's life are the most
decisive. It behooves us, therefore, to devote some time to this subject, though we must state that we will be limited in our conclusions by a body of experimentation and sound empirical study that
is almost in inverse proportion to the importance of the theme.

The unreflective citizen, with his face turned toward the future
and immersed in his adult world, is apt to classify his early religious experiences with his baby pictures. They are something to be
laughed at and depreciated if by some misfortune they are brought
to light, and like other transactions of these early years their importance is apt to be lost to memory. Yet even so, most of us have
at least a dim consciousness of the debt that our religious lives owe
to our childhood. Thus in the Braden study noted in the previous
chapter, early training was the seventh in a list of sixty-five reasons
given by different persons as to why they were religious; while such
items as conscience, duty, habit, and tradition, all of which point in

the same direction, also occurred, though farther down on the list.

The practical importance of this chapter will be readily grasped by parents and educators, who are concerned with knowing something of the characteristics of the religion of the child, as well as its dynamics; for even though not a treatise in religious education, nevertheless our chapter will supply background material. Indeed it should be of interest even to atheists, Communists, or others committed to keeping the young as far away as possible from such a heinous thing as religion. To them such a chamber of horrors will indicate what to avoid.

The tiny infant comes into the world such a helpless thing, and yet with so many latent capabilities, that two contrary courses are indicated. First of all, conditions *require* constant watching and care, particularly during the earliest years, if the child is not only to survive but also to receive that essential training in habits and attitudes so necessary in coping with the arduous course that lies ahead of him. Yet, in the second place, this supervision must not be overwhelming, but must gradually be relaxed to the end that the child's individuality, the potentialities of his essential nature, may unfold and develop with his increasing strength. The insights of many otherwise differing students of child life have yet been united in the happy use of the metaphor of the plant, which man must indeed tend and care for, but which is granted its increase by the Creator, expressing Himself never so cunningly as in human individuality. Like the good husbandman who knows that there is a time to till and a time to refrain from tilling, a "time to plant and a time to pluck up that which is planted," so the sensitive parent or the artist-educator mingles care with forbearance if the "tree planted by the river of water" is to bring forth fruit in due season.

In the main we will be concerned with answering but two questions: (1) What does the child's religion come from and how does it develop? and (2) What is this religion like? The first part of our chapter, then, will show a developmental and dynamic concern, while the second part will be mainly descriptive.

WHAT DOES THE CHILD'S RELIGION COME FROM AND HOW DOES IT DEVELOP?

A child is not born religious. Whatever Wordsworthian sentimentalists may hold to the contrary, the psychologist sees the newly born infant as a creature much nearer the animal state than the human. Indeed a highly developed ape is in some ways more "human" than is the newborn child.[1] The child is a human being merely *in posse*, not *in esse*. When even the more elementary human traits are slow in appearing, how much less can we expect at birth the appearance of religion, the most complicated and subtle of all man's infinitude of faculties! And yet it is with these humbler functions that religion is inseparably intertwined, and out of them it develops. What are some of the essential principles involved in the process?

Dependence and the "four wishes." When the infant emerges from the even and secure confinement of the womb to taste its first great adventure in life, namely the struggle for breath, its nervous system must sustain a considerable shock. We do not necessarily have to go all the way with the Rankians in their emphasis on the crucial importance of this, the *birth trauma*, as they call it. Nevertheless we can recognize that very probably this experience may have considerable importance for the future psychic development of the individual, particularly if the conditions surrounding the birth are drastic or abnormal in important respects. And it would seem certain that there is at least one psychological result.

This is that with dawning consciousness there should be borne in on the organism an inchoate but nevertheless very real sense of dependence. Of Thomas' four wishes,[2] the wish for security immediately grips the infant and mingles with those physiological reflexes that operate with the drawing of the first breath. Human hands assist him in this first of his earthly endeavors, while his small demands for creature comforts and his growing appetites can be sup-

---

[1] An ape of sixteen months brought up with a child, for example, showed more fondness for its "foster parents" than did the son in the family himself even at the same age. See Kellogg and Kellogg, *The Ape and the Child*.

[2] See Chap. 4, pp. 66–74 of this volume.

plied only in limited degree by initiative on his part. This sense of dependence will be with him all his life, in greater or less degree, and is the prototype of that sense of dependence on the Creator that Schleiermacher felt to be the essential core of the religious life. Certainly he could plead priority for this psychological reaction.

A second of the four wishes that shows itself almost as early is the wish for new experience. This is expressed, more physiologically than psychologically, as the limbs move about in a generalized, haphazard way. Within a few weeks of birth they begin to show undoubted signs of organization not merely to the pardonably prejudiced parents, but to the detached scientific observer as well. Indeed that this activity even at birth is not purely physiological is indicated by the fact that if the infant's waving arms and legs are suddenly pinioned, he will show signs of emotion, such as redness of the face and explosive crying that some psychologists call anger and others, more cautiously, simply excitement.[3] While not so insistent as the wish for security, the wish for new experience is another urge whose expression the infant learns is to some extent dependent on what others do with him.

The wish for response is also present in embryonic and mostly physiological form, for the infant will respond with apparent satisfaction to fondling and stroking, especially of the so-called "erogenous zones," a fact that helped to lead Freud to the concept of infant sexuality. Dependence is obviously important here too, and the infant soon begins to rely on those who care for him to satisfy this hunger along with his more physiological needs. As a matter of fact this satisfaction is almost as important as his food, even for his physical survival, and it is crucial for the wholesome development of his personality.

Pediatricians recently have become more aware of the fact that the most perfect physical care in the world is not sufficient to guarantee the survival of many infants. Without love, as if with nothing to live for, many will languish and die; with love, even though diet and sanitation may in some ways be deficient, they still may develop into robust, healthy children. It is for this reason that foundling homes and hospitals with the sole and extended custody of infants prescribe "mothering" along with diet formulas and hygiene for

[3] See Merry and Merry, *The First Two Decades of Life*, Chap. 2.

babies' care.[4] And it is in this way that the average infant gets his early lessons in response and love, and learns that for this too he is dependent on others.

The wish for recognition is operating less obviously at birth. Doubtless it might be demonstrated to exist in very elementary form, but in the ordinary sense it requires some degree of consciousness of self, and this does not develop until later, probably not until after the first year at the very earliest.[5] But during the second year it quite clearly is beginning to develop, and children of this age often show unmistakable signs of jealousy, which indicate its presence. This sense of personal worth is developed through that mirror of the self, the opinions and attitudes of other people, and once again the child experiences dependence.

While we might go on and list other areas where the child learns dependence, this is sufficient to make the point clear that in the most basic and essential way this habit develops. It is not the only trait that is growing, for like flowers in a garden, or weeds in the field, all traits are growing together.[6] They will all have their part to play in the religious consciousness, but enough has been said to make clear genetically why the sense of dependence is one plant that will be prominent in the garden of the individual's religious life. Man's feeling of dependence on God is made possible, in a psychological sense, by such experiences in the dawn of his existence.

The importance of the parents. If man is reduced to metaphor in speaking of the human mind because of its complexity, how much more is this true when he speaks of that still more inscrutable reality, the Divine. Many are the figures of speech by which God has been described, according to the experience of the worshiper, and also according to that aspect of God which one may wish to emphasize. It follows that in casting about for meaningful religious symbols the religious person will tend to prefigure his Deity in those human terms associated with his most meaningful, poignant, and satisfying experiences. It is not surprising, therefore, that the parent metaphor owns a universality that extends far beyond the Christian faith.

[4] See M. A. Ribble, *The Rights of Infants*, pp. 4–7.
[5] See Allport, *Personality*, Chap. 6, for a discussion.
[6] Cf. Pratt, *op. cit.*, p. 93.

We can then expect that a child's relations with his parents will have an important influence on his concept of God and hence on the whole quality of his religious life, dependent as in large measure it will be on the sort of emotional experience that the parent symbol originally evokes. Similarly will this influence the intellectual concept of God, though for the average person the intellectual factor will be of lesser importance. Allport tells of the case of a six-year-old boy who refused to say the Lord's Prayer with its opening words, "Our Father." The reason was that his earthly father was a drunkard and a renegade, and the emotional connotation of "father" as applied to God was more than he could bear.[7] It is for such reasons as this that sometimes one and sometimes another conception of God makes its appeal to different people. It is also an argument for flexibility in religious symbolism and custom.

We must not leave this subject before recalling Freud's observation on religion, as indicated in the previous chapter, for he makes the relations with parents and the consequent search for the father image the very core of the religious life. Freud's views are always to be treated with respect, though not necessarily with awe.[8] Though we wish to preserve a healthy skepticism with regard to his theories, it is noteworthy that he supports us in our emphasis on the importance of the child's relations with his parents for his future religious development.

Learning and maturation. The answer to the old conundrum, "What is everybody doing at the same time all the time?" is, "Growing older." An answer that might serve almost as well is "Learning," for that subtle and unresting change that goes on within our nervous fibres that the psychologist calls *learning* starts with birth and ends only with death. The less voluntary aspect of this change is distinguished by the name of *maturation*, and this is especially important in the earlier years. Psychologists have given more hours of thought and investigation to this subject than to any other in their field, with the familiar result that the more they learn about it the more

---

[7] *The Individual and His Religion,* p. 31.

[8] That empirical studies are far from verifying all of Freud's hypotheses, including those concerning parent-child relations, is made clear in R. R. Sears, *Survey of Objective Studies of Psychoanalytic Concepts.*

complex it becomes and the more confused they get. Yet the psychology of religion has a stake in this investigation, for religion develops through learning, and its ways will never be fully understood until learning is understood.[9]

It is obvious that many things, such as language and self-consciousness, have to be "learned" by the infant before the religious life can begin. This also involves maturation of both physiological and psychic functions, and the stage of this development limits the degree and quality of religious experience. To give a concrete example, in the parent-and-child relations of which we have just been speaking the child *learns* certain attitudes which will be woven into the texture of his religious life. The six-year-old, whose father was a drunkard, had *learned* certain attitudes toward his father which distinctly limited his religious response to the Lord's Prayer. On the other hand it was the *maturation* of his intellectual capacities that prevented him from repeating the prayer as mere rote and enabled him to make the connection between God and his father that caused his difficulty. Naturally more maturation and learning must take place before he will be enabled to comprehend the symbolic nature of the term "Our Father" and properly to integrate this concept into his own personal theological system.

The first and most obvious kind of religious learning develops by rote. The conditioned response, such as was demonstrated by the famous dog of Pavlov, doubtless is a mechanism sufficient to explain this popular method for inculcating religious words and religious habits. These include the memorizing of Bible passages, the folding of hands, and the bowing of the head at grace before meals. Great is the self-congratulation among fond parents and zealous religious educators when such instruction has been accomplished.

The author witnessed an example of the strength of such teaching when a young woman in church, who had forgotten her hat, felt it necessary to cover her head with a piece of tissue paper. Horrified though certain members of the congregation were at this breach of

[9] See E. R. Hilgard's *Theories of Learning* for a review of more than ten different theories influential in the field. For less advanced students Munn's *Psychology*, Part 3, or Merry and Merry *op. cit.*, Chap. 8, give a very satisfactory introduction to the subject.

ecclesiastical decorum they probably would have been more so if she had provided no covering at all!

Consequently it is a little disconcerting when a psychologist demonstrates that similar ritualistic maneuvers can be stimulated in pigeons.[10] It is not that a certain amount of this type of learning is not desirable and even necessary in religion. But it is important that its essentially simple and mechanical nature be understood so that it may be distinguished from processes that are either infinitely more complex though similar in quality, as Skinner or Thorndike would hold, or completely different in kind, as is the feeling of most Gestalt psychologists.

At any rate, children do not become capable of the higher and more complex processes of learning until they get older. This means that one should not expect anything more than the elementary forms of abstract and reflective thinking of the young child. This explains the emphasis on rote learning with them. Rote learning seems within their grasp while the higher kind appears to be beyond them. The danger in this view is that rote learning may become a habit that will crowd out other kinds so that the individual will become capable of no other. Furthermore, if we acknowledge the existence of the death urge,[11] we can readily see that the comfort of the security offered the child who dutifully fulfills the rote demands of his religion may become for him its chief attraction and source of solace. On the other hand, the child in whom the life urge is stronger may become impatient with this insipid brand of pap and so later on rebel at a religion so devoid of meaning. Perhaps these considerations may throw further light on a phenomenon we have noted before: the emphasis on rote in our churches and religious education may help to explain why the death urge is so much more prominent in popular religion than the life urge.[12]

Conscience and guilt. Some psychiatrists have made much of the ill effects on mental health of a sense of guilt and a rigid conscience. However, it is doubtful that many of the positive achievements of

[10] B. F. Skinner, "Superstition in the Pigeon."
[11] See Chapter 4.
[12] See Breckinridge and Vincent, *Child Development*, pp. 179–185, for good commentary on ineffectiveness of rote learning in the church.

modern civilization would be possible without the peculiarly human capacity for feeling guilt and the prick of that inner stimulus that we call conscience. There is no essential reason why guilt and conscience should be associated with religion, particularly as we have defined it, but in our Western religions and in all the more highly developed forms of religion this has always been true,[13] so that it is appropriate that we should say a few words about its genesis.

While the capacity for having a conscience may be God-given, the specific content of the individual's conscience is always learned. This we know since there is no matter of conscience—say that which involves the Ten Commandments—which anthropologists have not found to differ from the Western norm among some of the peoples who live elsewhere on our globe.[14] Even in our own culture lying, stealing, and killing will be tolerated by conscience under certain circumstances. Pangs of conscience do not trouble the average person who says he is feeling fine when he is not, who kills in war, or who steals from an enemy in order to keep himself alive. Also we differ from one another in what causes a feeling of guilt. The Catholic child feels guilt when he misses Mass; the New England conscience may trouble another who goes to a movie on Sunday; while the Jewish child may feel guilty if he neglects his religious duties on a Saturday.

The origin of these unique feelings of guilt is found in the teachings of the parents or parent substitutes, which started long before the individual can remember. However, most crucial to the process is the *identification* that the child at some point comes to feel with his parents, their ideals and wishes for him. In the ethical and religious areas this occurs most importantly sometime between the ages of three and six,[15] though of course the child does not understand the implications of what he is taught, nor is he able to reflect on the material. Indeed the strength of his feelings of conscience is partly dependent on this lack of understanding. Of course he may identify himself with people other than parents, and groups other than the family; his teachers or his playmates, for example. The teachings

[13] Cf. Rudolf Otto: "In every highly developed religion the appreciation of moral obligation and duty, ranking as a claim of the deity upon man has developed side by side with the religious feeling itself." *The Idea of the Holy*, p. 53.

[14] For examples see R. Benedict, *Patterns of Culture*.

[15] Cf. Hurlock, *Child Development*, p. 443.

and the attitudes of these others will modify his conscience and even influence his overt behavior to a marked degree. But the influence of the family will never be wholly erased. Long after the faces of his father and his mother have faded from his sight their silent influence will still be reflected in the conscience of the old man. Though he may pursue a very different road with never so jaunty an air, there will remain some acts that he never can perform without paying a price of inner distress, whether conscious or unconscious, in the form of a sense of guilt.

What we have been speaking of here is the development principally of what Erich Fromm would call the "authoritarian conscience," the content of which comes from sources to whom the child accords obedience and respect outside of himself. It is important for the child's adjustment, the fulfilling of his "wish for recognition," and for his finding his place in society. But when overdeveloped it is characterized by extreme rigidity, and its violation by an overwhelming sense of guilt that will hamper the creative development of his personality. Contrasted to it is the "humanistic conscience," made up of elements spontaneously developed by the individual, appropriate to his unique abilities and essential to his creativity.[16]

The development of both authoritarian and humanistic consciences in their appropriate degrees is necessary if the child is to realize happily his full potential. That is why he needs both discipline and freedom. Without an authoritarian conscience he becomes a law unto himself, a "psychopathic personality" or "moral imbecile," with no sense of responsibility to society or ability to conform. Without the humanistic conscience he becomes an uncreative cog in the machinery of the social system.

Conscience, then, is an important and basic part of the phenomena that behaviorists, psychoanalysts, and Jesuits have in mind when they chorus the importance of childhood training. It is another facet of religious growth that is important for our understanding of where a child's religion comes from and how it develops.

Harms' stages of religious development. One of the most original and resourceful, and, it appears to us, important empirical studies of the religion of the child is Ernest Harms' "The Development of Re-

[16] See Fromm, *Man for Himself*, pp. 141–172.

ligious Experience in Children," which appeared in the *American Journal of Sociology* in 1944. The method used was a variation of the projective technique and involved asking several thousand children aged from three through adolescence to imagine how God would look, then draw a picture of him and give a statement of what the picture represented. An analysis of the results indicated that the child's religious growth goes through three stages as illustrated in the accompanying reproductions.

(a) *The fairy-tale stage.* From three to six years of age the child's conception of God is highly fanciful and emotional rather than rational,

glorifying the highest fantasies with which the child at this age can catch with his little mind. . . . By liberating the pictorial forms of God experience we proved not only that a child, even at this early age, has a deep and original religious experience but that this experience is more deeply rooted in his nature and, therefore, more important than any other.[17]

This suggests that adults err in applying to children's religion rational standards which make this religion appear foolish. But one may wonder whether perhaps, in its reaction against literalistic and rote methods of setting a child's mind in the way it should go, modern religious educators have not sometimes made a similar error in their concern that the child's concepts should be as logical and clear as possible. For instance Santa Claus is a familiar *bête noire* in modern religious education, usually backed up with horrible examples of children who confused this engaging Christmas fairy with God.[18] Yet we are aware of no well-controlled studies which show that children who have enjoyed this pleasant fiction have grown into adults with more confused religious ideas than those whose early conceptions were purged of such delusions. We suspect that the not inconsiderable amount of confusion that exists probably has its roots elsewhere. At any rate, Dr. Harms' study indicates that intellectual re-

[17] Pp. 115–116.
[18] For instance, see Manwell and Fahs, *Consider the Children*, pp. 64–65. Every Christmas the *New York Sun* used to reprint a famous editorial, "Yes, Virginia, there is a Santa Claus," in answer to a little girl's inquiry. This illustrates one way of emphasizing the essence of the Santa Claus myth.

ligious concepts have little or no meaning for the child, and that the free play of the emotions and fantasy is to be encouraged at this level if the wholesome genius of the child is to be expressed.

Figure 1 on the accompanying plates is the drawing of a five-year-old boy at this stage. On being asked whether God should not look like a human being, he answered, "Why should he?"

(b) *The realistic stage.* From the time of going to school up to the dawn of adolescence the child's idea of God reflects more realistic concepts, which come to him through religious institutions and the teachings of his elders. The pictures of God at this time represent Him as a priest, with much use of conventional religious symbolism such as the Cross or the Star of David. In this stage emotion "creates ability for formalistic expression" since it cannot be expressed intellectually, hence the child's interest in symbolism; also he takes the institution with its forms and conventions seriously since he can see his elders do so.

Figure 2 is the picture drawn by a seven-year-old parochial-school boy. He has written on it, "I drew this picture because when I go to church I always see God on the Cross. I love God very much. The Blessed Mother is praying to her son."

Sometimes the realism of this stage goes beyond the ideas of the times, as in the case of the child who drew a figure of God who might have been either Christ or a priest with the words appended, "He is a Jew and a Christian and both kinds love him." This was similar to the ideas of a small boy at this stage, known to the writer, whose parents were of mixed faiths. He could not understand why he could not worship in both ways and was only puzzled by the conflicting requirements and prejudices of the differing churches. It is a sad commentary on institutional religion that growing up for so many children involves the acquiring of ideas and prejudices that would seem to draw attention away from essentials toward the distortions that owe so much to the secondary and tertiary expressions of religious life. Harms' example opens a psychological window which gives us insight into those wholesome aspects of the religion of childhood that Jesus must have had in mind in commending to his disciples the attitudes of the child.

(c) *The individualistic stage.* Logically we should reserve discussion of this stage for the next chapter, for it involves the religion of the adolescent, but we wish to treat Harms' findings as a unit. Of this stage he says,

Children of this age appear to have the highest degree of emotional sensitiveness they may ever reach during the course of life. In their individualized religious subjects they find an adequate medium for this keen emotional sensitiveness which, at this stage, is coupled with originality. . . .[19]

The individualistic stage is characterized by much greater variety than the first two, so much so that it is subdivided into three parts. (1) A large number of the pictures could be classified as conventional and conservative, with little fantasy, as in Figure 3, which represents God welcoming people into Heaven, by a fifteen-year-old girl. (2) A second group showed more originality and expressed personal views. Figure 4 depicts the personal religious experience of a fourteen-year-old boy, headed "Glory." (3) The third subdivision was "most astounding." Apparently spontaneously produced by American children, says Dr. Harms, were ideas similar to those of early Egyptian cults, Persian mythology, Chinese Buddhism, sun worship, German medieval mysticism, alchemy, Rosicrucianism, and other such unusual and far-removed movements. Figure 5 was the depiction by a thirteen-year-old boy, and is suggestive of Stonehenge and sun worship. A fifteen-year-old girl produced the picture in Figure 6. This is similar to a medieval concept of the magic bottle of life, with the primacy of human beings over the lower forms of life shown toward the margins. The children were not aware of copying these from anything.

In these empirical studies of Harms we find some substantiation and illustration of Fromm's concepts of authoritarian and humanistic expressions of religion. Subdivision 1 represents the ideas of those children in whom authoritarian influences have been strong, while the high individualism of subdivision 3 bears the stamp of a more "humanistic" variety. Harms points to the moral of his findings for religious education in the need for freedom, particularly for the adolescent to express his religion according to the pattern "which is congenital or, at least, profoundly connected with the child's natural disposition."

[19] *Ibid.*, p. 118.

Psychologists may differ as to the interpretation of the drawings collected by Harms. This is apt to be particularly true with respect to the third subdivision of adolescent pictures. One will agree according to the extent one accepts the theories of C. G. Jung concerning symbolic "archetypes" and the "racial" or "collective" unconscious.[20] But Harms' broad conclusions seem to make sense: the small child expresses fantasy in his religion, the older child's ideas are more realistically derived from his environment, while the adolescent shows much greater variety and creativity. These findings deserve to be checked by independent study, while the method is a most promising one for future elaboration.[21]

WHAT IS THE CHILD'S RELIGION LIKE?

The question of what a child's religion is like has already been answered in part in our discussion of development. In this section, however, we will emphasize the descriptive approach and will be more specific. Also we will be concerned principally with the conceptual or intellectual aspects of the child's religion. This is not because they are more important, for, as we have already pointed out, they may be wholly unimportant for an understanding of a particular child. In fact, if overemphasized they may lead to complete misunderstanding of the child and to distorted emphases in religious education. But intellectual concepts are more obvious and hence more accessible to the psychologist, so that we can be clearer in our treatment. More information is available. Also the ideas of children have importance as a kind of foil for the understanding of mature religion. Characteristics that are perfectly appropriate to the age of childhood are most inappropriate to a later age, and so much adult religion is "childish" in this derogatory sense that it is important that we recognize what these characteristics are.

Ideas accepted on authority.   We have already spoken of Fromm's concepts of the authoritarian and humanistic.[22] The child's ideas are

[20] For Jung's theories, see his *Modern Man in Search of a Soul* or *The Integration of Personality.*

[21] For Dr. Harms' theories and practice in the clinical use of child art, see his *Essentials of Abnormal Child Psychology*, Chaps. 8–9.

[22] For a development of these terms apart from the concept of conscience, see Fromm, *op. cit.*, Chap. 2.

almost wholly "authoritarian" in the sense that they come from other people. The child has been learning from his cradle to accept things from those who care for him, and his experience has been that most of these things are good. Also his elders are so much more powerful and able than he is that it is natural for him to believe in their omniscience. Obedience, also, is a habit that he has learned will pay, so that it is quite easy for him to accept the adults' ideas as soon as they begin to have any meaning for him—and even before. If any documentation of this characteristic is thought necessary, the reader will find it in a thorough empirical study by MacLean.[23]

Unreflective. Since children accept ideas on authority, it is not at all surprising that reflection on them is seldom encountered. Most adults are familiar with this characteristic of the child mind, and some even indulge in the dubious amusement of testing the limits of childish credulity. Thus a neighbor was heard to inform a child of five that Santa Claus had cut off his beard. When the child asked why, he was told that Santa's mother wanted to stuff a pillow with it. This explanation was perfectly satisfactory to the child despite his encounter the next day with a department store Santa in all the glory of his customary appendage. It is in this spirit that religious ideas are accepted, so that it is no wonder that the most inconsistent and bizarre ideas are entertained by children. Thus MacLean found that 73 per cent of a certain group of children agreed that "God has a face, hands, and feet, just like a man," while 58 per cent of the same group of children just as cheerfully assented to the view that "God is not like a person at all. He is something like electricity—just an energy that works, keeping things going and making them grow." [24]

This does not mean that there is no reflection among children, for a precocious child here and there may be remarkably keen in scrutinizing ideas that are presented to him. Pratt calls our attention to the following entertaining account by Edmund Gosse of an episode in his own life, purportedly when he was six:

My parents said: "Whatever you need, tell him and He will grant it, if it is His will." Very well: I had need of a large pointed humming-top

[23] *The Idea of God in Protestant Religious Education*, p. 116 and *passim.*
[24] *Ibid.*, p. 90.

which I had seen in a shop window in the Caledonian Road. Accordingly
I introduced a supplication for this object into my evening prayer, carefully adding the words, "If it is Thy will." This, I recollect, placed my
Mother in a dilemma, and she consulted my Father. Taken, I suppose, at
a disadvantage, my Father told me I should not pray for "things like
that." To which I answered by another query, "Why?" And I added that
he said one ought to pray for things we needed, and that I needed the
humming-top a great deal more than I needed the conversion of the
heathen or the restitution of Jerusalem to the Jews, two objects of my
nightly supplication that left me very cold.[25]

Pratt also cites the case of one eight-year old girl who, told that faith
would move mountains, prayed for three hours that Mount Washington be removed into the sea. The unsatisfactory result of this brand
of earth removal shook her faith so that she did not pray again all
summer.[26]

Two causes may be assigned to such unusual performances among
children. They suggest children of very high intelligence, and it is
usually found that the capacity for reflection begins with a mental
age of about twelve. Thus a girl of eight with an IQ of 150 would
have the required intelligence. On the other hand, even with less
intelligence the disappointment of a very specific and greatly desired
expectation might well stimulate a rebellion that would lead to
doubt. The case of Edmund Gosse and the humming-top suggests
some such process.

But despite exceptions like those cited above, which give us a
glimpse of the process of awakening doubt in childhood, we must
bear in mind that the rule is an unreflecting entertainment of the
most available ideas that present themselves, or are presented, to
the child's mind. Some of these find a lodgement while others de-
part after a brief stay; many are ill-assorted and contradictory, but
the hospitable mind of the child can contain them all with a minimum of reflection on their implications, or uneasy feelings that perhaps they do not all belong there.

Egocentric. A child is not born with a sense of self. This begins
to develop perhaps toward the end of the first year of life, though it
cannot be said to be firmly present until he becomes aware of his

[25] *Father and Son*, p. 49.
[26] *The Religious Consciousness*, p. 101.

name and the proper use of the personal pronouns.[27] Stimuli and experiences take on meaning and are organized around this sense of self, and so make possible memory and the growth of the ego. Of necessity these early impressions are rather narrowly focused on a selfhood crass and obvious. As it grows they take in wider and wider territory as the individual graduates from an exclusive concern with his personal interests to an identification successively with his family, his school, his country, until his awareness of his interests achieves those ideal heights where, in the words of John Donne, he seeks not to inquire for whom the bell tolls because he knows that a loss for any of mankind is his loss too, and that it tolls for him. It is this process of the expansion of the self for which the great religions show much concern, and the difference between selfishness and altruism is largely a matter of degree between the narrow and the wider ego.

In the child we see the self at the beginning of its journey. Consequently it is only to be expected that his prayers should abound with personal requests for protection and favors, while ecclesiastical apparatus and religious concepts are all referred in some way to his personal pleasure and welfare. Thus a small boy told his mother he was going to be a priest because it was "a good paying business," while Allport tells of five-year-old Tommy who saw the Cross in the chancel of the church only as "T for Tommy." [28]

Children who, on the one hand, suffer from too many frustrations in life or who lack the love of others, or, on the other hand, are surfeited with too much attention, are apt to be stunted in their capacity to develop the self. Or it may be that a drastic experience of frustration may throw the self back to a more childish, that is, a narrower, stage of the ego. Consequently we find adults who bear the ungracious marks of a concern for self appropriate to this childish period. They lack the capacity to "love their neighbors as themselves."

Anthropomorphic. The child, in common with his elders, derives his concept of deity from his experience with people. But he uses

[27] For an account of the development of the consciousness of self and its extension, see Allport, *Personality*, pp. 159–165, 217–220. Also for this and the next topic, cf. his *The Individual and His Religion*, pp. 28–32.

[28] *The Individual and His Religion*, p. 29.

only the grossest and most obvious aspects of human nature in ar-
riving at his idea of God. Thus God most commonly is a man with
gray hair and a beard, who occasionally walks the earth checking
up on evil-doers, but most of the time presides in a vague place
somewhere up in the sky where everyone is happy and which is
called Heaven.[29]

Tacked on to this anthropomorphic core are concepts that might
be called superanthropomorphic, namely characteristics that are
simply human ones writ large in terms of power and knowledge, as
with the heroes in the comic books. MacLean reports a number of
children who said that "God can see right through the roof," while
others conceived of God as sending floods in modern times "to kill
bad people." One child announced, "There was an auto accident in
our street and a lot of people were killed. God did it!" while another,
incipiently somewhat less bloodthirsty, said, "God saves people from
being killed. I know because I fell right in front of an automobile
and it never touched me."

Variations from the superhuman theme are ideas that represent
numerous bizarre embroideries on human nature, some called up by
out-of-the-way bits of the child's experience, some the expression of
the child's own fantasy. Pratt reports the conviction of a six-year-old
that "God is a face of a man with big ears. He doesn't eat anything
but only drinks dew." [30]

The features that chiefly distinguish conceptions like these from
adult ideas of God are literalness and concreteness. While it would
not be too difficult a task to find parallels among adult concepts, even
the literal-minded adult is apt to have a saving sense of the infinity
of God that broadens his range and enables him to transcend, even
though in small degree, his narrow prison of the actual. The mature
adult who reflects on the idea of God with any thoroughness of
course recognizes that our terms of personality when applied to God
are simply figures of speech which represent the best efforts of our
limited minds to reach out toward the secrets of unutterable mystery. The results of Harms' study, as we have indicated, show that
under proper conditions the child may indeed have a sense of some-

---

[29] The reader will find this statement well documented in MacLean, *op. cit.*,
Chap. 4.
[30] *The Religious Consciousness*, p. 97.

Figure 1

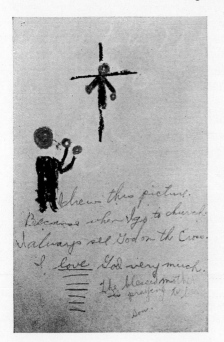

Figure 2

Figure 3

Figure 4

Figure 5

Figure 6

thing that fills him with awe. But for the most part the students in this field have found the overt ideas of children, derived largely from their narrow experience and what people have told them about God, to be mainly anthropomorphic.

Verbalized and ritualistic. A great deal of what passes for religion among children is simply the repeating of phrases by rote or the performance of religious motions. Parents and religious directors experience a dubious sort of satisfaction when they observe the obedient young folding their hands, bowing their heads, and mumbling phrases of piety. A little boy, used to saying his prayers before a religious picture, found himself without the picture and substituted, with no feeling that it was inappropriate, the cover picture of a popular magazine.[31] Another child was overheard praying this version of the Lord's Prayer: "Our Father who art in heaven, Harold be Thy Name." The fact that presumably he had never heard the deity addressed by the somewhat familiar name of "Harold" had not disturbed the rote repetition of the phrase.

There have developed much difference of opinion and some acrimony among religious educators as to the value of such ritualistic practices. The more progressive camp tends to dismiss such behavior with scorn. In view of the considerable amount of adult religion, from the time of the prophet Amos to the present, that has been on a hardly higher level and which doubtless got its start in the practices of childhood, we should applaud the wholesome rejection of such superficial training.

On the other hand, habit may be a good and useful workhorse in religion as elsewhere. Furthermore practices which started as meaningless habits in childhood often flower later on with a meaning which they could not have acquired if started at a time when their significance could be fully comprehended. For example, the most powerful single influence on the expression of the great masters of English style such as Shakespeare, Milton, Carlyle, Ruskin, Emerson, Hawthorne, and Lincoln seems to have been the English Bible. This has also been true for the common man. It is questionable whether this beneficent influence on language would have been exerted had not little children been introduced to its vigorous phrases and stately

[31] Allport, *The Individual and His Religion*, p. 29.

cadences long before they could have much sense of what these meant.

One of the controversies among religious educators is whether to use the obsolescent King James version of the Bible or one of the modern translations. My strong recommendation is for the King James with the use of modern translations as a gloss for clarity and to correct the obvious inaccuracies of the former. If my theories are sound, the intellectual experiences of the child are less important than the emotional, and the King James version is still superior in its capacity to stir the imagination of both children and adults. For example compare the rendering of I Sam. 3:11 by Moffatt: "I am about to do a deed in Israel that will make the ears of all that hear it ring." with the vigor of the King James: "Behold, I will do a thing in Israel at which both the ears of everyone that heareth it shall tingle." It is by such force and skill of phraseology even more than the literal clarity of ideas that children are moved, even though the experience may not come to full flower until many years later.

Whenever Sir Roger De Coverley was asked by two friends to arbitrate a dispute between them his shrewd habit was to pronounce that there was "much to be said on both sides." This is our conclusion as to whether there is value in verbalized and ritualized training among children. But there is no doubt that rote practice characterizes this stage of religious development. And whatever its use may be, it is important that it be recognized for what it is, a mere possible means to an end, and never to be mistaken for the real thing.

Imitative. As suggested by our discussion of rote religious practices, it is clear that much of the child's religious life must be learned through imitation and suggestion.[32] One of the amusing characteristics of childhood is the child's way of aping the superficial aspects of the ways of grown-ups, as when children "play church." Because the child's religious life is of necessity superficial, there are some progressive educators who advocate postponing the cultivation of its important aspects until much later on. The most extreme statement of this position is to be found in *Emile* by Jean Jacques Rousseau, where it is advocated that the child be carefully

---

[32] For a somewhat mechanical theory but a systematic treatment of how this takes place, see Miller and Dollard, *Social Learning and Imitation.*

removed from all contact with religion until adolescence, when it is expected that he will develop a religious life for himself.

However, it is very doubtful that most children would become religious all by themselves. If the scientist achieves his modern miracles because he stands on the shoulders of Titans, this is also to a large degree true of the religious man. Studies are pretty unanimous in indicating that few people are strongly religious in maturity who have not had a religious upbringing as children. For instance, the author, in his study of Moral Re-Armament, found that of fifty-five persons who had been influenced by the movement, not a single one had come from a completely non-religious home! [33]

The subtler aspects of early religious influence contain values that have never been measured. Doubtless some of these influences come from outside the family. Nevertheless, influence from within the family would still seem the most potent single factor in the child's religious development. Perhaps the classic tribute to the influence of the religious home comes from Carlyle, who was never in the habit of praising the merely conventional. He is thinking of his own home when he has Teufelsdröckh say:

My kind Mother . . . did me one altogether invaluable service: she taught me less indeed by word than by act and daily reverent look and habitude, her own simple version of the Christian Faith. . . . My Mother, with a true woman's heart, and fine though uncultivated religious sense, was in the strictest acceptation Religious. . . . The highest whom I knew on Earth I here saw bowed down, with awe unspeakable, before a Higher in Heaven: such things, especially in infancy, reach inwards to the very core of your being; mysteriously does a Holy of Holies build itself into visibility in the mysterious deeps; and Reverence, the divinest in man, springs forth undying from its mean envelopment of Fear.[34]

Spontaneous in some respects. Having pointed out that the child's religion is imitative, we will now mention a contradictory

[33] See *The Oxford Group*, Part 3, esp. p. 228. At the same time Allport, Gillespie, and Young report that a third of the college students they studied who reported no religious influence in their upbringing felt a need for religion. It is not clear how deeply they felt this need but obviously home training is not an absolute requirement. See Allport, *op. cit.*, p. 38.

[34] *Sartor Resartus*, p. 75.

tendency, which is a certain spontaneity that exhibits itself to the sensitive observer. For example the child, unlike the adult, does not have the strong need to seek a meaning for life. His attention span is short, his motives of short term, and while his little purposes may be as intense as those of adults while they last, the riddle of existence is never more than of passing moment to him. Yet, aside from motives of imitation and desire to please his elders, the child often shows signs of a surprising spontaneity and freshness in some of his religious interests. His interest in the green world of nature and the shining heavens above him is one sign of his religious spontaneity, while Harms, in the study alluded to above, has demonstrated it especially in the pictures of God drawn by the younger children in the "fairy-tale stage" of religious development.

It is of prime importance that the parent and religious educator recognize, respect, and nourish this spontaneity, for in it lies the hope for that primary type of religious behavior that we have defined as the core of religious experience.

Wondering. A final characteristic of the child's religion is that it is characterized by wonder. It is not the type of wonder that leads to creative reflection or thought in the intellectual sense, but a kind of immediate delight in the amazing new world opening around him. Some years ago an essay entitled "My Philosopher" appeared in a current magazine. In it the author described a philosopher friend with whom he often walked. The philosopher invariably showed great delight in the most commonplace activities of the everyday world, explored every by-way, took an interest in the vehicles passing in busy streets, and was fascinated even by the rows of multicolored canned goods lining the grocer's shelves. The philosopher, of course, turns out to be a child of three.

It is this delight in the wonderful, which is one form of the wish for new experience, that is expressed in the interest in fairy tales at this age. Consequently it is not surprising that this wonder is projected onto the idea of God suggested by older people, particularly when God is thought of as the creator of such striking marvels as the sun, the moon, and the whirling planets. Also this explains the appeal that religious myths have for the younger child—Adam and

Eve being driven out of Eden by an angel with a flaming sword; the three children of God walking in the midst of Nebuchadnezzar's burning, fiery furnace; or the Lord parting the Red Sea so that the children of Israel might walk through. It is true that the child who carries a literal interpretation of such things into adulthood may run into trouble, but there is little scientific evidence that this carry-over will happen if he is emotionally secure, and taught by those who realize that one of the needs of the child is not so much exact rational concepts as the feeding of this sense of wonder.

The existence of wonder is suggested by Harms' study, which we mention again to emphasize the fact that this fondness for fantasy is reflected in the pictures of God drawn by the children of pre-school age. Indeed there are those who question whether in this age of scientific realism and sophistication we adults would not be better off with more of the capacity to look at life with some of this sense of pristine wonder that we find in the religion of the child.[35]

This treatment of the religion of childhood is obviously a mere preliminary statement, a rational analysis in which there are still many elusive elements which escape our grasp. But it is enough to indicate that even in childhood religion is a complex affair. In it we see characteristics to be deplored; or, at any rate, elements that we hope to see the child slough off as he grows older. On the other hand there is promise of religious sensitivities. Due to the unfortunate pressure of religious agencies to make children into their images and the impingement of a culture in which material values take a very high rank, these are destined to come to flower, alas, among only a few.

Consequently, we are able to understand the idea current among intellectuals of Wordsworth's day that the child was the *only* religious person, and why bearded philosophers followed around the six-year-old Hartley Coleridge, the "Mighty prophet! Seer blest," as

[35] The emphasis on the need for an increased capacity for wonder was one of Carlyle's reactions against the extreme rationalism of his day. The two most effective literary passages for the re-creation of a sense of wonder for the adult of which I know are the pronouncements of Jehovah in the latter chapters of the Book of Job, and the chapter "Natural Supernaturalism" in Book 3 of Carlyle's *Sartor Resartus*.

if every word spoken by this babbling child had dropped from the mouth of a Nestor.[36] And we are better able to understand Jesus when he commends to us the children, "for of such is the Kingdom of Heaven."

At the same time we should be warned against sentimentality and equating the child's religious life with that of maturity. Just as the physical proportions of the child are appropriate to him while an adult with the same proportions would be a monster, so the once charming faith of a child becomes a proper object of scorn if carried unmodified into manhood; "when I became a man, I put away childish things." No thoughtful person wishes to perpetuate the credulity, egocentrism, and the anthropomorphism of the child, though what amount to such characteristics are often enjoined upon the faithful.

The lesson that we should be taught is respect for the child's religion, which we can improve only if we first respect it. Appropriate to the child's age, it must be expressed in the child's own way; if pruned too closely it will either yield but stunted fruit or become merely a third-rate mockery of what religion ought to be. Also respect it we must if we are to recapture those lost religious sensitivities that Jesus had in mind. In other words, we must be discriminative, and here is one place where psychology can help the religious person in his quest for the essential values of the religious life.

SUMMARY

The psychological importance of the early years in human development demands that some attention be given to religion in childhood. We note that the emerging religious consciousness owes much to more primitive sources, such as the need for security, response, recognition, and new experience. The parents play a role in satisfying all four, though particularly security and response. Thus it is clear that the kind of parents a child has will influence his concept of the divine, the result partly of maturation and partly of a very subtle process of learning. So also does conscience develop, and its content will depend on the child's training and culture. This will become a

---

[36] See Wordsworth's famous "Ode on Intimations of Immortality from Recollections of Early Childhood."

part of the growing adult as he identifies himself with his parents and internalizes their standards. However, no person is creative ethically and religiously whose conscience is wholly dominated by ideas from authoritarian sources. A study by Harms suggests that children's religious concepts go through three stages: the "fairy-tale stage," the "realistic stage," and the "individualistic stage." While the first of these is important for the development of a child's religious imagination, it is not until the last stage, at adolescence, that he becomes capable of true religious originality and creativity.

When we turn from development to a description of the child's religion we find a mixture of primitive and creative elements. Thus the religion of the child is unreflective and mainly accepted on authority. It is egocentric, and the child's ideas of God are palpably a projection of earthly authoritarian figures like a father or grandfather. Furthermore a child's religious convictions, such as they are, are verbalized rather than understood, while their expression tends to be ritualized and imitative. These characteristics are to a large degree inevitable and are not to be deplored when they can be demonstrated to be necessary stages on the road to a wholesome adult faith. The teachability of children, for instance, is a feature that gives them access to the religious wisdom of the ages, when the latter is presented under favorable auspices. Finally, the child is usually superior to the average adult in his capacity for wonder, one of the philosophical ingredients of the profound apprehension of spiritual reality. It is important that the child be treated with understanding and respect if his religious life is to come to full flower.

Chapter 6

RELIGION IN ADOLESCENCE
AND YOUTH

A boy's will is the wind's will,
And the thoughts of youth are long, long thoughts.
—Lapland Song

Psychologists are much more nearly agreed on the point at which adolescence starts than when it ends. It is pretty universally conceded that the onset of puberty marks the beginning of adolescence, while it is thought of as ending anywhere from sixteen to even the late twenties, though usually not as far along as this. Originally conceived as a physiological phenomenon, it is now recognized that its psychological characteristics in large part are socially produced. Margaret Mead [1] and other anthropologists report that in many primitive societies physical maturing brings along with it the expectation of the tribe that the youth promptly assume the responsibilities of an adult. Here the peculiar constellation of personality traits and stresses that we call adolescence hardly exists. The child becomes an adult all at once. Yet in our discussion we will have in mind the age that begins with puberty and extends to the period when the young man or woman has started to support himself and has a reasonably firm grip on the vocational ladder. We have in mind *the age of transition*

---

[1] See her *Coming of Age in Samoa*, for example. A discussion of the definition of the age of adolescence will be found in the opening chapters of any volume on the psychology of adolescence, such as those by Garrison, Cole, Landis, or Horrocks.

from childhood to adult maturity, which we will think of as adolescence.

This concept is admittedly somewhat loose, for there is a sense in
which none of us is wholly mature. We merely achieve that measure
of maturity at which we take ourselves very seriously and find that
most other people do as well. Some of us are still "adolescents" at
an advanced age, confused and irresponsible, as a look around at
nearly any college reunion will testify. Psychologically adolescence
ends with the achievement of a sense of responsibility and a reasonably well accepted philosophy of life effectively implemented. While
theoretically this puts no certain termination to the period, in practice what we are speaking about might conceivably end at fourteen
or fifteen for those on whom an adult role is forced that early. For
most it would end somewhere between eighteen and twenty-four,
though with those preparing for the professions it might be thought
to end even later. Thus it would extend through the period that is
often termed *youth*.

In the case of the religion of childhood, we first tried to trace its
origins and how it developed, after which we described its main
features. In the case of adolescent religion we will do both together,
remembering that adolescence is a continuation of childhood, so that
its religion has the same roots. Similarly the dynamics involved will
be much the same, though we will call attention to certain new elements and forces that are characteristic of this period. These will be
described chiefly under six heads: (1) ideas and mental growth, (2)
emotions, (3) social considerations, (4) moral growth, (5) attitudes
and interests, and (6) worship and prayer.

But before we begin this discussion we would like to make some
general observations on the significance of this period of artificially
extended childhood, and ask whether along with its obvious social,
economic, and intellectual utility, it extends its benefits to the religious life as well. It is no accident that adolescence is prolonged in
our complex culture as compared with its duration in more primitive
societies. In return for a longer period of protection, youth returns to
society larger dividends in the form of those advanced social and economic skills that enable our culture to maintain and advance itself.
The material foundations of our society are ministered to by such
experts as the engineer and the physician, who attain their measure

of competence thanks to the postponement of the day when they are required to be responsible for their full self-support.

Even more importantly, the cultivation of the intellectual life is made possible by the college years that are more and more becoming the expectation of the average American youth. While some who are closely in contact with the typical American campus may wonder just how much the intellect is being cultivated, nevertheless a mere five per cent yield in terms of intellectual curiosity and the pursuit of knowledge for its own sake would be sufficient to justify this postponement; for from it flows the delight in pure ideas which comprise that durable base which is the real foundation of our material progress.

Potentially adolescence and youth may do something similar for religion. We say "potentially" advisedly, for it is by no means automatically assured. But it would seem logical to assume that wasteful though youth may be of that most precious commodity, time, nevertheless the same lack of pressure that enables youth to waste time will allow young people to meditate and speculate, and also to attain insight into cosmic mysteries. In all ages the poet, the seer, and the religious prophet have tended to be young men rather than old. Indeed

> A boy's will is the wind's will,
> And the thoughts of youth are long, long thoughts.

If religion does not seem to be reaping its share of the benefits of this calculated pause before the youth leaps into that maelstrom that becomes his destiny in life, it is because his elders conspire to direct his attention toward more mundane affairs. Harms' picture of the adolescent's idea of God, referred to in the last chapter, suggests some of the richness and originality of the ideas of many youths in the religious area.

Yet a recent study indicates that among 1,798 young people between 18 and 29 questioned by the YMCA, about 70 per cent of the "long, long thoughts" comprised such things as "getting to the top," financial security, happiness, respectability, and other matters equally egotistic; while less than 14 per cent indicated that when alone these youths thought of such things as God's plan for their lives, philosophical concerns, or social problems, as indicated in Table 1.

Table 1

DISTRIBUTION OF REPLIES BY 1,798 YOUTH, AGES 18–29, TO QUESTION, "WHAT KIND OF THINGS DO YOU THINK ABOUT MOST WHEN YOU ARE ALONE?" *

	Per Cent
The future in terms of happiness, security, and respectability	25.4
Immediate associates	13.7
The future in terms of financial security	12.5
The future in terms of "getting to the top"	11.5
Personal adjustment	10.8
Recreation	10.2
Social problems	5.8
Philosophical concerns	4.2
The future in terms of God's plan for my life	3.6
The past—mistakes and lessons	2.3
	100.0

* Adapted from M. G. Ross, *Religious Beliefs of Youth*, p. 105.

However, the same study indicated that this latter, smaller group tended to increase as the individuals grew older. But the fault for its not being larger can doubtless be laid at the door of a culture that reserves its chief rewards for the winners in the fierce competition for more tangible goals; or perhaps to a religious educational tradition that possesses neither the skill to educe the creative religious potentialities of youth nor the understanding of the essential nature of youth prerequisite to the development of those skills. The opportunity is there, but it seems to be missed by the Church more often than it is seized.

But still another factor explains a certain capacity demonstrated by some youth in the religious field. We have spoken of the life urge and the death urge in Chapter 4. Youth, with its physical vigor and life before it, is influenced to a higher degree by the life urge. More often than not its very participation in delinquent behavior or its weakness for sowing wild oats is an expression of this urge toward the new, the dangerous, and the exciting. But in this case it has been turned aside from the creativity that is its more natural expression toward destructive acts.[2] This helps to explain the experience of more than a few young men, like <u>Augustine and Francis of Assisi, whose conversions marked the redirection of the strong currents of their youthful energies into religious channels</u>.

But once more it would seem that the Church has not made use of more than a small fraction of the potentiality that seems to reside in these energies. In the study noted above, Ross estimated that only five per cent of his full sample of nearly two thousand youth seemed to be totally effective, religiously creative personalities.[3] This would seem to be a measure of the proportion of what we have called primary religious personalities, the minority whose numbers may be small but whose influence is out of proportion to its size. While the roots of this type of expression may be found in the childhood religious upbringing of those primary personalities, the definition and first conscious flowering of their creative religious purposes comes in adolescence, or early youth. This makes of adolescence an age of opportunity for the Church, when for these reasons, and others we shall detail later, religion may exert a molding influence second only to the impressions of early home teaching.

In these opening comments we have strayed from the path of strict psychological considerations to touch on the concerns of religious education. This has been done to indicate the use to which our psychological information may be put. We will return to these concerns occasionally as the chapter proceeds.

Ideas and mental growth. <u>Though ideas and intelligence are closely associated, it is important that they be kept apart in one's thinking</u>. Religious ideas are conveyed in elementary form during childhood, often through rote methods of memorization, and while they may acquire more richness as their holder grows, they are not manipulated or criticized to any great degree until adolescence. It is this *corpus* of ideas that helps to make the difference between the Christian and the Buddhist, the Catholic and the Protestant, the Presbyterian and the Methodist. Though by no means the whole

---

[2] For a study of destructiveness, see the author's "Sex Differences and Motivation in the Urge to Destroy," esp. pp. 174 f.

[3] *Op. cit.*, p. 158.

story, ideas also help to explain the content of the conscience, which differs from person to person.

It is when we turn our attention to intelligence that we become aware of the dynamic and creative capacity to change ideas and even to bring new ones into existence. When we consider the nature of some of the ideas presented to the child, it immediately becomes apparent why they must be absorbed by rote or even by token if they are to be absorbed at all. In the traditional service of baptism, for example, the mewling infant is called on by proxy to "renounce the devil and all his works, the vain pomp and glory of the world." [4] Similarly, children are often required to recite the Apostles' Creed and to state their belief in such abstractions as "the Holy Ghost, the Holy Catholic Church, the Communion of Saints, the Resurrection of the body, and the Life Everlasting." It is obvious that comprehension of such concepts must be severely limited by the level of intelligence.

Binet found that even at the age of nine the average child could not be expected to go much beyond such mental activities as making change, naming the months of the year, and answering or comprehending easy questions. [5] The capacity to understand abstractions does not fully develop until about age twelve, if then, while the ability to integrate facts and reach a conclusion concerning them becomes clearly apparent only when the average child has achieved a mental age of fourteen. [6] It is also around these ages that the ability to resist suggestion as to ideas begins to show itself. It is quite understandable, then, that anything approaching real thought concerning religious concepts should be the exception rather than the rule before the age of twelve. We can also understand why questioning or doubt tends to be a characteristic of adolescents rather than of children.

But the mere development of intellectual power is not sufficient by itself to explain doubt, for there are many adolescents who are never troubled by doubt; many of these firm adherents are not handicapped by low mental ability. The tradition in which a child has

[4] The Book of Common Prayer, p. 276.
[5] Garrett, *Great Experiments in Psychology*, p. 5.
[6] Judging by the Binet Scale. See Terman and Merrill, *Measuring Intelligence*, or the account in Freeman's *Theory and Practice of Psychological Testing*, Chaps. 4–5.

been reared is one of the influences that will affect the probabilities of the experience of doubt. To question authority, for example, is more tolerable to the Protesant than to the Catholic, and studies seem to indicate that the Protestant youth is more questioning and independent in his religious beliefs and choices than the Catholic. One evidence of this would be the proportion of youth who change their religious allegiance to churches other than those in which they have been brought up. Allport, Gillespie, and Young, in a study of college youth, found that about 85 per cent of the Roman Catholic youth who were still religious had remained Catholics, while roughly only 40 per cent of the corresponding Protestant and Jewish youth still remained loyal to the specific membership preferences of their families.[7]

Doubtless another influence is the fact that in Western culture the adolescent becomes very conscious of the process of psychological weaning that occurs as he begins to separate his beliefs from those of his parents. In some cases it is the very sense of insecurity about his beliefs that leads the youth to rebel against those of his parents for fear that he be thought to have none of his own. Pratt quotes from a term paper of one of his students a passage suggesting this superficial and conventional kind of doubting: "A college youth passes through a wretched period of doubt and disbelief, he falters, the old dogmas seem mere rubbish—he sees the folly of it all, yet he yearns after the grand, the awe-inspiring, etc., etc." [8]

In addition, the newly found powers, the strange urges, and the confusions due to conflicts between peer-group and home, all stir emotions that disturb the intellectual foundations of religion laid in childhood. Those who, like youth in primitive communities, plunge immediately into the responsibilities of adults, quickly tend to become immersed in the practical problems of making a living. Such youth make a comfortable and ready adjustment to the practical world and to conventional religious ideas. These are apt to look down on their fellows who are privileged to live in a more leisurely way and so can indulge themselves in the luxury of speculation over airy

[7] "The Religion of the Post-War College Student," p. 13. Particularly the Protestant reader must avoid the fallacy of inducing from this data that skepticism and independence necessarily and always have wholesome spiritual results.
[8] *The Religious Consciousness*, p. 118.

nothings, as the practical-minded so often take theological considerations to be. Indeed, it must be admitted, our colleges and graduate
schools seem full of uncreative personalities who, like Hans Castorp
in Thomas Mann's *The Magic Mountain*, have escaped the demands
of the real world in an obsessive concern for the uncertain fruits of
the world of speculation.

But the temptations of such interests are part of the price that
must be paid if we are at the same time to produce those daring
voyagers among the seas of religious ideas; voyagers so necessary if we
are to gain a sense of the realities that lie so much deeper than mere
practical phenomena. A sensitive concern for truth usually has its
conscious birth at this time of life, and if it is not born in youth it
may never be born at all. Furthermore, it often shows itself in wholesome skepticism of the inadequate religious concepts of childhood.

The emotions. The human mind finds great difficulty in understanding itself except by considering things one at a time. There is
no field in which this is more regrettable than when dealing with the
emotions. For without some involvement of the emotions there is
hardly a psychological act that can occur. Indeed all the functions of
the human psyche make one whole and should be studied together.
This aspect of Gestalt truth should be considered or, at the very least,
kept in the reader's mind, whatever the aspect of the psychology of
religion under discussion.

This is particularly necessary in dealing with adolescence, when at
least the Western youth is apt to be tossed about on waves of such
conflicting urges that spiritually it can be declared that "nature doth
contend about them whether they live or die." The basis of the emotions is to be found in the physical equipment of man. Familiar is
the quickening of the pulse, the catching of the breath, the suffused
cheeks, and the sweating palm that accompany any marked heightening of his emotional life.[9] We can well understand that, with the ap-

[9] We cannot here go into any description of the intricate brain mechanism,
the glands, the complicated bodily functions, and the other fascinating things
about the emotions that every psychology student should know. See Munn's
Psychology, Part 6; Young's *Emotion in Man and Animal*; Mottram's *The Physical Basis of the Personality*; English and Pearson's *Emotional Problems of Living*,
or the works of W. B. Cannon. For a discussion of emotions in adolescence, but
at a more generalized level, see Hurlock's *Adolescent Development*, Chap 4,
or Merry and Merry, *The First Two Decades of Life*, Chap. 9.

proach of physical maturity, the emotions also will reach their peak. It is small wonder that an age not yet sure of its ideas and aims, and still short of that measure of control that characterizes the adult, tends to be one of emotional extremes.

Among the characteristics of emotional experience of importance to the student of religion is the fact that strong emotion makes possible feats, both physical and psychological, beyond the reach of the individual under more normal conditions. This may be desirable or undesirable depending on conditions. Consequently we may think of intense emotion as a kind of dynamite, to be handled very carefully and yet most useful under proper control.

One of the many stimuli that will initiate an emotional state is conflict between differing religious ideas, between religious and secular ideas, or between ideals of behavior taught by religion and the behavior itself. The adolescent takes such things seriously, for he does not yet know how easily many of his elders make the transition from whatever behavior may be sanctioned by society on weekdays to the modern equivalent of breast-beating on Sundays. It is out of such tensions that the possibility of conversion grows. Also this explains why conversion has always been found to be a characteristic of youth rather than of other ages. However, since this subject will be taken up in greater detail in a future chapter, the significance of conversion for adolescence will be left for discussion in that place.

There will not be space to detail all the tensions to which youth is subject and which have significance for the religious life. Of importance in Western culture, however, are the tensions growing out of the sex urge. It is not necessary to agree with Freud that sex is the central urge in human motivation. Studies with animals have shown sex to be far from the strongest physiological drive, and there is no good reason for supposing the case to be otherwise in human beings.[10] The preponderance of modern psychological opinion ascribes much of the seeming urgency of sex to the severe taboos with which society surrounds its expression. Since these taboos are often buttressed with religious sanction, it is no wonder that religion and sex are linked together in the mind of the adolescent.

Ethan Brand, in Hawthorne's powerful tale, traveled the world over in search of the unpardonable sin. Had he extended his research

[10] For a discussion see Munn, *op. cit.*, Chap. 11.

into the hearts and minds of adolescents, whether of his own day or of ours, he would doubtless have found a high proportion of these youth who identified the unpardonable sin with some form of sex offense. Kinsey [11] has sufficiently confirmed the insights and researches of psychologists and doctors to the effect that probably nine out of ten males have engaged in masturbation, most likely during adolescence, while a majority of women have similarly offended the mores. More severe forms of sexual offense are only less widespread, which means that a tremendous amount of guilt feeling plagues the youth of our land and serves as the source for emotional tension. Much of this behavior is solitary, all of it to some degree secret, and where not overt it is carried on symbolically in the imagination. This results in religion being the chief recourse for the average American youth as it seeks for a means of controlling this behavior and alleviating the sense of guilt.

These youth have nearly all tried prayer or other religious means of allaying temptation. Highly emotional religious exercises are sometimes successful but usually only temporarily, while the Catholic practice of confession doubtless is very effective in helping some youth in preserving balance, especially if they have a wise confessor. Of importance to religion is the fact that a youth's estimation of his religion will owe much to how helpful it has been to him in handling his sexual appetites. For example the author found, in his study of the Moral Re-Armament movement, that with a number of its early adherents a favorable or unfavorable attitude toward the movement was associated with a wholesome or unwholesome reaction to its program for cultivating sexual purity.[12]

It is possible that the higher frequency of satisfaction with their church of Catholic youth may owe something to the confessional process. It is noteworthy that Moral Re-Armament has owed the success of its program in part to the use of confession. The psychologist may not be able to plumb all the secrets of religion in trying to explain the undoubted fact that often it does succeed in giving man power over his sexual urges. But he can see that with reference to youth especially it involves (a) releasing the youth from an excessive

[11] *Sexual Behavior in the Human Male; Sexual Behavior in the Human Female.*
[12] *The Oxford Group*, pp. 229 f. Also see p. 61 for a participant's account of an early meeting at which sex was a prominent subject of discussion.

sense of sin by acquainting him with the plain fact that he is not alone in his temptations, and hence (b) restoring to him his sense of community with others together with the support that a sense of fellowship brings, and (c) distracting him from preoccupation with sex by supplying him with a sense of purpose which at its best transcends and includes all other lesser purposes.

Any religion worthy of the name will have theological concerns as well. But anyone responsible for a religious program for youth should ask himself the psychological question of whether his program is effective in these three foregoing ways.

It should be noted that emotional tensions are not always obvious to the observer and often express themselves in disguised forms. The intellectual doubts so characteristic of youth, for example, are frequently the expression of maladjustments in other fields. A team of evangelists were visiting a college campus; there one of them spent a long time in trying to resolve the doubts of two young men who had come to him saying that they could not bring themselves to believe in God. Finally in despair they were turned over to a more perspicacious member of the team. The latter was assailed with the theological difficulties of the two young men, but he refused to listen to them. "Your troubles are not intellectual," he said, "they are moral." Highly insulted, the young men rose and left the room. But shortly afterward they reappeared to admit that the evangelist was right. Further conversation led to the relief of emotional tensions, and ultimately to belief.[13]

But even when youth apparently succeeds in resolving intellectual doubts, the real conflict may be emotional. The wise pastor or religious worker with youth needs to cultivate the art of listening sympathetically to whatever the adolescent may have on his mind. Emotional clarifications far subtler than merely intellectual ones may be effected, and these may constitute the significant elements in what may appear to the individual himself as logical conviction. Any sensitive reader of Carlyle's *Sartor Resartus* will sense the essentially emotional and moral source of Teufelsdröckh's agonized wrestling with his spiritual doubts.

Most religious institutions utilize the beginning of adolescence to mark the period during which youth assumes mature responsibility

[13] *Ibid.*, pp. 105–106.

for his religion through "joining the church," confirmation, or the like.[14] One frequently hears comments from older adolescents to the effect that such was foisted on them too early, before the decision could really become their own. There is much truth in these objections, for such ceremonies are apt to be but routine affairs, and so quite likely may be repudiated a few years later. Furthermore some institutions are capable of a rather shameless dragooning of partially mature minds, through a shrewd sense that a larger number of brands will be saved from the burning if these are snatched while they are still somewhat green. Nevertheless there still remain many for whom the experience is a genuine one, which gives form and direction to the chaotic emotional urges of the age. From this point of view the time chosen would seem to be psychologically sound.[15]

Social considerations. The infant grows into a social being in the early years after birth, and the social aspect of his existence becomes steadily stronger as the years go on. But he does not develop full social awareness and self-consciousness until adolescence. At this time social self-consciousness normally becomes very acute, particularly with respect to peer relationships, as will be indicated later.

However, youth is also capable of becoming impressed with the importance of social status, a concept that is readily absorbed from older people; and the fact of being socially secure, or mobile in any direction, cannot fail to have its effect on the personality.[16] Naturally enough this influences the religious activities of youth, though probably more so those of young women than of young men.[17] For instance, Hollingshead has shown in *Elmtown's Youth* that lower-class youth are less often members of a church than are upper-class youth, and social class considerations may play a large part in the success or failure of certain church youth groups. To be sure, if adults are sometimes guilty of attending a certain church for largely social reasons,

[14] For a good discussion of confirmation practices, see G. Stanley Hall's *Adolescence*, Bk. II, pp. 261–280.

[15] Kupky found that their first communion was often reported by Catholic girls as marking their first real religious experience, Protestants much less often. See his *Religious Development of Adolescents*, p. 104.

[16] For well written case studies illustrating the effect of class on adolescent personality see *Children of Bondage* by Davis and Dollard.

[17] For evidence of more class-consciousness among girls than boys, see Landis, *Adolescence and Youth*, p. 281.

we can expect youth to resemble them in this, and sometimes they will better the instruction.

Closely allied with the concept is that of *social role,* or the concept that the individual has of the part that is his to play in society. For example the child's relation to the church is clear, and he plays a child's role without any special conflicts arising from uncertainties as to what is expected of a child. Similarly, the adult member of a church is equally clear about his place and the behavior expected of him. But the adolescent is neither one nor the other. He is apt to look on the youth group—particularly if it meets at the same time and in the same building as the conventional Sunday School—as merely an extension of the children's classes. Nothing mortifies his pride so deeply as the horrible thought that he might be mistaken for a child. On the other hand, though he may be the recipient of the right hand of fellowship after joining the church or after confirmation, along with receiving stirring homilies to the general purpose that he is now to take on adult responsibilities for his faith; nevertheless somehow the full glow of adult satisfaction seems to elude him, for he has not yet defined for himself the complete role of adult. This lack of definition of social role for the adolescent interferes with his integration into many adult groups, but nowhere more obviously than in the church. The youth group is notoriously that which gives the most concern to those responsible for religious education. Success with this group is bound up largely with the ability to define for youth an acceptable role in the church appropriate to its age.

On the other hand, the role that is clearest to the adolescent and hence most potent for influencing his conduct is that which relates him to his peers. As has been pointed out elsewhere [18] the adolescent peer-group represents a social hiatus between childhood and maturity, within which there exist very strong group loyalties and definite, though sometimes peculiar, concepts of how human beings behave. This has a tendency to withdraw youth from the general cultural tradition in favor of a tradition developed by youth itself. Indeed part of that tradition often consists of a kind of rejection of the adult world and its loyalties. At its worst this rejection fosters the rebellion and delinquencies that currently cause so much head-shaking among

[18] Landis, *Adolescence and Youth,* Chap. 22.

the law-enforcement fraternity. It also seems to develop particular strength with regard to religious matters, which may incur a very special kind of anathema in some youth circles.

A church youth worker told the story of an adolescent of junior-high age who was particularly interested in a certain youth program. But he explained that he had long set his heart on achieving membership in a certain very potent neighborhood gang, "The Dukes," with high prestige but delinquent interests. Should it be discovered that he had had any traffic with an organization sponsored by the church, the Dukes would refuse to look at him, and his peer-group social ambitions would be effectively thwarted. While not always as extreme as this, a measure of this kind of attitude will be found in nearly every society of adolescents, though particularly so among boys, and it behooves youth leaders to make allowance for it.

Yet paradoxically, there is also present among youth a contrary tendency toward hero-worship of its elders and a feeling of need for guidance and for confidants. This grows out of the necessity for the psychological weaning from the family and the feeling of the need at one and the same time for independence and for a parent substitute. For boys, a very manly young adult, preferably with athletic ability, such as the high-school football coach, may fill the role of such a hero, and he has the potential power to lead youth either for good or for ill. For girls, a young woman schoolteacher, with just the right combination of friendliness, dignity, and dash, may serve the same purpose. If the churches could enlist, preferably in a professional capacity, more youth workers of this general type, they would be taking another important step toward solving the problem of youth.

When one considers the religious potential of the average adolescent, it seems a cause for inquiry why the church so often misses the mark at this point in religious education. What is required is a study of the complex social patterns of youth with a program designed to take advantage of the social urges and to satisfy the social needs of this age. It is true that the religious needs involve deeper levels of the personality, but if ordinary psychological and social skill is not used properly to open doors, these deeper levels will never be reached and its treasures may forever remain locked away.

Moral growth. ⤬There is no necessary identity between morality and religion. The essential religious experiences of Presence, awe, wonder, mystery, and worship does not always bring moral behavior along with them, while on the other hand there are plenty of examples of people who are moral and ethical without being religious. But the two are closely associated, and in our definition of religion we allow for this association in emphasizing the evidence of the religious man's experience "when he actively attempts to harmonize his life with the Beyond." The evidence is often that of ethical and moral conduct. Hence it is that the psychologist of religion must inform himself on the dynamics of character, or that aspect of the personality concerned with right conduct.

Morality in its fully developed form is not possible before the time of adolescence. For one thing, ethics and morals require a certain degree of intelligence, notably the ability to form concepts and to generalize. We have already seen that these capacities ordinarily do not develop before the ages of fourteen or fifteen. It is true that the roots of the moral life are found in childhood, and in the previous chapter we have already treated the subject of conscience, another most important factor in this area; but it is probable that these influences do not develop in their full flowering until late adolescence. One study of college students has concluded that maturity in moral judgment is reached between the ages of seventeen and twenty.[19]

Klein,[20] in alluding to the fact that children seldom become insane but adolescents do, has noted that while departure from the moral code for the child may mean simply a threat of the withdrawal of his parents' affections, to the adolescent it may mean a catastrophic loss of self-respect. This is for the reason that moral principles, only superficially learned earlier, now have become interiorized and form a vital part of the individual's ego-structure. This gives them tremendous power for weal or woe within the personality. On the one hand, a breach of the youth's moral standards may bring on such guilt feelings as to drive him to psychotic symptoms as a means of escape. A too one-sided regard for such unfortunate results has led some psychiatrists to advocate what might almost be described as the repeal of the moral law and to denounce the meddling of the churches with

---

[19] Barkley, "Development of the Moral Judgment of College Students."
[20] *Mental Hygiene,* pp. 178 f.

such a sensitive thing as conscience. But, on the other hand, it is this spur which, applied to the sensitive spots of personality, has accounted for the heroic achievements of man in the realm of the moral life. Without these, cultural life as we know it would not be possible. Furthermore, particularly when wedded to the realities of a genuine religious experience, it enables man to achieve a sense of being himself, with a profounder satisfaction, delight, and keenness than does any other human experience.

Yet all who work with youth should know that this capacity for high moral expression is merely a capacity, not necessarily an actuality for any given individual. It is a paradox that we find among youth both a high incidence of idealism and of delinquency. The reasons for this are complex, though we may note in passing that both high morality and crime may involve that craving for adventure that is a noteworthy feature of the youthful temperament.

Hartshorne and May [21] found the moral behavior of adolescents extremely variable. An individual might be extremely honorable on the playing field yet most dishonest in the classroom, or vice versa. One is not necessarily bound to conclude, as do Hartshorne and May, that moral behavior is specific to the situation involved and that therefore there is no such thing as a *trait* or a general tendency toward honesty and morality.[22] This depends on many complex urges and the structure of the individual's personality. There are many youths whose self-respect is bound up with the passionate necessity for living a strict moral life, and whose intelligence is sufficiently keen to enable them to distinguish on principle ethical from unethical behavior. George Eliot, in her sensitive study of childhood and adolescence, *The Mill on the Floss*, draws from life her picture of the two Tulliver children, each of whom in his own way exhibits this firm moral structure. That such are in the minority is an additional reason to heed the caution voiced in our second chapter that in this field we must beware of putting too much reliance on the mere counting of heads and noting of averages.

Havighurst and Taba, in their study of adolescents, do justice to the complexity of urges and motives behind moral behavior, at the

[21] See their *Studies in Deceit*.
[22] See Allport, *Personality*, pp. 248–258, for a criticism of their doctrine of specificity.

same time that they make use of certain general distinctions. Of the five moral types described in the following section, only the Self-directive Person could be expressing religion in any essential sense:

Adaptive Persons take on the beliefs and principles of their social environment readily, without much question and without much inner commitment. They seem to have no moral struggles.

On the other hand, Self-directive Persons are reflective and critical concerning morality. Although their moral behavior may be very similar to that of the Adaptive group, they are characterized by self-doubt and turmoil over the moral choices they must make. They are engaged in the painful process of working out moral principles for themselves.

Submissive Persons too are very self-critical concerning their moral behavior, but their doubt springs from a very different source. Unlike Self-directive Persons, they are worried, not by the problem of whether or not they are living up to their own principles and whether or not those principles are the correct ones to follow, but by whether or not they are living up to the expectations of persons who are in authority over them. For Submissive Persons, the question is not "Is this really the right thing to do?" but rather "Is this really the thing to do to keep me out of trouble?"

The Unadjusted Persons are confused over moral beliefs and principles. Caught in an environment which fails to reward them sufficiently for good behavior, or which poses moral choices which cause them severe conflicts, they are unable to see a clear and consistent relation between a set of moral beliefs and principles and the feelings of personal satisfaction and social approval which they are striving for.

The Defiant Persons have rejected the generally approved moral beliefs and principles. They have not experienced satisfaction and social approval for good behavior to a degree sufficient to learn the beliefs and principles which lie behind good behavior. They are ruled by selfishness and aggressive impulses.[23]

Of the above categories, the largest would probably be that of the Adaptive Persons. As we have already noted in discussing social considerations, the average adolescent is very much concerned with standing in well with his peer-group. Typically, the desire to live ethically and morally comes second to social considerations, though

[23] *Adolescent Character and Personality*, pp. 182–183.

this does not mean that it may not have strength of its own. Also, the peer-group may have an ethical code that will stimulate ethical behavior even though for some individuals this will have no more moral significance than the behavior of a flock of sheep following the pattern of the strongest ram. At this point we encounter the paradox of moral behavior without moral significance. This warns us of some of the hazards of relying too much on the observation of behavior apart from considerations of inward psychological conditions, even though we must believe that ultimately the inward conditions will somehow become apparent in overt behavior.

At any rate, it is apt to be this concern for the peer-culture that explains what otherwise seem like anomalies in the moral life of youth. The athletic member of a school or college team plays a game of punctiliously good sportsmanship on the field because his team mates do; he cheats in the classroom because otherwise he might become ineligible to play. He resists the temptation to lift money from the pockets of his friends because to be discovered would mean social ostracism, though he may not hesitate to "borrow" their clothing; but "horsing around" and destroying property to the amount of hundreds of dollars is just good fun, because the whole gang is involved. Though one cannot summon up great enthusiasm for the moral qualities of such an average youth, under the same social influences he may nevertheless demonstrate much firmness of character in refusing to inform on his fellows or in upholding the honor of an organization with which he has identified himself. It is important for the psychologist to see such variant behavior for what it is, as *social*, rather than *moral* or *immoral*, behavior. Havighurst and Taba, in the work cited, show how much reputation for character owes to middle-class standards and social influences in Prairie City.[24]

When we attempt to relate moral behavior to religion we must remember that of the five types of individuals only the Self-directive Person can be considered to be truly moral and ethical, with a source within himself of principled living and creative behavior. While we cannot categorically state that only religion can be the source of such creative behavior, it is nevertheless notable that in point of fact the greatest creative moral personalities of the ages, such as Socrates,

[24] The July–August, 1954, number of *Religious Education* is devoted to a symposium on character education.

Gandhi, Schweitzer, and Jesus, have been religious men. It is in adolescence that such self-direction begins to emerge.[25]

Any worker with youth knows how rare such dedicated adolescents are. But, to hark back again to our opening chapter, we must note an influence far out of proportion in value to the numbers involved. Part of the problem of juvenile delinquency today is the number of Defiant Persons who supply the leadership for juvenile groups made up predominantly of the Adaptive, Submissive and the Unadjusted types. Happy is the church youth organization which has one or more Self-directive adolescents with leadership abilities whose sense of moral and spiritual realities enables them to inspire others.

The following case report relates in his own words the experience of such a Self-directive youth. He handed it to the author as a class assignment and gave permission for this use of it. The problem was whether he would be able to cope with the strains of Air-Force training without resorting to the relaxation afforded by alcohol. According to his own interiorized code, he held drinking to be wrong. Significant for our study is the fact that it was through religion and prayer that he developed the attitude making this abstention possible. More than merely a substitute for liquor, religion became an organizing principle of an effective life.

As I look back over my life with an increased insight into the psychological aspects of day-to-day conflicts, I feel now, even as I did then, that I have been mercifully free from great psychological disturbances. There was a time, however, when I was faced with a problem which threatened not only to shake that which I had always counted secure but also to change my whole outlook on life. It is with this problem which I wish now to deal.

The problem, to state it simply, was this—could an average young fellow undergo the extreme pressures of Air Cadet training for a period of nine to twelve months without seeking release now and then through the medium of alcohol? I had been confronted with this question before I ever volunteered for service but I felt then that the answer was simple and obvious. It seemed to me that anyone with average character and intelligence would have no great trouble refusing to drink and I expressed

[25] Cf. the thesis of Riesman's *The Lonely Crowd*, which holds that the typical American character is developing away from "inner-direction" to direction by other people.

this opinion publically. The fact that I expected it to be so easy to do was one of the factors which made it harder.

I was called to active duty in February, 1943 and sent to classification center at Nashville, Tennessee, to undergo a long series of tests. Thousands of young fellows like myself had come there in hopes of being classified for pilot training. The first day we were there we learned that on the average forty-five per cent to fifty-five per cent were reclassified for some other kind of training. We lived and worked for three weeks with the knowledge that we had only a 50–50 chance of getting the classification we wanted and that all the folks back home expected us to get. But three weeks is not such a long time and I had come prepared to work under pressure. The day finally came, the notices were posted, and two days later those of us who were eligible for pilot training were herded aboard an old coal burner and deposited at Maxwell Field, Alabama, for eight weeks of preflight training. The figures here were more encouraging; only about twenty per cent of the class was likely to "wash out" but we were subject to hazing of the most belittling kind, sixteen hours a day on the theory that we must learn to "take it" before we should be put in a position to "dish it out." We ate all meals at rigid attention, always walked at attention when outside our barracks, and were permitted only three answers to any question. These answers were: "Yes, sir"; "No, sir"; and "No excuse, sir." Thus when asked why we had broken this or that rule, even though we had not done so, we were forced to give the latter answer and take the penalty for breaking it.

It was during these eight weeks that the pressure began to bother me. We were not permitted to leave the post during the first four weeks and when we were finally given passes to go into Montgomery, Alabama, there was an invitation to go along with most of my classmates and "drown our troubles" or go do something else by myself. Being alone with nothing to do during the few times that the pressure was off made me feel as though I was bearing a greater burden than anyone else in my class and that therefore, I would be more likely to crack under it. At times like this it is very easy to rationalize almost anything.

Finally, the preflight training ended and we were sent to Arcadia, Florida, for our first phase of flying training. As usual the first information we sought, and got, was the "wash out" rate. Here where the actual flying started it ran from thirty-five per cent to fifty per cent of the class. Here the training became much more strenuous and the pressure more intense. One could be "washed out" for any reason, even being late for a ground school class without sufficient excuse. Here would be our biggest step in all of the training we were to receive, i.e., the step from never having flown (for most of us) to flying the airplane solo. We were given to understand that we should be able to solo after eight hours of dual instruction and that we would be given no more than ten hours of dual instruction.

It was here that the crisis came. The pressure became unbearable, more than once I resigned myself to failure. Once I even decided to tell the commanding officer that I wished to quit—anything to get out from under the constant, crushing pressure of wondering if I'd get through the next day.

There were four of us to a room and we often talked about quitting, but the main thing that made us each decide against it was the thought, What would all the folks back home say? I feel sure that if there had been no other consideration than our own feelings, some of us would have quit. I began to wonder if I were being too different from the other fellows because I didn't drink. Perhaps because I was different in this way I was running into more than a normal share of difficulty and trouble. I realize now that the reason I felt this way was that I was living with my tensions and frustrations right through the week-ends, while most of the other fellows forgot theirs, usually with help of a bottle.

The beginning of the answer to my problem came when I finally realized that I had to DO something. I either had to start drinking or find some other way to relax the pressure once in a while or else crack up completely and be washed out. At this time I was a nominal Christian, no more than that, but I decided that if my religion were ever going to be any good at all to me that it had to be now. I also decided that if I were going to test my religion I would have to go all out, not half way (which is probably what I would have done if I had decided to resort to drinking). So, I turned to prayer, like many people, as a last resort—but I tried to be as honest as I could. I admitted that I was licked, that the job was too much for me to handle so I turned the whole works over to God. I acknowledged that from here on He was the boss—if I were to go right on through, fine, if I were to wash out then I would just make the best of it. It was amazing how the pressure relaxed, and not only on week-ends but all the time. When I finally got myself off my hands and stopped being such a frustrated worrier, all sorts of things began to happen. I soloed the airplane successfully, I began to gain back the ten to fifteen pounds I had lost, and I met a very nice girl who thereafter occupied most of my time on week-ends and made me forget all about flying while I was with her.

The pressure remained through the next two phases of flying training and right up to the day we received our wings and gold bars, but now my confidence was restored and I had a new faith in the power of prayer. I felt sure that nothing could come up in my life that God and I together couldn't handle. The rest of my three years in the Air Corps were some of the most enjoyable and informative years of my life.

An experience of a young man considerably more complicated than this but nevertheless essentially similar will be found described in Carlyle's *Sartor Resartus* at the end of the chapter entitled "The Everlasting No," and in "The Everlasting Yea." It was a religious transaction that enabled Teufelsdröckh to escape nervous disorganization and to grow from an Unadjusted Person into a highly Self-directive one.

It is through close study of cases such as these that the psychologist and the religious educator may secure understanding of the function of religion in the moral behavior of youth.[26]

Attitudes and interests. Anyone who has spent much time discussing the "youth problem" has probably noted a pleasant fiction among grown-ups to the effect that this problem is a new thing, that teen-agers were much more wholesome and better behaved "when I was young." But those who are well acquainted with youth know that, if anything, youth is better than its parents and if the children's teeth have been set on edge it is the fathers who have eaten the sour grapes. The real corrupters of youth are neither the Socrates of the times nor the youth leaders themselves so much as the conventionally minded adults who insinuate their materialistic value systems into the minds of the coming generation.

This generalization can be illuminated at least in part by noting some of the attitudes of youth toward religion, and in particular toward church. For youth is both the most religious and least religious of ages. Most religious in that the surges of the life urge make possible an intensity of religious experience not likely to be achieved later on. Least religious in that—partly in response to the rebellion against authority that is a common symptom of adolescent struggle for psychological weaning and independence, partly in expressing a certain clearness of religious insight—youth tends to reject institu-

[26] The Character Research Project at Union College, Schenectady, N.Y., has made a systematic attempt to produce desirable character traits. See Ligon, *Dimensions of Character* for a report of theory, methods, and results.

tional religion and the petty concerns of the denominations. The following statement of a youth in Murray D. Ross's excellent study is typical of a rather large group:

I think the teachings of the church are changing and will continue to do so. The breakdown of the various sects is a sign of deterioration and the breakup of religion. On the other hand, the recent movement to unite the various sects is encouraging as in the former breaking apart they have lost fundamentals. They have dealt with and quarreled over techniques so long that they have lost sight of fundamental principles.[27]

Many adolescents, then, tend to reject the Church either consciously or else by omitting any regular performance of religious duties. Howard Bell found that less than 45 per cent of the 13,000 youth he studied in Maryland attend church regularly, while about 35 per cent attended either not at all or on religious holidays only.[28] Yet this is the age that Harms found to be highly individualized and original in its concepts of God,[29] while the chapter on conversion will demonstrate that the highest incidence of conversion experiences comes in the adolescent years.

Youth also is well known for its idealism, and while this is an impression that needs some scrutiny, nevertheless studies seem to confirm it at least in part. On one particular issue, for example, Ross found that 39 per cent of the youth he interrogated believed that there is no difference between Negroes and white people and that they should live together as one people in the community, while only about 15 per cent explicitly believed in segregation.[30]

Table 2
PERCENTAGE OF 1,927 YOUTH HOLDING CERTAIN POSITIONS ON NEGRO-WHITE RELATIONS *

Negroes are	Per Cent
Inferior and should be segregated	2.4
Not inferior but segregation desirable	13.1
Not different but better not to mingle socially	44.0
No difference. Whites and Negroes should live together as one people	39.0
Other	1.5
	100.0

* Adapted from Ross, *op. cit.*, p. 82.

[27] *Religious Beliefs of Youth*, p. 46.
[28] *Youth Tell Their Story*, p. 198.
[29] See Chapter 5, pp. 92–96.
[30] *Op. cit.*, p. 82.

It seems quite evident that the proportion supporting the liberal view is not nearly so large among their elders.

But at the same time Ross found that youth defined its aims quite largely in terms that suggested the influence of tangible and material-istic values current among the adult population at large. Over 73 per cent defined their major aim in terms of economic, financial, or marital success, while less than 21 per cent picked the sort of less tangible goal associated with idealism and religion, such as social-spiritual development, being of service, and doing God's will.

It seems obvious then that the situation is complicated, and that clear conclusions elude us. But it would seem reasonable to conclude that at least some of the disapproval among churchgoing adults of the ways of youth stems from youth's neglect of conventional reli-gious expression. Also not a little of youth's turning its back on spir-itual values, where it occurs, is simply a reflection of adult society.

We conclude this section with the statement of a college under-graduate which will show concretely some of the points we have made. Conventional in some ways, the beliefs of this young woman are essentially fresh and Self-directive. Typical of youth is the funda-mentally favorable evaluation of the function of religion and the Church at the same time that this approval is discriminating, original, and critical in certain ways. It is a mistake to hold that youth is irreligious.

I feel that a person needs a fundamentally religious viewpoint on life in order to be a complete person. I feel that religion is an aid in gaining a mature philosophy of life. I think we are more affected in our daily lives by Christian teaching than perhaps by anything else. For instance, I do not think we can ever be happy unless we can love someone or something. The personal traits which make for happiness and which we admire, such as devotion to something higher than ourselves, personal courage, mo-rality, etc., all stem from Christianity and other religious teachings. I do not know much about other religions but I think they are similar in many ways, from what I do know.

I think we are progressing in fulfillment of Christian ideals at the present, even though the world situation is so bleak. There have always been wars, but now the war crisis is a universal one. Still it is in daily relations where I think we can find hope; for example, in the treatment of children by parents and teachers, in the treatment of sick people, of the deformed and the mentally ill. I believe that science and education have been largely responsible for this even more than organized religion. I feel that God as the father of all men, and all men as brothers, is the true ideal which we must eventually reach. If we do not, I think the world will eventually bring about its own destruction.

I feel that one needs a strong religious training in the home (of the right kind) in order to have a strong faith from the beginning. That does not mean that I think one cannot find a faith later on. I think that God exists and that everyone can find Him. To some people this comes more easily than to others and not until after great grief or a traumatic experience or simply through a maturing experience or through nature, etc.

I feel that I gain the strongest sense of the presence of God when I am out of doors, quiet and at peace. Church gives me intellectual backing for my beliefs and helps to clear my mind on a good many things and gives me a feeling of fellowship, but I only really feel the presence of God out of doors and often in prayer.

I do not feel that I have a strong faith and I would like very much to gain one. Through faith I feel you can sense eternal truths and the really important things without being centered in self and in petty things.

I had the usual Sunday school training when I was young without a very strong home religious training. As an adolescent I felt that religion was romantic and something very beautiful. I learned to pray and to sense God after an illness when I felt completely disillusioned. I spent a good deal of time outdoors alone, one summer in Massachusetts, and it was then that I really began to think things out and to pray to God.

The church did not help in my seeking although I realize it did point the way. Reading the Bible was a much more influencing factor.

I feel that because a child's viewpoint is so limited he connects his own particular church with religion. Therefore it can have either a retarding or a beneficial effect on the religious faith of the child.

I think that churches are completely necessary for intellectual backing (I do not feel the highest types of church services should be emotional in content) and for the sense that you are not alone in your worship. However, religion still remains a fundamentally personal thing. It comes from one's innermost spirit. I feel that there are as many different concepts of God as there are people in the world, but the important thing is that it involves that sense of a higher power, of something finer than ourselves, which we worship and to which we hope to aspire.

I have no patience with dogma or ritual. Form obliterates meaning and spirit. I admit that to many people this is a great aid in religious thinking, but I do not feel that these people are really fundamentally religious until they can learn from the ritual and sense something within themselves and have a communion with God which does not come from outside things.

I feel that without any religious faith, life would be hard, almost intolerable and without much meaning.[31]

Worship and prayer. Either a preliminary to, or the object of, any effective act of worship or of prayer is an experience of the reality of the divine. Consequently anyone concerned about the religious development of youth will be interested in knowing something about the sources of this experience.

Here, as elsewhere in the sphere of religious life, there is considerable individuality and no generalization that will cover all cases. As an illustration of the variety of sources we may use a study of adolescent girls by the German scholar, Oskar Kupky.[32] Kupky asked 148 schoolgirls to describe in a composition an experience of "reverence," the term being described in such a way as to suggest a religious experience. Of the girls polled, 20 gave no indication of ever having had a religious experience, leaving 128 who had. Of the 128, 68, or over half, pointed to nature as that which evoked the experience. This recalls the statement of the college girl just quoted above, and suggests that youth leaders are on sound ground when they attempt to arrange for worship services amid scenes of natural beauty.[33]

Far behind nature came ecclesiastical forms and ceremonies, with 31 girls giving some aspect of these as a source of religious experience. That upbringing and background is an influential element in the process is indicated by the fact that in this group were many Catholic girls, none of whom made any mention of nature.

The life and fate of man were mentioned by 18 of the girls. Of an old woman whose son was killed in battle, one girl wrote, "You never hear a complaint from his mother. She bears her lot so calmly that

[31] From an unpublished study, in possession of the author, by Elizabeth Pierce and Elizabeth Dillingham, "Religious Doubts Among Middlebury Women." The statement has been altered slightly to preserve anonymity.

[32] *The Religious Development of Adolescents,* Chap. 10. See also Havighurst and Taba, *Adolescent Character and Personality.*

[33] "The Everlasting Yea" from Carlyle's *Sartor Resartus,* Wordsworth's "Tintern Abbey," Francis Thompson's "To a Snowflake," and Psalms 19 and 121 are all classical literary expressions of nature as a source of religious thoughts and experience.

one cannot but have an involuntary feeling of reverence for her." Of the death of an aged relative, another girl reported, "I had never really understood what death means, and this taught me the deepest reverence for God."

In the last place were nine girls who mentioned as the stimulating factor some work of art or music, such as the Sistine Madonna or Schubert's symphonies.

One cannot place too much reliance on the proportions in this sampling, for adolescents of the opposite sex or of another locale would doubtless show differences. One notices that neither religious poetry nor the Bible is mentioned.[34] We know that both the spoken and the written word under the right conditions are rich sources of stimuli for religious experience, while experimentally minded religious educators have found drama, properly used, another source.[35]

It is out of such ingredients as these that a psychologically effective experience of worship for youth may be wrought. But it must be added to childhood experiences, such as we have outlined in our

---

[34] For what it is worth, I would like to comment out of many years' experience in teaching the Bible to tenth-grade preparatory-school boys, about as obdurate a group as one could find with respect to any overt desire to absorb spiritual truth. I believe there is nothing better than Old Testament poetry to open the doors of the young masculine mind to the force of religious realities. When one points out to them the strength, the dramatic force, and the love of nature of Hebrew poetry, particularly with the help of the great King James translation, one often finds them, despite themselves, emotionally responding to the beauty of the lines with a sensitivity that they had thought worthy only of girls. I have found that the surest book to evoke these reactions is the Book of Job—Job cursing his day (3:1–26), the Lord's description of the creation paean (38:1–7) and the stars of the heavens (38:31–33), or the magnificent picture of the war-horse (39:19–25)—though some of the Psalms, Ecclesiastes, and parts of the Prophets are almost equally good. But the process should not stop here. With these experiences as a vestibule and a means of creating respect for the Bible, the religious-minded teacher can lead these aroused young spirits on to the spiritual truths that lie beyond. Yet the teacher is to be warned against the idea that simply a mechanical presentation of King James English to youth is sufficient to effect this result. The process combines intellect with emotion, and without a lively personal experience of the Bible the teacher is not apt to make much progress. The Bible indeed, and particularly the King James version, is a Goliath's sword not to be wielded by those of little stature.

[35] For an example, see Gertrude Fagan, "Worship in a Young People's Group," for an account of some experiments in worship at the Riverside Church in New York City.

previous chapter, and a religious sensitivity that is not the same in all adolescents.[36]

None of Kupky's girls mentioned prayer as a source of the experience of reverence, and indeed it would seem logical that such an experience should precede prayer rather than result from it. This, however, is psychologically questionable, and it may be doubted whether the subjects were able to introspect sufficiently accurately to note that regular prayer quite likely had had at least a confirming influence on their attitudes of reverence.

Yet, whatever the relation of prayer to religious experience, it is certain that the average youth prays with more or less regularity. Ross found that over 42 per cent of 1,700 respondents prayed at least once daily, while less than 15 per cent prayed not at all. When asked why they prayed, 33 per cent said that God listens and answers, 27 per cent that prayer helps in time of trouble, 18 per cent that one feels better afterward, while 11 per cent said that it reminds you of your obligations to man and society. Four per cent were perspicacious enough to see that habit was an important reason.

To examine the meaning of these responses further, a representative cross-section of the respondents were questioned verbally, of which 75 provided enough data for analysis. Of these only 17 per cent indicated that prayer constituted for them a meaningful way of communicating with God, while for 26 per cent it was more a means of self-analysis or meditation. The largest group, or 42 per cent, were those for whom prayer was a kind of magical technique to be used in case of need. A 19-year-old student said, "Well, usually before a test I pray to the Lord if He couldn't help me in some way. . . ." The 15 per cent who never pray of course had no comment.[37]

[36] Kupky, *op. cit.*, p. 102, mentions with some agreement G. Stanley Hall's opinion that, contrary to common belief and almost all empirical studies, boys are more religious than girls. I am inclined to think that in a completely non-ecclesiastical, essential sense this is quite likely so. Note the preponderance of men among the world's great religious teachers, prophets, poets, mystics, and leaders, though it is certain that most of these owed much to their mothers.

[37] Ross, *op. cit.*, pp. 60–67.

SUMMARY

To summarize our chapter on youth, we must note that this is the age of greatest religious potentiality, when the capacities of the individual mature and are seen in the freshness of their first flowering and pristine vigor; when the sensitivities are keenest and the world is a fairyland of opportunity and adventure. It is an age when the intelligence matures and true morality first becomes possible. But because of the unfamiliarity of its new-found strengths, the surge of new emotions and the stress of new desires, together with a vacuum of accepted adult functions for the adolescent to perform, youth becomes confused. Sometimes in rebellion it defies all convention and authority, religion along with them. Sometimes it conforms to the crassest demands of the competitive materialism of its elders—and betters the instruction. Sometimes it is content to conform in a colorless way and joins a church group or not according to the practice of the local peer-group. But sometimes, perhaps through favoring circumstances influenced by understanding elders whom it respects, or perhaps through a special disposition that grows from within, its religion becomes real and vital. It is then that it may become Self-directive and enables its possessors to join that creative minority of religious spirits that contributes so much to the civilizing of society and owes so much to youth.

Chapter 7

DOUBT AND CONFLICT

There lives more faith in honest doubt,
Believe me, than in half your creeds.
—Tennyson

We may then say the mature religious sentiment
is ordinarily fashioned in the workshop of doubt.
—G. W. Allport

"Doubt seems to belong to youth as its natural heritage." So says Starbuck,[1] and it is this consideration that persuades us to take up in this chapter and the next the subject of doubt and its frequent concomitants, conflict and suffering. Though distinguished from each other as different psychological functions, doubt and conflict both tend to cause distress to the individual. This distress cannot always be dignified by the term "suffering." Nevertheless, in the case of the most sensitive and often the most creative religious spirits, doubt will result in very acute psychological pain. This chapter, then, will be an account of some of the origins of religious suffering in doubt and conflict, while our next chapter will contain some observations on suffering itself.

DOUBT

Starbuck supports his thesis that doubt is prevalent among youth by citing 53 per cent of 142 women and 79 per cent of 95 men who reported doubts about religion going back to ages 11 to 26. The

[1] *The Psychology of Religion*, p. 232.

137

women reported that their doubts occurred somewhat earlier than
did those of the men; [2] doubtless this fact is influenced by the earlier
maturing of women. These percentages are supported, at least in a
general way, by a more recent study supervised by the author in 1951,
which showed 65 per cent of a random sample of 50 women at
Middlebury College reporting that at the time they had doubts concerning religion.[3] It is hard to compare these figures exactly with
other recent studies such as those of Allport and Ross, since their
data were collected in a somewhat different form. Yet by reading between the lines one can find support for our conclusion that religious
doubts are a major consideration in the religious attitudes of a sizable
minority of all youth, while it has played some part in the religious
development of a definite majority of all believing Americans.

People differ in their estimate of the value of doubt. The official
church attitude is that it is to be deplored as an obstacle to faith, at
the worst a temptation of the Devil, at the best a sign of weakness.
But the psychologist cannot dismiss it, for it is a fact. Neither can he
blink the fact that it is often a wholesome factor in religious growth.
Furthermore, liberally minded religious people, particularly among
Protestants and Jews, knowing the honorable place that doubt has
played in the consciousness of many of the most sensitive religious
spirits of the ages, have welcomed and even encouraged a certain
measure of religious questioning among those of the coming generation.

The fact is that not doubt itself but the kind of doubt and what
it represents are the crucial factors. Doubt may simply be a convenient means of shrugging off responsibility. Since belief in God, for
example, may seem to point to an inconvenient amount of attention
to church duties, it is much easier to deny the efficacy of all religion.
Or, since almost any theology is a hard discipline, it is much simpler
to discard the whole idea of God at once rather than waste time
resolving the many inconsistencies and *non sequiturs* that soon occur
to anyone who, starting with conventional ideas, is seriously concerned with hammering out for himself a rational faith. Or a sense

[2] *Ibid.*, Chaps. 14 and 18.
[3] Pierce and Dillingham, *op. cit.* The woman whose testimony was cited in
the previous chapter was of course one of these women. As in her case, the
doubts of a number were of relatively minor significance.

of the discrepancy between one's beliefs and practice may persuade one to throw over belief, though it must be confessed that the average religious mind manages a handsome disregard of the tensions that might be supposed to follow upon such inconsistencies. We might point out that some of the more punctilious ecclesiastical minds would have us believe that doubt is only the expression of indifference or escape or other negations. If this were the case, one could readily agree that doubt could be neither creative nor wholesome.

On the other hand, doubt may be the positive expression of a love of truth, essential to the growth of the individual and to religion as well. The process of putting away the childish furniture of the mind cannot take place without some form of doubt, even though in some individuals the process may be largely unconscious. Therefore the subject deserves treatment as a creative element in religious development. But before we examine some specific psychological sources of doubt, let us look at some generalized influences, partly external and partly internal, operating with peculiar force at the period of youth.

We have already discussed in the previous chapter the importance of advancing mental age as a prerequisite to doubt. Without the capacity for logical reasoning and the comprehension of concepts, the more serious expressions of doubt could hardly occur. This does not mean that emotional factors are not operating too, for frequently they are of great importance. A boy may reject the idea of God simply because he may unconsciously identify God with a cruel father. But even where it is not the essence of the matter, some intellectual activity is required to support the experience of doubt.

Another factor influencing doubt is the religious tradition in which the individual is brought up and the consequent valuation which is placed on it. If doubt is regarded as a heinous matter by his family and associates, the youth is less likely to exercise whatever inherent tendency he has in that direction. On the other hand, if doubt is the fashion, there are many who will follow along with it on that account alone. Consequently, empirical studies show pretty generally that the incidence of doubt is much higher among Protestants or Jews, for example, than among Catholics.[4] This would seem to be due to the

---

[4] Ross, in *Religious Beliefs of Youth*, p. 22, shows 48 per cent of the Catholics holding a completely orthodox idea of God, to 34 per cent of the Protestants and only 15 per cent of the Jews; however, the number in the latter

greater emphasis on individual responsibility in Protestantism and Judaism. Protestant and Jewish youth are more often *told* that they must work out their own beliefs. Suggestion doubtless operates cogently at an unconscious level as well.

That sex is still another influence on doubt is suggested by Starbuck's figures, quoted above, to the effect that 53 per cent of his sample of women reported doubts to 79 per cent of the men. This is what one might expect on the strength of the fact that nearly every comparison of *groups* of men and of women shows the women to be "more religious" than the men. But Starbuck goes further to show that men differ from women not merely in the fact of doubting, but also in the origins, and perhaps also in the quality, of their doubts. Of those who had doubts, 73 per cent of the men mentioned educational influences as stimulating causes, to only 23 per cent of the women; while 47 per cent of the women attributed their doubts to "natural causes," to only 15 per cent of the men.[5] This suggests that men's doubts may more often be the result of explicitly rational considerations.

But these figures also suggest a third influence that may not be negligible, namely obscure physiological processes in part tied to the physiology of the sexes. For, judging from Starbuck's analysis, this factor is what he chiefly means when he speaks of natural causes. For example, one of his woman respondents writes, "I have had times of doubt when I wondered almost if anything were true and how we could believe it. This would usually come at times when I felt unusually despondent and nothing went right; it would end as soon as I felt better." [6] This impression is strengthened by his figures showing that doubts come earlier among women than among men.[7] Since this is doubtless another expression of the earlier emotional maturation of girls, and since it is pretty generally agreed that this earlier matura-

---

sample was much smaller, and in a YMCA, where the responses were collected, this may not be typical of Jewish youth. The disparity between Catholics and the others on less fundamental religious beliefs was even greater. (See Chap. 3.) If one objects that the discrepancy might be explained on the basis of educational level, which might not have been as high among Catholics, he can find these findings in general borne out in Allport's study of Harvard and Radcliffe students in *The Individual and His Religion*, pp. 40 f.

[5] *Op. cit.*, p. 236.
[6] *Ibid.*, p. 237.
[7] *Ibid.*, p. 239.

tion is tied to the prior physical maturation of the female, it would seem clear that physical factors enter the picture. And even though it may be true that intellectual factors are more prominent in the doubts of men, it does not follow that physiological factors are of no account even among men other than the 15 per cent that Starbuck reported as ascribing their doubts to natural causes.

A fourth and final, even more generalized influence is that of the life and death urges. It will be recalled that the life urge stands for those basic psychic forces pressing for activity and change, while the death urge is the contrary force pushing the psyche toward quiescence. We have distinguished between doubt as an active expression of the love for truth and as a means of evading responsibility. With the latter the death urge doubtless plays its part. But, most importantly, the life urge is a factor in motivating doubt as the expression of positive concerns, such as a love of truth.

This will help to explain why doubt tends to be a characteristic of youth, the period when the life urge is so much more potent than it will be later on. For to youth doubt often means not only a necessary stage on the road to truth, but also a breaking with tradition and a means of asserting one's own personality. The accomplishment of these things represents an adventure in the life of the spirit that bears the mark of the life wish. But this adventure is not merely exhilarating; for the spiritually sensitive mind it may result in severe suffering when it involves tension, conflict, and a break with a tradition that has meant much in early life. Yet this suffering may be necessary for religious growth. Having in mind his own poignant wrestling with doubt as a young man, Tennyson wrote:

> There lives more faith in honest doubt,
> Believe me, than in half your creeds.

We are now ready to turn to the more specific sources of doubt in the psychology of the individual. Here we will be following, with minor alteration and rearrangement as well as with abridgement, Gordon Allport's excellent analysis in his chapter "The Nature of Doubt" in *The Individual and His Religion*.

Personal. Some doubts are personal in their origins. The most obvious of these are those that touch the self-interest of the individual, some trivial and others striking much more deeply into the roots of personality. Tom Tulliver, in *The Mill on the Floss*, stopped praying after he found that prayers would not get him through his Latin exercises. A youth in a religious family prayed long and fervently for the life of a sick sister; the death of the sister immediately plunged the youth into a paroxysm of doubt. There are few religious people who have not encountered these or similar psychological events in their religious growth. There are many variations in the way these crises are handled by different individuals, but only the insensitive survive them without some stirrings of doubt.

The influences that we have just described are for the most part at the level of consciousness. Somewhat more obscure happenings lead to negative attitudes toward religion that may be classed with what the psychologist calls defense mechanisms. One such means of defense involves violent antipathy toward something or someone, which obscures by its very violence the real source of the difficulty. The real source may be known to the individual, but more characteristically it is not. For example, the youth who unconsciously hates his father may grow up to reject the religion that his father represents. His defense reaction lies in his violent attacks on religion which grow the more violent as he strives unknowingly to prevent the real source of his negations from rising into consciousness. Many good and clear-sighted church people have been puzzled by the paradox that some self-styled atheists and agnostics seem yet to be more spiritually sensitive than the orthodox. Thomas Carlyle's doubts recorded in *Sartor Resartus* probably derived in some measure from an unconscious rebellion against his stern father.[8] As Allport indicates, the very doubts themselves may be an indication of spiritual concern, and the too-loudly protesting opponent of religion may be showing "a suspiciously deep concern about the whole matter."

Personal sources of doubt, then, include both obvious violations of the individual's self-interest and more complex personal experiences that unconsciously lead to generally negative attitudes toward religion.

Shortcomings of organized religion. Sometimes associated with defense mechanisms, though distinct from them, are doubts that

[8] For a psychoanalytic explanation of this, see J. L. Halliday, *Mr. Carlyle— My Patient*, especially Chaps. 2 and 18.

arise from the contemplation of the shortcomings of organized religion and religious people. We say that these are associated with defense mechanisms, for frequently the misdoings of the Church are cited by the critic of religion as justification for his position. This mechanism is, of course, rationalization, an apology that deceives the apologist even more than others as to the real source of the doubt. Those who have a genuine concern for religion are much more apt to remain its supporters in general, at the same time that they may be its most vigorous though constructive critics.

For there is no question but that there are many rents in the garments of church institutions, not to speak of the liberal supply of hypocrites and one-day-a-week practitioners among their patrons. One does not need to be partisan to note the cruelty of the Inquisition, the witch-hangings of the Puritans, or the lack of much evidence that the modern churchgoer is ethically any better than his neighbor. Such observations may well raise honest doubts as to whether the so-called truths of religion are really true. It is not surprising that even religious people should sometimes have their moments when they wonder whether religion in some of its forms may not do more harm than good.

Expression of human needs. Another source of doubt is the reflection that the religious life seems to be more an expression of human than divine needs and interests. History shows us that the Greek gods simply represented the vices and the virtues of the Greeks themselves, writ large. Though it is not so obvious, one can find the projection of human characteristics and human needs even in the most sophisticated modern conceptions. There are many who, with Freud, cannot but wonder whether the idea of God is nothing more than an illusion.[9]

Similarly, as we have shown in Chapter 4, the sources of religion may be found among the various urges, desires, and needs of human kind. While there are some people for whom this is the best kind of argument for the truth and value of religion, yet there are others who turn their reasoning the other way. If our religion grows out of our sense of dependence, for example, does it not follow that religion is an expression of weakness unworthy of a self-reliant human being?

[9] Cf. the title of his book on religion, *The Future of an Illusion.*

Again, can we not find the origins of much of our religious ritual and many of our religious customs in the superstitions of bygone times or the practices of primitive peoples? [10] These, then, are further sources of religious doubt.

Habitual. A fourth kind of doubt we will call habitual. Allport designates this as *scientific doubting*, since it particularly characterizes the thought processes of the scientist. For the success of scientific endeavor rests on the unwillingness to regard any particular scientific truth as final, and a continual skepticism with regard to the current picture of reality is one of the prices the scientist pays for progress. Had there been complete acceptance of the former scientific dogma that an atom cannot be split, there would now be no atomic bomb. While one might well question whether this is "progress," it certainly must be called that from the strictly scientific viewpoint and will illustrate our generalization. Furthermore it will also illustrate Allport's point that scientific knowledge is limited in its scope and properly cannot be extended to the fields of value and religion.

But the scientist, who performs such wonders with the assistance of the tool of doubt, naturally tends to apply his tool to these other fields.[11] Unlike Descartes, he is not likely to regard the idea of God as a clear and distinct concept. J. H. Leuba has shown that there is a considerable amount of disbelief among scientists, increasing with their eminence.[12] Such is the prestige of the scientists in our society that many people catch the habit of doubt from them. Just as it is hard for some people to believe that a man with a million dollars may be wrong, so it is hard for others to believe that an honored scientist with an IQ of 150 can err when he promulgates the dogma that God is an outworn superstition. Perhaps what has been noted as the current "return to religion" owes not a little to the fact that the scientists themselves, as they watch their scientific monsters grow, seem to be looking more humble than they used to and to be

[10] See Frazer's *The Golden Bough* if any documentation of this statement is thought necessary. For refutation of the idea that origin is a valid criterion of religious value, see Allport, *op. cit.*, pp. 109–110, or James' *Varieties*, pp. 16 ff.
[11] As an example, see B. F. Skinner's *Science and Human Behavior*, especially Chaps. 21, 23, and 28. The reader will find Aldous Huxley's *Brave New World* an excellent satire on this tendency.
[12] "Religious Beliefs of American Scientists."

returning to more positive positions on religious beliefs and the importance of values.

Literalism. [reverential] A fifth and very important source of doubt we will call literalistic. The responsibility for this lies very largely with religious bodies themselves and arises from the frequent insistence that religious language that was meant merely as metaphor be taken as fact. It is as if one should banish Aesop's *Fables* from his library because, since everyone knows that animals do not talk, all these tales are untrue. A similar mistake would be the rejection of the Parable of the Good Samaritan on the ground that research had failed to indicate that Jesus had known of any such actual happening.

An old lady of the author's acquaintance declared that if the Bible stated that the whale had swallowed Jonah, she would believe it; and if it had stated that Jonah swallowed the whale, she would have believed that too. If such literality represents religious thinking, then some people might be pardoned for doubting the religious position. At any rate it is certain that large numbers of seekers, spiritually only half sophisticated, are led to doubt through the patent nonsense which religious language often expresses when only its literal denotation is taken into account.

We have alluded elsewhere to the fact that psychologists, when discussing the human mind, are frequently forced to use metaphor.[13] If this is true with respect to something limited, like the mind, how much more will this be true when man gropes toward ideas of the Creator or speculates concerning spiritual truth. Hence it is that the believing parent or religious educator, as soon as the child approaches the years of reasoning, is well advised to make clear the distinction between *fact*, which frequently is a matter of not the slightest significance in the exchange of the spiritual marketplace, and *truth*, which often is so subtle that it may be suggested but never exactly defined. In this way the child will not see a picture of the Lord and Jacob tumbling about through the dark night in an undignified physical wrestling match which the Lord finally wins only by committing a

---

[13] The *tabula rasa*, or wax tablet, of John Locke, the closed hydraulic system of Freud, the connecting telephone exchange of Thorndike, and the mind-as-a-muscle concept of the faculty psychologists are all examples of explicit or implicit figures of speech used in discussing the mind. Cf. p. 63.

kind of foul.[14] But he will understand that, preserved through the darkness of many centuries, we have the echoes of an account by a spiritually sensitive and imaginative Jacob of a spiritual confrontation that shook him to his depths. The idea of this could be but partly conveyed, and then only by a metaphor drawn from an experience common to the average man of his day.

It is for this reason that religious belief is dependent on the believer being speculative and in part a poet. We have here two spheres: one the proper domain of the scientist, the sphere of fact; the other the sphere of speculative truth and faith, and here is where the religious mind operates. He who possesses a mind that is congenitally literal has but two options: either he must hold to his beliefs in a wooden or literalistic way, or he must give way to doubt when his intelligence shows him the inconsistency that the literalistic interpretation of Truth will always produce. The world of religion is largely the world of the poet, the prophet, and the saint; and here the scientist, as a scientist, cannot operate. The literalistic person becomes a doubter because he does not see the distinction, and because scientist and poet, though speaking two different languages, nevertheless must use the same words.

Confusion of magic with religion. A final category might be added to those which we have derived from Allport. It overlaps them, but can be distinguished in principle, and we suspect that it is a very common source of doubt. This is the confusion of magic with religion. Typical of the magical attitude is the idea that man may coerce or strongly influence God by adherence to proper rituals or imprecations. The examples of Tom Tulliver praying for help in his studies and the youth for his sick sister, noted above as doubts stemming from personal origins, will also fall into this category. For doubt followed as the result of what appeared to be no answer to prayer, the idea being that God is in some way obligated to produce results for him who prays. This is a very common attitude among conventionally religious people. We may suspect that the only thing that keeps many from doubt is the lack of very rigorous reflection on the obvious fact that such forms of religious activity pay very meager dividends.

[14] Genesis 32:24–32.

But, starting with this magical premise in place of a religious one, there are many vigorous minds who do reflect and develop into agnostics or atheists. They have not realized that true religion consists, not so much of the attempt to persuade God to perform the will of man, as it does of the efforts of man to come into communion with God, to the end that he may learn God's will and harmonize his life with it. For those who wish religion to be a thoughtful affair and yet want to minimize the possibilities of doubt, there is no more important duty than making crystal clear to believers this distinction between magic and religion.[15]

CONFLICT

The experience of conflict is one with which every person is familiar. It arises from the fact that we cannot be in two places at once, perform two incompatible operations at the same time, or hold two contradictory positions simultaneously, without damage to intellectual processes. A very simple form of conflict arises when we have to decide whether to go to see a good movie or stay at home to watch our favorite television program. On a religious level it may come from the desire to remain loyal to our childhood faith and also to embrace a radically different kind of faith which attracts us. While we may be very acutely conscious of some of our conflicts, others are buried in the unconscious where they may affect our behavior in irrational ways, unrecognized by our conscious minds.

Depending on how deeply rooted the religious sentiment is, conflicts involving religion may be among the most poignant and severe the individual ever experiences. Thus in commenting on the doubts of Teufelsdröckh in his "Everlasting No" stage, Carlyle states, ". . . it will be clear that, for a pure moral nature, the loss of his religious Belief was the loss of everything." [16] This state of mind was accentuated by that poignant source of doubt, lack of belief in oneself.[17] But just because the religious sentiment may often be superficial, many a religious conflict is resolved without the suffering visited on a Carlyle.

[15] The figures of Balak and Balaam in Numbers 22–24 represent the magical as opposed to religious presuppositions.

[16] *Sartor Resartus*, p. 122.

[17] Cf. *ibid.*, p. 125. "Alas! the fearful unbelief is unbelief in yourself; and how could I believe?"

This is reserved mainly for those we have called primary religious personalities, those who are sustaining the stresses of a first-hand religious experience together with basic neurotic tendencies. The secondary religious personalities will feel it less keenly, while the tertiary religious personality will be bothered not at all so far as the conflict involves real religious choices. This is not to say that the tertiary personality will not suffer from conflicts that involve religion, as for example when one must choose between a certain marriage and loyalty to a church forbidding the marriage. The true tertiary religious personality in such a case will feel conflict, but basically it will be a conflict between his love and *what people expect of him* in a religious way. Indeed it is possible for the conflict to be even more severe on this account.

Religious conflicts are of several kinds, though usually falling into one of three categories. They may involve a conflict between belief and doubt, which we have already discussed. Or they may involve loyalty to two different religious ideas or two religious institutions. This kind of conflict could be well illustrated by the experience of Martin Luther when through many months he found himself reluctantly pulled ever further away from the authority of the Roman Catholic Church toward the ideas of righteousness that he had made his own. A third kind of conflict is that between what one recognizes as a religious loyalty and a secular one, as in the case of the rich young ruler who longed for salvation yet could not give up his worldly possessions.[18]

One of the great introspective psychologists of the ages, St. Augustine, has set forth in his *Confessions* a lively account of his quivering spirit as the demands of his new-found Christian faith warred against the pull of the habits of his old way of life.

My will was the enemy master of, and thence had made a chain for me and bound me. Because of a perverse will was lust made; and lust indulged in became custom; and custom not resisted became necessity, by which links, as it were, joined together (whence I term it a "chain"), did a hard bondage to hold me enthralled. But that new will which had begun to develop in me, freely to worship Thee, and to wish to enjoy Thee, O God, the only sure enjoyment, was not able as yet to overcome my former wilfulness, made strong by long indulgence. Thus did my two

[18] Mark 10:17–22.

wills, the one old and the other new, one carnal, the other spiritual, contend within me; and by their discord they unstrung my soul.

Thus came I to understand, from my own experience, what I had read, how that "the flesh lusteth against the Spirit, and the Spirit against the flesh." I verily lusted both ways; yet more in that which I approved in myself. For in this last it was now rather not "I," because in much I rather suffered in myself than did it willingly. And yet it was through me that custom became more combative against me, because I had come willingly whither I willed not. . . . Nor had I now any longer my wonted excuse, that as yet I hesitated to be above the world and serve Thee, because my perception of the truth was uncertain; for now it was certain. But I, still bound to the earth, refused to be Thy soldier; and was as much afraid of being freed from all embarrassments, as we ought to fear to be embarrassed.

Thus with the baggage of the world was I sweetly burdened, as when in slumber; and the thoughts wherein I meditated upon Thee were like unto the efforts of those desiring to awake, who still overpowered with a heavy drowsiness are again steeped therein. And as no one desires to sleep always, and in the sober judgment of all waking is better, yet does a man generally defer to shake off drowsiness, when there is a heavy lethargy in all his limbs, and even though displeased, yet even after it is time to rise with pleasure yields to it, so was I assured that it were much better to give up myself to Thy charity, than to yield myself to my own cupidity; but the former course satisfied and vanquished me, the latter pleased me and fettered me. Nor had I aught to answer Thee calling to me, "Awake, thou that sleepest, and arise from the dead, and Christ shall give thee light." And to Thee showing me on every side that what Thou saidst was true, I, convicted by the truth, had nothing at all to reply, but the drawling and drowsy words: "Presently, lo, presently; leave me a little while." [19]

It is easily seen that conflict plays a part in all growth, and particularly in religious growth. For conflict fosters an uneasiness which is a stimulus, and forces those choices necessary to learning, which is so intimately bound up with growth. Furthermore religious choices involve the most significant and culturally sophisticated of all choices, the *choice between values*. It is growth in this area that lets man realize his tallest stature.

[19] St. Augustine's *Confessions*, Book 8, Chap. 5. A psychoanalytical account of Augustine's conversion may be found in Ostow and Scharfstein, *The Need to Believe*, pp. 102–109.

How are these religious conflicts dealt with? The principle is much simpler than the fact. The psychotherapist strives to help the divided self to bring its warring impulses to consciousness where either a compromise may be made or undesired elements may be banished forever.[20] What the spiritual person means, psychologically, when he speaks of being confronted by God is the bringing into consciousness of the demands of religion as compared with the more ordinary demands of the body and of everyday life. So radical are the demands of religion, when completely realized, that this comes as a shock to the sensitive spirit that the fully religious person is so often apt to possess. Usually a psychologically unsophisticated person, yet stirred to his depths by a clash of forces that reaches to the very ends of his being, the religious man is forced to many drastic devices to describe what has happened. This probably explains Jacob's use of the story of the wrestling match to explain his encounter with God, while we have just read St. Augustine's metaphoric handling of the matter. It is also this radical conflict between the religious way and the way of the world that explains the phenomenon conversion. The tensions aroused are so great that something must give way, and they are often resolved with dramatic suddenness. However, we must defer our discussion of conversion to another chapter.

Yet we would like to present just one more example of religious conflict; it gives another illustration of this dramatic representation of conflict from within, and, more significantly, it shows us this process of resolution through the confrontation of which we have been speaking. John Bunyan was hardly as psychologically perceptive as was Augustine, yet in his own way he was just as conscious of spiritual conflict and just as effective in describing it. It was as if his soul were a battleground between two very real personages. God and the Devil, conceived in characteristically Biblical terms. At one time in his life Bunyan found himself obsessed with the desire to "sell Christ," and somehow or other this idea became attached to the story of Esau selling his birthright for a mess of pottage, which attachment he ascribed to the maneuvers of the Devil. But about the same time

[20] A dramatic classical case is that of Miss Beauchamp, described in *The Dissociation of a Personality* by Morton Prince. Here various urges in the personality had split it into four distinct selves, which were finally remolded into a single personality by Prince who, largely through the use of hypnosis, brought these selves into simultaneous consciousness and integration.

the Lord, as it seemed to him, as a counter measure drew his attention to the passage of Scripture, "My grace is sufficient for thee." His internal struggle he dramatized as a contest between these two texts. Let us hear him describe the contest:

By these words ["My grace is sufficient for thee"] I was sustained, yet not without exceeding conflicts, for the space of seven or eight weeks; for my peace would be in it, and out, sometimes twenty times a day; comfort now, and trouble presently; peace now, and before I could go a furlong, as full of fear and guilt as ever heart could hold. And this was not only now and then, but my whole seven weeks experience; for this about "the sufficiency of grace," and that about Esau's parting with his birthright, would be like a pair of scales within my mind; sometimes one end would be uppermost, and sometimes again the other; according to which would be my peace or trouble.

The resolution of this conflict came as the result of Bunyan's desire to have the two texts come into his mind simultaneously and, so to speak, do battle for his soul. Of course we have no difficulty in discerning the wholesomeness of this process, which illustrates the psychotherapeutic principle of confrontation of conflict. We will let him continue with his picturesque phrases, and so describe to us the result:

Well, about two or three days after, so they [the texts] did indeed; they bolted both upon me at a time, and did work and struggle strangely in me for a while; at least that about Esau's birthright began to wax weak, and withdraw, and vanish; and this about the sufficiency of grace prevailed with peace and joy. And as I was in a muse about this thing, that scripture came in upon me, "Mercy rejoiceth against judgement." [21]

We have already noted the fact that some religious conflicts cause little disturbance within the personality, while others, like those of Augustine and Bunyan, are agonizingly disruptive. How can we distinguish between the two, and what is to determine whether a religious conflict will be disturbing or not?

Obviously some conflicts do not disturb because they are recognized as not important to the individual, and while nearly any professed believer will readily repeat the cliché that his religious faith

[21] The foregoing account based upon, and the quotations taken from Bunyan's *Grace Abounding* described in Georgia Harkness' *The Dark Night of the Soul*, pp. 44–51.

is of supreme importance, this is not often the case. If the individual's conscious mind does not recognize this truth, his unconscious does, one symptom being his apathy toward religious inconsistencies. Perhaps the effect is achieved because the mind has set up watertight compartments which keep the critical faculty from interfering with the religious sentiment.

Yet there are those who do not appear to fall in either of these classifications, who seem so well satisfied with their lives that self-congratulation leaves little room for preoccupation with doubts. The reasons for religious doubts may seem intellectually interesting to them, and conflicts a matter for discussion by those who are up-to-date and have read Freud, but otherwise are hardly disturbing to them.

Moreover, there is still another variety of person. The members of this group are not without their doubts and conflicts, and may be spiritually effective people, but so firm is their mental balance that such troubles are taken in their stride. Robert Browning was hardly a spiritually insensitive person, nor was he without his doubts, yet he never seems to have been what one might call profoundly disturbed by them. So invincible was his mental health that such facts as an invalid wife, approaching death, or religious doubts seemed to be only occasions for him to demonstrate anew how well oiled all the hinges of his spirit were.

> Poor vaunt of life indeed
> Were man but formed to feed
> On joy, to solely seek and find and feast:
> Such feasting ended, then
> As sure an end to men;
> Irks care the crop-full bird? Frets doubt the maw-crammed beast?
>
> Then welcome each rebuff
> That turns earth's smoothness rough,
> Each sting that bids nor sit nor stand but go!
> Be our joys three parts pain!
> Strive, and hold cheap the strain;
> Learn, nor account the pang; dare, never grudge the throe!

It would seem, then, that a certain constitutional wholesomeness of spirit protects some people from being emotionally jarred by religious doubt and conflict. We will have more to say about this subject in the next chapter.

This leads us to the query whether, *not* the fact of religious conflict and doubt, but rather their emotionally disturbing character may be the indications of an unbalanced nature. We know, for example, that John Bunyan was not a completely stable individual, while with respect to the quotation we have given from St. Augustine we might well wonder why he felt the demands of Christ and the world to be so sharply opposed. Would not a sensible person see that some compromise was inevitable anyway, and go ahead to make the accommodation? Why the misery of so long a period when Augustine wished to live a life of righteousness yet could not? Does this not argue for some measure of personality disorganization that would throw him into that rather large class of at least mild neurotics to which religion and culture through the ages has owed so much?

In our next chapter we will try to make a little clearer the distinction between these two types of religious people, the suffering and the healthy-minded.

SUMMARY

To summarize our chapter, we found religious conflict, and particularly doubt, to be experiences especially frequent among youth. Intelligence, religious tradition, physiology, and the strength of the life urge are all general factors that stimulate doubt in this period. More specific intellectual origins of doubt include personal considerations and reaction formation, the shortcomings of religion, the realization that religion is largely the expression of human needs, skeptical habits of mind transferred from other areas, the mistaking of the literal meaning of religious language for religious truth itself, and the confusing of religion with magic.

Religious conflict is a common experience, but the suffering caused by it will vary according to the depth of the religious sentiment and the disposition of the individual. Religious conflicts include those between belief and doubt with consequent choice between values, between loyalty to different religious ideas or institutions, and between the spiritual and the secular. Like all conflicts religious ones are best handled when they are faced on a conscious level and disposed of in a way that will leave the personality harmonious and well integrated.

Chapter 8

TWO ROADS
TO RELIGIOUS GROWTH—
HEALTHY-MINDEDNESS
AND SUFFERING

> God has two families of children on this earth, the
> once-born and the twice-born.
> > —Francis W. Newman

> Biological self affirmation needs a balance between
> courage and fear.
> > —Paul Tillich

Two of the best-known chapters of James' *Varieties* are those titled "The Religion of Healthy-Mindedness" and "The Sick Soul," in which he describes two different expressions of the religious sentiment. Like the expressions of the life urge and the death urge, these characteristics show themselves in areas other than religion, and as parts of the total structure of the psyche they interpenetrate other factors, so that the more one thinks about them the more blurred the picture becomes. Doubt and conflict, for example, which we discussed in the last chapter, are much more likely to be associated with the "sick soul," the individual for whom religion and life itself will mean suffering.

Yet the healthy-minded person will have his doubts and conflicts as well, but with his own characteristic way of handling them. Fur-

154

thermore, whenever we search for the simon-pure sick soul or the completely healthy-minded, we find neither, for each individual is a blend of the two; and some are such a good balance that it is difficult to identify their most characteristic expression. What we must do is observe both extremes of what in practice is a continuum, and describe what we find, even though our descriptions will sometimes appear caricatures.

It may be questioned whether these categories, taken from a book written at the turn of the century, are not out of date. It seems to us that James has proposed a descriptive dichotomy pervasive in the religious life and laden with implications for the religious educator or the student who wishes to understand variations in expressions of the religious life. It may have its roots in temperament and so be physiologically conditioned; yet that outward events have their influence also is indicated by the fact that whatever theology may be in vogue expresses now the sick soul and now healthy-mindedness as one proceeds from one era to another, or goes from place to place, or contemplates this religious movement or that.

HEALTHY-MINDEDNESS

The religion of healthy-mindedness we will describe chiefly under four heads: it is 1) optimistic and happy, 2) extroverted and unreflective, 3) usually associated with a more liberal form of theology, and 4) conducive to a gradual form of religious growth.

(1) *Optimistic.* Healthy-mindedness in religion, just as it sounds, finds religion natural, easy, and conducive of good cheer. People of this kind, says Francis W. Newman, "see God not as a strict Judge, not as a glorious potentate; but as the animating Spirit of a harmonious world, Beneficent and Kind, Merciful as well as Pure." [1] Robert Browning, whom we mentioned in the last chapter, was an example of a religious person who rejoiced in this kind of temperament.

> God's in His heaven,
> All's right with the world.

[1] Quoted in James' *Varieties*, p. 79.

This cry of Pippa sums up at the same time his philosophy and his temperament, and governed his relations with his fellow men.

> It is to be hoped [says William James] that we all have some friend, perhaps more often feminine than masculine, and young rather than old, whose soul is of this sky-blue tint, whose affinities are with flowers and birds and all enchanting innocencies than with dark human passions, who can think no ill of man or God, and in whom religious gladness, being in possession from the outset, needs no deliverance from any antecedent burden.[2]

One wonders how to explain this kind of attitude. Is it the result of an active thyroid gland and good digestion, a happy infancy, modern methods of religious education, or a correct philosophy of life? If we could only isolate the right prescription, most of us would be tempted to use it, since it produces so much of what most people seem to be living for. Doubtless there is much interaction among the various factors associated with it so that it would be hard to tell what is cause and what effect. We need more research in this area. Consequently for the most part we will have to confine ourselves to description, and even that will have to be done with a pretty broad brush.

(2) *Extroverted and unreflective.* One of the secrets of happy living is for the individual to be concerned with what goes on outside rather than inside himself. The healthy-minded person, consequently, is not particularly concerned with sin, least of all his own; and when he cannot avoid giving it his attention, his tendency is to exteriorize and get rid of it. If it is not his own sin he will tend to attack it and pulverize it, so to speak, while the very activity will do his spirits no end of good.

James presents us with an example of this type of temperament which, though not particularly religious, nevertheless represents in an exaggerated way the attitude of a good many so-called religious people. In answer to inquiries on a questionnaire as to what worked most strongly on his emotions and what his notion of sin was, the respondent answered as follows:

[2] *Ibid.*, p. 79.

Lively songs and music; Pinafore instead of an Oratorio. I like Scott, Burns, Byron, Longfellow, especially Shakespeare, etc., etc. Of songs the Star-Spangled Banner, America, Marseillaise, and all moral and soul-stirring songs, but wishy-washy hymns are my detestation. I greatly enjoy nature, especially fine weather, and until within a few years used to walk Sunday into the country, twelve miles often, with no fatigue, and bicycle forty or fifty. . . . I never go to church, but attend lectures when there are any good ones. All my thoughts and cogitations have been of a healthy and cheerful kind, for instead of doubts and fears I see things as they are, for I endeavor to adjust myself to my environment. This I regard as the deepest law. Mankind is a progressive animal. I am satisfied he will have made a great advance over his present status a thousand years hence. . . .

It seems to me that sin is a condition, a disease, incidental to man's development not being yet advanced enough. Morbidness over it increases the disease. We should think that a million of years hence equity, justice, and mental and physical good order will be so fixed and organized that no one will have any idea of evil and sin.

James' comment on the case is worth repeating:

If we are in search of a broken and a contrite heart, clearly we need not look to this brother. His contentment with the finite encases him like a lobster-shell and shields him from all morbid repining at his distance from the infinite. We have in him an excellent example of the optimism which may be encouraged by popular science.[3]

Not only the extroverted feature of healthy-mindedness, but also its unreflective characteristic is illustrated in the above quotation. Consequently the healthy-minded do not tend to become theologians, and when they think about religion it is apt to be in a superficial way. They function much more effectively as executives and administrators of religion than they do in defining it or in searching for its more cunning secrets. Such religious ideas as they have are apt to be conventional ones. Those religious people who have something of both the extrovert and the introvert about them would fall in the

[3] Ibid., pp. 91–92. Intimate statements about the inner workings of the minds of the healthy-minded tend to be scarce. I wished to find an autobiographical volume of this type to which I could frequently refer as I have to Sartor Resartus by Carlyle, a sick soul if there ever was one. Perhaps the most available would be Benjamin Franklin's Autobiography. Norman Vincent Peale is a modern exponent of healthy-mindedness.

middle between our two extremes.[4] Our description is fitted to types rather than individuals.

Benjamin Franklin is a good example of a well-known historic figure who will help to round out what we mean by this unreflective tendency. On the few occasions when he thought much about religion, to Franklin it meant mostly an active attack on vice together with a simultaneous cultivation of virtue. He was well aware of the fact that his character was not in every respect what it should be, and he had his moments when his conscience pricked him, some of which he sets forth with great candor in his *Autobiography*. But not one to entertain troublesome thoughts when there was anything that could be done about them, he set out to attain moral perfection in a well-planned campaign calculated to eradicate all his faults in several courses of systematic endeavor of just thirteen weeks apiece.[5] But failing in this endeavor he readily concluded that moral perfection might be nothing but a kind of "foppery in morals" which might make him envied and hated, and that "a benevolent man should allow a few faults in himself, to keep his friends in countenance."

Even more characteristic was his idea for organizing the "virtuous and good men of all nations" into a "United Party for Virtue." He went so far as to draw up an intended creed, which illustrates a healthy-minded emphasis on conventional religious ideas to appeal to the many, with an emphasis on doing good as follows:

That there is one God, who made all things.
That he governs the world by his Providence.
That he ought to be worshipped by adoration, prayer, and thanksgiving.
But that the most acceptable service of God is doing good to man.
That the soul is immortal.

We learn that unfortunately Franklin was never able to launch this project, <u>for in a somewhat typically healthy-minded way, he was at the time too busy with the details of his business.</u>

---

[4] The concepts of the introvert and the extrovert correspond very closely to those of the sick soul and the healthy-minded of James. The latter are simply introversion and extroversion expressing themselves in the field of religion. For a clear definition of introversion and extroversion, the reader is referred to C. G. Jung, who defined them in *Psychological Types*.

[5] See Chap. 9.

(3) *Usually associated with a more liberal form of theology.* The reality of sin is found most poignantly not by those who turn their attention outward but by those who look inward. Consequently it is the soul-searching introvert who feels its importance and is more likely to sharpen its implications into a theological system of discipline and rigor: the Calvinist Edwards rather than the Unitarian Emerson.

It follows from the healthy-minded man's extroversion that the fine distinctions and disciplined thinking which are ingredients in the great theologies will tend to be absent from his views. Consequently healthy-mindedness will be more apt to express itself through a liberal position that emphasizes right conduct and love rather than wrath, sin, and eternal perdition. The liberal, though he may be a stalwart champion in the fight for social justice, is not apt to *feel* so keenly the radical nature of the demands of his religion; and even if he does, the feeling is not apt to be a burden to him. This means that evil is not so sharply set off from good. The moral relativism that is one of the features of our day owes its existence to liberalism, which in turn derives in part from the psychological urge of healthy-mindedness.

Yet healthy-mindedness finds means to mitigate even the grim implications of rigorous theologies. The doctrine of Purgatory of the Roman Catholic church would seem, psychologically considered, to be a less rigorous form of the more radical Hell-or-Heaven insistence of Calvinism and thus is an expression of religious healthy-mindedness. Also, as James points out,[6] the Catholic practice of the Confessional is a means of exteriorizing sin and guilt and so getting rid of them. Furthermore, Penance is a practical method of doing something about the problem, psychologically the best way to treat any kind of morbidity. Thus we cannot say that liberalism has a monopoly on healthy-mindedness.

But, as we have indicated, Protestantism has not been without its expressions of healthy-mindedness. Some of these have been what James would call *systematic* forms of healthy-mindedness. In these, evil and suffering are deliberately excluded from the scheme of things by the thinking of the group, in much the same way that the existence of mind and consciousness is deliberately excluded from con-

[6] *Varieties*, p. 126.

sideration by behavioristic psychologists. The Biblical injunction, "If thy hand offend thee, cut it off," is translated by these super-healthy-minded religious people into "If sin and evil and suffering trouble you, pay no attention to them." And it must be admitted that this method often operates with admirable results.

Probably the most thoroughgoing familiar example of this systematic type of healthy-mindedness is that of Christian Science with its denial of disease, evil, suffering, and even death except as a kind of mirage caused by the admission of the idea of these "unrealities" to the mind. Accordingly the healing miracles of Jesus are explained as the refusal of Jesus to recognize that disease was real among those he cured. Furthermore Christian Science demonstrates its tenets by impressive citations of cures that it has effected. There is no doubt that many of these are real cures, and the psychologist has no difficulty in understanding how a resolute healthy-mindedness, supported by religious orientation, can well effect certain types of cures.[7] Morbid thinking has given way to a cheerful outlook on life, to the benefit of many an anxious, trying disposition. A few quotations from Mrs. Mary Baker Eddy's *Science and Health* will illustrate this systematic denial of the unpleasant side of life as well as the emphasis on its more positive aspects.

In order to pray aright, we must enter into the closet and shut the door. We must close the lips and silence the material senses. In the quiet sanctuary of earnest longings, we must deny sin and plead God's allness.

Life, God, omnipotent good, deny death, evil, sin, disease. Disease, sin, evil, death deny good, omnipotent God, Life.

You say a boil is painful, but that is impossible, for matter without mind is not painful. The boil simply manifests, through inflammation and swelling, a belief in pain and this belief is called a boil. Now administer to your patient *a high attenuation of truth* and it will soon cure the boil.

If you or I should appear to die, we should not be dead. The seeming decease, caused by a majority of human beliefs that man must die, or produced by mental assassins, does not in the least disprove Christian Science; rather does it evidence the truth of its basic proposition that

[7] See Weatherhead, *Psychology, Religion, and Healing*, Section III-3, for a discussion of Christian Science and healing.

moral thoughts in belief rule the materiality miscalled life in the body or in matter.

Stand porter at the door of thought. Admitting only such conclusions as you wish realized in bodily results, you will control yourself harmoniously. When the condition is present which you say produces disease, whether it be air, exercise, heredity, contagion or accident, then perform your office as porter and shut out these unhealthy thoughts and fears. Exclude from mortal mind the offending errors; then the body cannot suffer from them. The issues of pain or pleasure must come through mind, and like a watchman forsaking his post, we admit the intruding belief, forgetting that through divine help we can forbid this entrance.[8]

Though less systematically and clearly than Christian Science, another vital modern religious expression of healthy-mindedness is the movement now known as "Moral Re-Armament," under the leadership of the Reverend Frank N. D. Buchman. Moral Re-Armament does not go to the extreme of denying the reality of sin and suffering. Indeed, Dr. Buchman has been guilty of artificially stimulating distress of mind in order to effect conversion.[9] Yet the net effect of the movement, with its emphasis on a religious activism, better personal relations, and a kind of lay practice of confession which succeeds more often than it fails, is that of healthy-mindedness.[10]

But this feature of healthy-mindedness is more especially evident in Moral Re-Armament's systematic refusal to entertain any but the very simplest forms of theology. This may be partly due to the movement's desire to bring all nations and faiths within its scope, but it has always shown this characteristic more fundamentally because it expresses an aim of its leader. One of Dr. Buchman's oft repeated slogans has been, "Read people, not books"; and since the early days of his evangelistic career he has consistently refused to discuss theological questions with those he has attempted to convert, according to his principle of "win your argument, lose your man." Attendants at Moral Re-Armament functions almost invariably have a good time, as another Buchman slogan, "Brevity, Sincerity, Hilar-

---

[8] Pp. 15, 113, 153, 164, 392–393, as quoted in Weatherhead, *op. cit.*

[9] See cases of Arnold Bullock, pp. 146 ff., and Mrs. Rose Danforth, pp. 208 ff., in my *The Oxford Group*.

[10] From a randomly selected cross-section of 55 cases, only three of whom were then active members, there was considerably more testimony of benefit than of harm. See *The Oxford Group*, Part 3.

ity," might suggest. Here there is little moaning or groaning of the spirit, and nothing in the way of the dry study of theology. The movement is a vigorous expression of primary religious experience, very definitely not oriented toward suffering but of an admirably healthy-minded variety.[11]

Owing much to the Oxford Group, an earlier phase of Moral Re-Armament, Alcoholics Anonymous is another expression of religious healthy-mindedness which testifies to the value of this type of religion. Norman Vincent Peale's movement has already been mentioned as an expression of healthy-mindedness.

(4) *Conducive to a gradual form of religious growth*. So sane and well-balanced are the lives touched with religious healthy-mindedness, that growth proceeds not by fits and starts nor by violent convulsions but like a steady stream, provided only that the religious life expresses primary religion and not its partially pseudo forms of the secondary or tertiary varieties. The sense of well-being and confidence that it engenders stimulates a wholesome progressiveness of spirit and willingness to look for more spiritual worlds to conquer. Obstacles are simply spurs to greater activity for the healthy-minded man who "welcomes each rebuff which turns earth's smoothness rough." As a child, the healthy-minded most typically finds himself surrounded by loving parents who prepare him in easy stages, both by example and by precept, for the mature religious life. As a man, girded well for the battle against spiritual darkness and esteeming iron as straw, he goes on from strength to strength.

Quite naturally this is the type of religion that appeals most to college professors, religious educators, and writers of textbooks. Growth of this kind is so reasonable, predictable, and controllable that it pleases the academic mind. Also it obtains the indulgence of psychologists as a wholesome process quite in accord with most of the psychological rules, and a boon to mental hygiene. It is a rational, orderly process, the benefits of which are clear.

Indeed it is hard to see how a religious educator could counte-

---

[11] See *ibid.* for a discussion of Moral Re-Armament methods and some of these emphases of which I have been speaking, especially pp. 25–36 and 107–112. Scholars who wish more detailed documentation of points made will find it in my unpublished doctoral dissertation at Harvard, *The Oxford Group: Its Work in American Colleges and Effect on Participants,* available on Interlibrary Loan.

nance any other process. The sick soul grows through stress and suffering, perhaps through the cataclysm of conversion. A responsible religious person with any humanity could hardly justify the deliberate promotion of suffering for the purpose of stimulating religious growth. The church school cannot aim to turn out neurotics simply because so many of the great achievements of religion were the work of neurotics. Even in cases where religious bodies have insisted on conversion as a requirement of membership, excesses due to the stimulation necessary for such an emotional experience usually result in the requirements being toned down with the passage of time.

An example of this healthy-minded emphasis in religious education we can see in the movement known as "Christian Nurture," which takes its inspiration from the work of Horace Bushnell. Bushnell opposed the violent revivalism popular in his day, the idea that infants were the children of sin until regenerated by a conversion experience in their later years. His proposition was that "the child is to grow up a Christian and never know himself to be otherwise."

In other words, the aim, effort, and expectation should be, not, as is commonly assumed, that the child is to grow up in sin, to be converted after he comes to a mature age; but that he is to open on the world as one that is spiritually renewed, not remembering a time when he went through a technical experience, but seeming rather to have loved what is good from his earliest years.[12]

Bushnell gives a hypothetical case of religious growth which clearly shows the framework of his thinking to be that of healthy-mindedness:

A young man, correctly but not religiously brought up, light and gay in his manners, and thoughtless hitherto in regard to anything of a serious nature happens accidentally one Sunday, while his friends are gone to ride, to take down a book on the evidences of Christianity. His eye, floating over one of the pages, becomes fixed, and he is surprised to find his feelings flowing out strangely into its holy truths. He is conscious of no struggle of hostility, but a new joy dawns in his being. Henceforth, to the end of a long and useful life, he is a Christian man. The love into which he was surprised continues to flow, and he is remarkable, in the churches, all his life long, as one of the most beautiful, healthful, and dignified

[12] *Christian Nurture*, p. 10.

examples of Christian piety. Now, a very little miseducation, called Christian, discouraging the piety it teaches, and making enmity itself a necessary ingredient in the struggle of conversion, conversion being no reality without a struggle, might have sufficed to close the mind of this man against every thought of religion to the end of life.[13]

As one would expect, the family plays an important role in Bushnell's concept of gradualness in spiritual growth, for his psychological intuition showed him how much is owed to the early and impressionable years. He rightly divined that sudden conversions in the average family are superficial,[14] and he knew that for the long pull the process of gradualism is to be preferred. The following excellent passage not only illustrates Bushnell's psychological insight but summarizes well the gradualistic philosophy of Christian Nurture:

At first, the child is held as a mere passive lump in the arms, and he opens into conscious life under the soul of the parent, streaming into his eyes and ears, through the manners and tones of the nursery. The kind and degree of passivity are gradually changed as life advances. A little farther on it is observed that a smile kindles a smile; any kind of sentiment or passion, playing in the face of a parent, wakens a responsive sentiment or passion. Irritation irritates, a frown withers, love expands a look congenial to itself, and why not holy love? Next the ear is opened to the understanding of words, but what words the child shall hear, he cannot choose, and has as little capacity to select the sentiments that are poured into his soul. Farther on, the parents begin to govern him by appeals to will, expressed in commands, and whatever their requirement may be, he can as little withstand it, as the violet can cool the scorching sun, or the tattered leaf can tame the hurricane. Next they appoint his school, choose his books, regulate his company, decide what form of religion, and what religious opinions he shall be taught, by taking him to a church of their own selection. In all this, they infringe no right of the child, they only fulfill an office that belongs to them. Their will and character are designed to be the matrix of the child's will and character. Meantime, he approaches more and more closely, and by a gradual process, to the proper rank and responsibility of an individual creature, during all which process of separation, he is having their ways and exercises translated into him.[15]

[13] *Ibid.*, pp. 18–19.
[14] See his semi-humorous picture of the newly-converted family, *ibid.*, p. 78.
[15] *Ibid.*, pp. 28–29.

By reading such a passage we can understand William James when he uses Francis Newman's expression "once-born" to describe the healthy-minded. The development of such a child under Christian Nurture is a steady, one-dimensional progress. Such crises as there are are minor and easily surmounted. The difference between the individual as an infant and as an adult seems one of degree rather than of quality.

We have already suggested some of the reasons why healthy-mindedness is a stimulus to growth. In the first place healthy-mindedness, whether religious or otherwise, is associated with bodily vigor. This means that necessary energy is available as a kind of internal stimulus for the production of growth. In the case of the healthy-minded man quoted from James, the factor of bounding physical health seems quite apparent, and while this element is far from being an invariable source of spiritual growth, it plays its part in that type of growth of which we are now speaking. In fact even the sick soul requires a certain minimum of bodily vigor, although the salient sources of his stimulation are so very different. However, we should note that physical health is not the only source of healthy-minded growth, for there are many examples of almost invincibly healthy-minded people who nevertheless have been sickly in body. Robert Louis Stevenson attained a considerable measure of healthy-minded spiritual maturity, and yet his life was one long battle against disease. But typically it is fair to say that bodily health is an important source of spiritual growth in the religion of healthy-mindedness.

But we can note the prominence of optimism that is one of the hallmarks of the healthy-minded life. In general it may be stated that optimism is more of a stimulus to almost any kind of higher learning and growth than is pessimism. Any good teacher knows that praise and encouragement are more conducive to learning than is blame, while psychological investigation has pretty well supported this generalization.[16] The sense that one is succeeding and that others are working with him and for him is a powerful stimulus to putting forth greater effort. It is with this consideration in mind that the advocates of the gradual type of religious education emphasize the love of God

[16] For one of the most often cited of these demonstrations, see Elizabeth Hurlock, "The Value of Praise and Reproof as Incentives for Children."

rather than the grimness of His justice and His wrath. Said the distinguished Unitarian, Edward Everett Hale:

A child who is early taught that he is God's child, that he may live and move and have his being in God, and that he has, therefore, infinite strength at hand for the conquering of any difficulty, will take life more easily, and probably will make more of it, than one who is told that he is born the child of wrath and wholly incapable of good.[17]

In the extreme case the individual conceives a sense not only of making progress toward a goal but of being *bound to succeed*. This puts on failure and disaster a very different complexion from the outlook of the person expecting failure as a normal thing. This optimistic certainty is a common source of that steadfastness which is an element necessary for any sustained growth, whether internal or external, and which helps to explain the peculiar effectiveness of religion as a source of motivation. The hopelessly outnumbered Christians huddling in the catacombs were able to defy the might of the Roman Empire because they *knew* that, though they might die in the arena, this was merely a way station on the road to eternal bliss. The extraordinary survival of Judaism among a people for ages without a country has rested on the conviction that they were God's Chosen People. The only effective organized resistance to the Nazi terror in Germany was supplied by religious people who had faith through all their defeats that in the end the Church was sure to triumph.[18]

Though in a very different context, we see this same psychological principle operating in Communism, a religious substitute or quasi-religion, in which economic determinism is an article of faith. The good Communist *knows* that capitalism is bound to lose and Communism is bound to win. He endeavors to harmonize his life with the forces of victory. Thus we can understand psychologically the force and drive that Communism exhibits and why it will be defeated only by a faith that can surpass it in vitality. It is from roots such as these that the religion of healthy-mindedness draws the strength that fosters its spiritual growth.

[17] Quoted in Starbuck, *op. cit.*, p. 306.
[18] For documentation and an excellent discussion of this statement, see C. L. Hunt, "Religious Ideology as a Means of Social Control."

A final source of spiritual progress is the fact that, since healthy-mindedness directs its efforts outward, its fruits tend to be visible, and thus are a much more lively stimulus to growth than if they were unseen. Art is long, and education is a slow process; but probably religion is the chief of all activities in which results are hidden from the eye. Thus the religion of healthy-mindedness has the advantage over the religion of suffering in that results are *more* visible. One of the fascinations for amateurs in painting, whether on canvas or the side of a house, is that results are so visible. Once begun, it is the obvious progress that keeps the neophyte at his task. By analogy, it is the religious practitioner who directs his attention outward to good works, who sees the sick healed, who binds up the wounds, and who finds that his sympathy comforts those in distress, who discovers his faith to be quickened and enlarged.

But we must make explicit some of the shortcomings of the religion of healthy-mindedness before we leave the subject.

The most unattractive feature of religious people as a whole is a certain smugness and sense of superiority that grow out of the sense of certainty of which we have been speaking, especially when religion has gone to seed. This is a particular temptation for the healthy-minded, for whom religion has paid such handsome dividends in the way of happiness that a certain amount of self-congratulation can hardly be avoided. The healthy-minded Walt Whitman never tired of "singing of himself," though his readers might. There are few people who have not been bothered at one time or another during their lives with evangelists whose professional healthy-mindedness had made them certain that the secret of health and happiness is bound up with their own particular brand of religious expression.

The following quotation is from the testimony of a member of Moral Re-Armament whose conversion led to what seems to have been an experience of this healthy-minded type. One senses in it more than a hint of this cocksureness on spiritual matters. The question was whether a conversion experience had seemed religious at the time it occurred.

My feeling is *absolutely* the same *now*. Different persons, different methods may help bring one to a spiritual experience and knowledge of the guidance of God—but it is not a thing you "see through." You either know it or haven't yet experienced it.[19]

Another weakness of healthy-mindedness is the tendency to over-emphasize the active life at the expense of thought. Psychiatrists are familiar with the extreme overactivity of the manic patient, and it has been suggested that this is an "escape into reality," a device by which the afflicted person distracts his own attention from thinking about his real problems by a feverish concern with the insignificant details of his immediate environment. There is a strong suggestion of this in the religion of healthy-mindedness, and it breeds a kind of shallowness in thinking which we have implied in the foregoing pages.

The healthy-minded cults have not been those which have produced great thinkers and theologians. The systematic denial of evil by Christian Science is not echoed by any theological thinker of the first rank, while Moral Re-Armament [20] specifically denies interest in any theology except the simplest common denominator of religious concepts necessary for the concert of its activist program. The emphasis on good works and right living is a wholesome feature in healthy-mindedness, but, emphasized out of proportion to other aspects of the religious life, it may simply turn into its own peculiar brand of escape from reality.

Our last objection to the religion of healthy-mindedness grows out of the preceding, and is perhaps simply another way of stating the same thing. This is its tendency toward a very narrow view of reality. Certainly any picture of human nature with sin left out or even minimized is plainly a distortion. True, it is not necessary to wallow in the contemplation of the seamy side of human nature, as certain recent novelists and playwrights would have us do. Their picture is just as distorted. Neither is it necessary to make the weeping Jeremiah the standard for the religious life. But the fact that one knows that God is in heaven does not require one to believe that all is right with the world, and the healthy-minded person who insists on

[19] See *The Oxford Group*, pp. 250–252 for a brief discussion of this aspect of Moral Re-Armament, or, for a more searching treatment, see J. C. Bennett's *Social Salvation*, Chap. 2.

[20] Cf. my *The Oxford Group*, pp. 107–112, 117–120.

this is more and more, especially in the present day, being met with head-shakings and bewilderment.

Indeed, the present state of world tensions at this very moment is making the religion of healthy-mindedness more and more difficult, and the nineteenth-century liberal cult of steady progress toward a better world has for many years now been out of fashion. It has been the psychological impact of the world's tensions, sin, and suffering that has caused liberalism to be subjected to a re-examination.[21] Neo-orthodox emphasis on the fact of sin and the inadequacy of man is a reaction against religious healthy-mindedness which, in the interest of optimism and good spirits, has espoused a world-view that has become so broad as to distort reality.

It would seem not only that the religion of healthy-mindedness has had its day, but that its unreflective shallowness may have played some part in lulling people into a dangerous disregard of the evil forces in society that require only to be disregarded if they are to become unleashed. As Screwtape points out, the Devil does not sleep, but many comfortable optimists among the religiously healthy-minded do. It would seem that the religious habit of mind is changing toward something which, though more distressing, is a little more real. We have been paying for the optimism of the nineteenth century with the suffering of the twentieth, and the only question is whether the change will take place fast enough.

It is not our province to pronounce on theology, politics, or social conditions, but simply to point out a possible connection between these and certain psychological characteristics of the religious mind. Consequently we will now turn from a concern with the religion of healthy-mindedness which, though it certainly should have its place, perhaps has not as essential a function in the world of today as the religion that expresses itself in suffering.

[21] Even the healthy-mindedness of Moral Re-Armament has undergone some correction in the last few years in lessened emphasis on its function in freeing the individual of personal tensions in favor of more emphasis on solving national, racial, and economic problems. An indication of this is found in the photographs in its literature. The ubiquitous smiles of ten years ago have given place to a much higher proportion of expressions of a grimness more appropriate to a contemplation of the steady advance of Communism or the cruelties of racial antagonism in South Africa.

SUFFERING

Much neglected by the formal psychologies of religion is the subject of suffering. Considering its importance in the history of religion, this is strange. Doubtless this neglect owes much to the fact that the psychologist doesn't know exactly what to make of it. Modern psychology has studied extensively the subject of physical pain, fears, anxieties, and depressions. These all involve suffering and have their bearing on religion, but we have little precise data on religious suffering as such. This comes from a reluctance of the psychologist to approach the subject, especially with a measuring instrument in his hand, for how is he going to produce his phenomena or even recognize them when they have been produced for him? Here indeed is a rich area to tempt the daring explorers among the social scientists, but for the time being we will have to fall back on the methods used by William James over half a century ago. His data were the documentary outpourings of religious spirits in anguish, his measuring instrument that most sensitive though most unreliable of all measuring instruments, the human mind.

In his famous chapter in *Varieties,* "The Sick Soul," he provides us with what is perhaps the only systematic attempt by a psychologist to describe religious suffering and even here he is forced to emphasize philosophical and theological considerations. More than in any other aspect of the subject, the psychologist of religion is here forced to join hands with the theologian and the poet in order to achieve understanding. No doubt the appalling thought that he might be classed with such people explains why the psychologist has been so reluctant to approach this important area, at the same time that it explains why poets and religious men have so much more to tell us of human suffering in its religious aspects. Nevertheless, when we consider the subject of religious growth we must at least glance at suffering, no matter how ill-equipped we are to understand all its complexities.

We can start our consideration of suffering by noting a simple fact that the scientific psychologist has sufficiently demonstrated. This is that some form of stimulation to produce un-ease and restlessness is necessary for any kind of growth and learning. On the animal level the rat psychologist starves his subject, or perhaps applies voltage to an electrified grid in order to hasten learning. Living matter in all its forms, when faced with destruction, has the peculiar tendency to resist, the generalized life urge, as we have called it; and it is discomfort that calls forth this tendency.

The higher we get in the animal scale, the greater is the capacity for discomfort, and it is in man that this capacity reaches the acme of its refinement through the sharpening of sensitivity by the spiritual life. Let the healthy-minded rail though they will against the unwholesome conflicts fostered by the grim theologies; nevertheless the fact remains that suffering is bound up with humanity. The person who is incapable of suffering or who too deliberately dulls its edge is crippled in his capacity for spiritual growth and in danger of degenerating into a mere vegetable.

This fact has been recognized by the attention that suffering has received from all major religions and the keenest spirits of many countries and ages. "Man's Unhappiness," says Carlyle, "comes of his Greatness; it is because there is an Infinite in him, which with all his cunning he cannot quite bury under the Finite." [22] Kierkegaard makes essentially the same point in *The Sickness Unto Death* when he says, "The possibility of this sickness is man's advantage over the beast, and this advantage distinguishes him far more essentially than the erect posture, for it implies the infinite erectness or loftiness of being spirit." [23] The ancient Biblical writers divined that suffering was somehow connected with growth, for in many places and in many ways the praises of suffering are sung. "My son, despise not thou the chastening of the Lord: For whom the Lord loveth he chasteneth." [24]

Perhaps there have been no greater stumbling blocks to the determinedly healthy-minded theologians than the fact of suffering in the world, and the problem of evil. While no religious thinker has adequately solved this problem, it is the sick soul rather than the healthy-minded who has come the closest to the heart of the matter in the minds of most sensitive readers. Browning, with his, "Grow old along with me, The best is yet to be," seems to be whistling in the dark compared to the "Nature red in tooth and claw" that shrieked

[22] *Sartor Resartus,* p. 143.
[23] Pp. 147–148.
[24] Hebrews 12:5–6.

against the creed of his less gifted but more spiritually discerning contemporary, Tennyson. Horace Bushnell with his movement of Christian Nurture shows common sense and much understanding of psychology, but theologically he skims merely the surface of the stream and leaves many of the problems of the religious life safely undisturbed under the waters. Compared with his introspective predecessor Jonathan Edwards, with predictions of hell-fire and torment, or the outpourings of his sick-souled contemporary Søren Kierkegaard, the theological contributions of the healthy-minded Bushnell are mere bubbles soon to be forgotten. For the discovery of truth James casts his vote against healthy-mindedness and in favor of the sick soul with its more drastic experience of reality.

The method of averting one's attention from evil, and living simply in the light of good is splendid as long as it will work. . . . But it breaks down impotently as soon as melancholy comes; and even though one may be quite free from melancholy one's self, there is no doubt that healthy-mindedness is inadequate as a philosophical doctrine, because the evil facts which it refuses positively to account for are a genuine portion of reality; and they may after all be the best keys to life's significance, and possibly the only openers of our eyes to the deepest levels of truth.[25]

But what are the characteristics of the sick soul, and what constitutes the psychological background against which suffering is experienced? We have already described it in reverse in our account of healthy-mindedness. The sick soul is simply at the opposite pole from healthy-mindedness, and in between there are all gradations.

Where healthy-mindedness is optimistic, the sick soul is steeped in pessimism. Healthy-mindedness is extroverted and unreflective; the sick soul is an introvert and much more thoughtful in his approach to life. If the healthy-minded man tends to be a liberal in his theology, the sick soul, though by no means always orthodox, is nevertheless apt to espouse a much more drastic and demanding type of theology. Healthy-mindedness tends to stimulate a gradual, smooth, and rational type of religious growth, while the sick soul is prone to a religious development that moves by fits and starts. Much more frequent are visions, overwhelming encounters with God or the Devil, long periods of meditation and melancholy, and sudden flashes of

[25] *Varieties*, p. 160.

spiritual light or conversion experiences. We will not take the time
to document these statements at this point, for their force has already
been made partly clear and will be further apparent in the ensuing
discussion. But it is obvious that it is the sick soul on whom the
burden of the world's evil falls.

There are a number of varieties of suffering that we can discern,
the differences arising chiefly from the source of the suffering; though
naturally in any given case several of the varieties will be operating
together. In general they may be put into two broad categories, those
where the cause has less personal significance or is external to the
personality, and those where the cause is more personal and internal
in origin. All of them, however, have their importance for the religious life, though more so where the cause is internal.

SUFFERING FROM EXTERNAL SOURCES

Catastrophe. An obvious outside source of suffering is catastrophe
that touches the individual closely. Its religious significance will obviously depend on whether any religious reference is made. The death
of a son would have a different significance for an atheist and a
theistic believer. In many cases religion may have the healthy-minded
effect of reconciling the individual to facts and enabling him to
accept them. Though it took many long years, this was the ultimate
effect of Tennyson's loss by death of his close friend, Arthur Hallam.
"In Memoriam" records the inner struggles of poignant religious
doubts and sufferings before Tennyson could accept this loss and
reconcile his religious faith. Had he been more healthy-minded his
reconciliation would have come sooner, but literature would have
been poorer in the loss of what has been called the finest flower of
his genius.

The capacity of religion to transform suffering into insights of profound significance is nowhere better seen than in the aftereffects of
the Exile and Dispersion of the Jews. High though the religion of the
Prophets of the pre-Exilic period may have been, the post-Exilic
prophecies were finer. Not only did the belief in Jehovah and the concept of the Chosen People hold the nation together during these
times of trouble, but in a paradoxical way both sharpened the edge
of suffering and increased the valuation put on it. This resulted in

such sublime concepts as that of Chapter 53 of Isaiah with its description of the Servant of the Lord as "despised and rejected of men; a man of sorrows, and acquainted with grief." Without the suffering on the one hand, and the religious interpretation of it on the other, it is inconceivable that tradition would have much more to record of the Exile than the mere fact of its occurrence. It is through empirical discoveries such as this one, when testing their comfortable religious presuppositions in the fierce crucible of suffering, that religions come to estimate the experience so highly. In this connection it is well to reflect that the poet Goethe referred to the Christian religion as a "Sanctuary of Sorrow."

The contemplation of evil. Another important external source of suffering is the contemplation of evil. We have seen how the healthy-minded tend to minimize evil and even systematically to deny its existence. The sick soul not only acknowledges evil when it touches his own self-interest, but by very virtue of being a religious person becomes more sensitive to evil in the form of the suffering of other people. This leads to the experience of vicarious suffering, when one becomes as distressed with others' suffering as he is with his own. This was the experience of Hosea when he understood the suffering of his unfaithful wife, and this enriched religion with the concept of the God who may be just but also participates in the suffering of his wayward people.

Another result of vicarious suffering may be the sharpening of the conscience of the religious person, perhaps through an insight into the interrelatedness of all human kind and the realization that everyone in some way participates in the sorrows of everyone else. Through this there develops a sense of responsibility that leads to a concern for society, expressing itself in such emphases as the Social Gospel and forms of social service and reform that can be justified so much more successfully on a theological basis than on any other.

For it is the religious sufferer who dwells on suffering. No one has a satisfactory explanation for the existence of suffering, though the religious thinkers have come closest to it. At any rate it is through the contemplation of evil and suffering that mankind has found and expressed some of its most moving thoughts. It is not merely the rhetoric of the Book of Job that makes it the most eloquent of all the books of the Bible, but its matter also, which is the problem of suffering. Doubtless the unknown writer had experienced in his own life poignant periods of suffering through outward personal catastrophe, but very probably he had also observed unjust suffering in others, which troubled him though he could not explain it. He knew merely that "man is born unto trouble as the sparks fly upward," and that much of this trouble is undeserved.

SUFFERING FROM INTERNAL SOURCES

Temperament. Some people suffer because of their temperament. They seem to have been born that way. Mrs. Gummidge in *David Copperfield* was always complaining of being a "lone lorn creetur," and "everythink went contrairy" with her, particularly when everyone else was having a rousing good time. Religion for this type of person is apt to be a very mournful affair, and the subjects of death, sin, sacrifice, and the high cost of church collections are just the things to fit in with the mood. The cause here is in a sense internal, but it is pretty much a matter of glands, chronic dyspepsia, and low blood pressure, clearly physical in nature, for which the individual has little personal responsibility. Temperament in this case may affect one's outlook on life as well as one's theology. Carlyle's dyspepsia was noted for the influence it was supposed to have had on his preoccupation with the sins of his contemporaries. Though there were other roots as well, no doubt his temperamental cast was one of the sources of the sufferings about which Carlyle groaned so eloquently during most of his existence.

Neurosis. The most obvious type of religious suffering, the sources of which are intimate and internal, is that which is neurotic. Strictly speaking, this is not religious suffering at all but neurotic suffering. Yet neurotic suffering with a religious reference is in part religious suffering, and we cannot close our eyes to the fact that in the teachings of such people as Jeremiah, John Bunyan, and George Fox, religion owes not a little to teachers who have been neurotics.

Religious neurotic suffering may be of various kinds, too numerous to be reviewed here. The most frequent is recognized by the common man under the term "martyr complex." This has elements of paranoid thinking—the tendency to feel that one is being singled out for persecution—and also of masochism, the enjoyment of pain. Like Elijah languishing under the juniper bush,[26] the prophet who feels he is preaching God's word is under the necessity of justifying his opposition, and convenient justification involves the feeling that one is the special object of other people's animus.

But paranoid thinking usually spurs one to action, and provided it is not too marked, it may be a tonic to a wholesome activity that will bring an end to miseries. Elijah did not enjoy his mood of splendid despair very long, but soon was up and doing the Lord's work, with happy results, as every good Bible student knows. Much less creative is suffering in the form of masochism. Since the masochist, for various complicated reasons, unconsciously enjoys his suffering, this is a particularly harmful expression of the religious sentiment and may even be subtly very dangerous in its effects on personality.[27]

Masochism in its extreme forms may involve deliberately inflicted privations, tortures, or even mutilations for the sake of religion. James quotes from the autobiography of the Blessed Henry Suso, a fourteenth-century German mystic and ascetic, as an example of pathological extremes.[28] Suso devised for himself such comforts as an undergarment studded with a hundred and fifty brass nails, sharpened and so fixed as to pierce his skin; gloves with sharp tacks in order to discourage him from disturbing the noxious insects with which, by a sort of invitation, his body teemed; a door to sleep on, and to make sure that this should not be too comfortable, a cross with thirty protruding needles and nails just under his body. In winter he slept on the bare floor of his cell and froze, his body covered with scars and his throat parched with thirst. He boasts that over a period of twenty-five years he never took a bath, and strove to "attain such a high degree of purity" that he would neither scratch nor touch any part of his body other than hands and feet. All these torments he endured "out of the greatness of the love which he bore

[26] Cf. I Kings 19:10: "I, even I only, am left; and they seek my life, to take it away."

[27] One will find descriptions of paranoia and masochism in any good text on abnormal psychology. For a particularly thorough treatment of masochism, see Reik's *Masochism in Modern Man*.

[28] *Varieties*, p. 301 ff.

in his heart to the Divine and Eternal Wisdom, our Lord Jesus Christ. . . ."

While we cannot say that the luxury-loving culture of modern Christianity is in every respect a gain over that of the fourteenth century, nevertheless it is hard to see just how the sufferings of Suso were turned to religious advantage. The tone of his autobiography makes it clear that he took a good deal of satisfaction in his exploits, but we suspect that the more wholesome fruits of his undoubted piety had other sources than his masochistic urgings.

Conflict and doubt. We have pointed out that the healthy-minded person is no stranger to conflict and doubt, but he is able to handle the situation much more easily. The sick soul, on the other hand, reacts much more like a neurotic and indeed is often clearly a neurotic and on occasion even a psychotic.[29] In these cases the suffering may take the form of a drastic sense of inner catastrophe. The best account of such an experience is given us in *The Exploration of the Inner World* by A. T. Boisen, himself a religious man who suffered an attack of catatonic schizophrenia.[30]

His theory of this form of schizophrenia, in which the patient often remains inert and motionless for long periods of time, is that the individual has been so struck by the conflict of loyalties that the whole force of his attention and his being is given over to the painful duty of decision. This involves an experience of suffering so keen that it can be appreciated only by a person who has passed through it. In the case of the religious person it is brought on partly by the individual's sense of the radical nature of the demands of religion and the making up of his mind to the sacrifices involved. Boisen believes that his experience not only helps him to understand the significance of the psychotic episodes in the life of George Fox, but also throws some light on the experience of normal persons and the suffering that doubt and conflict often bring. It is noteworthy that a period of meditation has often preceded action in the lives of many religious leaders. We have seen the effect of conflict on Augustine before his

[29] It must be remembered that extreme healthy-mindedness may develop neurosis too, as in hysterical symptoms of psychic blindness or paralysis; or even psychosis, as in the excessive extroversion of the manic patient.

[30] For a good brief summary of Boisen's theories, see Klein's *Mental Hygiene,* pp. 164–170. These matters will be given fuller treatment in Chap. 16.

conversion became effective, while Boisen suggests that the period of the Temptations in the Wilderness may have had somewhat the same significance in the life of Jesus.

We can taste some of the internal psychological flavor of suffering brought on by conflict in Carlyle's vivid phrases. The description comes from "The Everlasting No" chapter of *Sartor Resartus*, where he describes his state of mind due to doubt and denial.

Having no hope, neither had I any definite fear, were it of Man or of Devil:, nay, I often felt as if it might be solacing, could the Arch-Devil himself, though in Tartarean terrors, but rise to me, that I might tell him a little of my mind. And yet, strangely enough, I lived in a continual, indefinite, pining fear; tremulous, pusillanimous, apprehensive of I knew not what: it seemed as if all things in the Heaven above and the Earth beneath would hurt me; as if the Heavens and the Earth were but boundless jaws of a devouring monster, wherein I, palpitating, waited to be devoured.[31]

Distance from God. The category of conflict and doubt shades into the last and, religiously speaking, most significant of all the sources of suffering. This is the suffering that comes from realization of the great distance between the actuality of man's condition and the purity and splendor of the nature of God. Of course this distance is often expressed in religious forms, and the conventional worshiper repeats in many ways the idea that he is a miserable sinner. But outside of the words, one notes surprisingly few signs of the suffering that might be supposed to claim those individuals who felt what they said. As a matter of fact, were such signs to be produced, as in the days when Jonathan Edwards' parishioners screamed with terror at the thoughts of their unworthiness, any respectable church body would quickly see to it that such unwholesome forms of religion were suppressed. Suffering from the consciousness of sin seems more often mouthed than experienced.

The truth is that most congregations are sufficiently healthy-minded not to take such statements too much to heart. Since most church members are religious only in a secondary or tertiary sense, they could not be expected to understand the full extent of the great gulf that lies between God and man. It is therefore not only in the

[31] P. 127.

ranks of the small band of primary religious personalities that we find suffering of this type, but more especially in those primary religious personalities who are of the sick-souled variety. But again we can see the importance of a small minority in religion, for the fruits of this type of suffering are out of all proportion to the numbers of individuals involved.

Quite clearly this sort of suffering is dependent on religious sensitivity and will vary in different individuals partly as this factor varies. One's sensitivity grows with thinking about it, and this helps to explain why it is that the sick soul in his preoccupation with the state of his own inner processes is so much more apt to be sensitive to his own comparative degradation than is the healthy-minded. It also helps to explain the incredulity and scorn with which the healthy-minded have traditionally looked upon those sick of soul. Says Walt Whitman:

I could turn and live with animals, they are so placid and self-contained,
     I stand and look at them long and long;
     They do not sweat and whine about their condition.
     They do not lie awake in the dark and weep for their sins.[32]

But not all the keenness of religious lamentation is mere neuroticism, and the scorn of the modern liberal is due to his inadequate background of psychological understanding. It is only by postulating a certain genuineness and value in this religious sensitivity that we can make sense out of much of the theology and of accounts of religious experience of former ages. Those who live in a once-born world have the obligation at least to gain some intellectual comprehension of the two-storied dwellings of the twice-born.

And so it may be instructive to turn briefly to a thinker who demonstrates this kind of sensitivity and suffering, the Danish prophet, Kierkegaard. So subtle is the writing of this philosopher that one not a thorough student of his thought is never quite sure of his meaning. Nevertheless it is quite clear even in merely noting the titles of some of his works that the concept of suffering, in one form or another, played an important part in his life and thought.[33]

[32] From "Song of Myself."
[33] E.g., *Fear and Trembling, The Sickness Unto Death, The Concept of Dread,* and *The Gospel of Sufferings.*

In *The Sickness Unto Death* he focuses on suffering in the form of despair, both in its conscious and unconscious forms. Despair, he says, derives from the radical opposition of the finite, as represented by man and the infinitude of God. This despair is unconscious as man goes about his everyday tasks of making a living, accommodating his neighbors, and getting ahead in the world, whether under the form of a healthy-minded acceptance of conventional Christianity or not. It is only when he becomes conscious of sin, or the distance between his own state and that of God, that man has any possibility of spiritual growth. The shock of this realization involves suffering, or despair made conscious.

Those, on the other hand, who say that they are in despair are generally such as to have a nature so much more profound that they must become conscious of themselves as spirit, or such as by the hard vicissitudes of life and its dreadful decisions have been helped to become conscious of themselves as spirit, either one or the other, for rare is the man who is truly free from despair.

Ah, so much is said about human want and misery—I seek to understand it, I have also had some acquaintance with it at close range; so much is said about wasted lives—but only that man's life is wasted who lived on, so deceived by the joys of life or by its sorrows that he never became eternally and decisively conscious of himself as spirit, as self, or (what is the same thing) never became aware and in the deepest sense received an impression of the fact that there is a God, and that he, he himself, his self, exists before this God, which gain of infinity is never attained except through despair.[34]

For this twice-born child of God there was no easy road into the Kingdom of Heaven. His *Training in Christianity* might almost have been a direct denial of the theories of Christian Nurture.

In Christianity there is perpetual Sunday twaddle about Christianity's glorious and priceless truths, its sweet consolation; but it is only too evident that Christ lived 1,800 years ago. . . . People have mutually confirmed one another in the notion that by the aid of the upshot of Christ's life and the 1,800 years (the consequences) they have become acquainted with the answer to the problem. By degrees, as this came to be accounted wisdom, all pith and vigor was distilled out of Christianity; the tension

[34] *The Sickness Unto Death*, pp. 159–160.

of the paradox was relaxed, one became a Christian without noticing it, and without in the least noticing the possibility of offense. . . . Christendom has done away with Christianity without being quite aware of it.[35]

That the despair and suffering arising from a sense of unworthiness that Kierkegaard felt were so important to spiritual growth was exemplified with less subtlety yet with vivid poignancy in the experience of Bunyan:

But my original and inward pollution, that was my plague and my affliction. By reason of that I was more loathsome in my own eyes than was a toad; and I thought I was so in God's eyes too. Sin and corruption, I said, would as naturally bubble out of my heart as water would bubble out of a fountain. I could have changed heart with anybody. I thought that none but the Devil himself could equal me for inward wickedness and pollution of mind. Sure, thought I, I am forsaken of God; and thus I continued a long while, even for some years together.[36]

Though the introspective personality capable of such reflections may often be tinged with more than a modicum of neurosis, nevertheless it is out of the spontaneous awareness of the distance between God and man that the profoundest insights into spiritual reality come. Heavy though the price in individual suffering may be, yet these insights are the flowers grown among nettles that have stimulated the growth of the spiritual life.

The foregoing will have given the reader some insight into the sources and varieties of religious suffering. It should be noted that suffering is neither an infallible means nor the sole source of spiritual growth. Were this the case it would be the duty of the church deliberately to create conditions of stress and to muddy the waters of the personality whenever they threatened to run smooth and clear. Though religion has been guilty of this at times, this would be an unnatural forcing of the situation, as the case of Suso suggests. Any person who faces life thoughtfully and honestly will encounter suffering enough.

Furthermore, just as "hope deferred maketh the heart sick," so

[35] *A Kierkegaard Anthology*, pp. 396–397. I have rearranged the order of the passage.
[36] *Grace Abounding*, as quoted in James' *Varieties*, p. 155.

suffering too long endured will disintegrate the personality, not
strengthen it. Even the sick soul must have his moments of exalta-
tion and victory. But typically the pleasant fruits of life are not the
ends of life but its by-products. Carlyle expressed the sick soul's emphasis when he said, "The only happiness a brave man ever troubled
himself with asking much about was, happiness enough to get his
work done." But psychologically, suffering must be looked upon
neither as a good nor an evil but a condition which puts an edge on
man's sensibilities whether spiritual or otherwise. Emily Dickinson
had this idea in mind when she wrote:

> Not one of all the purple host
> Who took the flag to-day
> Can tell the definition,
> So clear, of victory,
>
> As he, defeated, dying,
> On whose forbidden ear
> The distant strains of triumph
> Break, agonized and clear.[37]

Yet after a time suffering ceases to sharpen and begins to dull.
Boisen cites the catastrophic nature of certain types of schizophrenia
and their tendency to make or break the personality.[38] He points out
that in psychoses the issue may sometimes depend on the support
given by religious aims. This is also the case in more normal troubles.
The capacity to make use of suffering to strengthen rather than to
weaken depends largely on the individual's ability to fix his aims on
something beyond the suffering or, in other words, to make sense out
of it. It is this function that religion performs *par excellence* among
all the sources of human motivation. Under no other form can the
human mind project an aim so ultimate, all-embracing, and profound
than in his conception of the divine. It is not the business of the psychologist to examine the truth of this conception but simply to
record its effect on the human mind.

The following sensitively written and moving case history will serve
to illustrate this capacity of religion to transform suffering in such a

[37] Emily Dickinson's *Poems*, p. 13.
[38] *The Exploration of the Inner World*, pp. 159–160.

way as to lead to spiritual growth and creative human service. The author was a young woman of vigorous intelligence and firm religious faith who turned in the account as an assignment in one of the writer's courses, and gave permission for its use.

Though this brief report is not to be a case history, nevertheless a mention of certain background facts will be made which it is felt are relevant to the presentation. I am now twenty-five years of age and have come from a happy family of seven children. Even as a child, a large family such as we were seemed to me to be the ideal of any marriage. Though it cost them much in the way of personal sacrifice, my parents have made it possible for all their children to have a college education, and there it was that I met my husband. A few months after our marriage we were on our way to Africa for the first term of missionary service of four and a half years.

We had talked together of our family plans, and as in most other subjects, felt and hoped the same things. However it was not as simple and automatic to have children as most newlyweds take for granted it is, and not till after surgery had corrected a minor defect did conception occur. The following nine months were perhaps the happiest of my life, at least in a physical way. I suffered none of the discomforts of pregnancy; instead the whole experience was an exciting and new adventure, full of plans and dreams and busy days. There wasn't the slightest inkling that anything could go wrong, and if the doctor had any such, he did not tell me. As I was waiting those last weeks, the nurse joked with me, saying, "You're going to have an easy one, I bet!"

The details of the difficult delivery of a still-born baby are not necessary to this report; my husband witnessed the entire event and it was his tears which first pierced the fog of anesthesia with the sharp realization of reality: our baby was dead and with him the dreams and hopes and joys of anticipation, doomed to be not realized.

Perhaps the last part of the above statement is too strong, for rising above the first tidal wave of disappointment and sorrow, there came the strength of faith and the sustaining power of the presence of God. There was the great comfort of friends who shared our sense of loss and gave us of their friendship and sympathy. There was the hope of Easter, together with the hope of other babies that would come—"the next one" was in my thoughts as I put away the layette and crib. There came also from the experience a deepened sensitivity to the sorrows of others, for not until one has experienced first-hand such sorrow, can the heart be attuned to the aching in the hearts of others; I realized how blind I had been when our beloved Africans had faced similar bereavements, how unreal had been my sympathy. I had never been able figuratively to weep with those who weep, but now God had turned a difficult experience into one which brought blessings of many kinds into my life and the lives of others, I believe. The crisis was met and faced by the grace of God, and I was enriched by it in the realization of God's Hand upon me through it all.

In the months and now years which have followed the events described above, another kind of adjustment has had to be made, different from that of the initial experience; though there seems to be little physical reason, conception has not yet taken place. This has brought a different kind of situation, for there has been through these months a continual hope that it would occur, and consequently a continually recurring disappointment of the hope. In some ways the rise and fall of such hopes has been a cycle more dangerous to mental health than the bereavement itself; it has brought the possibility of pessimism following discouragement, the temptation to wonder what could be the purpose of the denial of hopes, the temptation to be "blue" and even envious when friends continue having children easily and normally, to be angry and jealous when news of "unwanted" babies or "undeserved" babies was heard of, especially if such babies were deserted or given away. I recognize clearly that such temptations are dangerous not only to mental health but to a positive Christian witness, and though giving in to such feelings has been rare, occurring usually at times of physical illness; yet I recognize their existence, and in facing the reality of my situation, I take into account the wearing influence of disappointed hopes.

Another facet of the situation as it exists today is the possibility of adoption. This step we have considered favorably, but on the advice of doctors who feel that we should eventually have our own, we have postponed application till thorough check-ups could be made for both my husband and myself under the care of specialists who were not available in Africa. If we should consider starting adoption procedures, it would mean delaying our return for the second term of missionary service. To an outsider such a delay would seem of small importance, but in our particular situation, though it would be possible, it does not seem the best step to take at this time. This statement is made advisably after considering the possibility of the next five years in Africa being childless years. There are other factors which are of significance too, which I need not elaborate on here. This decision, however has not come easily, and yet now that it is made, I do not continue to fret over its implications. We still have the possibility of adoption when we return again to the States in 1957, if at that time it should be necessary; then the procedure could be well-planned and there would be plenty of time for the carrying out of the legal detail.

In closing, there are four factors which have been and are of great help to me. First of all, has been my husband whose patience and faith have been transmitted to me by his own loving example, whose love and sympathy have cut sorrows in two and doubled my joys. Then there has been the objective and yet sympathetic help of doctors who have made our problem theirs, seeking to do all they could to make conception a more likely possibility and whose encouragement still gives us good hope of eventually having children of our own.

Another factor which has been of help is the therapeutic effect of a busy and engrossing and worthwhile vocation. In our mission work, one's own problems often get lost in much bigger ones which demand all the energy and devotion that participants can give to them. There have also been opportunities on the field to help with the care of others' children, and many have been the little ones whom we have had the opportunity to love and care for even if only directly for short periods of time. All children seem more precious to us than before, and we find joy in all such opportunities to know and to help. We have learned also to rejoice with them that rejoice.

The last, which to me is the most important and in which others find their greatest significance, is the great peace that comes with knowing that we can leave in our Father's loving Hands all of our wants and wishes, trusting and knowing that He cares. He has given me the grace to pray, "Use me" instead of "Give me", and in being able to transcend the unwholesome emotions that tempt me by facing them realistically and finding resources to overcome and change them, there has come grateful joy for His strength made perfect in weakness.

Two of the authors whose works I've been reading for this course seemed to have described what I've tried to say: "One often feels ashamed that, having endured great crises, he seems unable now to endure a continuing succession of minor irritations. Whether we ought to feel shame depends on many things. If self-pity obsesses us, as it is altogether too prone to do, the sooner it is banished the better for all concerned. Yet for balanced judgment one needs to remember that long-continued irritations become major matters. If they cannot be eliminated they, too, must be accepted with as much good grace (which means God's grace) as can be brought to bear upon them." [39]

"Serenity comes not alone by removing the outward causes and occa-

[39] Georgia Harkness, *The Dark Night of the Soul*, p. 174.

sions of fear, but by the discovery of inward reservoirs of strength to draw upon." [40]

It is this capacity of religion to transform suffering that explains the hold that it has on the human spirit. It is this that makes psychologically credible what would otherwise be incredible—Christian martyrs meeting wild beasts with joy and singing, the Jews wresting sublime concepts of Jehovah out of the sorrows of the Exile, Mohammed turning flight into victory, or Christ finding triumph on the Cross. Suffering has been the matrix out of which have emerged life's greatest creativities.

Yet we must remember that the way of suffering is not the whole story of spiritual growth, but only half, even though the profounder half. It is the way of the sick soul. He more than the healthy-minded is the pioneer of the spirit, the sick soul who is outwardly so passive and inwardly so active because of his distress of mind. But the healthy-minded way is more outwardly active. The healthy-minded man perhaps has never wept over his inward condition. Reared in a wholesome and loving environment he has never known what it is not to be religious. His vigorous temperament and active mind cause a continual unfolding to him of the wonders of God's world and His ways with men. Difficulties and defeats come to him, but because he meets them actively he resolves them quickly. His growth is more apt to be bound up with his works than his speculations. He is the pragmatist and the executive of the religious life as the sick soul is its prophet, theologian, and poet.

We talk about the sick soul and the healthy-minded person, but in actuality neither exists in unadulterated form. Either one in all his purity would not be a man but a monstrous fiction who could not lead for long a profitable spiritual existence. But each religious person carries something of both around with him, and it is this fact more than anything else that enables us to understand each other. Both are necessary to the religious enterprise. Movements as well as individuals have given predominant expression to one way or the other; one era chiefly expresses one, and then is corrected by the next. It would seem that the wars and threatening dangers of our times are so forcing our attention upon evil that the mood of the sick soul is

[40] Rufus Jones, *The Testimony of the Soul*, p. 22.

balancing the optimistic healthy-mindedness and liberalism of the nineteenth century. Perhaps our religious values are soon to be tested by suffering beyond belief so we will need all the fortitude and optimism that healthy-minded religion can supply, but it is the sick soul who will have the function of meeting most effectively and solving most profoundly the great issues of life and death.[41]

SUMMARY

The religious consciousness may grow through two opposed psychological modes, that of healthy-mindedness or suffering. The healthy-minded religion is optimistic, extroverted, unreflective, more often associated with a liberal form of theology, and is conducive to a gradual form of religious growth. The religion born of suffering tends to develop opposite characteristics. It is more sensitive to the impact of catastrophe, and is more distressed at the contemplation of evil. But it may also have its roots in the inward condition of the individual, his temperament and lack of psychological integration, his conflicts and doubts. Most poignant is the suffering experienced by the sensitive religious soul who senses the gap between his own imperfect life and the law of his God. But suffering may be a spiritual liability rather than a wholesome stimulus to growth unless the individual sees meaning in his suffering. This latter is one of the functions of a religious view of life. While it is the healthy-minded who are the executives of religious action, it is those who are able to face and give meaning to their sufferings from whom come the profoundest interpretations of the spiritual life.

[41] It is the facing of the more pessimistic aspects of life that helps to explain the turning of many contemporary Christian intellectuals to the existentialism of Kierkegaard. An example on the American scene is Paul Tillich. In *The Courage to Be* he deals with the problem of anxiety of which the chief modern form is the anxiety derived from the sense of the meaninglessness of life. The result of this is suffering. Yet Tillich is not without his healthy-minded emphasis on the possibility of transcending the anxiety through the "courage to be."

Chapter 9

CONVERSION

Then said I, Woe is me! for I am undone; because I am a man of unclean lips, and I dwell in the midst of a people of unclean lips: for mine eyes have seen the King, the Lord of hosts.

Then flew one of the seraphims unto me, having a live coal in his hand, which he had taken with tongs from off the altar:

And he laid it upon my mouth, and said, Lo, this hath touched thy lips; and thine iniquity is taken away, and thy sin purged.

Also I heard the voice of the Lord saying, Whom shall I send, and who will go for us? Then said I, Here am I; send me.

—Book of Isaiah

For students of religion and religious psychology there is no subject that has held more fascination than the phenomenon called conversion. Yet of recent years a kind of shamefacedness becomes apparent among those scholars who mention it. They hasten to explain that conversion was much overemphasized in the old-fashioned theology, that it is largely abnormal and unnatural, and that much more satisfactory results can be obtained by the gradual process of religious growth. This attitude is characteristic of the liberal clergy as well.

This depreciation is even more obvious among the more conventional psychologists of the present day, who infrequently concern themselves with the study of religion and practically never with the subject of conversion. It is quite obvious that the latter is regarded as a kind of psychological slum to be avoided by any really respectable scholar. For example, one will find much interest in the process of creativity among psychologists, and nearly every text in general psychology will allude to the sudden character of much creative thinking; how the chemist Kekulé emerged from a drunken stupor with the solution to the structure of benzine, how Coleridge woke from a dream with the lines of *Kubla Khan,* or how Henri Poincaré solved complicated mathematical problems in a flash of insight.

Yet similar and equally creative experiences in the religious field are completely ignored. St. Paul's conversion on the Damascus road transformed not only Paul himself but influenced the whole course of Western history. Luther's sudden decision in the thunderstorm set in motion a process whose end is not yet. Wesley's conversion changed the religious face of England and created Methodism as a force to be reckoned with throughout the world. Can we ask for more creativity than was effected by these transformations, whether we are interested in the psychological process itself or merely in its fruits?

In their rejection of conversion it is as if some psychologists had on *a priori* grounds decided that conversion were a mere emotional bubble not deserving the encouragement of being noticed. If human nature has the effrontery still to demonstrate religious conversion despite the solemn conclusion of scholars that the phenomenon is illogical and reprehensible, then it must take the consequences of their neglect! We notice, for example, that even though religious conversion beautifully illustrates the working of the unconscious mind which the great Sigmund Freud was so anxious to describe in all its varieties, this astute thinker hardly mentions the subject.

We can agree that conversion has been abused by many evangelists. It has been overemphasized, forced on people, and often distorted. It is also true that it has to large degree gone out of style. The proportion of those who even *say* they have been converted, especially in recent years, has been much smaller than formerly. E. T. Clark,[1] in perhaps the most extensive study of conversion ever undertaken, reported sudden conversion in only 6.7 per cent of 2,174 cases, a figure approximately confirmed more recently by Allport, Gillespie, and Young in their study of Harvard and Radcliffe students.[2]

But here again we must return to one of our central theses. Primary religion is the experience of a small minority whose influence and significance is out of all proportion to its size. This may also be the

[1] *The Psychology of Religious Awakening,* p. 47.
[2] "The Religion of the Post-War College Student," p. 17.

case with conversion, whether we are interested in what it is that is creative in religion or simply in an experience that throws light on the dynamics of personality. Consequently we find ourselves once again ranged on the side of William James, whose *Varieties* treats conversion as a subject of major importance. We will not be able to treat the subject exhaustively. The more one scrutinizes it the more complicated and baffling it becomes. But at the outset of our discussion we wish to record our conviction that conversion is a psychological force to be reckoned with. It must be recognized and understood by the churches; it points to realities of supreme import in religion; and it discloses subtleties in personality of particular interest to the psychologist.

Definition of conversion and its study. At first glance the term "conversion," as used in a religious sense, would seem to have a pretty clear meaning. Actually it is used very loosely to cover, not only the dramatic event of a sudden religious illumination, but also all gradations from this to the gradual experience of religious growth that we have described as associated with the religion of healthy-mindedness. The essential root meaning of the word suggests a complete and thorough change, so that strictly speaking conversion may be said to have occurred whenever this change is evident, whether it takes place over a long period of time or "in the twinkling of an eye." Yet it must not be thought that all conversions are profound, for many are exceedingly superficial.

However, there is a difference between gradual conversion and a process that is simply an unfolding of powers and capacities in a direction already evident. There is no "conversion" involved, for example, in the development of the intelligence or the emotions that is the normal process of a child's growth. Likewise in the growth of spiritual capacities envisioned by Christian Nurture there is no real conversion.

On the other hand, when a firmly held religious idea or allegiance is given up for a radically different one, or when an asocial, sour nature is sweetened through the influence of religion, we can call this change *conversion* whether it takes place suddenly or gradually. Isaiah's conversion and St. Paul's are described as being of the sudden type, while Augustine's seems to have displayed more gradualness, perhaps because the latter's superlative powers of introspection led him to see that the sudden dispelling of his conflict through the chance reading of a Bible passage was merely the end point of the long process that he describes to us.[3]

The confusion doubtless arises from the fact that probably there never was a dramatically sudden conversion that did not have some unconscious elements of growth and gradualness about it, often considerably more than the subject suspects. On the other hand, there very likely never has existed a spiritual progress of such ideal Bushnellian evenness that never a jerk or a jar disturbed its well-oiled consistency of growth. When we use the term conversion, then, we will have in mind the idea of change in direction. We cannot separate it from the concept of growth, for the two form a unified Gestalt. But the emphasis is on change, particularly of the sudden and radical type, though we by no means exclude the more gradual process providing it involves the all-important change in direction. This may involve change away from religion.

To sum up, we can define religious conversion as *that type of spiritual growth or development which involves an appreciable change of direction concerning religious ideas and behavior. Most clearly and typically it denotes an emotional episode of illuminating suddenness, which may be deep or superficial, though it may also come about by a more gradual process.*

It is obvious that if the term itself is uncertain, the study of the phenomenon is not apt to be characterized by the highest precision. As with all religious phenomena, one encounters the usual obstacles not only of definition but of controlling conditions of observation. Many conversions occur at revivals; but since revivalists are not prone to setting up booths with one-way screens through which the psychologists may observe what happens, and most are exceedingly chary of cooperating in any way, scholars must worry along with what methods they can devise.

The two methods traditionally most popular in the psychological study of religion have been the questionnaire and the study of docu-

[3] See his *Confessions*, especially Book 8. A fascinating collection of modern testimonies of conversion, most of them of the gradual type, is found in D. W. Soper's *These Found the Way*, for instance that of Joy David who turned from Judaism and Communism to Christianity, or Chad Walsh from atheism to the ministry.

mentary accounts, mostly autobiographical, of conversion experiences. These have been supplemented by interviews where possible, often as a means of checking on the questionnaire, and the results have been treated statistically or written up in the form of case histories. Since nearly all psychologists of religion have experienced to some degree the phenomenon they describe, it is quite likely that in many studies of conversion the participant-observer technique has been involved unconsciously and informally.[4] A unique attempt to substantiate the validity of the questionnaire is reported in George A. Coe's *The Spiritual Life*, where in one of the early studies he checked on the reports of his informants by using hypnosis.

While there have been a number of studies of conversion, especially around the turn of the century, few have been recent and there is space to mention only two. One of the earliest and in some ways the most thorough of these studies is that of Edwin Diller Starbuck, the results of which are now most available in his notable *The Psychology of Religion*, first published in 1899. Conversion loomed larger in the religious consciousness of that era than it does today, and attention to the subject comprises well over half of the book. Though the statistical treatment of the several hundred statements that Starbuck patiently studied was without the benefit of more modern conventions and methods, no student of conversion can afford to neglect Starbuck's findings, observations, and pregnant insights.

More recent and even more extensive is the aforementioned study of college men and women by Elmer T. Clark, *The Psychology of Religious Awakening*, published in 1929. Clark's study was done when liberal theology in Protestantism pretty well ruled the field, and conversion was considered not nearly so essential to salvation as it was in Starbuck's day. It is clear that while Clark does not distinguish between conversion and gradual growth in quite the way that we do, there is general agreement. He divides religious awakening into three categories: the classical or *definite crisis* type, represented by 6.7 per cent of his subjects; *emotional stimulus* (27.2 per cent) by which Clark denotes either a turning point with little emotion involved or

---

[4] All of the foregoing methods are illustrated in some way in my *The Oxford Group*. Though not with participant-observer intent, I had attended some of the meetings with sufficient sympathy to feel the attraction and value of the Moral Re-Armament movement. This experience stimulated my interest and later study. Many studies of conversion have begun in a similar way.

simply a point in normal growth which stands out for some reason in the subject's memory; and *gradual awakening,* 66.1 per cent. Since Clark allowed the subjects to define conversion for themselves, one cannot be certain how many of his latter two categories would qualify under our definition of conversion. Yet we can be sure that it still is a well-distinguished phenomenon which to some degree touches perhaps over a fourth of the better educated segment of our population. Doubtless we need further surveys using more up-to-date statistical tools and a more precise definition of conversion.

The process of conversion. When we come to describe our chief concern in this chapter, the crisis type of conversion, we note that, like other religious phenomenon, it is to a certain extent unique in each individual. But converted people in particular are apt to try to universalize their own cases and use them as touchstones by which to test the piety of others or to force their own experiences on them. The psychologist, with his fondness for searching out general laws, must beware of a similar fallacy. Nevertheless, provided it is well understood that we are flourishing a broad brush, we will venture to make a few generalizations.

Study of documentary records of conversions suggests that the convert passes through at least three fairly well-defined stages. The first is a period of unrest, the causes of which may or may not have definition in the consciousness of the subject. In the old-fashioned theology this usually made its appearance as a "conviction of sin," though Starbuck showed that even in his day this was not nearly so common as might be supposed.[5] Pratt demonstrates several cases, particularly some from India, where conviction of sin seemed to play a very minor role.[6] Yet inspection will show that the unrest proceeds from a sense of unworthiness or incompleteness closely resembling a sense of sin or associated with it in most cases. Occasionally there is merely a vague depression, perhaps springing from pathological sources. In the case of the conversion of Tolstoy, the sense of the meaninglessness of life was a potent factor.[7]

While this unrest may be in varying degrees artificially stimulated,

[5] *Op. cit.,* Chap. 5.
[6] *The Religious Consciousness,* Chap. 7.
[7] See his *My Confession* or Pratt, *The Religious Consciousness,* pp. 138 f.

it nevertheless often arises from a certain measure of insight into one's soul and a sense of the great gap that inevitably exists between a presumably religious person and the God he worships. The practice of some form of confession just prior to a conversion crisis is a re-action to this sense of unworthiness, and the resulting exteriorizing of it through confession goes far toward explaining the ultimate sense of joy and relief that ensues.[8]

The second stage is the conversion crisis itself. With or without what would appear to be an adequate stimulus, there is a sense of sudden and great illumination, a feeling that one's problems have been solved. The new life, which a moment before seemed so harsh a road of thorns, now seems easy. Augustine read the verse, "Not in rioting and drunkenness, not in chambering and wantonness, not in strife and envying; but put ye on the Lord Jesus Christ, and make not provision for the flesh, to fulfil the lusts thereof"; immediately his doubts vanished and the temptations with which he had been struggling for many long years no longer troubled him.

Often the individual is conscious as well of autonomic bodily changes that accompany the surge of emotion. This was the case with Frank Buchman who, recalling the moment of his conversion, de-scribed "a vibrant feeling up and down the spine, as if a strong current of life had suddenly been poured into me."[9] A somewhat parallel experience was that of John Wesley, who reported on the oc-casion of his conversion that he felt his heart "strangely warmed."[10]

While the first stage of the conversion process tends to be charac-terized by conflict and active mental struggle, the second stage is often ushered in by relaxation, or "surrender" as piety usually de-notes it. This surrender was a feature of Buchman's conversion, and helps to explain why the term was so often used in conversions he stimulated in others. In *Sartor Resartus* the "Everlasting No" cor-responds to the period of unrest, the "Center of Indifference" to the relaxation and cessation of active struggling, and the "Everlasting Yea" to the climactic stage.

[8] Note similarities in the theory and practice of modern psychotherapy, as in psychoanalysis or Rogers' client-centered therapy.
[9] *The Oxford Group*, p. 39.
[10] *The Heart of Wesley's Journal*, p. 43.

The third stage of conversion grows logically out of the second. As the emotion of the climax dies away, it leaves the convert with a sense of peace, release, and inner harmony. He feels at one with God, his sins forgiven, his problems solved, and his miseries fled away. John Milton's Satan said, "To be weak is miserable." This home truth of psychology helps to explain the sweetness of the post-climax stage, for the newly converted feels strong enough to attack any spiritual mountain. Says Carlyle's *alter ego*, Teufelsdröckh, "And as I so thought, there rushed like a stream of fire over my whole soul; and I shook base Fear away from me forever. I was strong, of unknown strength; a spirit, almost a god."

While these three stages comprise the essence of the psychological process, another stage is necessary if the experience is to have any permanence. This is the concrete expression of the conversion. It is for the lack of this factor that many conversions made by traveling evangelists do not last. They are not followed up either by the individual himself or by an effective organization to provide opportunity for this expression. A large share of the credit for the success of the preaching of John Wesley, an itinerant if there ever were one, belongs to his genius in organizing Methodist societies which enforced spiritual discipline for his converts. This included an iron-clad rule for rising at five in the morning for prayers and preaching! [11] And it is quite appropriate that Isaiah ends the account of his conversion with the words, "Here am I; send me." [12]

Curiously enough this stage may even *precede* the crisis, when it doubtless plays an important part in bringing the crisis about. When Wesley was in his stage of uncertainty and doubt he questioned whether, not being sure of his own faith, he should preach. With practical wisdom his mentor replied, "Preach faith till you have it, and then, because you have it, you will preach faith." [13] When a neophyte applies to Alcoholics Anonymous and is told he must rely on a Power higher than himself for strength, he often objects that he believes in no Higher Power. The reply is that he must behave

[11] See *op. cit.*, p. 451 and *passim* for accounts of this and other facts about the societies.
[12] Isaiah 6:8.
[13] *Op. cit.*, p. 36.

as if there were a Higher Power. This frequently results in what is in effect a true conversion in which, whether by slow process or swift, atheists and agnostics often arrive at a belief in God.

The reader may verify the foregoing description by reference to various cases.[14] Isaiah's account of his conversion—quoted at the beginning of this chapter—brief though it is, suggests all four of the stages we have described. We will here present at some length two cases. The first is the case of Thomas Carlyle, whose mouthpiece, Teufelsdröckh, with splendid verbosity describes the inner experience that led him from the "Everlasting No," his period of doubt and trial, through the "Center of Indifference" to his final conversion in the "Everlasting Yea."

Carlyle's spiritual difficulties, as we have indicated in Chapter 6, arose from conflicts between his early religious beliefs and the skepticism he acquired at Edinburgh University. There were also uncertainties about his life work and some pathological elements besides, which played upon and accentuated his miseries. Previous references to Carlyle will have supplied the reader with some of the background of his life. The quotations are taken from the chapters "The Everlasting No" and "The Everlasting Yea" respectively.

The speculative Mystery of Life grew ever more mysterious to me; neither in the practical mystery had I made the slightest progress, but been everywhere buffeted, foiled and contemptuously cast-out. A feeble unit in the middle of a threatening Infinitude, I seemed to have nothing given to me but eyes, wherein to discern my own wretchedness. Invisible yet impenetrable walls, as of Enchantment, divided me from all living: was there in the wide world, any true bosom I could press trustfully to mine? O Heaven, No, there was none! I kept a lock upon my lips: why should I speak with that shifting variety of so-called friends, in whose withered, vain, and too-hungry souls Friendship was but an incredible tradition? . . . Now, when I look back, it was a strange isolation I then lived in. The men and women around me, even speaking with me, were but Figures; I had, practically, forgotten that they were alive, that they were not merely automatic. In midst of their crowded streets and assemblages, I walked solitary; and (except as it was my own heart, not another's, that I kept devouring) savage also, as the tiger in his jungle.

[14] The chapters on conversion in James and Pratt include very full case material.

Some comfort it would have been could I, like Faust, have fancied myself tempted and tormented of the Devil; for a Hell, as I imagine, without Life, though only diabolic Life, were more frightful: but in our age of Down-pulling and Disbelief, the very Devil has been pulled down, you cannot so much as believe in a Devil. To me, the Universe was all void of Life, of Purpose, of Volition, even of Hostility: it was one huge, dead, immeasurable Steam-engine, rolling on, in its dead indifference to grind me limb from limb. O, the vast, gloomy, solitary Golgotha, and Mill of Death! Why was the Living banished thither companionless, conscious? Why, if there is no Devil; nay, unless the Devil is your God? . . .

Thus had the EVERLASTING NO . . . pealed authoritatively through all the recesses of my Being, of my Me. . . . "Behold, thou are fatherless, outcast, and the Universe is mine (the Devil's)! . . ."

In reaction to this exquisite suffering, Teufelsdröckh summons up enough healthy-mindedness to confront himself with the fact that whatever catastrophe he fears is at least endurable, and at the end of the chapter describes a kind of preliminary conversion in which he musters enough courage to face the fate in store for him. This leads him to the "Center of Indifference," which is easily recognized as the illustration of the relaxation of active striving or the "surrender," though not in the usual religious sense. The transition and crisis, experienced as he reposed on a high hilltop, he describes as follows:

Here, then, as I lay in that CENTER OF INDIFFERENCE; cast, doubtless by benignant upper Influence, into a healing sleep, the heavy dreams rolled gradually away, and I awoke to a new Heaven and a new Earth. The first preliminary moral Act, Annihilation of Self, had been happily accomplished; and my mind's eyes were now unsealed, and its hands ungyved. . . .

Beautiful it was to sit there, as in my skyey Tent, musing and meditating; on the high table-land in front of the Mountains. . . . And then to fancy . . . the straw-roofed Cottages, wherein stood many a Mother baking bread, with her children round her:—all hidden and protectingly folded-up in the valley-folds; yet there and alive, as sure as if I beheld them. . . .—If in my Wayfarings, I had learned to look into the business of the World in its details, here perhaps was the place for combining it into general propositions, and deducing inferences therefrom.

Often also could I see the black Tempest marching in anger through the Distance: round some Schreckhorn, as yet grim-blue, would the eddying vapour gather, and there tumultuously eddy, and flow down like a mad witch's hair; till, after a space, it vanished, and, in the clear sunbeam, your Schreckhorn stood smiling grim-white, for the vapour had held snow. How thou fermentest and elaboratest, in thy great fermenting-vat and laboratory of an atmosphere, of a World, O Nature!— Or what is Nature? Ha! why do I not name thee God? O heavens, is it, in very deed HE, then, that ever speaks through thee; that lives and loves in thee, that lives and loves in me?

Fore-shadows, call them rather fore-splendours, of that Truth, and Beginning of Truths, fell mysteriously over my soul. Sweeter than Day-spring to the Ship-wrecked in Nova Zembla; ah, like the mother's voice to her little child that strays bewildered, weeping, in unknown tumults; like soft streamings of celestial music to my too-exasperated heart, came that Evangel. The Universe is not dead and demoniacal, a charnel-house with spectres; but godlike, and my Father's. . . .

I see a glimpse of it! . . . there is in man a HIGHER than Love of Happiness, and instead thereof find Blessedness! Was it not to preach forth this same HIGHER that sages and martyrs, the Poet and the Priest, in all times, have spoken and suffered; bearing testimony, through life and through death, of the Godlike that is in Man, and how in the Godlike only has he Strength and Freedom? Which God-inspired doctrine art thou also honoured to be taught; O Heavens! and broken with manifold merciful Afflictions, even until thou become contrite, and learn it! O, thank thy Destiny for these; thankfully bear what yet remain: thou hadst need of them; the Self in thee needed to be annihilated. By benignant fever-paroxysms is Life rooting out the deep-seated chronic Disease, and triumphs over Death. On the roaring billows of Time, thou art not engulfed, but borne aloft into the azure of Eternity. Love not Pleasure; love God. This is the EVERLASTING YEA, wherein all contradiction is solved: wherein whoso walks and works, it is well with him.

The foregoing will give the reader a glimpse of the inner forces at work in Carlyle's conversion as well as a hint of the philosophy of life which, though at times imperfectly executed, found expression in the literary activity that left many volumes to posterity. The experience was highly original and unique, yet at the same time it demonstrates our generalized stages of conversion.

We will add another, more modern and more pedestrian, case, from the author's collection of conversions effected in the early stages of the Moral Re-Armament movement. The subject supplied the information by filling out a questionnaire some fifteen years after the event.

Samuel Hoffman was brought up in a religious family of means. His mother was strongly religious, the other members of the family not so much so, but they were active in altruistic enterprise. He was sent to a well-known church preparatory school and to a large and respected New England university. Indistinguishable from many other youths with a similar background, his personality was pleasant but not positive or effective. His church attendance was limited pretty much to what was prescribed by academic requirements at his school except for "a curious or hungry visit to Church once in a while." After college he went into business, perhaps because it seemed the thing to do, yet with little enthusiasm and feeling divided, self-centered, and ineffective. His job gave him a moderate living.

Shortly after this he came in contact with Moral Re-Armament in the period when it was known as the Oxford Group or Buchmanism. Here he found an answer to his unrest in an experience of conversion in which he describes himself as definitely "changed." Of the religious reality of the experience he has no doubt. He says, "Nothing else could have done the same in me—or through me, in subsequent years. It gave direction, purpose; showed me The One Thing worth giving your life for." The experience he felt was beneficial in every way. It gave new awareness of the meaning and value of life, a new direction for energies and a zest for living. His attitude toward life was changed constructively, and he believes that what he experienced is "the one thing most needed by individuals and the world."

It seems clear that the experience made him a much more dynamic person. For the first time he realized that he had latent powers for leadership and "in personal interviews lives were changed or helped." He rejoiced in finding himself "an influence for good instead of just a 'nice fellow.'"

He does not make clear that the movement added anything to his intellectual equipment as such, but indicates that the experience indirectly caused him to do a great deal of thinking and eventually led to his entering a theological seminary. He describes the experience as "naturally and rightly attended with some emotion" but hastens to add to this comment that he has been a far less emotional person ever since.

Nothing in previous church or school training had led him to expect a conversion; this he thought of as something that happened only in rescue missions until his reading of Begbie's *More Twice-Born Men* suggested its possibility for him. For thirteen years he was an active worker in the Oxford Group, but he withdrew about the time that its Moral Re-Armament phase began, since he believed that it had departed too much from its earlier Christ-centered program. On the other hand he acknowledges his own great debt to it and wishes that the conversion experience which it features were the natural and expected thing for upper class Americans. He has now been for a number of years a loyal clergyman in the Protestant Episcopal church.[15]

This case illustrates particularly clearly the sense of power and personality integration which frequently follows a conversion experience. Also it is noteworthy that the implications were followed up. The thirteen years of active work with the movement and Hoffman's vocation as a minister were doubtless powerful factors in consolidating the newly formed habits and attitudes. Not all the cases from this movement, it should be pointed out, have similarly happy results, though many do. Of the negative cases in our study, a much smaller proportion had had an extended period of active service with the movement.

It is necessary in the psychological study of conversion that one divest his mind of the customary pious belief that God directly engineers the change in much the same way that a magician on the stage might change a rabbit into an elephant. And to those orthodox souls disposed to hold up their hands in horror at the idea of divesting the experience of all spiritual significance by leaving God out, we must reply that the psychologist is not competent to define the place of God in the transaction. The spiritual significance comes not from the psychological experience but the interpretation of it. The idea that God's influence involves direct intervention in normal psychological processes of a push-button nature is simply an arrogation by the theologian of the right to describe just how God works. This is the fallacy committed by the comforters in the Book of Job. It will be recalled that the conclusion of this great spiritual work is that God's ways with man are inscrutable. Hence it is hardly likely that the finite psychologist with merely human powers of comprehension will be able to pronounce on the ways of an infinite God

---

[15] Adapted from *The Oxford Group*, pp. 174–176. The name is a pseudonym and the facts have been altered in non-significant ways to preserve anonymity. Other cases with varying outcomes will be found in Part 3 of the same volume.

beyond what he is able to observe. The psychologist, *as a psychologist*, can neither include nor exclude the influence of God in the conversion process.

This being the case, it is pertinent to observe that the mechanics of conversion are found to operate not only in the interests of religion but also in other directions, and even sometimes *against* the interests of religion. For example Pratt, in *The Religious Consciousness*, cites the "counter-conversion" of the Italian philosopher and priest Robert Ardigo.[16] Ardigo had devoted years of intellectual labor to defending his faith against the Protestants, and especially against the scientific positivism of his day. What was his surprise one day to awake suddenly to the realization that he was a Positivist!

> The new system I found, to my very great amazement, already complete, and unshakably settled in my mind. At that moment I had observed, as I sat under a shrub in the garden which I had laid out near my canonical residence, how my last reflections had snapped the last thread that still held me bound to belief. Now it suddenly came to me, as though I had never in my life believed, and had never done otherwise than study, to develop the purely scientific tendency in myself. This arose, as I believe, out of the zeal with which I had sought to experience as far as possible all the conflicting grounds of religion, to be able to believe on good security, and to defend my belief against all attacks.

His new position he held to with great steadfastness until the end of his days.

Allport, in a discussion of sudden reorientation, relates the case of an almost hopeless college student in an English class, who was customarily and monotonously berated by his instructor for his poor work. Finally, during an altercation in which the youth declared he would *never* like English, the harried instructor retorted, "It isn't English I'm talking about at the moment, it's your life." The thrust struck home with the result that the youth totally revised his attitudes and study habits almost on the spot. He eventually made Phi Beta Kappa and became an English teacher![17]

[16] Pp. 126–127.
[17] *Personality*, pp. 207–212. A similar discussion and examples will be found in Starbuck, Chap. 11.

It should also be pointed out that conversion experiences may be influenced by abnormal factors and may even be wholly abnormal in their significance.[18] Since conversion is so often, or perhaps always, associated with conflict, it would be strange if neuroses or even more serious disturbances were not often involved. Some cases are normal, some borderline, and some wholly pathological. But, as James points out, this has little to do with the spiritual significance of the experience, which must be judged by its fruits. He points out that both John Bunyan and George Fox were unstable personalities, yet their religious influence was creative and wholesome. We have noted also that Boisen has found religious significance in some cases of catatonic schizophrenia.

We must, then, regard religious conversion, psychologically considered, as a special case of a wider psychological category. Consequently it is our business to approach it in the same way that we would study similar phenomena of the sudden reorientation of personality.

FACTORS OPERATING IN CONVERSION

Conflict. The most basic psychological element in conversion would appear to be conflict, or at any rate tension, which most frequently is associated with conflict. It is the striving for something one cannot attain, or the attraction of two incompatible ways of life, as in the case of St. Augustine. Most characteristically there is the conscious espousal of unattainable religious ideals. There is always a certain amount of this within any religious person. All of us know what we *ought* to do, but too often we don't do it. "For what I would, that do I not," said St. Paul, "but what I hate, that do I." [19] But with the individual headed for a conversion, the tension builds up partly consciously, but, more importantly, unconsciously, until it reaches a considerable pitch.

Psychologically it is the recognition of the inner unrest due to this tension that constitutes what is often theologically termed "conviction of sin." While conscious recognition of this does not always involve conversion, nevertheless it tends to make it possible in the

[18] See Starbuck, Chap. 13, for a full discussion.
[19] Romans 7:15.

confrontation by the individual of his choice. The decision has been evaded and compromised and shoved off into a corner, perhaps for many years. The willingness to make the decision allows the repressed clash of issues to come to the surface to be met, and the fact that so much is there that never has been consciously known surprises the person. Not the least of the surprise is the discovery of how easy most problems become when they are resolutely faced and their implications clearly seen. The convert, of course, is usually not a psychologically sophisticated person, and this sudden seemingly mysterious influx of power to solve his problems is often ascribed to the immediate miraculous intervention of God.[20]

And so we may note that, the greater the tension, and the larger its proportion lying in the unconscious, the stronger the likelihood that a sudden transformation of personality may take place. This, of course, confirms a principle which Freud demonstrated in many of his cases without any reference to religion.[21] But the demands of religion are so radically at variance with the everyday habits of the average person, and are also so deeply ingrained in the individual conscience, that tension in this area may become extraordinarily poignant. Hence the dramatic and astonishing nature of the release when defenses yield and the whole of the half-buried conflict is opened to the light of day. We may consider conflict, then, the background out of which conversion may develop.

Contact with religious tradition. The typical revivalist, with that dramatic flair that is part of the stock-in-trade of the species, makes much of the miraculous nature of conversion by emphasizing that it may occur "in the twinkling of an eye." Indeed we have demonstrated that this is true so far as the conscious crisis of many conversions is concerned. But no conversion ever occurred without a history, and a most important consideration in this history is what the

[20] The psychologist may point out these facts without denying God. He is simply indicating that the process is considerably more complicated than the believer is apt to think. God stands much farther back in the process than immediate intervention. A believing psychologist may hold that all phenomena are the expression of the Creator and intend to learn psychologically as much about His ways as he can, even though with no chance of plumbing all the depths of Infinite Mystery.

[21] See, for example, Freud's lectures in Van Teslaar's *An Outline of Psychoanalysis*, or other volumes of his introductory lectures.

influences were. Ordinarily the crucial factor is family training in religion, the significance of which we have outlined in Chapter 4. Though many of the cases in the writer's study of the Oxford Group were very lukewarm or even agnostic about their religion just prior to their conversion, there was not a single person involved who had not been brought up in a religious family. In *The Confessions* of St. Augustine we note that though his father was not religious, he owed much to his Christian mother, Monica, while we have already remarked the religious influence of early life to which Carlyle testified.

But, though the most common and usually the most profound influence on the average convert, the family is not the only agent of tradition. Though much less potent, the Church also plays its part, yet most often through its human representatives. Another's example of devotion to religion may be a crucial factor, particularly as a stimulus which initiates the growth of ideas which may lead to conflict and tension. It is difficult for a person with a belief in his own way of life not to be impressed by the example of someone sincerely suffering for a belief entirely different. It seems quite clear that the conversion of St. Paul had its roots not only in his strict training in religion but very importantly in the spectacle of the martyrdom of Stephen, to which Paul often made reference.

Suggestion and imitation. This last observation points to the importance of suggestion and imitation in many cases of conversion. In some cases of course there is little but imitation involved. If there is ever a case of skim milk masquerading as cream it is when, in an atmosphere of emotionalism, penitents by the dozen hit the revivalistic trail. Such people may consider themselves "converted" even to the end of their days; but, though there are exceptions, studies of this type of conversion have shown very little permanent behavioral evidence of personality change, unless one is satisfied to consider mere church attendance and Bible reading profound changes. This was the conclusion reached in an investigation of 73 converts made during revivals in Boston from 1948 to 1950.[22] It is this brand of conversion that brings the term into disrepute.

Yet imitation and suggestion have a legitimate part to play in

[22] P. A. Sorokin, *The Ways and Power of Love*, p. 180.

conversion, as they do in all of life. They are not only part of the cement which holds social groups together but stimuli to new experience as well. The possibility of conversion may be suggested to those who need it as well as to those who do not. Moral Re-Armament makes it a practice to have converts openly witness to what "surrender" and a "changed life" have done for them,[23] thus suggesting it to others. Many of these undergo lasting and beneficial personality change. Documentary evidence of the suggestibility of those who report themselves converted, whether with or without definite personality benefit, is found in *The Spiritual Life* by George A. Coe.[24] Of a population of 77 that he studied, 24 had undergone striking religious transformations. This group, according to testimony of friends as well as corroboration by hypnotic test, was more suggestible than those who had not had conversions of the crisis type.

Emotion. In the same study Coe made a comparison of temperaments and found that the converted group tended toward the category where "sensibility," or emotion, is predominant. Since Coe's study was finished before the turn of the century, it is not necessarily certain that the experiences he studied would be typical of conversions today. At the time, revivals were very frequent and great pressure was brought on members of several important denominations to undergo conversion as an evidence of salvation. Under these conditions we might expect suggestible and emotional natures to be those who succumbed. Consequently we must be cautious in accepting Coe's findings.

Nevertheless emotion of some sort is prominent as an almost invariable concomitant of religious conversion and is not merely confined to the revivalistic brand. Even where it is not explicitly described, the tone of the report of the experience betrays the emotional charge. This is seen in Carlyle's description of his "Everlasting Yea" experience.

It is for this reason that popular evangelists make emotional appeals combined with suggestion which are pretty patent to anyone who attends such a service in a detached and critical frame of mind. Gospel music of a soul-stirring nature is part of the formula at certain

[23] *The Oxford Group.* See Chap. 2.
[24] P. 120 ff.

points, while soft, sentimental music of a tears-provoking band is the prescription when the sinners are asked to come forward. Near-hypnotic and sometimes even dishonest suggestion has been known to be used on occasions to maintain the emotion and start the trek to the mourners' bench. Coe tells of one evangelistic virtuoso who, with no one at all on the way, bawled out, "See them coming! See them coming!" and so started the parade.[25]

Yet sometimes, perhaps because the individual is otherwise ready for the experience, or perhaps because it is followed up more skill-fully, the crass arousal of emotion through deliberate suggestion may lead to genuine and profound religious experience. Frank Buch-man is one of the most effective revivalists of the present day, yet he has not been averse to the pretty obvious stimulation of a sense of conviction of sin as a preliminary to confession and the conversion crisis. In his earlier days he could usually rely on drinking, smoking, or particularly sex among college youth as a fertile ground for such an arousal. However, now and then he was trepanned by happening on someone so conventionally "good" that the master was forced to resort to considerable manipulation before a suitable "sin" was uncovered. The following case was one of his earliest women con-verts, which perhaps explains an ineptitude unusual for him. But the case is given to demonstrate our point that even artificial manipu-lation, though hardly to be recommended, may not be without its benefits, particularly if applied by an evangelist with real concern for the individual.

Mrs. Ross Danforth was attending college about the year 1922 when Dr. Buchman, after many years of evangelistic work almost exclusively devoted to men, first began to interest himself in the conversion of women as well. Mrs. Danforth had been well brought up in a family of not more than nominal religious interests and had none of the bad habits that Buchman could usually rely on in men to lead to a sense of sin. This resulted in using attendance at a dance to serve the purpose.

She describes her experience as follows: "His attempt to convince me of the error of my ways (which chiefly consisted of my having gone tea-dancing at the Copley-Plaza during Christmas vacation) ended in nervous shock and illness for me and great disapproval and concern on the part of several professors. I might add two things:—Frank was not

[25] *Ibid.*, p. 145.

nearly so narrow as time went on and was infinitely thoughtful with most of us and truly kind—and I, in spite of the nervous upset, continued to be grateful to him and loyal for many years. In the three years spent at college it was Frank who gave me that which was most real and vital, and for which I had the deepest need.

"I feel the experiences to have been genuine although influenced by strong emotion. I think they had a direct relation to God and that the fellowship of the Group stimulated a growth that would have been more gradual and far less rich otherwise. It gave me a rigorous training in self-discipline, it gave entrance to a deeper Christian fellowship than I have ever found since, it gave color and glow and a sense of fine adventure to life."

This conversion led Mrs. Danforth to be active in the movement for the following six years. Then, because she sensed that Christianity could be expressed in other ways, and after her marriage to a fine Christian clergyman, who was not a member of the movement, she withdrew. However, despite the original nervous collapse, she testifies to the lasting positive benefit of the total experience. Like others, she deeply wishes that the Christian Church were more conscious of the values of this type of emphasis.[26]

Adolescence. The first great student of the psychology of adolescence, G. Stanley Hall, was much ridiculed in 1881 when in a public lecture in Boston he pointed out that this was the most characteristic age for conversions. Since then the researches of many students have confirmed this judgment, and Starbuck's figures indicate the typical age for the conversion of males to be 16.4 and for females 14.8.[27] Other studies agree in general with Starbuck that the common age for men is somewhere around the sixteenth year, with the occurrence of conversion in women about two years earlier.[28]

It may be noteworthy that there is also about a two-year difference in the onset of puberty between boys and girls, with the latter maturing sooner. At any rate there has been much speculation among psychologists of religion as to whether puberty was a significant factor in the stimulation of conversion. But Starbuck found cases where conversion was reported five years *before* the onset of puberty, and a considerably larger number occurring several years *after* it.[29] Tol-

[26] Adapted from my *The Oxford Group*, pp. 208–210.
[27] Hall, *Adolescence*, pp. 11, 292; Starbuck, *op. cit.*, p. 204.
[28] For instance, E. T. Clark, *op. cit.*, Chap. 3.
[29] *Op. cit.*, p. 44.

stoy's conversion occurred when he was about fifty, while the author found a member of Moral Re-Armament, a clergyman, who reported conversion when nearly sixty.[30] Though conversion is obviously more commonly a phenomenon of youth, it can be confined within no certain limits. If puberty is a causal factor it does not operate in all cases, though in some it may well help to put in motion growth experiences that eventuate in conversion.

E. T. Clark points out that when conversion occurs by the more gradual process the "awakening," or the beginning of a more lively sense of the values of religion, occurs earlier by three or more years than with the crisis type.[31] He suggests that this may be explained by the fact that no hindrance is placed in the way of the normal unfolding of the religious powers. On the other hand, when impediments intervene and blockages are set up, then an emotional disturbance is necessary to release the pressures of growth. Whether any strict analogy can be drawn between the process of religious growth and the developing flower is extremely doubtful, and, if pushed to the wall, most religious educators would admit this; nevertheless this figure of speech is so common among those who see Christian Nurture as the best and only way for all, that it is well to inquire whether some loose thinking is not involved. The use of this figure begs the question of whether there might be some values in sudden conversion over gradual awakening. It pre-judges the issue and stacks the cards in favor of what is assumed to be the normal process of religious growth. We will return to this and kindred questions later in the chapter.

Other factors operating during adolescence that help to explain why it so often is the age of conversion include all of the new powers accompanying the early bloom of maturity, such as the new perceptions of intelligence, the sensitivities arising from surging emotions, the chafing urge to be up and about the work of grown-ups, the nudging and the kicking about that the body receives from newly released hormones, the strangely new form and texture of the body with its assurance of new strength and powers, and the strange clearness of sight about things moral and spiritual that sometimes comes to these adventurers into a new land. Then there are the

[30] *Op. cit.*, pp. 222–224, the case of the Rev. Henry Sampson.
[31] *Op. cit.*, p. 65.

paradoxical confusions that come at other times and lead to the term "storm and stress," which sages so often use to describe the age. We have described these factors in Chapter 5 and have not the space to analyze in detail their exact relationships. We merely have said enough to hint at the reason why adolescence and conversion are so closely associated.

Theology. If there were any evidence needed to refute the idea that conversion is a purely spontaneous affair mediated *in toto* by the Grace of God and subject to His initiative, this will be found in the studies showing a relationship between the incidence of the experience and the theological ideas held by the individual. If conversion is suggested or required by the Church, the individual is much more likely to undergo an experience that he will at least report as conversion. This helps to explain why conversion was so much more common during the last century than it is today. The stern theology of the Calvinists and the insistence of the Methodists on an experience of justification patterned on the conversion of John Wesley were important factors in stimulating conversion.

E. T. Clark found that whereas only 2.2 per cent of 133 respondents who belonged to the sacramental churches where Confirmation was the rule reported conversion experiences, 34.6 per cent of 176 who had been brought up on the stern theology reported it.[32] Many of these latter were older people whose upbringing extended back to the time when the churches were benighted, and had not been freed by the enlightened doctrines of Christian Nurture and liberalism. Typical of the reports by which such background was evaluated was that of the respondent who spoke of remembering teachings about

Sin, its loathsome effects; hell and the damned; punishment forever and ever, if not converted, if converted and faithful to the end happiness and contentment forever.[33]

Prudent persons hearing and believing such horrendous and minatory ideas bestirred themselves to see whether they could not bring themselves to emotional experiences which would constitute

[32] *Op. cit.*, pp. 86–87, and all of Chap. 4.
[33] *Ibid.*, p. 85.

a reasonable facsimile of what they had observed in others as conversion. This would sometimes be the real thing and sometimes not, as converts often observed for themselves when a second or a third conversion was much more thorough than the first.

On the other hand a person taught to rely on the Sacraments could much more easily be satisfied by going through the sacramental type of religious motion. Even the mystics complain of periods of spiritual "dryness." There is no sacramentalist who has not had at least some approximation to this experience and so knows what we are talking about. When Confirmation is accompanied by emotionally toned religious experience, this is much more likely to be described as "religious awakening" or simply "religious emotion" than "conversion." Since it is usually a much milder occurrence it fits in much better with the gradual type of growth and is not often accompanied by those dramatic transformations of character that are much more apt to accompany a crisis conversion.

The will. The problem of the freedom of the will can hardly be described as settled. Both among psychologists and theologians there are differences of opinion, and it may seem that to assume such freedom will lead the psychologist onto marshy ground. But the common-sense belief most generally held is that the will is a reality. It would certainly *appear* to play its part in certain conversions.

William James pointed out in a famous essay that belief was often the product of the will to believe. If this is true of belief it is also true of conversion. Some conversions come about largely through the intention to be converted, or an active struggling toward some further goal that may involve conversion. We can see this element at work in Carlyle, for a large part of his transformation involved his determination to seek the truth, regardless of what havoc it might play with comforting religious beliefs. And so he makes Teufelsdröckh say,

One circumstance I note . . . after all the nameless woe that Inquiry, which for me, what it is not always, was genuine Love of Truth, had wrought me, I nevertheless still loved Truth, and would bate no jot of my allegiance to her. "Truth!" I cried, "though the Heavens crush me for following her: no Falsehood! though a whole celestial Lubberland were the price of Apostasy." [34]

We know that it was not *merely* this active struggling that led Teufelsdröckh to the Everlasting Yea, but that the relaxation of the Center of Indifference had an important part to play as well. So, in more orthodox conversions, periods of effort culminate in "surrender," which serves the same psychological purpose. And so there are people whose passion it is to make their lives true, just, pure, lovely, and of good report, and yet who know that they are not any of these things. But the striving toward that goal may one day give way to a conversion experience in which they surrender their own desires, and, even if they cannot attain perfection, they nevertheless in seemingly miraculous ways acquire strength to achieve a larger measure of it than ever before. The surrender does not mean abdicating the will, but rather a narrow and selfish conception of it.

Following Starbuck, James distinguishes two types of conversion, the *volitional* and *self-surrender*.[35] The former is largely identified with gradual growth, since growth through active striving is more apt to be slow and logical; while the latter is characterized by stress and emotion. Yet the prominence of the emotional factor often hides from the subject himself as well as from observers the part played by will. The crisis, unless it be superficial indeed, is likely to be merely the climax of many years of painful conflict and effortful straining toward a goal. Their effects are registered in the unconscious, where they are bottled up, so to speak, and perhaps deliberately neglected, as in the case of Ardigo. Yet they are indispensable to the final result, no matter how much emotion is expended at the moment of change.[36]

THEORY OF CONVERSION

If conversion is a rare phenomenon today as compared to the past, one may question why we spend so much time over it. Is it not old-fashioned and pretty much outworn in our enlightened day, a

[34] *Sartor Resartus*, p. 124.
[35] *Varieties*, p. 202.
[36] For more extended discussion see *op. cit.*: James, Lecture 9; Starbuck, Chap. 8; and Pratt, Chap 8, also the dissertation by Joseph Havens.

theological curio and a psychological antique? One answer is that it is not outworn, but is still going on today, as Moral Re-Armament, Alcoholics Anonymous, and other religious movements show. But a more pertinent answer is that the study of conversion helps to throw light on the dynamics of the religious life as well as on personality dynamics in general. Whatever will help him to understand the workings of the human personality is of interest to the psychologist.

One question is whether the experience of conversion is the expression of healthy-mindedness or of the sick soul. One's immediate reaction is that of course, with the emphasis on sin that usually accompanies it and the suffering that comes from the dividedness of mind that usually precedes it, conversion is a phenomenon of the sick soul. There is no denying that in *conversion itself* this is the case.

But it may be simply a way-station on the journey of a divided spirit toward a healthy-minded religious integration. While the first stage of the conversion involves suffering, the crisis brings on a feeling of peace, joy, and strength. Carlyle was a typically sick soul in his Everlasting No phase but a much happier, better-adjusted person in the Everlasting Yea stage. Yet he could never, even at his best, be described as healthy-minded, and like Tolstoy, was beset with moods and troubled thoughts to the end of his days. His conversion simply made him *more* healthy-minded than he had been before.

But there are those for whom conversion is simply a temporary cloud in the sunny sky of their religious lives. Despite its emphasis on conviction of sin and conversion, the Moral Re-Armament movement fits better into the category of healthy-mindedness than of suffering as we have pointed out in a previous chapter. Its uncomplicated solutions for the problems of life, the almost professional good fellowship practiced by its leaders, and the activism of its program are all factors that turn the conversion process into what most of its adherents experience as a good time. It is true that Moral Re-Armament talks much about sin and recognizes its reality, but the conviction of sin that characterizes most of the experiences of "change" constitutes merely a kind of necessary initiation ceremony to a cheerful and sometimes even hilarious life of spiritual effectiveness. One of the converts commented on his conversion, saying that it came "through Buchman's suggestion. I felt I must need it if he said so. I was extremely happy until he pointed out to me how wretched I was." Apparently for this individual conviction of sin was merely an isolated dark spot imposed upon a spirit predominantly healthy-minded. Conversion led to happy adventures of evangelism and spiritual good fellowship.

But assuming that the soil in which conversion grows is likely, in the more genuine cases, to be suffering, rather than good humor and lightness of heart, we may well ask whether this suffering is necessary or wholesome. Does crisis conversion accomplish anything for the individual or for religion that gradual growth might not? This is a difficult question and one on which it would seem that we will get no certain light. Perhaps an objective study may one day be devised to answer this question, which is of such great importance to religious education. In the meantime we are forced to go on as we have in the past with the problem a matter of intense controversy, to which we will now proceed to add some matter on our own account.

At the beginning we must admit that the average, revivalist-stimulated, highly emotional type of conversion is not impressive. What with the catchy tunes of the gospel hymn, the trumpets, the rapid-fire warnings of destruction given out by the excited evangelist, and the mass influence of hysterical suggestion, it is hard to imagine that lasting good may result. If one sees this sort of thing as a kind of escape from the drabness of reality, there may be little harm in it except that some people may become scornful of all religion as the result of an experience of this variety. We have seen that tangible benefits in the form of overt personality change are apt to be meager.

But the trouble with statistical surveys of conversion by means of questionnaires, which ask whether the individual has been converted, is that in most analyses little distinction is made between the conversion that has occurred on the spur of the moment in the gospel tent and that which is the culmination of years of inward struggle. Even the individual himself seldom has great insight into the meaning of the conversion he reports. It may have been merely the emotional equivalent of a visit to the movies, and yet, because of the prestige that conversion brings in his religious community, he maintains its genuineness. This should hardly be classified with religion of the primary type, and yet in statistics it would be lumped with experiences of profound influence in changing personality. It is for this reason that the case study is so necessary in investigations of conversion as a means of deepening the psychologist's understanding of the meaning of the varying experiences undergoing survey.

In a large population of individuals who say they have been converted there is likely to be a very high proportion whose conversions have been of this superficial variety. Yet the significance for religion lies not in these people, but in the few for whom conversion has been a vital experience. For it is from these few that religious truth may come, and it is from them that the ranks of religious leaders are replenished. Our study of the Oxford Group showed that many of the young men converted by the Group afterward entered the ministry, and some of them are now among the leaders in American religious life. E. T. Clark's study showed that a much higher percentage of young preachers and missionaries reported definite crisis awakening than did those in his sampling not in religious work.[37]

Furthermore we note the rather high proportion of the saints and prophets and religious leaders in history whose mission among men and whose effectiveness was derived from a crisis experience of some kind. Isaiah, Paul, St. Augustine, Socrates, Mohammed, Buddha, Luther, Ignatius Loyola, and Tolstoy are merely a few of those whose development was marked by periods of sudden enlightenment. If gradual awakening is in every respect to be desired, it is a little hard to explain this seemingly high incidence of crisis among the spiritual *élite*.

We have no rigorous data with which to support most of our speculations, but it would seem that one of the benefits of the experience is the tension involved. We do not usually think of tension as psychologically welcome, because the term has come to connote the

----

[37] *Op. cit.*, pp. 112–115. His figures are a little confusing, for p. 115 appears to show 70.6 per cent of the religious workers reporting crisis, while on p. 113 only 17.7 per cent are so listed. This compares with 6.7 per cent crisis in his population of 2,174 cases including religious workers. If, by his use of figures on p. 47, we subtract the religious workers from the total group we find that only 45, or 2.8 per cent non-religious workers reported crisis conversion. This means that even if the lower percentage of 17.7 crisis is used, crisis conversion is more than six times as prevalent among religious workers than among those who are not. These figures should give some pause to advocates of gradual growth who at the same time are concerned about the recruitment of religious workers.

undesirable. But without some tension nothing would be accomplished, and the tension that may be an uncomfortable burden to the individual may also be the means of his achieving heights of which he had never dreamed. The conflict of the divided self, poignant and troublesome to the sick souls as it may be, may involve a kind of toning up of the psychological system so that an emotional charge is available for spiritual achievement.

The emotional discharge, so much deplored by the average educated observer, seems to be the instrument of effecting a change in personality impossible through less drastic and by more gradual means. This does not mean that emotion alone is sufficient. That is why the isolated emotional indulgence of the gospel tent accomplishes so little. The effective crisis is simply the climax of a process that has been building up for some time, and its final expression depends on intellectual elements previously absorbed. Psychotherapists are aware of the fact that a single emotional "trauma" or shock may condition an individual for life. As the result of one episode he may learn to fear closed spaces, sex, the sound of bells, or some other stimulus.[38] This fear may become a part of his personality throughout life unless it is removed either through patient re-education or possibly through a cognate therapeutic experience equally emotional. We can readily understand that through some parallel process, which we might call *conversion shock,* a conversion experience can condition the habits and attitudes of a lifetime. Unfortunately many so-called conversions are simply superficial emotional indulgences. Furthermore, not all deeper experiences are oriented in a wholesome direction. The emotion itself is significant neither for good or ill. But it should not be difficult for us to understand that conversion shock may have a deep and lasting influence on personality simply *because* an emotion is involved. It is the agent of the change.

The value of the emotion lies chiefly in its capacity to overturn habit. We have seen that usually it is long-time and ingrained habit that is the chief enemy of those striving for life on a higher spiritual plane. The individual knows how he *wants* to live, but finds it impossible to accomplish his aim by gradual methods. But under proper

[38] For an example see the movingly written *The Locomotive God* by William Ellery Leonard, the story of how one experience of fright caused a little child to develop a lifelong fear of trains.

auspices and the enlivening capacity given to him by extreme emotion, a new way of life is momentarily achieved, and what has seemed hard suddenly becomes easy. St. Paul, from hating the Christians, suddenly became their most intrepid supporter. However, in most cases the discipline of the will is necessary to confirm and strengthen the gains against backsliding.

Geologists tell us that one violent storm may do more to change the face of the landscape than all the lesser storms of a century. In somewhat the same way, directed by the intelligence and supported by the will, an emotional episode of floodgate proportions seems to do its psychological work.

There is no reason to believe that these changes in personality are not in some obscure way physical as well as psychological. The autonomic changes in blood pressure, heart beat, and chemical composition of the body due to glandular activity that accompany emotional states are well known. It is becoming better understood in mental treatments that electric shock treatments, brain surgery, and drug application will accomplish sudden and often dramatic personality changes. Consequently it is not far-fetched to believe that subtle but actual physiological changes inextricably and wonderfully linked with ideas may play their part as agents of the conversion process.[39]

SUMMARY

We have tried to show that there is value in conversion, that it can transform men who can transform society, and that many of our religious leaders have experienced it. We have also shown that stern theology with its emphasis on sin, and sometimes even the artificial stimulation of conviction of sin, are often associated with conversion. Genuine conversions may not often derive from the excitement of the gospel tent, but a profound experience may be derived from a sense of inadequacy, incompleteness, and evil-doing. In proportion as people are made clear-sighted and sensitive to spiritual truth they begin to sense that yawning gap between what things are and what

[39] For an interesting and illuminating discussion of similarities in physical treatment, psychotherapy, and religion, see "Psychiatry and Spiritual Healing" in the *Atlantic Monthly*, August, 1954, by an anonymous writer described as a distinguished English psychiatrist. It is also suggested that perhaps the modern "brain washing" may take advantage of the same principles.

they ought to be. It is in this discernment that dividedness of self and the seeds of conversion are sown. Awakening may come by a gradual road. The psychologist must acknowledge two manners of spiritual growth. But the fact of the matter is that the demands of the great religions of history are so radical in their essences that no comfortable citizen can contemplate their demands without inwardly drawing back.

The Celestial City seems to him so glistening when seen from a distance, and yet the road in between is beset by so many frightening horrors. The healthy-minded see these latter as through a mist which softens the outlines of all forms, so that the pilgrim wanders and may lose his way. The spiritually sensitive, whose eyes have been sharpened through suffering, sees these things clearly. He is both attracted by his vision and repelled by the rude changes implied for his way of life, and it is the sharpness of the difference that stuns him into temporary, perhaps permanent, inactivity. Like Kierkegaard, he sees his own life and society as a shambles, and the great portion of what passes for religion as merely a piece of pious play-acting. Whatever teaching enables man to discern evil and so to force aside that façade of respectability that hides the realities of life will increase the sense of the sinful and so make more likely the experience of conversion that we have shown is associated with it. This need not involve the cheap and artificial stimulation of conversion, but simply an emphasis on truth that in some personalities will lead to a transforming and creative experience of conversion.

To those who may object that this is not good mental hygiene the religious man may reply that what passes for good mental hygiene is not always what it is supposed to be, either for the individual or for society. Nevertheless, whether good mental hygiene or not, the pursuit of truth seems to him to make the concept of mental hygiene cheap and ridiculous. St. Paul and St. Augustine and Tolstoy, Bunyan and Fox and Gandhi were not concerned with mental hygiene and in their lives achieved something less than its perfection. But they bequeathed to society values that their followers have used and civilization has celebrated. All of these had undergone deeply emotional religious experiences that changed their lives. We can ascribe these changes to conversion shock, a process psychologically similar to and perhaps identical with emotional traumatic shock which deeply conditions the personality during an experience of brief duration. The psychologist has neglected this area of study so that we do not have as much exact information about it as we would like. Otherwise it might be possible to make more use of it for the creative transformation of human lives. That there should be a distinguished minority of individuals in history and contemporary life who demonstrate these creative possibilities suggests that psychologists should revive the attention given to conversion in earlier years by Starbuck, E. T. Clark, and William James.

Chapter 10

THE PROBLEM OF FAITH

Love of wisdom is only one phase of the complete religious intention.
—Gordon W. Allport

One of the most subtle and important problems of religious development is that of faith—what it is, how it comes about, and how it may be nurtured and continued. The shallow-minded may suppose that it is simply a matter of thought and reasoning; that he who wants to arrive at religious truth merely sits down and thinks about it until he comes to some logical conclusion, a conclusion which thereupon becomes his faith. It must be granted that there may be a tiny minority to whom this description would in some sense apply. But though the reasoning process is an honored part of any educated person's religious faith, it is only a part. The psychological problem of faith is considerably more complicated. We have been leading up to it in the last few chapters.

The matter of belief. To discover whether or not people are believers is no problem. It is easy to find out, verbally at least, simply by asking them, as many investigators have done. The evidence seems abundantly clear that most people do believe. Even among those supposed enemies of religion, men of science, Leuba discovered—and this at least a generation ago when scholars were less ready to admit to religious interests—that nearly half would confess to a belief in God and more than half to a belief in immortality.[1] Allport, Gillespie, and Young demonstrated that only 12 per cent of the students at

[1] *Man or God?*, pp. 258–260.

Harvard and Radcliffe described themselves as atheists, with another 20 per cent claiming to be agnostics.[2] This leaves over two thirds of the students who were in some sense believers. Ross showed that among youth approached through the YMCA well over 80 per cent were believers in God.[3] In Chapter 3 we referred to Barnett's study, which showed 95 per cent of Americans to be believers. There is no doubt that we live in what Lewis Browne called "this believing world."

But when we begin to delve into the matter more closely, beyond simply trying to discover the facts of belief or unbelief, we find the situation more complicated. Belief demonstrates many different levels of manner and intensity, four of which are perhaps salient.

Four levels of belief. (1) *Stimulus-response verbalism.* This level, also called "verbal realism" by Allport,[4] begins its development with the life of the child. To the child, *saying* religion is the same *as* religion, and his belief is bound up with a magical reliance on the power of words, as we have pointed out in Chapter 5. The mechanism of the learning process here can be persuasively explained by reference to the conditioned response. The adult speaks, while the child's repetition is accompanied by reward. This cultivation of belief is on a hardly higher intellectual level, at least at the beginning of things, than was the salivation of Pavlov's famous dog.

This type of belief has its beginning in childhood but does not necessarily end there. Long after childhood has passed, many adults still hold beliefs on this verbal level. It is hard to find that religion makes any more difference to them than enabling them to rattle off a list of their religious beliefs, sometimes with an air of great power and conviction.

Aiding and abetting the conditioned-response process, and to some degree a part of it, are authority, imitation, suggestion, social pressure, and the search for security. Most of these influences are clear, with the possible exception of the search for security, which requires a brief comment. The child has learned that the proper vocal expressions will bring him the protection of his parents. It is a simple gradation

---

[2] "The Religion of the Post-War College Student."
[3] *Religious Beliefs of Youth*, Appendix C.
[4] *The Individual and His Religion*, p. 122.

from this to associating similar attitudes with the idea of a "heavenly father." And so the individual learns to "believe" through his need for security.[5]

Despite its superficiality, this verbal type of belief has astonishing vitality, a fact that behavioristic psychology would lead us to expect. The early, ingrained, habitual responses are very difficult to modify. The Freudian psychologists would agree in an emphasis on the importance of early influences. However, we cannot ascribe all the vitality in religious belief to these causes alone. It is quite evident that the individual soon develops "ego involvement" concerning his beliefs. The Catholic child discovers that his verbalisms do not agree with those of his Presbyterian or Baptist fellows, while the Methodist may discover that his ideas are not consistent with those of the Jews. In the schoolyard these verbalized differences have been known to be defended by recourse to fisticuffs. On an adult level we see the same ego mechanisms operating almost as obviously with tools of hardly greater subtlety. So we have the spectacle of Christians belaboring one another in defending their verbalizations of Christian belief, in the process proving to the hilt that their version of the teachings of the gentle Carpenter of Nazareth is nothing more than verbalization.

But in a more wholesome way, verbalization of belief may be consolidated through the accretion of experience and of time. After all, most beliefs, aside from denominational irrelevancies, have a core of truth that takes on meaning through the years. Consequently what started as a mere verbalism may end as a living truth. It is this fact alone that provides whatever justification there may be for teaching beliefs to children before they can understand their implications. Some of these symptoms of accretion will appear in our description of other levels of belief.

(2) *Intellectual comprehension.* This level involves truly creative processes considerably more complicated than those of simple conditioned-response verbalism. This is the level at which the religious intellectual chiefly operates, though it is by no means confined to the intellectual alone. All religious persons who reflect at all are bound to use logic and reason to some degree in attempting to think through

[5] This is essentially the Freudian explanation. See Freud's *Totem and Taboo, The Future of an Illusion,* or the last chapter of Ostow and Scharfstein's *The Need to Believe.*

their beliefs. The important point to remember is that no matter how meaningful religious beliefs may be through the process of thought, they need have no relation with life nor affect it in the slightest degree. Reason *may* and *should* play its part in any total process of religious belief, but a keen interest in the intellectual validation of belief does not guarantee the existence of any level beyond it.

At this level belong such processes of thought as the Thesis, Antithesis, and Synthesis of Hegel—or belief, doubt, and new belief. The mind pursues its theological adventures through the reception of truth, the doubting of this truth, and then the formation of a new insight embracing both the original partial truth and the doubt itself. We see this process beautifully illustrated in the Book of Job, while one can also discern it in the pronouncements of the prophets.

In this category also belong the so-called proofs of the existence of God. These include the *ontological* proof, derived from man's idea of God; the *cosmological* proof, that there must be a Creator of such an orderly universe as ours; the *teleological* proof, that this Creator must have intelligence and purpose; the *pragmatic* proof, that belief in God brings good results; and so on.[6]

But reason and logic, the chief tools of intellectual comprehension, may be poor instruments if relied on exclusively. We may deplore the insulation of religious thought from behavior, but even worse, on occasion, may be the forcing of logic, derived perhaps from dubious assumptions, on a situation that calls for a much more subtle and sensitive approach. Such would be the witchcraft trials approved by the colonial theologians in the Massachusetts Bay Colony, or the persecutions of the Inquisition. The latter are often explained and partly excused on the grounds that the administrators of the Inquisition firmly believed that salvation was wholly dependent upon acceptance of the Catholic faith. Since the loss of the believer's soul was of infinitely greater moment than the mere loss of his life, heretics and Jews were more dangerous than murderers and therefore deserved to be exterminated if they were unwilling to accept the "True Faith." Thus we see what a dangerous instrument logic may be even when based on what appears to wise men as a perfectly reasonable assumption. Religious logic must never be detached from the total situation. Mere beliefs do not constitute the life of faith.

[6] See Allport, *ibid.*, pp. 135–141.

(3) *Behavioral demonstration.* This category shows belief of a much more fundamental and thorough nature. A man's actions demonstrate his real beliefs much more clearly than do his words. This kind of manifestation of belief is often severed both from any verbalization of belief or any conscious intellectualized comprehension of the real meaning of the behavior. The Good Samaritan is the classic demonstration of this manner of belief.

Nevertheless, behavior is not the inerrant indication of belief that at first thought one might suppose. In the case of inarticulated conviction, it is. But conviction is not the only cause of behavior with seeming religious significance. Religious behavior, as opposed to verbalization, may be just as much a matter of habit or stimulus-response as verbalized belief. Of course, being more demanding on the organism, it is less often simply a matter of lazy habituation. But it may also be compulsive in nature; and instead of the positive expression of unspoken conviction, it may be the negative expression of an unconscious sense of guilt. This is a plausible explanation for many of the extravagant forms of mortification of the flesh practiced by medieval mystics.[7]

There are scores of beliefs and disbeliefs, feelings of guilt, loves, and hates lying unspoken and uncomprehended under the surface of consciousness. Ultimately none of us really can be sure what manner of person he is until some crisis or extremity wakes the sleeping convictions by which we live. The result is an open and occasionally dramatic expression of what sometimes are affirmations or sometimes rejections, of our religious beliefs.

(4) *Comprehensive integration.* But these three levels of belief are all partial expressions. They are all, taken alone, unsatisfactory in some manner or other, for the capabilities for heroic behavior may forever slumber. Even when virtuous action breaks forth we are never quite sure that a positive religious conviction lies at the root of it. A belief becomes totally wholesome and fully admirable only when verbalized conviction is well comprehended through critical and creative thought, the whole well integrated with behavior to form a Gestalt perfectly convincing even to a misanthropic observer. The true saint has a universal appeal. Few can resist the goodness of a Schweitzer, while even his enemies admitted the sincerity of Gandhi.

[7] See Ostow and Scharfstein, *op. cit.*, especially Chap. 4.

Of course not all comprehensive beliefs of this kind are equally valuable or profound. The beliefs of St. Margaret Mary Alacoque, founder of the cult of the Sacred Heart, seem to have been either quite conventional or very self-centered. A great many of them concerned favors from God to her own person.[8] But according to the lights of her feeble intellect she appeared to live up to her beliefs and to leave a spiritual legacy which her own Church at least has valued.

At this level all elements of the act of belief are working together, religious behavior being consistent with the beliefs that support and justify it. Jews treasure a story of the martyrdom of Rabbi Akiba, which well illustrates this point. He was being horribly tortured, when a bell announced the hour for him, along with every pious Jew, to say the Sh'ma, "Thou shalt love the Lord thy God with all thy heart, and with all thy soul, and with all thy mind." The old man recited as far as "with all thy heart," then stopped and smiled. "How can you smile," said one of the onlookers, "when you are dying in agony?" "Every day of my life for many years," he replied, "I have repeated these words, and I knew that I loved the Lord with all my heart, but can a man say that he has loved Him with all his soul until he comes to the end of his life? Now that the day of my death has come and the hour for repeating the Sh'ma has returned, and I have loved the Lord with all my life, why shouldn't I smile?"[9]

The distinction between belief and faith.   Thus far we have used the word "belief" and avoided its synonym "faith." The distinction between the two is largely psychological but very important, principally involving the connotation of the two words. "Belief" is a more static term and does not suggest a strong positive emotional attitude toward the object or proposition believed in. I may believe in the existence of Greenland or believe that it will rain tomorrow without the belief's affecting me very much or making me feel like doing anything in particular as a result. This is the case with belief in God at the level of stimulus-response verbalism. Although of a richer kind,

---

[8] See accounts in James' *Varieties*, p. 336 ff., or Leuba, *The Psychology of Religious Mysticism*, Chap. 4.

[9] Adapted from Kirsopp Lake, *Landmarks in the History of Early Christianity*, pp. 12–13.

religious beliefs at the level of intellectual comprehension are also in this category, with the exception that beliefs at this level may stimulate the urge for more intellectual activity.

"Faith," on the other hand, is a much more dynamic term. It suggests a warm, even passionate attachment and implies the urge to some kind of action as a result. The phrase "faith in God" connotes not merely a verbalized belief in Him but a loyalty that implies duties on the part of the believer. On this ground we can see that the old argument as to whether justification comes by faith or by works is psychologically an empty one since faith would include works. This means that the categories of belief by behavioral demonstration and particularly by comprehensive integration, can better be denoted by the term "faith."

Another connotation of the term "faith" is that there is an element of risk to the believer. There is no risk involved in my belief that it will rain tomorrow, for it makes little difference to me anyway. But with respect to my belief in God at the fourth level, there is a difference. Since I do not really *know* that God exists, in the same way that I *know* that two and two make four, it follows that anything I do based on that assumption is a kind of risk investment in the existence of God. It is a betting of my life on my belief. To the extent that this makes a real difference in my attitudes and my behavior, it is proper to call my belief *faith* in God.[10]

The problem of faith. With the foregoing discussions as background, we are ready to consider the problem of faith. This is not only of immense theoretical importance to the psychologist, but it is of utmost practical importance to those who are concerned with fostering the religious life. Actually this problem breaks down into two closely related questions: (a) How does belief become faith? (b) How is faith kept creative?

Psychology has much empirical data with which to answer some of the lesser questions concerning the religious life, such as, how widespread is religious belief? how often do people pray? and, why do people go to church? But it knows very little about how the simple verbalized beliefs of childhood grow into a mature faith or how this

[10] Cf. Allport, *op. cit.*, p. 123; also H. M. Kallen, *Secularism is the Will of God*, Chap. 8.

mature faith flowers in acts of creative service to mankind. It does not know with any precision what the conditions are that maintain creativity nor why the creativity may decline or perhaps lapse altogether.

Perhaps this is another way of saying that psychologists do not yet know all they would like to know about the secrets of personality itself. Since the religious life may be the most complex of all aspects of personality, we ought not to expect to answer such questions until we have first answered the simpler questions. Yet psychology may be of some help here in offering what data it has. Also, if allowed a certain latitude, it may speculate and offer theories to be tested. And, most important of all, the psychologist of religion may perform a service in asking the question and underlining its importance. If religious scholars and social scientists focus on the problem, there is hope that real progress may be made.

With respect to an empirical attack on the problem, social science has at least made a start. Although Benjamin Franklin may have had his doubts,[11] Americans in general, ever since the days of George Washington's Farewell Address, have assumed that religion is one of the pillars by which public morality is supported. The term "religion" here usually means church membership and the activities that go along with it. However, the Hartshorne and May studies were among the first to suggest that this hypothesis is very doubtful. This doubt has been strengthened by most studies of the problem, even though these studies show that church members do tend to be the better behaved citizens of the community. But when social class is comparable, there usually is little choice between the citizenship of church members and that of non-members. These were the findings of Havighurst and Taba, Hollingshead, and Lloyd Warner in their studies of Prairie City, "Elmtown," or "Jonesville," as the community was variously called. E. L. Thorndike would doubtless agree.

However, there are some scraps of empirical findings that point more optimistically in the other direction, though it must be admitted that they are less impressive in sum total. A. B. Hollingshead in *Elmtown's Youth* reports that the reputation in the community for probity and reliability of the Norwegian Lutheran youth was higher than might have been expected from their class status. Pro-

[11] See *Autobiography*, pp. 86 f.

fessor Erland N. P. Nelson of the University of South Carolina studied the religious attitudes of 851 students there and compared these attitudes with certain aspects of their overt behavior fourteen years later. There were positive correlations of .42 with church activities, .36 with community activities, and .23 with voting in state and national elections.[12] The present author with Caroline M. Warner made a study of the relationship between church attendance and reputations for kindness of 72 individuals in a small homogeneous community. Correlations were .41 for kindness and .64 for honesty, being positive in both cases and significant at considerably better than the one per cent level of confidence.[13] Other studies might be mentioned, but these will provide a sampling.

How does belief become faith? We have indicated that though this question is very complex and little empirical light has been thrown on it, the asking of it is important. One of the few social scientists concerned with this question—or a question closely allied to it—is Prof. P. A. Sorokin, of Harvard University, Founder of the Research Society for Creative Altruism. Among several books written by Dr. Sorokin on this general subject is *The Ways and Power of Love*. In this he analyzes various forms of altruism and considers how it is produced. While he does not confine himself to religion, nevertheless he takes it seriously as one of the sources of altruism. The volume is rich in speculative theory, with considerable empirical material in illustration and support.[14]

We will review a few of the influences that appeal to us as important in stimulating the growth of belief into faith, referring to Sorokin when appropriate. There are many points that might be made, of which we will select but six.

(1) *Gradual maturation, especially through family influences.* We have touched on aspects of this road to faith in our treatment of religious growth, particularly in dealing with the religion of childhood and the religion of healthy-mindedness.[15] It will be remembered that

[12] "Religious Attitude Shifts and Overt Behavior."
[13] "The Relation of Church Attendance to Honesty and Kindness in a Small Community."
[14] A psychological approach at a descriptive level is P. E. Johnson's *Christian Love*.
[15] See Chaps. 5 and 8.

healthy-mindedness represents a normal, gradual unfolding of the religious life with very little inner conflict. This type of experience is facilitated by a normal family experience in which the individual is surrounded by love and wholesome religious influences. If it were practicable, the best single piece of advice we could give one seeking a sound experience of religious faith would be, "See that you are born into a genuinely religious family."

In a study of Christian saints, Sorokin indicates that 43 per cent of the Catholic saints belonged in what he calls the "fortunate altruist" category, equivalent to healthy-mindedness, while the same could be said of 69.9 per cent of the Russian Orthodox saints.[16] He also found that 43 per cent of these had been started on the road to sainthood through family or kinship agencies.[17]

(2) *Persons.* The example of a person whose beliefs have become a living faith is another subtle but potent stimulus to this kind of growth. A classic specific example is that of the influence on Saul of Tarsus of the martyrdom of Stephen, while Sorokin reports that 27.9 per cent of the saints in his study were started on their career toward sainthood through the influence of particular persons outside of their families.[18]

(3) *Institutions.* It is heartening to note that that much-maligned factor in the religious life, the religious institution, exerted an important influence on Sorokin's saints. Of those he studied, 29.2 per cent were strongly conditioned by the Church or by monastic and educational institutions.[19] Since in nearly all cases the schools or universities embraced by the category "educational" were religious in their sponsorship and influence, it is fair to class them as religious institutions.

In a sense this category is an extension of the second type of influence, for institutions are collections of persons, and doubtless the institutional influence was so intertwined with that of the individuals who comprised them that it would be hard to separate the two. So much is this true that the power of an institution to stimulate the growth of a vigorous religious faith is bound up with the morale of

[16] *The Ways and Power of Love*, p. 153.
[17] *Ibid.*, p. 202.
[18] *Loc. cit.*
[19] *Loc. cit.*

those of whom the institution is composed. We can easily understand that a monastic community fired with the freshness and zeal of a newly found truth or mission, as the early Franciscans or the band of devoted followers surrounding Loyola in the early days of the Jesuits, would have a more creative influence than the same community a hundred years later under more conventional conditions. Sorokin has pointed out that the incidence of sainthood differs in different times, while we will refer, in our chapter on mysticism, to the fact that the Middle Ages and the seventeenth century were more productive of mystics than other periods in the history of the Western World. Obviously the potency of religious institutions is subject to many outside influences. Yet this should not blind us to the fact that as instruments these institutions have figured importantly in the growth of faith in the large sense in which we have defined it.

(4) *Mystical experience and conversion.* Mysticism and conversion are two closely related roads to the livelier expression of religious belief. Though both may be unwholesome in certain cases, or have very trivial influence in many others, for the most part they occasion a quickening process that marks a positive step in the development of mere belief into mature faith. It is hard to say whether these experiences are true causes or merely symptoms of developing belief. However, it seems clear that to some degree at least, they are causes. This, together with the fact that their influence is often so powerful and dramatic, justifies their being listed among the important stimulants of faith. Sorokin's figures indicate that from 30 to 57 per cent of his Christian saints experienced some variety of catastrophic conversion experience.[20]

(5) *External trauma and crisis.* Mankind reacts to crisis in unpredictable ways. Some theorists emphasize the beneficial effects of misfortune, while others feel that more often psychological damage results. It is clear that since much depends on the individual, examples may be accumulated to prove either theory. Many of the heroes of faith have been the type who were able not only to survive misfortune but also to turn it to advantage in their spiritual development. While the distress and suffering of James' "sick soul" variety of religious growth [21] is often due to inward conflict, the stress of

[20] *Ibid.*, p. 153.
[21] See Chap. 8.

public or private misfortune can be an important positive factor in the development of faith. The ills of the times seem to have been an important factor in the development of the religious consciousness of both Isaiah and Jeremiah, while Ignatius Loyola would have been a hero of the battlefield of war rather than the battlefield of faith had not an unlucky cannon ball struck his leg.

In order to account for both the beneficial and deleterious effects of crisis, Sorokin has developed what he calls the "Law of Polarization." Society, he points out, is ordinarily composed of a few heroes, saints, and altruistic leaders at one end of the scale, with another small, anti-social group composed of criminals, ruthless psychopaths, and assorted non-creative derelicts at the other. In between come the great body of reasonably well-behaved, colorless followers and fitters-in to the general social pattern, good citizens because they eschew any very dynamic expression of their personalities. But in times of stress the neutral middle mass tends to gravitate to one pole or the other, with some people performing acts of courage, sacrifice, and leadership which amaze themselves, while others degenerate into anti-social baseness.[22] Through some such process as this, latent beliefs are thrust naked before the world.

Of course this information is of little practical use to us since we cannot go around inflicting misfortunes on people in the fond hope that these will bring about strengthened religious faith. In many cases the results would have little or no religious significance even though they might be beneficial, while in other cases the results would be just contrary to what we had intended. The kind of information we are discussing here tends in the direction of helping us to *understand* the development of religious faith, for understanding must precede any practical significance our studies may eventually have.

(6) *Deliberate behavior and the operation of choice.* We have already stated that the extent of man's capacity to choose is a matter of much debate and skepticism among psychologists. Relying on appearances, however, we are assuming that, no matter how restricted, certain free and potentially creative options rest with the individual as sources of the development of faith. Doubtless the *desire to choose* in a certain way precedes the choice. Probably the verbalization of a

[22] P. A. Sorokin, *ibid.*, pp. 226 ff.

belief biases the choice to some degree, and it would seem that the Gestalt principle of *closure*, the psychological urge to complete anything the mind perceives as unfinished, may well be operating here. At any rate, the tension or sense of guilt, sensed by many people who feel they are not living up to what they profess, affects the choice and enhances the likelihood of developing a creative faith. But it is the decision to do something about the situation and the consequent action that often win the day for a more mature faith.

William James treated this problem in his famous essay, "The Will to Believe." He once said he wished he had titled it "The Right to Believe," for people get the impression that he was defending a kind of gritting-of-the-teeth determination to believe in the face of any amount of contrary evidence however plausible. What he meant was that to believe or not to believe was equally respectable intellectually and that an individual had the right to make the choice that seemed best to him. James also pointed out that, creatively speaking, belief, as opposed to non-belief, was "the livelier option." It generates those activities which, when joined to belief, become what we have called faith.

But also, once performed, acts consistent with belief tend to strengthen belief. This theoretical truth is put to good use by the practitioners of religion. For instance, Frank Buchman, the leader of the Moral Re-Armament movement, and one of the world's more successful evangelists, has never insisted that a prospective convert believe in God. His experience had taught him that it was usually sufficient if the individual could be persuaded to behave *as if* there were a God, on an experimental basis, so to speak.[23] The conviction came afterward. As another example, alcoholics who are atheists often apply to Alcoholics Anonymous and are confronted with the second of AA's famous "Twelve Steps." This is that, having admitted they cannot cure themselves, they must rely on the help of a "Higher Power." It is suggested to them that if they cannot believe, they should try to follow the steps anyway. Of this type of person the Founder once said,

He sometimes eliminates the "spiritual angle" from the "12 steps to Recovery" and wholly relies upon honesty, tolerance, and "working with

[23] See my *The Oxford Group*, p. 28.

others." But it is curious and interesting to note that faith always comes to those who try this simple approach *with an open mind*—and in the meantime they stay sober.[24]

This is analogous, in the production of altruism as analyzed by Sorokin, to what he calls the "factor of the retroactive influence of the first good deeds." [25] Frequently all that the person needs is the deliberate performance in the direction of faith of those first good deeds. But "will power" is not all there is to it. The man who jumped up from his chair and ran around the block every time his chair felt particularly comfortable to him, found his "will power" just as feeble at the end of a year as before he set out to train it. Similarly one does not in cold blood go out to perform his chore of goodness for which he receives his faith for value given. This is not to say that no one tries this method; the term "do-gooder" probably owes its existence to this hollow imitation of genuine faith. Neither intellectualized religious belief nor a mechanical performance of the acts of virtue severed from any kind of psychological warmth is what we mean by faith.

But faith is not only a discrete and specific psychological function, but also to some degree a kind of conversation between the beliefs of the mind and the acts of the organism, a resultant of tension between belief and action. This rhythm of faith is one of the great truths to which the seers and thinkers of the ages have testified in one form or another, whether in ancient times by the figure of the Cave of Illusion of Plato or the Biblical dichotomy of Faith and Works, or in more modern times by the Principle of Alternation of W. E. Hocking and the Withdrawal and Return of which the historian Arnold Toynbee speaks.[26] We are suggesting that in this process of circular stimulation there is a place for the deliberate performance of acts that help to commit the individual to that much larger life venture which is called faith. Faith is an acting out of deeds supported by emotional warmth and ratified by intellectual assent.

How is faith kept creative?   One of the characteristics of true religious faith is that it is socially and culturally creative. By this we

[24] Anon., "Basic Concepts of Alcoholics Anonymous," p. 6.

[25] *Op. cit.*, p. 203.

[26] See Hocking's *The Meaning of God in Human Experience*, Chap. 28, and Toynbee's *A Study of History*, Vol. III, pp. 248 ff.

mean that it eventuates in ethical behavior and stimulates cultural achievement. Too often the study of history and society, pursued with the omission of references to religion, presents only a distorted and partial picture. This is because faith has been and continues to be a cultural force of vital importance. But it has not always been positively creative, either for the individual or for society, and it is the business of the psychologist to throw what light he can on this complex problem of how faith is kept creative.

We will not have space to suggest more than one idea of scores that might be put forward, for doubtless the true solution would fill many volumes. In a sense the present work is a continuing attempt to solve the problem, but in this section we will not be proposing the more familiar activities of daily religious life, such as prayer and worship, that might be thought to be closer to the answer.

The point that we have in mind concerns the two contrary forces of faith and skepticism. The two are not always necessary for a life to be productive both religiously and culturally, but one can see these factors at work pretty obviously in much cultural achievement. That faith should be one of the sources of the good things of the cultural life should be no surprise—at least to religious partisans. The benefits of religion to society are celebrated by every preacher, with a lyrical exuberance almost equal to that of an auto salesman describing his latest model. But skepticism is spoken of by the preacher in terms less ecstatic. The psychologist, however, notes that, just as faith is one of those things by which people live, so skepticism is part of the process by which faith grows. "Skepticism cannot, therefore," says William James, "be ruled out by any set of thinkers as a possibility against which their conclusions are secure." [27] In a somewhat similar vein Allport notes the importance of doubt in the development of religious faith:

Doubts of the many sorts we have considered flood into one's life. They are an integral part of all intelligent thinking. Until one has faced the improbabilities involved in any commitment one is not free to form an independent conviction based on productive thinking and observing.

Mature belief . . . grows painfully out of the alternating doubts and affirmations that characterize productive thinking.[28]

[27] *Varieties*, p. 325.
[28] *The Individual and His Religion*, p. 122.

This growing process is not only part of religious faith itself but also constitutes the heart of a creativity that leaps the confines of what may narrowly be thought of as religion and confers its benefits on fields beyond.

Perhaps the place where the creative influence of faith and skepticism best shows itself is the realm of literature. Anyone with an acquaintance with world literature will note that doubt or skepticism is a favorite theme, not just in writings by professional doubters like Voltaire or Lucretius, but more often in the writings of the profoundly religious. The Book of Job is a supreme example, while the works of Tolstoy, Dostoevsky, Goethe, and Milton, Carlyle's *Sartor Resartus,* Tennyson's "In Memoriam," and Emerson's *Essays* are just a few in an almost endless list. Furthermore, it is being added to every day. These are not merely religious works but also works of art which survey the wider field of values in respect to philosophy, economics, politics, and society, as well as human nature in general.

It would seem that the tension generated by the opposition of belief and skepticism is no inconsiderable source of the psychological energy by which the works were created. Belief, in order to become creative, should not come too easily, and while we cannot say that severe conflict with skeptical ideas is a situation to be desired, nevertheless it would seem apparent that the greater the tension the greater the *potentialities* for achievement, even though the risks are greater too. Naturally this is not the only kind of tension that operates, since it is more apt to be found prominent in the introspective type of "sick soul"; in the healthy-minded individual it is much less prominent, even though usually present. Tension for the latter is more apt to be supplied by conflict with the outward environment. The "sin" that he fights is more apt to be found in conditions around him rather than within.

The enemy of all creativity, religious or otherwise, is of course complacency, offspring of the death urge. The trouble with any formulation and expression of faith is that so easily and imperceptibly it becomes routine. Through its own psychological momentum it begins to reproduce merely itself. That subtle traffic with the field of events outside of one's own habit system ceases. Psychological energy, which may be the happy instrument of creativity, degenerates into a mere repeated stirring in the same pot. The tension, without the need for a fresh and radical adjustment, diminishes and is replaced by those pleasant and easy tensions that move one away from the exciting inquietude of creativity toward the mundane satisfactions of a more vegetative existence.

There is good reason why this particular polarity, the opposition between faith and skepticism, should eventuate in literary forms of creativity. Necessary to its activity is the manipulation of verbal symbols, which achieve their greatest cultural permanence when congealed in literary form. But we may conjecture that for each creative effort deriving from this source that achieves the dignity of print there must be a hundred verbalized only through the spoken word; while for every one that is made articulate for others there must be scores given voice in the mind alone, or existing there unrecognized and therefore never vocalized at all. It is such "mute, inglorious Miltons" who, happening on the words of the poet, the philosopher, or the religious prophet, and dimly recognizing their own experiences, are partly stimulated to further creative activity on their own account.

Though we can cite many illustrations to make our theory plausible, it must be admitted that there are no very precise studies to make its exact application clear. To be sure, the religious prophet is a person who frequently has become dissatisfied with previous formulations of truth and therefore is in part a skeptic, even though he is more vigorous as a mouthpiece of religious affirmations. Doubtless Amos' views on religion must have undergone drastic remodification when he concluded that those who presided at the Temple worship were not serving the Lord. And it is hard to see what significance the Temptations in the Wilderness had for Jesus had they not been doubts out of which grew faith.

The business of stimulating skepticism in the growing generation doubtless can be overdone, and we would not like to minimize its dangers; but some variety of heretical opposition is essential for all growing individuals and all forms of institutional faith. Martin Luther is much abused by Catholics, yet a good case can be made for him as the savior of the Roman Catholic religion. For whether or not Western Christianity would have reformed itself from within, as is often claimed, we may note that in actuality it was the Lutheran movement of the sixteenth century that supplied the chief pressures for reform both from within and from without the Catholic church. It is also noteworthy that since that time Catholicism's most wholesome branches seem to be those in closest contact with Protestantism, as in Germany, Holland, the British Isles, and the United States. Furthermore it is likely that the religious freedom and the mutual respect for one another's differing religious views that characterize most democracies would have developed neither out of the monolithic Church of the Middle Ages nor from any of the theocratic states that Protestants have attempted.

There is evidence that, from the point of view of literary creativity, the Catholic emphasis on orthodoxy may be depriving Catholicism of the fructifying influence of heterodox opinions and the wholesome influence of doubt, at the same time that Western culture, particularly in America, is deprived of the full benefit of intercourse with Catholic culture. Catholics themselves have been among those who have recognized that Catholic education has not produced its share of writers and scholars.[29] An informal study made by the author of 91 writers, born since 1500 A.D., represented in an anthology, *The World's Great Catholic Literature*,[30] showed that 16 were mentioned in the volume as converts and four as skeptics at some time during their lives. The same might have been said for an indeterminate number of others where the fact was not specifically mentioned.

That the total may have been considerably larger is suggested by a study of 30 names selected because additional biographical information was elsewhere readily available. Of these, 20 were converts, while some measure of dissent from authoritative views was suggested in the case of 11 of the 30. Naturally these 30 constituted a more eminent selection, otherwise their biographies would not have been so accessible. In other words, a considerable number of prominent Catholic writers have clearly had the experience of questioning and casting aside previous views, while the incidence of this seems higher among the more eminent. It is to be presumed that, whatever other values the education of a child in a Catholic family and Catholic schools may have, deprivation of the tension that comes from contact with

[29] For example, see "Problems of Christian Culture" by Christopher Dawson in *Commonweal*, April 15, 1955; also letters to the Editor, July 15 and August 12, 1955, pp. 374 and 470.

[30] Ed. by George N. Shuster. I am indebted to Adolf Rindlisbacher for most of the labor of research, and to the Psychology Department of Wesleyan University for supplying funds in support.

non-Catholic ideas may make an eminent literary achievement less likely.

But tension may be caused by many influences other than those of skepticism and faith. The world is full of many tensions, some creative and others destructive. The question arises as to whether this particular type of tension has any advantage over other kinds. The answer is a tentative "yes."

It would seem that both faith and skepticism have their peculiar functions to perform in the process of creativity. The function of faith is to give meaning to life; and it would seem clear that, on the whole, there is no value orientation that is subjectively superior to religious faith in supplying this meaning and energizing man's actions. Religious faith has made more martyrs in the course of the world's history than any other cause. It is true that religious faith may become narrow, as too often it does, but in proportion as it is anything more than simple verbalism it directs and stimulates the believer. Indeed this energy tends also to be *in proportion to the narrowness of his belief.*

Anyone can verify this for himself. The narrower, stricter sects and denominations of believers tend to be the ones that enlist the fiercest loyalties and demonstrate the greatest sacrifices. The more liberal denominations are apt to look down on such groups, for they tend to class them with the lower orders of society and the lunatic fringe; yet they envy them the ease with which their budgets are raised and their churches filled. The conservatives, on their part, may return the scorn of their more liberal friends, whom they see as unwilling to make the full commitment to the life of faith. But this is just the trouble with those who hold the narrow faith. They tend to become bigots, and to take refuge in such a narrow definition of faith that if it is creative at all its creativity is very restricted. They tend to identify salvation too closely with their own creeds, their own churches, and their own narrow communities.

It is just here that the function of skepticism comes into play. For skepticism, with its questioning of old ideas, immediately suggests new ones. It raises horizons, and with its promise of freshness, freedom and adventure, with just a touch of danger, it provides a heady and exhilarating draught. The habit of seeing life as meaningful is left over from the old faith, which has acted like a dam impounding vast quantities of water with energy potential. Skepticism makes a breach in this dam and so releases the water for a spectacular and creative work.

But the dangers of skepticism may be worse than those of a narrow faith. For if skepticism goes all the way, undermines all faith and becomes absolute, its very triumph destroys its motive. "Vanity of vanities," said the Preacher, "all is vanity," and this represents the final end of the confirmed skeptic. Believing in the equal importance of all values, he believes in nothing, and, like the water that has gone over the dam and reaches the plain below, he no longer has the capacity to do any work. Having won over his old antagonist, religious faith, the skeptic has destroyed the tension by which he lived. Even the narrowest religious belief, though held never so grimly and bitterly, was better than this. For at least it was belief in *something*.

So far as it relates to belief and skepticism, the solution to the problem of how faith is kept creative lies neither with belief alone nor with skepticism alone, but with maintaining an equilibrium between the two. This equilibrium, however, is an unstable one, running always to the easy solutions now of narrow belief, now of complete skepticism. Unproductive is the church that tries to maintain a creative faith by insisting on too-narrow orthodoxy in belief, for by so doing the institution may be preserved a few years longer, but the purpose for which it has been founded will have been defeated. Less productive are the freethinkers who think so freely that they believe in nothing. But, if our insight is sound, fortunate are those individuals and those churches who, by vigilance, discipline, and a proper balance between thinking and doing, between doubt and belief, maintain that creative psychological entity that we call faith.[31]

---

[31] The interested reader will find an empirical attempt to verify this theory in an article by the author entitled "A Study of Some of the Factors Leading to Achievement and Creativity With Special Reference to Religious Skepticism and Belief." This gives partial support to the theory, in that a group of more eminent persons rated themselves to a significant degree more skeptical than a less eminent group. However, contrary to what the theory would seem to suggest, they rated themselves less intense in religious faith, though not significantly so. Even so, they considered themselves somewhat above average in faith, so that in many there must have been tension between belief and doubts. However, it is quite possible that if the study had been confined to writers and thinkers, instead of being general, the results would have been more positive and clear. A total of 301 persons were included in the study.

SUMMARY

Most people, at one time or another, hold religious beliefs on four ascending levels: (1) stimulus-response verbalism, the most superficial and mechanical; (2) intellectual comprehension, which involves merely the mind; (3) behavioral demonstration, which involves the area of good works; and (4) comprehensive integration, the highest level, in which the three preceding levels are welded into one psychological whole. We must distinguish between the term "belief," which is a static term more appropriate to a primitive level of religious expression, and "faith," a much more dynamic and comprehensive term connoting greater psychological investment and appropriate action.

The problem of faith is two-fold: How does belief become faith? and, How is faith kept creative? What empirical evidence we have about people's behavior suggests that most belief remains at a very static and unproductive level. But when we turn to examine outstanding examples of religious faith we note at least six influences that have had dynamic and creative effects in particular lives. These are (1) most importantly, the family, (2) other persons, (3) religious institutions, (4) mystical experience and conversion, (5) external trauma and crisis, and (6) deliberate behavior and the operation of choice.

The problem of how faith is kept creative is a most complex one. The suggestion that we have to offer is that the maintenance of just the right amount of tension between the forces of skepticism and those of faith has yielded creative fruit both for religion and for the wider culture as well.

Chapter 11

CRITERIA FOR A
MATURE RELIGION

The best fruits of religious experience are the best things that history has
to show.

—Wm. James

Never send to know for whom the bell tolls; it tolls for thee.

—John Donne

In the previous seven chapters we have sketched a developmental psychology of religion. It remains to cap these by a consideration of the finished product toward which this development has been tending. Through childhood and adolescence, whether through a healthy-minded gradual growth or the stresses of conversion, the sensitive religious spirit approaches some sort of resolution which we will now try to describe. This will be a difficult task for several reasons. 1) The process of religious development is never complete. 2) Religious maturity is by no means coincident with physical maturity. Indeed most adults can in nowise be said to be religiously mature. 3) Depending on one's concept of religion, religious maturity may be defined in a number of ways, each with its element of validity. Consequently our discussion will be more speculative and arbitrary than objective and precise. Yet we have already implied some concept of religious maturity, and it is appropriate that we give more formal consideration to this.

240

Accordingly we will first look back to the previous chapters to note what they imply for maturity. Then we will consider what light some other writers have thrown on the subject and comment on their ideas. We will finish with a few additional ideas of our own in order to round out the concept.

One can define religious maturity in two ways. From the point of view of the individual we can think of it as the highest point of adult religious development, which might be inconsiderable in one individual and distinguished in another. Or we can think of it as an idealized concept by which, as by a kind of yardstick, all religious development may be measured and compared. While the first point of view has its significance, it is the second approach we will adopt here, with but occasional glances at the first.

In discussing mature religion, we will think of religion at its best, its most effective, reminding the reader also that a consideration of the great religious spirits of history will help him to test our clues. For our basic idea we will return to our definition of religion as given in the second chapter: *the inner experience of the individual when he senses a Beyond, especially as evidenced by the effect of this experience on his behavior when he actively attempts to harmonize his life with the Beyond.* Consequently in the normal person the concept of religious maturity will involve an awareness of God or some cosmic reality, an inward experience, and an outward expression.

We cannot say that all of the urges that we suggested in Chapter 4 as sources of the religious sentiment are satisfied by its mature form. Some may have served simply to initiate development toward religious maturity. Thus extreme physical need may drive an individual to seek divine help, yet we would hardly define mature religion as that which satisfies pangs of hunger. Yet if religion develops from human needs we should expect its mature expression in some degree to satisfy them, at least in a psychological sense. And though we cannot demonstrate the satisfaction of these needs in any rigorous way, it will be sufficient to remind ourselves of some of them to make clear their connection with mature religion.

For example, the intellectual expression of religion demonstrated by an interest in theology will satisfy the desire to exercise one's reason. Concepts such as that of the fatherhood of God may satisfy the adult's needs for dependence. Again, curiosity about the mystery of existence may be heightened and come to fruition in mystical experience, the counterpart of Otto's sense of the numinous.

Just as in its immature forms, mature religion likewise will satisfy Thomas' four wishes for security, response, recognition, and new experience. It will be heightened through conflict and may help to resolve it. It should express both the life and death urges; while it will fulfill in the most satisfying form the eternal quest of the human spirit for values and life's meaning. These are all sources suggested earlier as part of the universal psychological needs of human nature which find expression in mature religion.

As we look back to Chapter 5, on the religion of childhood, we note that mature religion may in some sense be defined as the opposite of childish religion. The very fact that we identify certain religious traits as childish implies a judgment as well as a standard of maturity, whether or not that standard is very well defined in our own minds. Hence reflection about some of these traits at this point should help us to clarify what we mean by mature religion.

Thus, when we remember that the child is heavily dependent on his elders and on authority for his religious ideas, we realize that mature religion is considerably more critical, creative, and autonomous. It does not necessarily follow that maturity will have no need of authority nor that every critical view of religion is mature, yet the adult's capacity for reflection and self-reliance should find some expression in his religious life if it is to possess any measure of maturity. The childlike credulity that leads so readily to religious exploitation does not characterize a developed religious sense, nor does an extremely anthropomorphic concept of the Deity that has never changed from the earliest dawn of one's crude concepts about God.

Perhaps the most flagrant vitiation of the religion of adults—as opposed to mature religion—is the continuance of the egocentric concerns of the child. Particularly in their private prayers adults are continually casting a cloak of sentimental religiosity over all sorts of requests for personal favors which God, as a glorified errand boy, is expected to perform. Without in any way losing his sense of self-regard, the mature person has expanded that self to include much wider concerns. An inventory of the nature of one's prayers is a good indication of the maturity or immaturity of one's religion in this respect.

But similarly universal among adults is the childish reliance on ritual and verbalization in religion. When solemn ecclesiastics perform religious rituals or promulgate religious dogmas, one tends to feel that participation or repetition will rain down celestial blessings on the head of the faithful one. Furthermore, it is difficult to distinguish between those for whom this verbalized and ritualistic form of religious expression is a stimulus to a genuine spiritual life and those in whom it is only a hardened reflection of the habits of childhood. It was this aspect of religious immaturity that the Catholic satirist, Alexander Pope, in part suggested.

> Behold the child, by Nature's kindly law,
> Pleased with a rattle, tickled with a straw;
> Some livelier plaything gives his youth delight,
> A little louder, but as empty quite:
> Scarfs, garters, gold, amuse his riper stage,
> And beads and prayer-books are the toys of age.[1]

The religion of maturity is not satisfied with a mere ritualistic repetition of imitative verbalization of any type.

But it would be a distortion to depreciate childhood to the extent that we should suppose mature religion to be the opposite of that of childhood *in every respect*. We who wish to enter the Kingdom of Heaven are enjoined to become as little children, and it behooves us to be discriminating in our attempt to define maturity as in all respects the opposite of childhood.

For it is in children rather than in tired, owlish adults, or in inhibited, self-conscious adolescents that we are most likely to find the qualities of spontaneity and wonder which have characterized the great religious spirits of the ages. The mature religious personality has found a way to preserve these admirable traits of childhood. In similar fashion he has preserved an appropriate humility, that teachability to which Jesus undoubtedly was referring when he set the child in his Apostles' midst as an example. This quality is something very different from credulity and is in no way incompatible with a proper critical sense. These two characteristics are ingredients in the capacity for creative religious expression which Harms found

[1] "An Essay on Man," Epistle II, ll. 275–280.

in his study of the religious concepts of children, and this same creativity, conditioned and enriched in manifold ways, finds its most appropriate expression in maturity.

Reviewing Chapter 6 and the religion of adolescence, we recall that the powers and capacities of the adolescent are practically equal to those of the adult in the very fundamental fields of intelligence, emotions, social interests, and moral sensitivities. But mature religion as opposed to that of the adolescent tends to be less confused and fluid, more stable and tempered by a sense of responsibility, better organized and more effective when it is genuine. Adolescence usually is the vestibule or approach to mature religion. It may have provided experiences leading to the gradual unfolding of religious powers; or through suffering and a conversion of crisis these powers may have acquired a sharper edge.

G. W. *Allport's concept of mature religion.* One of the more thoughtful psychologists who have considered the concept of maturity is G. W. Allport. In his volume *Personality* he describes the mature personality as chiefly characterized by three factors: the ability to enlarge and extend the personality, self-objectification or insight, and an adequate philosophy of life.[2] Using these as his generalized base, he has considered the mature religious personality as a specialized form of maturity, and so developed this concept of religion in Chapter 3 of his *The Individual and His Religion.* It will be worth our while to note his ideas in some detail.

(1) The mature religious sentiment is first of all *well differentiated,* or self-critical. In other words, the person possessing this feeling has insight into himself. The average religious devotee tends to become defensive when his religion is criticized. To him it seems, of course, the highest form of religion ever developed; its dogmas are sure; and its expression, though not quite perfect, is much more so than that of any other religion. This attitude is reminiscent of the "my father can lick your father" stage of youthful development. On a slightly more advanced scale, it resembles the loyalty of the super-patriot who not only trusts in the capacity of the armed forces of America to wipe off the face of the earth all other armed forces but who spurns with high indignation any suggestion that the mo-

²   Chap. 8.

tives of the United States in its international dealings have been other than of the highest moral purity.

But just as the mature patriot can love his country despite her faults, so the maturely religious individual loves his church and is firm in his allegiance to it, at the same time that he sees its flaws and acknowledges that it might be improved. His is an informed partisanship, and he is able to accept criticism knowing that some of it may have a firm foundation and that he may be able to benefit from it. Though presumably he is able to deal vigorously with slender and uninformed criticism when vigor will be appropriate and effective, nevertheless he avoids an undifferentiated and invariable violence in defending his views, which will only betray an unconscious lack of confidence in his beliefs.

Still another aspect of this *differentiation* is that the mature person may reject aspects of the religious institution to which he gives allegiance at the same time that he accepts others, aware of their relative importance. Consequently his belief is better organized and articulated than that of the immature person. In other words, the mature religious sentiment features reason as an integrated and dynamically functioning factor in the whole.

(2) Next, Allport finds that mature religion has a *motivational force of its own* wholly independent of the original organic drives and psychological hungers which may have marked its origin. This concept he has developed from his view of "functional autonomy" as a characteristic of motivational drive.[3] Thus religion becomes a goal to be sought for its own sake, and so becomes capable of enlisting the total energy of the individual to an extent far surpassing the capacity of lesser goals.

Allport believes that this characteristic, more than any other, is the key to mature religion and explains its power to transform lives. Though this ingredient may suggest the possibility of fanaticism, if a dynamic and self-sustaining drive is properly curbed by a differentiating and critical understanding there will be no danger of this development.

(3) Allport's third mark of mature religion is the *consistency of its moral consequences*. A logical development of the dynamic influence of religious motivation is its power to influence the behavior

[3] See *Personality*, Chap. 7, for a description of "functional autonomy."

of the individual. We have already remarked that there is often a large gap between profession of religious belief and the behavior that the belief might be supposed to foster. When this is the case, we can be sure that full development of the religious sentiment is lacking and to this extent it is immature. Or, more often, morality will be demonstrated in some areas and not in others. A businessman may be very solicitous for the welfare of his family yet completely ruthless when it comes to taking dishonest advantage of his business rivals. Thus the influence of his faith is *inconsistent*.

Or perhaps the individual confines his religious observances to narrowly conceived aspects of his religious duty. He may, for example, be very scrupulous in the performance of the requirements of church attendance and participation in ecclesiastical rites, and he may study his Bible, pray, generously support his church, and fulfill all that is required of a "good church member." Still, the quality of his life away from the church, both public and private, may negate the church's teaching. This inconsistency would mark his religion as immature, no matter how respectable his gray hairs and his standing as a pillar of the church community.

Mature religion, on the other hand, is characterized by consistent moral behavior. The genuineness of the religious dynamic is testified by outward acts. This is what Jesus meant when he said, "By their fruits ye shall know them."

(4) Related to the consistency of mature religion is its *comprehensiveness* as a philosophy of life. Religion makes sense out of life and does so by relating all its happenings and facets not to man but to the Creator of man, the Divine that lies outside of man's immediate experience. Thus does the religious person possess a motive ultimately of more profound and compelling power than any merely humanistic type of sub-religious belief.

Furthermore, Allport points out, a comprehensive faith is also a tolerant one. The reflective believer who knows that religion must account for every last aspect of the world's experience also knows that there is much of which he has no knowledge. Truth is therefore much wider than the measure of any single person's belief. "The religion of maturity makes the affirmation 'God is,' but only the religion of immaturity will insist, 'God is precisely what I say He is.' "

(5) If all life is to be comprehensively related to a common

source, it follows that mature religion will also be *integral*. This means that in seeking to explain the relationship of experience to God the mature believer will find in life an integrated and harmonious pattern that will also demonstrate the relationship of its discrete parts to one another. Thus there is found a place for modern scientific thought and discovery with religious significance in appropriate relationship to the more characteristic activities of prayer and worship, when rightly considered.

This does not mean that the religious person can fully integrate and explain all aspects of life. There are bound to be mysteries difficult to explain, like freedom of the will and the problem of evil. But the religious person who is mature has thought about these difficulties and has not turned away from them or admitted easy solutions that do violence to the facts as he knows them. The integrated pattern that seems to him to be working itself out in history is too vast and complicated to be perfectly clear to him. Yet on the whole this picture testifies to sustained reflection on his part and is characterized by sufficient coherence to supply his own life with harmony and purpose.

(6) Allport's final point is that mature religion is *heuristic* in nature. This means that the believer is always seeking for more light, and recognizes an inevitable tentativeness about his belief which decrees that he will be forever a searcher. This does not mean that he will be uncertain in his quest, though in a paradoxical way he can never be assured of full certainty. He is realist enough to know that no high endeavor has ever been assured of successful completion. Therefore he will risk a commitment to a religious view of reality with the feeling that only this will give point to his life. But the map which he has accepted to guide his journey will need corrections as he pursues his way and senses its inaccuracies. This is why the cocksure expressions of religious bigots are immature. Maturity requires an admixture of humility that makes it possible for the true believer to absorb new points of view into his truth system and so to make his religious progress a genuine quest.

It will be noted that these criteria of Allport are not only thoughtful but fertile. It also is to be noted that they betray not only the approach of a psychologist but the bias of the intellectual as well.

They appeal to the reason and so are particularly welcomed by the undergraduate and the scholar. But in applying Allport's own criterion of the comprehensiveness of a mature faith, it is well that we should consider other criteria as well. Practically anyone interested in religion could present some ideas of his own as to what characterizes it at its best. The artist would have a different set of specifications, as would the anchorite, the politician, the social worker, or the businessman. Each would specify according to his own value system. But we will compare with Allport's the ideas of another psychologist who has taken the trouble to be aware about the subject, namely William James.

James' views of mature religion. James made no particular attempt to define mature religion as such. True to the pragmatic tradition he simply examined religious lives as he saw them and abstracted therefrom certain characteristics that he felt resulted from religious striving at its most intense. These he describes in his lectures on "Saintliness" in *Varieties*.[4]

It should be remarked that James' picture of the developed religious life would doubtless find more favor with the monk in his cell, who might very well turn up his nose at the concepts of Allport. Though James was hardly a pious person himself, his criteria nevertheless exude more nearly the odor of piety, and while Allport might plead that he is simply describing religion as it ought to be in maturity, James could reply that he is describing it as it frequently is. Since the saint shows us how religion is lived when at its best, he is presenting a model which all ought to follow. In this sense James is describing mature religion. He describes four marks of the inner disposition of the saint, and then four practical consequences which he conceives as flowing from the inner condition.

(1) The first mark of the saint is his *feeling that he dwells in a larger life* than that bounded by the petty interests of this world, "sensible of the existence of an Ideal Power." This power is usually identified as God, particularly in the Christian tradition, but it may sometimes have a less definite focus of reference, as in the case of nature mysticism.

(2) Close to this characteristic comes that of a *sense of the con-*

[4] Lectures 11–13.

tinuity of the friendly power with one's own life and a surrender to its control.

(3) As a result of the self-surrender there comes a *sense of immense elation and freedom*, as concern for self diminishes.

(4) Finally there is *a shifting of the emotional center toward loving and harmonious affections*, "toward 'yes, yes,' and away from 'no,' where the claims of the non-ego are concerned."

The key to the saintly life as James describes it is to be found in the latter two of the above characteristics. For he emphasizes the pure abandon and giving up of the saint's formerly habitual and conventional life as he loses himself in the hot urge to serve his God. The saint is carried away in a kind of passion to disregard caution and all lesser considerations in the fulfillment of what he feels is his divine destiny. It is this transcendence of self that makes possible the feats of asceticism, strength of soul, purity of mind, and charity that form the substantial substrata of the folklore of sainthood and that cause the plain, unimaginative man to blink his eyes with incredulity. We honor a St. Francis, a Gandhi, or an Albert Schweitzer, but we can hardly bring ourselves to imagine imitating them. Indeed it is quite commonplace for one who has undergone a profound spiritual experience to be amazed at changes that he had not previously considered possible in his own habits and thought.

True to his avowed purpose to examine religion in its extreme forms, James, in describing the saint as the flower of the religious life, is obviously describing a spiritual rarity. He is setting up not so much a norm as an "abnorm." Yet he makes it very clear that this "abnorm" is a phenomenon of great value to society, and is therefore an ideal to which every truly religious person should aspire. In this sense it is a standard by which we can measure religious maturity.

But it is clear that Allport and James have somewhat different approaches to the concept of the religion of maturity. In a certain sense it may not be fair to either to compare them, yet a comparison will help throw a clearer light on each.

Allport's standards betray much more of the typical academic approach with its emphasis on the critical faculty and the orderly, coherent unfolding of a personality pattern of religious value. His excellent and thoughtful survey of maturity consequently appeals to college professors, intellectuals, undergraduates, and others with whom things of the mind enjoy high prestige.

But where Allport presents us with a restrained and relatively domesticated concept of mature religion, James' brand is wild-eyed, passionate, and strange. Allport's religious man we often find walking among us, and even if this ideal is found in its perfection no more than any other, nevertheless it is recognizable as partially but definitely developed in many of our friends and acquaintances. Furthermore, unlike some of James' saints, he tends to be sufficiently proper so that if we appear in public with him we do not secretly hope that no one will recognize us.

In his picture of the saint, on the other hand, James is much less conventional, and doubtless was disapproved of by his professorial friends at Harvard (who, incidentally, were quite used to looking on their distinguished colleague's views with a certain amount of academic dismay). Where Allport suggests the critical faculty and reason, James speaks of the "abandon" of the saint. In place of the careful co-ordination of all facets of the personality in the service of religion, James' saint throws all considerations to the winds and is interested only in expressing the one thing that seems to him of paramount importance.

The respectable citizen distinctly does not want to have too much to do with an authentic saint, who often proves to be a very inconvenient companion. Who would wish to attend services with George Fox, afraid that at any moment he might rise to his feet to castigate the preacher in the middle of his sermon; while a Saint Francis who insisted on licking the sores of afflicted people might soon find himself afoul of the Board of Health. Within modern times, the prophet Gandhi was the subject of much sophisticated merriment as he traveled among London society in his loincloth, while many who have chaperoned Schweitzer in his ill-fitting black suit have been consoled only by the knowledge that others knew them to be in the company of a very distinguished man.

Yet there are points of contact between James and Allport. One of these involves Allport's concept of the dynamic nature of the mature religious sentiment as an urge that becomes deeply rooted in the psyche, needing no motive other than itself to drive it onward. This would seem eminently to describe James' saint, the chief difference being that James does not mention anything to parallel the differentiation within the sentiment that Allport feels is so important. And certainly both James and Allport would agree on the latter's third point, namely, that high religion is productive of a consistent morality. On other aspects of Allport's criteria it is not clear that the two would differ, yet neither is it explicitly clear that they could get together. We may conclude then from our examination of both that religion at its best involves at the least a firmly rooted source of personal motivation and drive which has clearly consistent results in personal morality.

Ideas from the Wiemans and Fromm. Others who have made important contributions to the concept of religion at its best include the Wiemans and Erich Fromm. In *Normative Psychology of Religion* [5] the former describe what they call "norms" or standards for measuring religious development. These are not norms in the sense of *normal* or *average*, but rather ideal standards of excellence that will help in determining how nearly the religion of an individual approaches perfection or how far short it falls.

The norms are six in number: (a) *worthfulness* of the objective from the point of view of all humanity, (b) *completeness* of the loyalty, (c) *efficiency* in attaining the objective, (d) *sensitivity* in sensing and discriminating between values, (e) *progression* of loyalties as lesser aims are outgrown and higher aims take their places, and (f) *social effectiveness* of the loyalty in pervading and influencing society. A little reflection will show us that there is much overlapping between the Wiemans' views and those of Allport and perhaps some with those of James. However, it will be noted that there is more emphasis on the social implications of religion. Allport and James both discuss some of these implications; indeed it might be argued that in his pragmatic emphasis on the fruits of religion the latter, like the Wiemans, emphasized social usefulness as a standard. Yet the focus of their interests is on the individual, while religious maturity for the Wiemans to a greater degree is concerned with the interaction between the individual's religious life and society. In other words, the Wieman approach is closer to that of the social psychologist or sociologist.

[5] See especially pp. 376 ff.

Fromm, on the other hand, swings to the opposite extreme. He distinguishes between what he calls *authoritarian* and *humanistic* religion.[6] The former is derived from other people and tyrannizes over the native impulses of the individual. The latter has its springs in the creative forces of the individual himself, though it can never become completely independent of social forces. In spite of this, Fromm reserves his warmest accolade for the religion that wins its way against the opposed definitions of others to express the deepest convictions of the creative self. Thus to him *humanistic* religion represents religion in its finest flower.

Additional ideas. Certainly one of the criteria for mature religion is its capacity to grow. Allport emphasizes this in his listing of the capacity to extend the self as one of his three fundamental requirements of the mature personality, represented more specifically with respect to religion in his insistence on its heuristic and comprehensive quality. Wiemans' progression of loyalties gets at the same idea in a somewhat different way.

In this connection it will be appropriate to give a brief picture of the growth of the self. The new-born child comes into the world with merely the rudimentary equipment of self and no conscious notion of it whatsoever. In another year this concept is beginning to dawn, and the focus of consciousness lies in the infant's gratification of its own desires. The self, in other words, is a very narrow one; yet paradoxically it is the core out of which the most exalted altruism grows. For first the child identifies his self and well-being with that of his mother and his narrow family circle. From there the widening circle of the self may take in his school, his community, his country, and finally all of mankind. The fully mature religious person never sends to know for whom the bell tolls, knowing that it tolls for him.

But all of us lie between these two extreme poles of the completely narrow self and the completely full and all-embracing one. The ideal, total identification of ourselves with the larger community is never quite an accomplished fact. There are always flaws and incompletenesses so that our neat description of the expansion of the

---

[6] See his *Psychoanalysis and Religion*.

self is always more theoretical than real, regardless of the individual to whom it may have specific reference. The stages of one's development have been only more or less thoroughly consolidated.

But one notices that there are certain persons who, when it comes to a conflict between the claims of the wider and the narrower self, tend always to the narrower; the bias of their natures is toward contraction rather than expansion. They can usually be depended on to choose their own comfort in preference to that of other members of the family; they prefer the well-being of their own social class rather than the interests of the country as a whole; while they are the super-patriots who are sure that any yielding of the national treasury or sovereignty in the interests of the world community is a most deplorable soft-headedness. In the field of religion, these same people constitute the denominational watchdogs, jealous of the success of any creed but their own. They are simply immature. Chronically fearful because of weak development of their egos, they reveal the selfish person for what he is—a person who has never properly grown up.

Another type of person, faced with the same conflicts of interests, habitually chooses the wider interest, not irresponsibly, like Rip Van Winkle, but with the capacity to identify the welfare of others with his own. This is one of the facets of the mature religious nature that we see demonstrated in so many of the great personalities of the ages. It is for this reason that they belong, not to their own countries or denominations, but to the world.

Still another hallmark of the mature religious person is his humility. Anyone who has enjoyed the privilege of meeting persons like Albert Schweitzer, Toyohiko Kagawa, or Sir Wilfred Grenfell, has noticed that they are unpretentious men. They are not without a certain native authority when things important to them are to be done or said, but are far from overwhelmed at thoughts of their own goodness. Indeed, they appear so little impressed with their own eminence that a meeting with them seems at first an anticlimax.

Perhaps this quality is simply a demonstration in practice of Allport's trait of differentiation of the mature religious sentiment. No wholesomely critical person can ever be impressed with his own spirituality. His insight into himself is so keen, and his vision is so vast, that perspective does not allow him to see himself as anything but a poor representative of something much better than himself. It is this that makes growth possible.

Another thought springs from our definition of religion as "the inner experience of a person when he senses a Beyond, especially as evidenced by the effect of this experience on his behavior when he actively attempts to harmonize his life with the Beyond." We have already noted that magical religion is characteristic of the child. Much of what passes for religion is not religion but, psychologically interpreted, nothing more than magic. The attempt of the average worshiper to inflict the petty desires in his own breast on the Almighty is exactly the psychological objective of the average primitive who practices magic, different though the external trappings of the act may be.

The truly religious person is not only sensitive to what appear to him to be apprehensions of the Divine nature, but he takes these insights as guides in the practical business of putting his life into harmony with them. These apprehensions may come to him together with experiences of greater or lesser conviction. Yet important to the process is the attempt to actualize them in his own life. As he succeeds or fails, so will these experiences condition his next encounter with spiritual Presence. This attitude of *active attempt to conform with the Will of God* is another of the identifying qualities of mature religion.

A final consideration concerns religion as a force giving meaning to life. The mature religious person sees his religion as a central concern throwing light on the mystery of existence in such a way as to give point to it with a depth, comprehensiveness, and satisfying quality that is equaled by no other means of explanation. He is to be distinguished from the superficially religious, for whom religion is an interest lying on the periphery of life. This characteristic helps to explain the dynamic nature of mature religion, as noted by Allport. A faith that derives from a sense of the meaning of life that transcends the limits of the known is best calculated to generate the motivational strength and participation in life which lead to the joy of pursuing an activity for its own sake. At this point "functional autonomy" becomes possible for the religious motive.

This quality alone will not mark a religious life as mature. Other standards must be met as well. In his *Travels with a Donkey*, Stevenson remarks on the bloodthirsty career of one Pierre Seguier, a French Protestant leader, whose singleminded devotion to what he supposed was the Lord's work wrought destruction among his Catholic antagonists in an eighteenth-century religious feud. Yet when he was brought to justice and a martyr's death, he declared, "My soul is like a garden full of shelter and of fountains!" He demonstrates that not all religion that gives meaning to life and comes to be pursued for its own sake is necessarily mature. Furthermore, honest observation forces one to acknowledge that there are other motives than religion capable of high intensity and functional autonomy.[7]

But we can say that, failing this, religion cannot be mature. It must give a meaning to life that is a central factor in the motivational system of the individual.

In conclusion. We have been trying to describe religion when it is most effective, or religion operating at its best within the individual. In view of the vast area comprehended under the term "religion," and in view of the varying forms it takes in different individuals, brief reflection is sufficient to impress one with the enormous complexity of the subject. Our brief survey is but an introduction.

It is furthermore complicated by the added consideration that it involves value judgments. No description of the characteristics of mature religion is lacking the taint of the subjectivism of him who describes. We have tried at least to infuse some balance into our subjectivism by confining our discussion largely to the ideas of others. The subject obviously has importance, for we often have occasion to appraise the value of religious experience. When this concerns the experience of others we may do well to heed the injunction to "judge not that ye be not judged," yet there are occasions when this dangerous procedure may not be escaped. Furthermore there is no doubt of its value in that old-fashioned but wholesome process of self-examination.

[7] Evidence that people in general feel that interest and satisfaction in work for its own sake is the most important factor in their creative and constructive achievements is to be found in my "A Study of Some of the Factors Leading to Achievement and Creativity, with Special Reference to Religious Skepticism and Belief."

It is at this point that the psychologist may be of help. We will not assume that he has the last word but simply that his discipline qualifies him to raise issues which should be considered. Consequently we will summarize by casting the main points made in this chapter in the form of questions that should lend themselves to the sort of appraisal of which we have spoken. The questions will not be all-inclusive, nor will they match the paragraphs point for point, but they will attempt to distill the chief insights to be derived from our consideration of the reflections of psychologists on the problem of mature religion. What, then, are these questions that will help us to recognize mature religion when we encounter it?

Ten questions for appraising mature religion. (1) *Is it primary?* Does the religion derive from a sense of compelling individual need, or is it a piece of pious, imitative play-acting? This will not always distinguish it from immature religion, but it will from dead religion. Whatever else it is, mature religion must always be alive.

(2) *Is it fresh?* Has it, like religion in childhood, a fresh sense of curiosity and cosmic wonder?

(3) *Is it self-critical?* Can the individual see weaknesses in his religious position at the same time that he remains loyal to it?

(4) *Is it free from magic?* Does the individual sense a source of Ideal Power to which he gives free obedience in his attempt to harmonize his life with the Divine? In other words, is his a genuine religion as we have defined it or merely a magical substitute conceived of by the individual as a means of securing favors from a cosmic source?

(5) *Is it meaningfully dynamic?* Does his religion give meaning to life in such a way as to enlist and motivate his total energies so that it is capable of becoming a satisfaction for its own sake?

(6) *Is it integrating?* Does it relate itself to all of his experience, thus integrating his life and demonstrating moral results consistent with his own aims as well as those of a wholesome society?

(7) *Is it socially effective?* Does the individual's religion strengthen his sense of community with others in such a way as to be ultimately creative of a more wholesome society?

(8) *Does it demonstrate humility?*

(9) *Is it growing?* Is his faith an expanding one both in his search

for deeper truths and in his progressively wider, willing identification of the interests of others with his own?

⁄(10) *Is it creative?* Does the religious life of the individual contain elements and show characteristics of its own, or is it in every respect a mere repetition of the religion of others? In a sense this is the supreme test of the mature religious life.

Part 3

ASPECTS OF THE RELIGIOUS LIFE

Chapter 12

MYSTICISM

When we speak of mysticism we have now before our mind a great historic phenomenon, found everywhere that religion is found.
—W. E. Hocking

Even so, this organ of knowledge must be turned around from the world of becoming together with the entire soul, like the scene-shifting periact in the theater, until the soul is able to endure the contemplation of essence and the brightest region of being.
—Plato

We have now finished the task of examining the process of psychological growth as it relates to religion. In the chapters remaining to us we will consider various aspects of the religious life, the first of which will be that of *mysticism*.

In approaching this subject we will be approaching an area which at the same time is one of the most fundamental and basic aspects of the religious consciousness and one of the most puzzling and controversial. On the one hand there are those who deplore anything mystical as a relic of superstition, the Dark Ages, and the primitive. On the other, there are those who look on almost any disordered imagination with a pretense to mystical experience as directly in touch with God Himself, provided only that the words used in describing the experience are sufficiently pious.

The psychologist, because he is a scientist and is well equipped with information about the aberrations and self-deceptions of human nature, is apt to be skeptical of the claims of the mystic and regard him as at least a neurotic, if not worse. Even the religious mind, particularly if in the liberal tradition, may disclaim mysticism. Yet mystical experience has always received warm support among sensitive religious natures, not merely among those who are orthodox, but quite often even among those otherwise agnostic. Though there are religions with little of the mystic component, in general it may be said, with Hocking, as he is quoted at the head of this chapter, that it is found wherever religion is found.

There is a good reason for this. It is that there is no experience that will bring to the individual a vividness of religious certainty equal to that enjoyed by the mystic. This is not to say that *only* through the mystical experience can a conviction of the reality of the Divine be obtained. The rational theologian, through a process of logic, may convince himself that God exists. But this is a derived, not an immediate experience, whereas the mystic feels that he has met God face to face. It is the difference between reading about a person in the newspaper and actually spending an evening in conversation with him. The latter is so much more likely to generate conviction and loyalty. Hence we can sense the importance of mysticism in keeping religion alive and vigorous.[1] It is for this reason that mysticism deserves the attention of the psychologist.

What is mysticism?   One of the things that makes mysticism so much of a bone of contention among scholars is confusion about what the term means. To some it is simply a word of general opprobrium denoting anything dealing with the vaguely supernatural. To others, it suggests the occult—second sight, mind reading, clairvoyance, prophecy, and magic, with the esoteric rites connected with the same. Unfortunately, for semantic purity, there is some affinity between what might be termed "pure religious mysticism" and these other more doubtful concepts.[2] This makes for confusion. Furthermore, the scholar is forced to be somewhat arbitrary in defining what mysticism means for him.

But what we will be discussing in this chapter will not be mysticism in the foregoing senses. We will be speaking of mysticism as

[1] Cf. William James: "One may say truly, I think, that personal religious experience has its root and centre in mystical states of consciousness." *Varieties*, p. 370.

[2] See Evelyn Underhill, *Mysticism*, Part I, Chap. 7.

the subjective experience of a person who has what he tells others is a direct apprehension of some cosmic Power or Force greater than himself. This Power is not necessarily experienced as a personal God; Emerson did not feel it so. But usually it is. The experience is intuitive rather than sensuous or rational, though it may have associated with it rational and sensuous components, as for example a mystical theology or the hearing of voices. All of these elements were present in the mystical account most familiar to Christians, the conversion of Paul on the Damascus road, with his subsequent teachings based upon it.

Most characteristically, the mystic who has experienced God, and often before the experience, develops an intense desire, not only for the experience, but for living the kind of life in harmony with his intuition of God. In the most thoroughgoing and self-conscious type of mysticism the worshiper attains what he calls "union" with God, denoting the acme of this harmony, or identity with God in act and will.

When in our second chapter we defined religion as "the inner experience of the individual when he senses a Beyond," we did not intend to denote an exclusively mystical type of experience, for after all there is more than one way to "sense a Beyond." But very definitely we meant to include mysticism as probably the most characteristic and essential type of religious experience. Certainly the mystic who is in active search of the Divine Will with the idea of conforming himself to it is very clearly engaged in a religious quest as opposed to the practice of magic, as we have defined these two terms.[3]

As we have already intimated, mysticism finds its expression in many religions. In the Old Testament the stories of Moses meeting God in the burning bush and the wrestling with God by Jacob at Peniel both seem to refer to some ineffable religious experience that was mystical in nature. The Fourth Gospel is an interpretation of the life of Jesus by one who seems to have been a mystic. Pagan mysticism with an influence, not only on the Christian tradition but Jewish and Mohammedan as well, finds its roots in Plato. The celebrated analogy of the Cave in the seventh chapter of *The Republic* is one expression of that philosopher's mystical insights. So-called *Neo-Platonism*, particularly as interpreted by the great third-century

[3] See pp. 23, 146–147.

Greek mystic, Plotinus, has always been a force in the Christian tradition.

The Christian Era saw two great periods of the flowering of
mysticism, the Middle Ages and the seventeenth century. The influence of the life of St. Francis of Assisi was a powerful one in the
former, and Dante represents a poetic outpouring of the mystic
consciousness in that period. The great theological figures of this
time were often mystics, as in the cases of St. Bernard and St.
Thomas Aquinas. In the seventeenth century Brother Lawrence,
St. Francis de Sales, and Madame Guyon represent Catholic mysticism in a variety of forms, while Jacob Boehme and particularly
George Fox, founder of Quakerism, represent Protestant mysticism.[4]

But Christians especially must not be so parochial as to suppose
that mysticism is developed principally in their own tradition. It
looms even larger in the religions of India, particularly in Hinduism
and Buddhism, though with somewhat more emphasis on its passive
aspects. Lao Tze represents the tradition in China. Several centuries
before Plotinus, Philo and the Kabalists mark a very vigorous movement in Jewish mysticism, while about the twelfth century Mohammedan mysticism reached its height in Sufiism, whose leading
exponent was Al-Ghazzali.

It is quite obvious that the mystical consciousness is the monopoly
of no one time or religious tradition. Hence we are on firm ground
in recognizing in mysticism a universal religious experience deserving
the attention of the psychologist.

Probably the best way to make clear the meaning of mysticism is
to cite concrete examples.

One of its commonest forms is nature mysticism. Perhaps some
of the readers of these words may be surprised to discover that in
this form they have had mystical experiences of an elementary nature. The contemplation of the wonder and the beauty of nature
will often give one an immediate intuitive sense of a creative and
moving Presence behind it all. The greatest nature poet of England
was William Wordsworth, who in "Tintern Abbey" describes his
experience in these characteristic lines:

> . . . I have felt
> A presence that disturbs me with the joy

[4] For a brief history of Christian mysticism, see Underhill, *op. cit.*, Appendix.

> Of elevated thoughts; a sense sublime
> Of something far more deeply interfused,
> Whose dwelling is the light of setting suns,
> And the round ocean and the living air,
> And the blue sky, and in the mind of man;
> A motion and a spirit, that impels
> All thinking things, all objects of all thought,
> And rolls through all things. . . .

Again, it was the philosopher Kant who found the evidence of God equally from his contemplation of "the starry heavens above" with "the voice of conscience within."

A somewhat more representative religious expression may be found in some lines written by the Hindu mystic and statesman, Mahatma Gandhi.

I do dimly perceive that whilst everything around me is ever-changing, ever-dying, there is underlying all that change a Living Power that is changeless, that holds all together, that creates, dissolves, and re-creates. That informing Power or Spirit is God; and since nothing else that I see merely through the senses can or will persist, He alone is. . . .

But He is no God who merely satisfies the intellect, if He ever does. God, to be God, must rule the heart to transform it. He must express Himself in every smallest act of His votary. This can only be done through a definite realization more real than the five senses can ever produce. Sense perceptions can be, and often are, false and deceptive, however real they may appear to us. Where there is realization outside the senses it is infallible. It is proved, not by extraneous evidence, but in the transformed conduct and character of those who have felt the real presence of God within. . . . To reject this evidence is to deny oneself.[5]

Another description of a concrete mystical experience of a rather advanced nature may be found in the words of the renowned Spanish mystic, St. Teresa of Avila. The occasion was the climax of two years of prayer, according to her account, when she experienced a vision of Christ. Her confessor was somewhat skeptical of its genuineness, but she justifies it in these words:

For if I say that I see Him neither with the eyes of the body nor those of the soul—because it was not an imaginary vision—how is it that

[5] Quoted in Phillips, Howes, and Nixon (Eds.), *The Choice is Always Ours*, p. 472, from *Mahatma Ghandi's Ideas* by C. F. Andrews.

I can understand and maintain that He stands beside me, and be *more certain of it than if I saw Him?* If it be supposed that it is as if a person were blind, or in the dark, and therefore unable to see another who is close to him, the comparison is not exact. There is a certain likelihood about it, however, but not much, because the other senses tell him who is blind of that presence: he hears the other speak or move, or he touches him; but in these visions there is nothing like this. The darkness is not felt; only He renders Himself present to the soul by a certain knowledge of Himself which is more clear than the sun. I do not mean that we now see either a sun or any other brightness, only that there is a light not seen, which illumines the understanding so that the soul may have the fruition of so great a good. This vision brings with it great blessings.[6]

Such experiences, so immediate, intuitive, and inward, leave the poor psychologist at somewhat of a loss as to how to study them. Not only must one largely rely on what the subject says about it but, as St. Teresa suggests, even the subject himself has difficulty finding words. Certainly it is hopeless to expect exact measurement.

Furthermore, as with other aspects of the study of the psychology of religion, another difficulty rears its head, but here more threateningly than in any other connection. This is the temperament and experience of the psychologist. If he happens to be susceptible to mystical experience, he, like other mystics, is apt to have been convinced by the experience. Consequently, his estimate of the phenomenon is apt to be quite different from another's whose temperament and experience has kept him from any participation in the mystic life. One senses this difference in reading about mysticism as discussed by George A. Coe and by James H. Leuba, where one encounters a maximum of critical questioning tempered with a modicum of appreciation, as compared with writings by Evelyn Underhill or Rufus Jones, where one finds a maximum of appreciation and a modicum of questioning. Yet all of these are honest and capable scholars. The latter two, mystics themselves, though not psychologists, are nevertheless far from being unaware of what psychologists have to say. William James and James B. Pratt keep more to the middle of the road, probably because, on the one hand, they had good training in the scientific tradition, and, on the other, had

[6] Quoted in Underhill, *op. cit.*, pp. 284–285.

first-hand intimations of the mystic consciousness due to their dispositions.[7]

Consequently, though mystics themselves seem quick enough to understand and to agree with one another—at least about the reality if not the details of their experiences—scientists and scholars exhibit the widest range of differences of opinion in estimating and evaluating this subject. This is greatly at variance with the scientific ideal, which requires that two or more scientists who observe the same phenomenon should agree on it.

However, there are two more or less objective though indirect manifestations of mysticism for the psychologist to study. These are, first the spoken and written accounts of their experiences by the mystics themselves and second, the facts about their lives and observable behavior. These are the data traditionally used by psychologists of mysticism, who have made only sporadic and mostly abortive attempts to set up experiments to gain more exact knowledge. And it is a paradox that the participation in mystical experience itself gives the psychologist profounder understanding at the same time that it may cause his analysis to diverge from that of his "scientific" brethren who, being completely innocent of any taint of practical mysticism, may suppose themselves more objective. We do not pretend to be able to resolve this puzzle but feel that a student's mind should be directed to it as he approaches the subject.[8]

The characteristics of mysticism. Each student of mysticism is apt to note certain characteristics that distinguish it from other psychological states. Those that impressed William James were four: (1) Ineffability, (2) Noetic quality, (3) Transiency, and (4) Passivity.[9]

By *ineffability* he means that the mystic has difficulty in com-

---

[7] Though James modestly disclaimed any first-hand knowledge of mystical states (*Varieties*, p. 370), his letters indicate that he was subject at least to mild experiences of a mystical nature. See R. B. Perry's *Thought and Character of William James*, pp. 362 ff.

[8] The thorough scholar always approaches as near as he can to primary data in its totality. Consequently, in examining the statements of the mystics the student is advised not to be content with brief quotations, such as he finds in this and other volumes on the subject, but to do extensive reading in the writings of individual mystics. See Underhill, *op. cit.*, for a bibliography.

[9] *Varieties*, pp. 370–372.

municating his experience. We have already noted and illustrated this characteristic through the quotation from St. Teresa. The mystic says that he has had a perfectly definite experience but that he cannot explain it by any words he has available. He feels like a person trying to explain the experience of sight to one born blind. He has no trouble making himself clear to other mystics, but to the uninitiated he is often simply puzzling.

One of the most dramatic examples of this characteristic is Pascal's account of the one great mystical experience that preceded and shaped the most fruitful period of his career. After his death the description was found sewn into his coat where he had worn it for years as a kind of amulet. Its eloquence lies in its very incoherence, for here we have one of the clearest of all French writers and masters of style so shaken and moved that he is reduced to a few broken phrases in describing the most significant experience of his life:

> From about half past ten at night, to about half after midnight,
> Fire!
> God of Abraham, God of Isaac, God of Jacob,
> Not of the philosophers and the wise.
> Security, security. Feeling, joy, peace.
> God of Jesus Christ.
> Deum meum et Deum vestrum.
> Thy God shall be my God. . . .
> Joy, joy, joy tears of joy.[10]

It will be noticed that most of this Memorial merely describes the effect of the experience or comments on it, the description of the experience itself being confined to but one word, "Fire!"

The term *noetic* means that the subject feels that through the mystical experience he has achieved knowledge. This seems paradoxical when he cannot describe it or make clear to others just what the experience is. But the mystic says that through his vision he knows certain things in a way that he never knew them before. "And then at last I saw Thy invisible things," says St. Augustine, "understood by means of things that are made. . . ." [11] These are

---

[10] The entire Memorial, less than forty lines in length, may be found in the translation of Pascal's *Thoughts* by C. Kegan Paul, p. 2, or almost any life of Pascal.

[11] Quoted in Underhill, *op. cit.*, p. 331.

frequently concrete things or propositions, for instance, the existence of God, the mystery of the Trinity, or the "wheels within wheels" of Ezekiel. Such conventional symbols do not exhaust the significance of the experience, and St. Teresa, for one, after ecstasy, is able to particularize with considerable lucidity "the intellectual vision of the Trinity in the Seventh Habitation." [12] St. Francis Xavier mystically divided "the truths of the human sciences." [13] William Blake at the same time one of the most mystical and most turgid of English poets, was equally certain that he understood mysteries, but was not so successful in conveying clear ideas in his poem "Jerusalem" or the "Book of Thel."

For James the ineffability and noetic qualities were the most authentic characteristics of the mystic life. Transiency and passivity were of lesser importance. By *transiency* he referred to the uneven intensity of the mystical life. It is true that the influence of even one mystical experience may exert a steady influence throughout a life, but mystical visions themselves are episodic. Furthermore, in their most intense and ravishing stage, they are not apt to last very long— perhaps a half hour or a little longer. [14] We have seen that Pascal's vision lasted for two hours, but this is longer than is usual. One can sense through Pascal's words the intense emotional character of the vision, so that it is easy to see that physical limitation of the human frame is one of the conditioning factors here.

By *passivity* James refers to the fact that the subject in mystical experience feels himself in the grip of a Power other than himself. He feels that his thoughts and his feelings, even his bodily motions are somehow not the product of his own efforts but that of another. "Our satisfaction," said John of Ruysbroeck, "lies in submission to the Divine Embrace.[15] This does not mean that the experience is not prepared for. Sometimes, it is true, it is completely unexpected. Carlyle was not expecting the experience that he describes as "The Everlasting Yea." Even this was prepared for in an involuntary sense, while those who are often described as the "Great Mystics" almost invariably went through an intense period of active training as a prel-

---

[12] *Ibid.*, p. 108.
[13] Quoted in Pratt, *The Religious Consciousness*, p. 407.
[14] Cf. James, *op. cit.*, p. 372.
[15] Quoted in Underhill, *op. cit.*, p. 356.

ude to vision. But during vision the attitude is one of passivity, and part of the "art" of the mystic is giving himself up to "surrender" at the proper moment and allowing himself to be carried along by influences that seem to "blow in" from outside.

Not all students of the subject are impressed with the same features, and Evelyn Underhill has another list of four which in part contradicts William James.[16]

(1) "True mysticism is *active and practical*," says Miss Underhill, "not passive and theoretical." To support her position she quotes many mystics, among them St. John of the Cross:

> In an obscure night
> Fevered with love's anxiety
> (O hapless, happy plight!)
> I went, none seeing me,
> Forth from my house,
> Where all things quiet be.

Obviously, this suggests aloneness but not quietness and passivity; rather the turning of one's back thereon in favor of adventure. Furthermore she points out that, like a child in a progressive school, the mystic must learn not out of books but by *doing*. This *doing* consists not only of the active purification of one's daily life but, for best results, a rigorous course in meditation. This latter is the purpose of the celebrated *Spiritual Exercises* of St. Ignatius of Loyola, required of every Jesuit.

However, Miss Underhill does not so much contradict James, for she herself says that mystical achievement is in part an "act of surrender." [17] She simply shifts the focus of the emphasis; moreover, her point deserves respectful consideration because of her profound sympathy with the mystics and of her own not inconsiderable mystical achievement.

(2) The aims of mysticism "are *wholly transcendental and spiritual*. It is in no way concerned with adding to, exploring, re-arranging, or improving anything in the visible universe. The mystic brushes aside that universe, even in its supernormal manifestations. He does

---

[16] *Ibid.*, p. 81 ff. In the following discussion we will make frequent use of Miss Underhill's own words. In several places for clarity we shall use italics not found in the original.

[17] *Ibid.*, p. 84.

not, as his enemies declare, neglect his duty to the many, his heart is always set on the changeless One." [18] This suggests that the mystic conforms with at least one of Allport's criteria for mature religion in that his quest is dynamically supplied with motivation as an end in itself, quite apart from any considerations of earthly improvement. Perhaps it would be more accurate to say that any benefit to the world that may result from the mystic's way of life he regards as a perfectly normal and proper, but wholly incidental result of his aim of union with the Infinite. "His spirit," says Tauler, "is as it were sunk and lost in the Abyss of the Deity, and loses the consciousness of all creature-distinctions." [19]

(3) The changeless One for the mystic is "not merely the Reality of all that is, but also a living and personal object of Love; never an object of exploration." [20] By "love" Miss Underhill is not speaking of it in its more popular sense but as "the ultimate expression of the self's most vital tendencies." Time and again the language of the mystic suggests that in his encounter with God he has experienced the ultimate. He feels that all his longings have at last had an answer and that finally he can give himself completely over to the Destiny for which he has been made. This was the psychological experience to which Augustine gave utterance in his fine phrase, "for Thou has framed us for Thyself, and our heart is restless until it finds its rest in Thee." [21]

(4) "Living union with this One . . . is a *definite state or form of enhanced life*. It is obtained neither from an intellectual realization of its delights, nor from the most acute emotional longings. Though these must be present, they are not enough. It is arrived at by an arduous psychological and spiritual process—the so-called Mystic Way—entailing the complete remaking of character and the liberation of a new, or rather latent, form of consciousness; which imposes on the self the condition which is sometimes inaccurately called 'ecstasy,' but is better named the Unitive State." [22]

We have quoted at some length here because this passage seems to epitomize what Miss Underhill feels to be the most important

[18] *Ibid.*, p. 81.
[19] *Ibid.*, p. 84.
[20] *Ibid.*, p. 81.
[21] Phillips, *op. cit.*, p. 491.
[22] *Ibid.*, p. 81.

things she has to say in her description of mysticism. The lesson that it has for the psychologist is that mysticism is a clearly recognizable state of consciousness, just as is the case with hypnosis or being in love. It is not necessary to agree with all her emphases, but her four points, like William James', call our attention to important facets of the mystic life.

Perhaps, before we leave her analysis behind, we should note an important corollary to her four points. This, she emphasizes, is that *"true mysticism is never self-seeking."* We can accept this statement at the same time that we might remark an element of defensiveness as Miss Underhill seeks to protect her beloved mystics from an obvious accusation. For, as we will note later, some of the mystics are not without a certain egotistic strain.

To these points of James and Underhill we would like to make three emphases of our own, though nevertheless closely correlated with what has already been said.

(1) *The language of mysticism makes extensive use of figures of speech and paradox.* This, of course, is a corollary deriving from the ineffability of mystic experience. The mystic is forced to be a poet, for no matter how definite his experience appears to him, he can convey its nature to those who have not had it only through riddles and by saying it is like something else. It is similar to being in love. How is this commonplace young man to make clear to others what a remarkable person is that young woman, so plain and untalented in the eyes of others? Perhaps this is one reason why the favorite metaphor of the mystics is that of love and marriage. Furthermore, this is not merely a convention of the Christian tradition. Thus the Mohammedan Sufi mystic Jalalu 'd Din:

> With Thy sweet Soul, this soul of mine
> 　　Hath mixed as water doth with wine . . .
> Thy Love has pierced me through and through
> 　　Its thrill with Bone and Nerve entwine.
> I rest a Flute laid on Thy lips;
> 　　A lute, I on Thy breast recline.[23]

This characteristic, so unfortunate from the semantic point of view, simply compounds the problem for the scientist. For it is difficult to say whether the romantic figure is used simply because

[23] Underhill, *op. cit.*, p. 426.

it is the analogy best understood by ordinary people, or whether it represents merely an imperfectly sublimated sex impulse. The psychologist tends to favor the latter explanation, for here he feels himself on firm ground. A partisan of the mystics, such as Evelyn Underhill, will emphasize the purely spiritual interpretation. There is something to be said on both sides of the question. Yet we might here issue a warning against taking the words of the mystics too literally. This is a mistake made probably as often by those who suppose themselves the friends of religion as by its enemies. Consequently, it is hard to see how the psychologist can wholly renounce the unfamiliar role of the poet in studying mysticism. For just as the skillful psychotherapist must read through his patient's words to the meaning behind them, the psychologist will misinterpret the mystic's consciousness unless he uses a certain amount of intuition in trying to understand what the mystic is trying to say.

There is perhaps less of a problem with respect to the mystic's use of paradox. For here the literal interpretation makes such obvious nonsense that at least the investigator will not proceed on any surface understanding. And so when we read the words of Walter Hilton as he speaks of "lighty murkness and rich nought . . . purity of spirit and ghostly rest . . . a lively feeling of grace and privity of heart, the waking sleep of the spouse and tasting of heavenly savour, burning in love and shining in light . . ." we are inclined to agree with the quaint conclusion of this fourteenth-century mystic that "they are divers in showing of words, nevertheless, they are all one in sense of soothfastness." [24] Otherwise one is forced to relegate these dark sayings to the category of the abnormal and treat such utterances merely as the symptoms of illusion.

(2) Indeed this is exactly what the scientist is almost forced to do in self-defense, for a second characteristic of the mystics is that *they regard what the ordinary man considers the Real as the Unreal, and what the ordinary person considers the Unreal as the Real*. The most famous philosophical expression of this point of view is found in Plato's analogy of the Cave in the seventh chapter of *The Republic*, to which we have already made reference. In this image it seems that Plato must have been instructed through mystical experience of his own as well as that of his master Socrates. For the mystic, the world

[24] Quoted in *ibid.*, p. 307.

of sense and thought is a mere shadow land, a point of departure, a "far country," as Master Eckhart called it, from which the individual finds his way "home," via the mystic path, to the land of the untouchable but Real.

As one of the results of his mystical experience Pascal divided men into three "orders," each separate and distinct with characteristic values and functions, *body, mind, and charity*.[25] Just as the man who is content to live a merely vegetative existence has no inkling of the delights of a life of thought, so the man whose function is thought can have no inkling of the illumination of him who has seen the mystic vision and therefore understands what Pascal calls "charity." It is interesting that the possessor of such a fine scientific mind as that of Pascal should confirm the experience of other mystics in their empirical discovery of what appeals to them as another dimension of experience. This is another of the marks of the mystic.

(3) The third and final mark of the mystic is his *tendency toward extravagance in behavior,* especially as seen from the point of view of ordinary common sense. This follows from the radical views of reality that we have just mentioned. The mystic completely reverses the ordinary view of what constitutes reality and unreality, and with it the generally accepted value systems. Hence it is inevitable that most of us should regard his behavior with somewhat the same degree of incredulity with which a miser might see a spendthrift acquaintance bestow Cadillac cars and diamond rings as dinner favors.

Famous in the annals of mysticism are the efforts of the Blessed Henry Suso to mortify and so purify his sensitive body. We have noted his wearing of an undergarment studded with "a hundred and fifty brass nails" sharply pointed to sink into his flesh, submission to the attacks of voracious insects, and the sleeping alternately on the freezing floor in winter and in a cell too small to allow him properly to lie down.[26] Such behavior would seem obviously pathological.[27] But only a little less so was much of the behavior shown

[25] Blaise Pascal, *Thoughts,* pp. 226 ff.
[26] James' *Varieties,* pp. 301 ff., and see pp. 176–177 of this volume.
[27] In other respects Suso was more winning and equally courageous. Falsely accused by an enemy of fathering a bastard child, he risked his reputation by having the child cared for at his expense rather than to have it suffer neglect as the innocent instrument of his own discomfiture. See Underhill, *op. cit.,* pp. 410 ff.

by St. Francis and his followers. Complete improvidence seems to characterize the story of the Flemish Antoinette Bourignan. At eighteen this strong-willed young woman left her home with its bickerings, to live a life dedicated to poverty with but a penny to sustain her. But hearing a voice, "Where is thy Faith? In a penny?" she threw it away as a reinforcement of her resolve.[28] Compared to these, the American Quaker and mystic John Woolman was a monument to common sense and the practical life. Yet he chose for himself the trade of tailor rather than a more lucrative one because it involved him in less "cumber," and he was capable of sleeping all night in the woods rather than avail himself of the hospitality of a friend whose household was run by slaves.[29]

Fully understood, such behavior is not as Quixotic as it sounds, particularly if we can allow the mystics *the validity of their characteristic value systems*. Such extravagant behavior is simply the downright and drastic expression of the desire for integration of the psychic life. This tendency is seen in nearly all expressions of the religious life, and the almost universal emphasis on purity of life in all the great religions simply represents the craving for singleness of mind that even the most worldly of us occasionally feel. The mystic not only feels it, he does something about it, while mankind stands by partly appalled that any should exist who dare put into practice what most of us merely profess.

To summarize briefly, then, the foregoing discussion and to integrate in little space the three points of view, we may describe the characteristics of mysticism as follows: *Mysticism is a definite but sporadic state of the religious consciousness partly active and partly passive, involving an experience so unusually personal as to defy description in any but the most figurative and cryptic language. It involves the apprehension of a transcendental Presence which radically influences the individual's point of view and way of life. The consequent passionate devotion to this Presence tends to lead to an extremely unworldly value system. These values foster extravagant behavior which nevertheless stimulates integration of the psyche centered on this devotion.*

[28] *Ibid.*, p. 213.
[29] See *Journal and Essays of John Woolman.*

The mystic life and growth. As with all aspects of the religious life, mysticism is subject to change and growth, not to speak of regression as well. Though strictly speaking, conversion is a different psychological process, yet it is obvious that mysticism is closely related to conversion. As a matter of fact, nearly all religious conversions involve some intimation of mystic vision. The reader will find this well illustrated in the "Everlasting Yea" chapter of *Sartor Resartus,* from which we quoted in the chapter on Conversion,[30] as well as in the story of the conversion of Saul of Tarsus. Consequently, we may say that in some cases mystical experience may be an accompaniment or an expression of religious growth.

But as an end in itself we can think of it as a religious experience subject to growth and as such it may be deliberately cultivated. This self-conscious cultivation is not necessary, particularly in the case of the milder types of mystical experience, as our remarks on Carlyle's experience have already indicated. St. Paul's experience seems to have descended on him with an unexpectedness that involved considerable shock. But the devotee of mysticism is apt to wish to expand and enhance his delicious minutes with God. For this purpose he will find at hand many prescriptions.

Various mystics have described stages of mystic ascent. St. Teresa, in her *The Interior Castle,* described "Seven Degrees of Contemplation," while Bunyan's *Pilgrim's Progress* is simply the most popular expression, in allegorical form, of Bunyan's own personal growth, which was at least partly mystical in nature. Carlyle lists "The Everlasting No," "The Center of Indifference," and "The Everlasting Yea." Evelyn Underhill uses five steps in her analysis of the subject. There would not be much profit in quibbling over what the steps might be, for in most of these cases the mystic is simply generalizing from his own experience. It is sufficient to remark that there is such a thing as progress in the Mystic Way, whether in well-defined stages or gradual unfolding of the subject's mystical powers.

Miss Underhill's five steps will serve to indicate by their names the general outlines of this progress. They are (1) Awakening, (2) Purification, (3) Illumination, (4) the Dark Night of the Soul, and (5) the Unitive State or Spiritual Marriage—often referred to as the

[30] See pp. 196–198.

Ecstasy. Of these, the "Dark Night of the Soul," a term taken from St. John of the Cross, requires special mention. It indicates that the course of the mystic experience, like that of true love, seldom runs smooth, for the mystic's most poignant experience is that of finding that he has lost the Vision. For a time nothing that he is able to do seems to be able to restore it. Physical and mental exhaustion may well have their influence on these states, which are well known to mystics of all times and conditions. The Forty-Second Psalm gives eloquent expression to an experience of this kind from the lips of an unknown Hebrew mystic.

As the hart panteth after the water brooks, so panteth my soul after thee, O God.
My soul thirsteth for God, for the living God: when shall I come and appear before God?
My tears have been my meat day and night, while they continually say unto me, Where is thy God? . . .
Why art thou cast down, O my soul? and why art thou disquieted in me? hope thou in God: for I shall yet praise him for the help of his countenance.

As the steps of Miss Underhill suggest, however, the Dark Night of the Soul, sometimes also referred to as a time of Spiritual Dryness, is seldom permanent. The traveler in the Mystic Way who perseveres will eventually reach his goal of union with God.

The most general and common means of stimulating mystical experience and growth are the forms and ceremonies of various religious faiths which frequently, though not always, have this purpose as one of their aims. Within the Christian tradition the Catholic liturgy has been considerably more prolific of mystical experience than has Protestant worship, though Protestantism is by no means without its mystics. Probably Quakerism, with its emphasis on silence and the Inner Light, has been the best-known Protestant stimulant to mysticism, although of a brand very closely linked with the active practice of Christian ethical principles. Yoga will serve as an instance of an Indian form of mystical discipline highly developed and with remarkable features.[31]

Manuals and directives have appeared, particularly some designed

[31] See Ernest Wood, *Great Systems of Yoga.*

by Catholics. The *Spiritual Exercises* of Ignatius Loyola is an example of a very thorough and detailed prescription for the practice of mysticism. On the other hand a more popular, yet more discursive, manual of meditations is the religious classic, *The Imitation of Christ* by Thomas à Kempis.[32] Beside the liturgy of worship and directives for meditation, various forms of art have been enlisted as auxiliary stimuli to the mystic life. And so we have religious sculpture and painting, stained-glass windows, and Gothic architecture, which at its best is an attempt to symbolize in stone the magnificence and mystery of spiritual transcendence. Again, the color and pageantry of religious ritual has been heightened by music such as the Medieval Plainsong or Gregorian Chant.

All this is evidence of the fact that growth characterizes religion in its mystical as with its other forms, also that this growth may come about both through the voluntary attempt to foster it as well as involuntarily by means of influences working from without and within. Obviously, differences in temperament make for differences in aptitude, and it would seem that not only the temper of the times but also individual psychological make-up would render many people peculiarly unfit for any participation in mysticism.[33] But just as almost any Philistine can be taught at least some elementary appreciation of art if he desires to learn, so it seems likely that nearly anyone may acquire for himself some small first-hand experience of the mystic life.[34]

Roots of the mystical life. Any attempt by a psychologist to explain mysticism is bound to seem superficial and fruitless to the mystic himself, since the psychologist must leave out the only fact the mystic considers worth bothering much about, namely God. We must concede that it would appear sensible first to settle the metaphysical problem of the nature of the object of the mystic's quest,

[32] Now thought by many scholars to have been written by Gerhard Groote.

[33] Such a person would seem to be Starbuck's respondent quoted on p. 90 of James' *Varieties*, and in our Chap. 8, p. 157.

[34] The reader may wish to try a simple experiment described by Evelyn Underhill. She asserts that nearly anyone who in complete quietude will steadily contemplate any simple object, resolutely shutting out from the mind all ideas and thoughts except those derived from the object, will come to have some elementary first-hand understanding of mystic contemplation. See *Mysticism*, pp. 310 ff., for her full description and comment.

but since we have renounced any competence in theology by espousing the scientist's point of view, we will have to confine our-selves to less exalted themes. To use Pascal's conceptions, we will be operating within the order of "mind" rather than "charity," even though the mystic life itself belongs to the latter order.

But at this point we wish to remind the reader that we do not subscribe to the "nothing but" fallacy. It does not follow, simply because we point out various psychological factors, some quite un-complimentary, which obviously condition the mystical life, that we claim that mystical experience is "nothing but" the expression of these factors. Since mysticism is a psychological state, we will do what we can to account for it, but psychologically it considerably exceeds in complexity the competence of a whole separate volume to do justice to it. We will have space only to present a few brief hints, especially because we have already in Chapter 4 touched on many of the factors that will help to explain mysticism along with other phases of the religious life.

In the previous section of our present chapter we mentioned *temperament* as an important prerequisite of mystical experience. People differ in their capacity for mysticism. As one reviews the lives of many mystics one receives the impression that the "sick soul" rather than the "healthy-minded" [35] is much more fully repre-sented among their ranks. Suso, George Fox, Antoinette Bourignan, St. Augustine, Madame Guyon, William Blake, Saints Catherine of Genoa and Siena, and Pascal were just a few in whose lives suffering played a prominent part. In Miss Underhill's steps of the Mystic Way both Purgation and the Dark Night of the Soul suggest suf-fering.

One feels that this suffering is at least partly due to the mystic's superior capacity for it because of his general sensitivity to all stimuli. Yet there is no doubt but that external circumstance has often played a part. For example, with the exception of St. Catherine of Siena, all of the women mentioned above suffered from unhappy home situations. These difficult situations acted on sensitive per-sonalities.

Also, the very unusualness of the mystic's temperament sets him apart from the crowd. The fact that his value system is different,

[35] See Chap. 8.

and that he acts in accordance with it, tends to bring him into conflict with family and society. St. Francis, we note, could not reconcile his wealthy family to his espousal of poverty. The spiritual
pioneer is not apt to be a favorite among the group with whom he
has been brought up.

A second factor is the *tradition* in which the mystic grows up as
well as the temper of the times. The fact that certain religious traditions and certain ages have produced more mystics than others is
a sufficient demonstration of this point. Another is that, despite the
novelty and noetic quality to him who experiences a mystic illumination, the substance of these revelations is not normally at
sharp variance with the orthodoxy of his own particular group. Thus
the Blessed Angela of Foligno in "marvellous illumination" was
"inspired to a consideration of the blessed union of the Deity and
Humanity of Christ," [36] while St. Teresa is shown the secret of the
Trinity. Despite the fact that the mystics are often bold individual-
ists, nevertheless this boldness often expresses a zeal for orthodoxy
and The Cause which is keener than that of the superiors they are
sworn to obey. Thus Teresa was capable of circumventing her immediate superiors in her urge to found many monasteries,[37] while
Loyola ran the risk of being declared a heretic before his famous
campaigns against Protestantism got under way. The mystic may be
more orthodox than the orthodox.

A third factor about which there has been much controversy, is
that of *self-hypnosis and psychosomatic suggestion*. To certain pious
minds this idea will seem almost blasphemous, but no candid student of mysticism can fail to note certain similarities between the
hypnotic state and some of the more extreme cases of mystical
trance. Similarly other psychosomatic principles, whether dealing
with hysterical conditions or otherwise, can also be seen to operate
in such cases. An illustration is the phenomenon known as *stigmatiza-
tion*, demonstrated first in medieval times on the persons of St.
Francis of Assisi, St. Catherine of Siena, and other mystics. This
consists of marks, sometimes open wounds, paralleling the wounds
on the body of Christ at the Crucifixion.

[36] Quoted in Thorold, *An Essay in Aid of the Better Appreciation of Catholic
Mysticism*, p. 120.
[37] See Leuba, *Psychology of Religious Mysticism*, p. 109.

The following excerpts from an account of phenomena observed on a nineteenth-century French mystic, Louise Lateau, is based on accounts by several responsible eyewitnesses. There would seem to be no reason for doubting their accuracy, though there might be difference of opinion as to the significance.

. . . they found the young girl occupied in working her sewing-machine. Blood was flowing abundantly from her feet, her hands, her side, and from all round her head. . . . Soon the machine stopped suddenly, the two hands of Louise became immovable, she was ravished into an ecstasy. . . .

M. l'abbé Mortier . . . wanted to place the vessel with the holy oils near the lips of Louise. When he was about two yards from the chair upon which she was sitting, she exhibited an extraordinary trembling, lively movements and a transport of joy. She rose, and fell suddenly upon her knees in adoration, her trembling hands joined and held out toward the sacred vessels; her face was truly seraphic. M. l'abbé Mortier drew back, always holding the blessed instrument in his hands; she followed the priest, who retired slowly. She was half-kneeling, half-standing, leaning forward, her hands joined; she looked as if she were drawn by a magnet, and if she were gliding rather than walking. M. l'abbé Mortier and Mgr. d'Herbomez made her go right around the room in this way, and, each time they stopped, Louise fell upon her knees in an attitude of adoration. When they had come back close to her chair, they removed the sacred vessels and placed them at some distance from her; she sat down, returned to her immobility, and the ordinary scenes of the ecstasy went on again, just as upon other Fridays.[38]

Anyone familiar with the phenomena of hypnosis or psychosomatic suggestion will think of similarities between this performance and conditions long recognized by the psychologist and studied by him.[39]

It is also quite likely that the possession of some of the personality qualities of the typical hysteric is a contributory factor in some

---

[38] Thorold, *op. cit.*, pp. 177 ff. The account goes on to relate the miraculous clairvoyant recognition of the presence of a morsel of the consecrated Host reposing in one of the vessels unknown to the priests. It is interesting that modern parapsychologists report evidence of similar phenomena of wholly secular nature produced by them under controlled conditions. See *The Journal of Parapsychology* or J. B. Rhine's, *The Reach of the Mind* for various accounts.

[39] See Weatherhead, *Psychology, Religion, and Healing*, Sec. 2.

cases. These include not only the tendency to split-off or trancelike states of consciousness and physical symptoms of psychic origin, but also the desire for the limelight and attention even at the cost of the welfare of others. In her zeal for a life of conspicuous piety, Madame Guyon seems to have been something less than an ideal wife and mother.[40] The Blessed Angela of Foligno in one of her visions heard God tell her that He loved her "more than any other soul in the Spoletan valley." In another passage (which she must have regretted could she have foreseen its effect on her posthumous reputation) she tells of begging God to deliver her from her family and her "great consolation" in losing by death within a short space of time her mother, husband, and all her sons! [41]

We have warned against the too literal interpretation of the figurative language that is so usual with the mystics. Yet it seems likely that at least some of these romantic metaphors represent a sex urge sometimes more and sometimes less wholesomely sublimated. Thus we can look on *sex* as a fourth source conditioning mystical experience. We know, for example, that both St. Catherine of Genoa and Madame Guyon lived lives of frustrated marital fulfillment at home, and it seems likely that there was more than a modicum of earthly feeling represented when the latter told God that she loved him "more passionately than the most passionate lover ever loved his mistress," or when she craved "the love that thrills and burns and leaves one fainting in an inexpressible joy and pain." [42] Furthermore, she herself seems completely unaware of how much her relations with at least two priests seem to have been largely a gratification of her thwarted sex impulses.

However, one must recognize that this does not necessarily vitiate the value of a mystic's life and insights. It is easy to manufacture a picture bordering on the sensational by snatching ejaculations out of context and reading into them what must be largely conjecture, no matter how probable. It is for this reason that the reader must be encouraged, before he passes any final judgment on the explanation of a mystic's experience, to examine the mystic's life and writ-

[40] See account and comments on life of Madame Guyon and other mystics in Leuba, *op. cit.*, Chaps. 4 and 7.

[41] Thorold, *op. cit.*, pp. 124, 96.

[42] Leuba, *op. cit.*, pp. 145–146; see the whole section for a discussion of this problem.

ings in their entirety. There is much more inspiring matter to be found in the lives of all of the mystics we have been citing. Nevertheless, no matter how much he may deplore the necessity, every mystic is irrevocably tied to a body. It would be strange if bodily conditions did not in some way affect its possessor's experience, and one of these conditions is most certainly sex.

Closely allied with sex is the fifth and final factor which we will mention. This is the *childish desire for security and escape*. Freudians of course link this with the sex urge through the experience of childish love for the parent. We have seen, in Chapter 3, that Freud regards the "search for the father image" as the root of all religion. His followers have applied this same formula to mysticism in particular. Ostow and Scharfstein in *The Need to Believe* develop this theme in their work, which is in essence a modern psychology of religion from the psychoanalytical point of view.[43] Here they tell the story of the eight-year-old Plotinus and his love of returning to the breast of his nurse. "The tendency to retreat and to demand the love and security granted an infant," say these commentators, "had already been established, and his later longing to join God in a union of love was a reappearance on a new level of the old desire." Similarly, they cite the nirvana of Buddhism:

It is a return to what some psychoanalysts call the "oceanic reunion", the world of the fed, satisfied baby on the delicious edge of sleep. All one's pleasure impulses are withdrawn from external objects and located inside oneself. And the variegated responses of the mind are narrowed and merged until they approximate the semiconscious, slumbrous, undifferentiated pleasure of the baby immersed in the uniform ocean of his feeling. It is a state of both omnipotence and dependence, and often the mystic feels his absorption to be a happy helplessness in which a force that is greater than himself but includes himself handles him as a parent handles a child.

Interpreted in this way, mysticism becomes little more than a weak, abnormal withdrawal into a land of illusion. The mystic is seen as a kind of schizophrenic, as Ostow and Scharfstein imply. It is interesting to contrast their interpretation with Evelyn Underhill's, which looks on mysticism as a life of intense positive activity.

[43] Pp. 115–125.

Nevertheless we must accept dependency and escape as one of the many roots of the mystic life. It is not surprising if in some cases it becomes the chief one.

A final comment, as a kind of footnote to our subject, may be made on the use of drugs in the stimulation of the ecstasy—or perhaps we should say pseudo-ecstasy. James, in his chapter on mysticism in the *Varieties,* remarks on similarities between mystical states and those produced by alcohol, nitrous oxide, and other anesthetics. More recently, in *The Doors of Perception,* Aldous Huxley celebrates the virtues of mescalin, as a safe and sane, non-habit forming means of producing mystical insight. He supports this by an account of a personal mystical experience induced by mescalin. In his book *Mysticism* R. C. Zaehner sharply attacks Huxley's views, citing an experience of his own with mescalin that failed to produce the spiritual values that Huxley claims. At the very least it seems that it is safe to conclude that the presuppositions that one brings to such an experience will affect its value. Also we may note the danger that people may fall into the easy assumption that the swallowing of a pill or the jab of a hypodermic needle is all that is necessary to open the eyes to heavenly secrets. Doubtless the scientist may learn something about mystical experience with carefully controlled experiments with appropriate drugs. But, to be effective, mystical experience must be integrated into a much larger whole. Drugs here as elsewhere may be found chiefly to play their familiar role as an escape from the real problems of life.

The significance of mysticism.   It is not properly a part of the psychologist's duty to evaluate, yet it is important that he show the relevance and significance of the phenomena that he studies. This inevitably involves some evaluation, implicit or otherwise.

We have already said that views on the value of mysticism differ. To those who hold that it is primarily an escape from life or a phenomenon of self-hypnosis the evaluation is foregone. "In seeking intercourse with God in the disappearance of diversity, in the peace of utter surrender, in excruciating delights, in a sense of freedom and illumination, the mystics have followed a wrong way," says Leuba.[44]

[44] *Op. cit.,* p. 316.

For him the passivity of the vision and the subordination of the conscious intelligence in the ecstasy is an abdication of the highest power of man, namely his reason.

But we would like to point out that the value of mystic intuition does not stand or fall with the extreme expressions of that way of life. Spranger in *Types of Men* [45] defines his religious type as essentially mystical, but then points out that there are two kinds: the *Immanent Mystic*, who finds God in the infinite affirmation of this world, and the *Transcendental Mystic*, who finds him by withdrawing from the world and by denial. Most mystics are a mixed type which combines the two forms, and it would seem that the value of any particular life would rest in large degree with the proportions involved. Thus we should not expect to find the lives of greatest significance among the extreme ecstatics such as Margaret Mary Alacoque, Madame Guyon, or Louise Lateau.

As a matter of fact few of the prominent mystics of history have been the pure Transcendental type, for many of them contributed a considerable work to the world beyond the expression of their visions. Teresa and Loyola were extremely able organizers, Francis of Assisi one of the world's most inspiring servants of the unfortunate, and George Fox the founder of one of the most notable sects among Christians. While God may have been the focus of their striving, their lives in practice expressed some sort of rhythm between contemplation away from the world and active striving in it. One of the earliest mystics to have divined this rhythm and express it in his philosophy was Plato. The prisoner in the Cave of Illusion who works himself free of his fetters, and so is able to contrast the glory of the sun with the miserable shadows in the cave, is in duty bound not to enjoy the sun forever but to go back into the cave and release his fellows, even though they do not wish to be free. This freed prisoner is the counterpart of the mystic who must not contemplate the sun always, but must alternate his vision of Spiritual Truth with work in the world where his vision fits him to help illuminate others.

In other words, wholesome mysticism balances the active and the passive functions of man. It expresses both the life urge and the

[45] Part II, Chap. 6. See also Pratt, *op. cit.*, Chap. 20, for a well-balanced appraisal of mysticism.

death urge. Furthermore, by withdrawing attention from the busy affairs of men, it helps to give perspective to the mystic as well as a focus that intensifies for him in passionate form an aim which gives meaning to his life. It is for this reason that frequently one intense mystical experience is sufficient to become the organizing point about which a whole life will revolve. Carlyle never forgot the "Everlasting Yea"; Pascal's experience was written down, sewed up, and carried around with him in his coat throughout his subsequent career.

The mistake that the mystics and their sentimental admirers have made is to take the experience of the presence of God out of its context and naively assume that because it *seems* to come from God this must be so. The context in this instance is the whole life of the individual and his relation to society.[46] The Roman Catholic church, for example, insists that a mystic's claims be carefully studied to ascertain whether they meet certain external conditions, among them that there should be nothing in the visions that runs counter to commonly accepted Christian principles and ethics. When thoroughly understood, it is seen that the value of the mystic's concept of truth may come partly from his idea of God, partly from his own common sense and intuition, partly from emotion, partly from his subconscious drives, partly from the perspective afforded by the experience, and partly from the life he lives.

Hence we may say, if we wish, that the Reality that the mystic feels is nothing more than an illusion. Yet we should not fail to note that the mystic himself feels this Reality to be the chief element in his experience and that this is the expression of one trying desperately to know and obey the Infinite. Where the fruits of this experience seem to be beneficial both to the individual and society we are entitled to wonder whether some kind of reality has not been tapped, despite the fact that we may question the literal validity of the mystic's views. St. Teresa, on being accused of receiving her mystical promptings from Satan, retorted, with great common sense, "I could not believe that Satan, if he wished to deceive me, could have recourse to means so adverse to his purpose as this, of rooting out my

---

[46] Cf. W. E. Hocking, *The Meaning of God in Human Experience*, Chap. XXVIII. In his Principle of Alternation, Hocking develops some of these ideas. Furthermore, writing before the time of Gestalt psychology, he anticipates its principles.

faults and implanting virtues and spiritual strength, for I saw clearly that I had become another person by means of these visions." [47]

Yet in quite another way mysticism has value not because of the relationship of the mystic with society but because, to some degree, these experiences cut him off from society to develop in solitude the resources of his individual inner life. Of these two somewhat contradictory truths about the mystic consciousness this appeals to us as the more profound.

In the psychology of our times it is the social context that is receiving the play, with the sociologist, social psychologist, and anthropologist in the ascendancy; the passwords to professional acceptance being "field theory," "interpersonal relations," "group dynamics," and the like. It is not to disparage the progress made along these lines to note that interest in the individual with his unique value and significance runs the risk of being submerged. We tend to neglect the concerns of William James, whose emphasis on the "individual in his solitude" in his definition of religion, betrayed his recognition of this value. There are not as many psychologists as there should be who follow the lead of Gordon Allport with his insistence that the psychological aspects of personality be sought in the study of the individual as such, not just as the representative of a group.[48] Perhaps this also explains why the mystics have been neglected by modern psychology.

In practical ways one symptom of this individuality has been the boldness of the mystic in asserting the truth of his divinely inspired insights. Of course, as we have pointed out, mystical intuitions have been strongly conditioned by doctrinal preconceptions so that a great many mystics fit pretty comfortably into orthodox grooves; in so doing they have sometimes outstripped ecclesiastical authorities, whose righteousness they have sensed as inferior to their own. But even a mystic so well disposed toward the authority of the Church as Angela of Foligno was capable at times of showing originality and fire. Consider the freshness of this passage: "I then understood how He is present in all nature, how in all things He has being—in the Devil, in the good angel, in Paradise, in Hell, in the adulterer, in the

---

[47] Quoted in Pratt, *op. cit.*, p. 466.
[48] See the first chapter of his *Personality* as well as his emphasis in *The Use of Personal Documents* and *The Individual and His Religion*.

murderer, and in everything having being, in some way or another, in fair things as well as filthy." [49] Or note the independence implied here:

But this time was given me a desire of expropriating myself with my whole will, and although I was much assaulted by the Devil, and frequently tempted not to do so, and was prevented having communication with the friars minor, and with all from whom it was fitting for me to take counsel, on no account, whatever good or evil things might have happened to me, could I have abstained from devoting all my goods to the poor, and, even if I should not have been able to do this, from at least stripping myself completely of them all. For it did not seem to me that I could keep anything without gravely offending Him who had so enlightened me. . . . I cried to Him saying: "Lord even if I am damned, I will nevertheless do penance and will strip myself of everything and serve Thee." [50]

Such a spirit of independence has frequently caused church authorities to cast a suspicious eye toward any mystic who comes forward and, on the basis of what he describes as an encounter with God, claims authenticity for some new truth. In this respect the mystic plays a prophetic part. Furthermore the estimate of the mystic's value will be influenced by the ecclesiastical bias of those who do the judging. Catholics will minimize the insights of the mystic who strays from the path of orthodoxy, while Protestants tend to have a warm spot in their hearts for any mystic, however mistaken, who has come in conflict with the properly constituted authorities. But despite the natural conservatism of any religious institution, its very lifeblood flows in those individual hearts whose possessors have met God face to face in an experience of vital immediacy. This is perhaps the real secret of the continued vitality of the Catholic church, which continues to amaze and confound her critics through the ages, for there is no branch of the Christian church that so systematically cultivates the mystic way.

The solution to the riddle of human creativity is to be found in a study of the causes of human individuality. This is nowhere more apparent than in the religious tradition where the mystic and the

[49] Quoted in Thorold, *op. cit.*, p. 154.
[50] *Ibid.*, p. 102.

prophet have put forth the new leaves that tell us that the organism is alive. Mystics are the poets of the religious life who, partly through their individual insights and partly through their passion, bring life, vigor, and conviction to religious acts. It is not necessary for us to determine whether religion is good or bad. Doubtless some expressions of it are good, while others are evil. But this much may be said with certainty: the person who has had an immediate experience of the godhead may multiply his religious dynamic. The effectiveness of Pascal's career dated from his vision.

Therefore, if religion is good, this strange and ineffable expression of human individuality that we call "mysticism," properly integrated into the whole structure of individual religious consciousness, is good also. It is unfortunate that there is so much false mysticism and pseudo-piety masquerading as religion, and so much sentimentality and exploitation of the undoubtedly unwholesome aspects of mysticism. Here again is another example of a point we have made before: the truly religious élite are a pitiful minority, yet they invigorate and leaven our whole society. In this connection we can do no better than to bring our chapter to a close with a quotation from the distinguished emeritus professor of Philosophy at Harvard, William Ernest Hocking:

But it matters not to us if some or even most prophets have been vain or false *if there are any true prophets.* In this, as in other great matters, nature makes a thousand failures to bring forth one consummate product. The existence of the genuine mystic—Bernard, Mohammed, Lao Tze, Plotinus, Eckhart, John of the Cross—however seldom he is found, is the momentous thing: sufficient to command respect for the tradition of mysticism, sufficient to justify the attention which, through religious history, has been focussed upon these individuals.[51]

We end the chapter, therefore on a note struck at its beginning. Mysticism is necessary to the vitalizing of the religious life and in some form is inseparable with it. It is for that reason that it is important that psychologists take it into account in their study of the religious consciousness.

[51] *Op. cit.*, p. 349.

SUMMARY

Mysticism, the direct apprehension of God, is a fundamental religious experience, though difficult for psychologists to study and even more difficult to agree on. Knowledge of the state must come mostly from the subjective reports of mystics, and its characteristics would seem to include the following: ineffability, noetic quality, transiency, and passivity; active and practical in some ways, at the same time it is essentially transcendental and life-enhancing. It follows that the descriptions of the mystics are full of figures of speech and paradoxes which frequently reverse the reality values of the common citizen. This has led many mystics to a form of behavior which is a logical consequence of their value systems and may be highly integrating for their personal lives but which seems wildly extravagant to ordinary common sense.

Mystical experience is subject to learning and growth, as with other aspects of the religious life. Sometimes, as with Loyola or the yogis, the mystics are highly self-conscious and systematic in their attempts to develop their sensitivities. Progress may involve periods of "spiritual dryness" and find its culmination in the experience of mystical ecstasy. The mystical life cannot wholly be accounted for by what we now know of its psychology. But rather obviously it is conditioned by temperament, tradition, suggestion, sexual urges in some cases, and the desire for security or escape in others. One should be critical of drugs as a means to mystic vision.

Since no two mystics are exactly alike, it follows that each one must be evaluated on the strength of his individual merits. Psychological analysis does not compel us either to approve or disapprove. However, the psychologist is biased in favor of those mystics who have been able to retain some grip on what he calls reality, and he notes that many have been enabled to attain no mean heights of achievement along paths esteemed by the culture of the ages. Furthermore he remarks that through mystical experience many mystics have integrated their own lives and invigorated religion.

Chapter 13

PROPHET, PRIEST,
AND INTELLECTUAL

And ye shall be unto me a kingdom of priests.

—Exodus

Would God that all the Lord's people were prophets and that the Lord would put his spirit upon them!

—Numbers

And I gave my heart to seek and search out by wisdom all things that are done under heaven.

—Ecclesiastes

Three other areas of the religious life which, like mysticism, have been neglected by psychologists are the psychology of the prophet, the priest, and the religious intellectual, together with the distinctions between them. A good deal on these subjects may be found in religious literature, but almost nothing in the writing of those few psychologists who have written about religion. Yet it is important that they be described in order to clarify two more aspects of the religious life, and two contrasted types of religious leaders. Furthermore the religious functions and psychological processes that they represent are important to keep in mind in connection with the subjects of prayer and worship, which will have our attention in a later chapter.

The mental processes of none of these constitute as clear-cut a state of mind as do those of the mystic. The concepts are further confused by the fact that in practice they not only overlap one an-

291

other but also overlap that of the mystic. The same person may be prophet, priest, intellectual, and mystic rolled into one. This means that all four terms are merely constructs invented by the scholar for the purpose of clarifying his thinking. For example, it would be hard to find an actual person to exhibit as a simon-pure specimen of a priest, and even more difficult to find an unadulterated prophet. Consequently when we describe the mental characteristics of each, we will be describing not something that exists in actuality but rather ideal types.[1] We will be oversimplifying nature in the interest of clarity.

Furthermore, it may be said that particularly the prophet and the priest, more than the mystic, perform for religion an institutional, social, or perhaps political rather than a psychological function. Perhaps this in part justifies their neglect by psychologists of religion. Certainly we find counterparts in fields other than religion, such as art, politics, society, and the world of thought. For the prophet is the religious liberal, while the priest is the religious conservative, generally speaking. Along with the function they perform are characteristic states of mind and attitudes, which, for the most part, we will attempt merely to describe. We will not analyze in any great detail their psychological sources.

The prophet. The classical examples of the religious prophets are those of ancient Israel, the record of whose doings and sayings are found chiefly in the great prophetic books of the Old Testament. The amazing religious vigor and fertility of the Hebrews was due in no small degree to their prophetic tradition, and many of our examples will be drawn from this source.

The religious prophet is not primarily concerned, as popular fancy would have it, with predicting the future. Although he is very much concerned with the future, prediction is a very incidental part of his function. Also, though so-called prophets have been given to visions, trances, dancing, and other strange behavior, these are not the prophet's essential characteristics. On the whole we may say that the following five characteristics are salient in the prophetic consciousness: 1) immediate experience of God, 2) a sense of mission

---

[1] This is the method of psychological description used by E. Spranger in his *Types of Men*, though he does not use these distinctions.

as the mouthpiece of God, 3) a concern for rightness of living, 4) a reliance on intuition, and 5) a highly individualized interpretation and expression of religious truth.

(1) *The prophet feels himself to be in immediate contact with God* or whatever to him is the ultimate Reality. In this respect the prophet and the mystic are one, so that the careers of most prophets have begun with some kind of mystical experience. The conversion which marked the opening of Isaiah's ministry was characterized by an ineffable mystical experience that reduced the prophet to symbols in his description of it.

In the year that King Uzziah died I saw also the Lord sitting upon a throne, high and lifted up, and his train filled the temple.

Above it stood the seraphims; each one had six wings; with twain he covered his face; with twain he covered his feet, and with twain he did fly.

And one cried unto another and said, Holy, holy, holy, is the Lord of Hosts: the whole earth is full of his glory.

And the posts of the door moved at the voice of him that cried, and the house was filled with smoke.[2]

The Apostle Paul would be another example of a religious personality whose experience—on the Damascus road—as we have pointed out, was mystical. This experience was the basis for a ministry mainly prophetic in nature. To come to more modern times, Thomas Carlyle might be cited. We have described his "Everlasting Yea" experience as mystical, yet the career of Carlyle and his literary messages of doom mark him more as a spiritual descendant of the Hebrew prophets than of the medieval mystics. Again, Martin Luther was another in whom the prophetic consciousness predominated, overshadowing the mystical elements in his nature.

We have pointed out that the mystic's immediate relationship with God is what imparts liveliness and a sense of reality to his religious experience. The passion of the prophet is nowise inferior to that of the mystic, and his emotional fire derives in part from the same sources.

(2) *The prophet feels a sense of mission as the mouthpiece of God.* Therefore he regards himself as a kind of messenger from God and a proclaimer of the truth. Thus we find among the Old Testa-

[2] Isaiah 6:1-4.

ment prophets that their most often repeated phrase is, "Thus saith the Lord," through which the authentic prophet is not shrewdly maneuvering for a hearing among the people but expressing his inward conviction that God is speaking through him.

So strong is this sense of mission that frequently the prophet has a sense of his words actually being formed by God. At any rate he may so interpret the compulsion that he feels to deliver himself of what he has to say. Of all the prophets Jeremiah is famous as one of the most reluctant. So disagreeable were the truths he felt he must proclaim, together with the unpopularity they brought him, that he would have been relieved could he have forgotten the whole business of prophecy. Because the word of the Lord makes him a "reproach and a derision," he resolves to speak in His name no longer, but, as he so vividly put it, "His word was in mine heart as a burning fire shut up in my bones, and I was weary of forbearing and could not stay." [3] It seems probable that such an attitude may have had its roots in a true compulsion, for the prophet is not seldom a neurotic, though one who may bring much of value to religion and to society.

(3.) *The prophet is concerned with rightness of living*, not as a means to an end so much as an *end* in itself. At least in its classical form among the Hebrew prophets the concept of righteousness is the supreme aim of the prophetic message. Of course righteousness is represented as the will of God and, so far, is conceived as a means of pleasing God; but the idea of righteousness is so bound up with God that the two are thought of as practically synonymous. This is different from the attitude of the mystics, who are also interested in right living, but very much as a *means* of making themselves worthy of the heavenly vision. Furthermore to this end they are preoccupied with their own righteousness, whereas the prophets are concerned about the righteousness of the people.

Rightness of living in itself is apt to be extolled as the sole condition of salvation and almost equivalent to it. "When the wicked man turneth away from the wickedness that he hath committed and doeth what is lawful and right, he shall save his soul alive." [4] To the prophet truth is pragmatic and works itself out in the practical life

[3] Jeremiah 20:9.
[4] Ezekiel 18:27.

of the people; hence prophecy is much more immediate in its social benefits than is mysticism.

This concern for righteousness was not only characteristic of the classical exemplars of prophecy but is also true of prophets of more modern times. "No, it is not *better* to do the one than the other," says Carlyle, speaking of Right and Wrong; "the one is to the other as life is to death,—as Heaven is to Hell. The one must in nowise be done, the other in nowise left undone." [5] Again, the prophets and their followers of our own times are those who see the mission of the Church bound up with social justice. Religion in their eyes is dead unless it expresses itself in good works.

(4) *The instrument of the prophet is his intuition.* He may make use of meditation and prayer, and he certainly does not neglect observation, which may be one of the ingredients in his sense of mission. It was the shocking spectacle of the venality of the priests in Samaria which supplied the spark in the coming to Amos of his sense of mission, while the keen political observations of the statesman-prophet Isaiah led him to warn Jerusalem not to rely on help from the waning power of Egypt. But the method of the prophet is not the scientific, methodical balancing of evidence, but the sudden, subconscious fitting together of the evidence and values in one profound insight into the meaning of things. In this respect he is identical with the poet and the mystic, which his language often betrays him to be.

Of course intuition is as notorious for its unreliability in the service of religion as it is in other areas. The Israelites were as aware of this as anyone, so that we frequently run across allusions to "false prophets" in the Old Testament. But even though prophecy may be more often wrong than right, when it is right its rightness is so profound that people through the ages have been delighted to honor these pioneers in the discovery of the world of religious truth. It is this ability to divine the nature of things that frequently leads the prophet to sense the direction of history and to declare it in his prophecy. Thus he is apt to acquire the reputation of soothsayer.

(5) It follows from all we have said that *in the prophet we have a highly individualized interpretation and expression of religious truth.*

[5] *Heroes and Hero-Worship,* pp. 309–310.

In fact the prophet is the individual *par excellence*. Despite his concern for the people he is not apt to be a highly socialized person but rather walks aloof. He is Elijah sitting alone, deserted, under the juniper bush, or John the Baptist with a girdle of camel's hair, feeding on locusts and preaching in the wilderness. On the other hand he may be Jeremiah thrown into a well because people are tired of hearing his gloomy warnings, or George Fox cast into prison because of the violence of his dissent. On the whole the prophet is not a pleasant person to live with, and he is apt to be no more popular than other determined speakers of the unvarnished truth. As Ahab, King of Israel complained of his one true prophet, Elisha, "I hate him; for he never prophesied good concerning me, but always evil." [6]

But it is in this very individuality that his function lies, for it is individuality that supplies the roots of creativity, and it is the prophet who, more than any other representative of the religious life, supplies its growing edge. And so it was Amos who first and forcibly showed the people of Israel that ritual can never supplant righteousness; Hosea who, from his experience of pitying a wayward and faithless wife divined that God may be merciful too; and Ezekiel who refuted the common view that the fathers' sins were visited on the children. The founders of nearly all strong religious movements have for the most part been prophets, who either proclaimed a new idea or gave fresh emphasis to an old one. Such were Moses, Jesus, Mohammed, Buddha, Luther, Fox, and Gandhi. They are primarily the expressers of the life urge, and it is on such as these that civilization puts its highest valuation. It is for this reason that it is worth the psychologist's while to mark their characteristics.

The prophet and the mystic. It will help us to clarify the psychology of both the prophet and the mystic to compare and contrast them.

As we have said, both prophet and mystic start from the same base, their immediate experience of God. It is this which justifies one's reference to many prophets as mystics, for seldom is there a prophet without some element of the mystic's turn of mind, just as there are few mystics who have not had their moments of prophecy. It is this truth that Spranger seems to be representing when he divided the

[6] II Chronicles 18:7.

religious type into the *Transcendental Mystic*, the thoroughgoing
mystic who withdraws from the world and makes union with God
his single-minded aim, and the *Immanent Mystic*, who finds God in
the world.[7] The *Immanent Mystic* is often identical with the prophet,
who might be thought of as *the mystic in action.*

But in action the ways of the prophet and the mystic diverge.
Since the prophet is of this world, it follows that he will have to
wrestle with certain things that the mystic can afford to neglect.
The mystic not only finds that the limitations of time and of space
grow hazy, but he makes a virtue of denying their very existence.
The prophet, on the other hand, lives in history, appealing to the
past for his exemplars and to the future for his vindication. Herein
lies the urge for forecasting events that few prophets seem to have
been able to resist. Also, since the prophet is so much more concerned with events than the mystic, he is much more likely to be a
politician. When the mystic becomes a politician, it is a sign that
he has deserted the purely mystical path in order to don the prophet's
mantle. And so we see this process actually at work in Isaiah, Luther,
Ignatius Loyola, and even with so thoroughgoing a mystic as St.
Catherine of Siena.

This means that the prophet affirms life rather than denies it,
as the mystic does in his "purgative" stage, his love of fasting and
mortification of desire, and his rejection of normal contacts with
others. The prophet is more apt to be found preaching rather than
praying and meditating; and even though he may have no particular
gift for friendship, he is much more socialized than the mystic in
his concern for the general welfare of society. Consequently, he is a
less thoroughgoing introvert than the mystic and more of an extrovert. Luther is a good example of the prophet. We read of his many
difficulties with his early monastic training and the obsessive recur-
rence of his sense of sin. Quite likely it was the tradition of medieval
mysticism in his monastery that, unknown to himself, struck across
the grain of his predominantly active religious nature. Hence in his
more prophetic days he looked back on his introspection as unwholesome and was inclined to condemn generally a system that
merely was not meant for him. Hence also that much misunderstood
adjuration of his, "Sin boldly!" In this he was not encouraging evil.

[7] See Chap. 12, p. 285.

Far from it! It simply represented the manly protest of an active religious nature against a system that encouraged interminable search for sin in one's inward nature rather than combating it in outward circumstance. Better to make a few mistakes in carrying the fight to the forces of evil in the world, where they dwell in such power, than to waste too much of one's time in ferreting out the last iota of evil within oneself. It was the prophet in him protesting against the mystic.

Yet it is this interest in the actual that gets the prophet into trouble. The mystical components of his nature make him very sensitive to religious values and religious truth. Consequently he reacts strongly when he considers these flouted by those who, though they may be in places of religious authority, nevertheless lead lives of dulled religious sensitivities and serve interests that may be very secular or even anti-religious. It is for this reason that the prophet is so apt to found a new church or a new movement. This also explains why the churches have always been so much less tolerant of their prophets than of their mystics. The latter can be troublesome too, but this usually is when the mystic turns into the prophet, as not infrequently happens. It was not so much the visions of St. Ignatius Loyola as what he proposed to do about them that gave the church officials some bad moments during his early ministry. Much the same were the cases of Wyclif and Luther and Hus, though the results for the Church were not so happy in these instances. The transcendental mystic, however, is apt to be more docile. The Church can afford to leave him to his own devices as long as he does not get the urge to publish abroad his mystical insights when they become heretical. So he is usually allowed to go his own solitary way, while his ecclesiastical sponsors point to him, with proprietary satisfaction, as a model of piety and obedience.

One notices that among prophets women are not so prevalent as among mystics. In the sense in which we have defined the prophet it is hard to think of a single prophetess of the front rank in all of history comparable in stature to Amos, Isaiah, Jeremiah, Luther, or Gandhi. St. Joan of Arc might be cited as a possible exception, but she was as much a mystic as a prophet, while her accomplishments were more prominently political and military than religious. On the other hand it is as easy, if not easier, to think of great mystics among women as among men. Probably no Christian mystic has been more written about than St. Teresa, while St. Catherine of Genoa, and St. Catherine of Siena are among the very great. In the Moslem tradition, Rabi'a was a woman mystic who is often listed along with the men, despite the depreciation of woman in Mohammedanism.

When one reflects on what we have said about the prophet and the mystic, he can see that the virtues of the mystic come closer to what in popular thought is considered the feminine temperament than the masculine, while with the prophets it is the other way around. Evelyn Underhill overworks the active emphasis among the mystics. While passivity and docility are by no means the invariable mark of the woman mystic, nevertheless there is considerably more of the passive component to be found among the mystics as a whole than among the prophets. The latter are almost all what one conceives of as the masculine type. On the other hand, this is not always the case among the men who are mystics. Whether we have here a distinction that is genetic in nature or simply a matter of social roles and expectations we cannot say, though the fact of this difference would seem pretty clear. It is more common for women to become mystics than prophets.

It is with some diffidence that we approach the question of whether Jesus was more prophet or mystic. It would seem evident that despite what appear to have been mystical episodes in his career, such as the Temptations in the Wilderness and his need to withdraw from the crowd at intervals for meditation and prayer, he is to be classified much more definitely with the prophets than with the mystics. Certainly Spranger's category of *Immanent Mystic*, which we have identified with the prophet, would fit him much better than *Transcendental Mystic*. If one runs back over the characteristics of the prophet, it will be found that there is hardly one that will not fit Jesus. On the other hand, it could hardly be doubted that, had he been a typical mystic, he would have been much more concerned with teaching his disciples the truths of the mystic way. As it is, the Synoptic Gospels contain a record of One who was much more intent on righteousness than on mystical experience, while the Gospel of St. John is thought by scholars to have received its mystical imprint as much from the temperament of the writer as from the words of Jesus. Yet there would seem little doubt that Jesus did partake of mystical experience which informed and inspired his life of prophecy.

The prophet, then, we can see as a kind of link between the inward life of the spirit and the concerns of society. He is an innovator, devoted to God as single-mindedly as the mystic, though in a different way. He strives to express the life urge and eschews the nirvana of the Buddhist mystics, which so perfectly exemplifies the passive goal of the death urge. Yet the prophet is dependent on the mystical insights, both of himself and of others. He is the liaison man between the visionary realities of the mystic and that great tide of history which the spirit of religion seeks to direct.

The priest. Another liaison man between the spiritual world and society is the priest, who differs from the mystic and especially from the prophet. The priest is the expression of the death urge in the religious life, by which is meant that his function is a conserving and more passive rather than a creative one. The priest may be a disciple of the prophet. At any rate, he exists to preserve the values of the past chiefly by means of providing for them institutional and ritualistic expression.

The priest may know God through first-hand religious experience, but this is not necessary to his function, however desirable it may be. He knows God primarily through tradition, and often speaks of the revelation of God through the religious institution. Or he may speak of the religious institution as the guardian and guarantor of religious truth. At any rate his first loyalty is not to himself or any personal experience of the Divine, nor even to the people or a concept of righteousness, but rather to the institution, whose servant he is.

Since one form in which values are conserved is by law, and since order is important to liturgy and the running of any institution, the priest tends to be a legalist. He will appeal to law in order to preserve tradition and to fortify the institution. "The Law" in Judaism comprises the first five books of the Bible, the fundamental core of Judaism. Anyone whose memory is hazy concerning these will find through cursory reference that the better part of these "Books of Moses" consists of a myriad of laws affecting nearly every aspect of Jewish existence. This represents the priestly psychology in Judaism just as "the Prophets" stand for the more liberal and prophetic strain. "The Law and the Prophets" then, represent the fusion of these two psychological facets of Hebrew religious tradition.

It might be added that it is not necessary for an individual actually to be a priest in order to share in the priestly psychology. For every properly appointed priestly servitor, there are three or four self-appointed curators of institutional punctilio. Every pastor is familiar with the problem of satisfying the fussy concern of one of these individuals that everything be done in due order lest some supposed ecclesiastical catastrophe overtake the Church. A candle lit or unlit here, or a person improperly admitted to Holy Communion there, are apt to lead to a degree of distress that transmits itself like a case of measles to all members of the congregation likewise susceptible. People of this kind seem to have a certain gift of nature that predisposes them to the conservative kind of priestly thinking. The prophet and even the mystic are apt to be bewildered as to what the fuss is all about. Fortunately actual incumbents of priestly offices are not often of this extreme type.

The prophet and the priest. Just as it was instructive to compare the prophet with the mystic, it will be similarly helpful to compare him with the priest.

It has been pointed out that the prophet is the religious liberal while the priest is the conservative. In their extreme forms, the prophet may be a radical while the priest becomes the religious reactionary. While religious history is full of services performed by the extremist, nevertheless, under ordinary circumstances, religion is best expressed by those with a saving balance of common sense and sanity.

In worship the priestly type of mind tends to prefer ritual and liturgy to freer forms. The priest rejects and distrusts the enthusiasm of the prophet, and to some degree he feels that a highly traditional, liturgical order of service is the Church's protection against those who might lightly leave the tried and true for dangerous experiments. For the same reason he is benevolently disposed toward creeds, even those which he does not quite understand himself, for at least he is sure that they have always been associated with tradition. It is the priest who stands in judgment at the heresy trial, while the prophet is the defendant. The authority the priest cites is that of the Church or an instrument sanctioned by tradition, for it must not be thought that a movement like Protestantism, with its reliance on the Bible, is without its priestly emphases. On the other hand the prophet, in appealing to his conscience, or his own religious experience, may be destroying the Church, or at least splitting it into fragments. One of the dramatic scenes of history ranged the prophet against the priest when Luther stood before the Princes of the Church at Worms. The prophet represents the authority of the individual, the priest that of the institution.

Both the prophet and the priest, ranged though they often are against one another, have their part to play and their function to perform in the religious drama of life. But they also have their characteristic dangers and weaknesses.

The prophet may become extremely egotistic, while the priest may become simply fussy and dull. The prophet may advocate change simply for change's sake, while the priest may resist all change. The prophet may stimulate disorder, while the priest fosters rigidity. The prophet may fragment the religious institution, while under the priest it may die of dry rot. The prophet may conceive a vested interest in stirring up people, while the vested interest of the priest may be to keep the people contented. If religion is in any sense the "opium of the people," it is the priest who stands guilty of having prepared the prescription.

It is obvious that religion as a total enterprise has need of both the prophet and priest. The prophet is religion's creative artist and seer, and its conscience as well. He asserts religion's right to be heard among the councils of men and to enter meaningfully into the transactions between man and his fellow. He is the Church's protection against itself and the tendency, which it shares with all institutions, of simply preserving itself long after its real function has been forgotten. The priest exists because many of the religious advances of past ages were good. Each generation cannot be expected to start anew and by its own unaided insights achieve and surpass the levels of all previous generations. For this reason the institution is necessary. At his best the priest sees the institution as a means of conserving those profound truths which do not lose freshness or power to move men with successive presentation. Further than this, he has his own way of encouraging the application of religion to life, by the proper use of the authority, the ritual, and the stability of the institution.

The religious intellectual. We have then studied and marked the psychological characteristics of three common types of religious leader, the mystic, the prophet, and the priest. There is yet a fourth type of religious leader whose function is important to the religious enterprise. This is the religious intellectual, the man of thought, most often materialized as the theologian, and it is to him that we next turn our attention.

Edward Spranger, in *Types of Men*, classifies people according to their dominant value system into six groups, Theoretical, Economic, Political, Esthetic, Social, and Religious. The religious intellectual in his purest form is not so much concerned with religious values *per se* as he is with abstract truth. Consequently he deserves to be classified as the Theoretical man rather than the Religious man. He is an explorer in the realms of the intellect, and just as the research scientist pursues truth by research in the field of nature, and the philosopher searches for it in the field of pure ideas, the religious intellectual is similarly caught up in the passion to know, but happens to use religious data and ideas for his field and his materials. He is no more the Religious type, described by Spranger as a mystic seeking unity with God, than he is the Political type interested in the pursuit of power.

This is not evident because in actual practice none of Spranger's types appear in their pure form. They are simply ideal types or abstractions to make psychological realities clear by oversimplifying them. Any individual to demonstrate in his life the type in its pure form would be a psychological monstrosity, and the religious intellectual is no exception to this rule. Indeed, if he is a religious leader at all, he owes his place of leadership largely to his sympathetic participation in the values of the Religious type. St. Augustine and St. Thomas Aquinas are among the great intellectuals of the Christian tradition, and yet both were so passionately devoted to religious values that they are better classified as Religious rather than Theoretical men, mystics rather than intellectuals.

However, among religious intellectuals and scholars of religion the concern for religious values tends to diminish as their passion for abstract truth develops. This is partly due to the rigors of the demands of the religious life. Since no value is more comprehensive than the religious value and, as Spranger reminds us, "nothing is outside the realm of religion," [8] it follows that when religion is mature there is no discipline more demanding. Hence there begins to operate the natural human preference for the lesser discipline of the intellectual life as compared with the heightening demands of religious maturity.

But this is not to say that the pursuit of truth is a bed of roses. Far from it. It is often to be noticed that in actuality most of those who *suppose* that they are religious people are subject to little or no discipline, while the discipline of the scholar is much more apt to be actual and real. Hence there is another factor operating, the tendency for a person to become more and more immersed in and motivated by whatever he happens to be doing if he finds in it any intrinsic satisfaction at all. This is one aspect of the phenomenon that G. W. Allport calls the "functional autonomy of motives," [9] as we have pointed out before. In other words the religious man may turn to the intellectual examination of faith and become so fascinated with it that as he grows older he tends to become nothing more than an intellectual. This helps to explain the complaint, voiced so often on campuses at theological schools by students, particularly the less intellectual ones, that their professors are taking their religion away from them.

As we have pointed out, the religious intellectual is never the purely Theoretical man, and he has his own way, different from the mystic, of becoming aware of aspects of spiritual reality. This is through logic and reason. He can be called religious because he does really "sense a Beyond" through these intellectual processes, which may even start, as they did with Descartes, with skepticism. But the psychological experience of awareness of God by the intellectual is quite different from that of the mystic. The intellectual also may feel quite certain of his belief, but psychologically it differs from the faith of the mystic in much the same way that belief in the existence of a foreign land by one who has read about it differs from belief in it by one who has been there. The belief of the intellectual is secondhand.

[8] *Types of Men*, p. 211.
[9] See his *Personality*, pp. 191 ff.

Consequently the intellectual is apt to be highly distrustful of mental processes that run counter to those he relies on. He suspects intuition, for his researches teach him how unreliable it is, and he cannot abide enthusiasm. This means that to the mystic, on the other hand, the blood of the intellectual seems of the thinnest variety, while to the prophet the religious thinker is a splitter of hairs and a chopper of logic, a mere legalist. Says Jeremiah:

How do ye say, We are wise, and the law of the Lord is with us? Lo, certainly in vain made he it; the pen of the scribes is in vain.
The wise men are ashamed, they are dismayed and taken: lo, they have rejected the word of the Lord; and what wisdom is in them? [10]

The intellectual is apt to feel that his function is to *appraise* righteousness rather than practice it. Hence in contrast to the prophet, or even the priest, the intellectual is not apt to become a martyr. No one had a keener appreciation of the evils of his age than Erasmus of Rotterdam, who pointed them out in words of incomparable precision. Yet for himself he sensed that he probably lacked the iron to endure martyrdom,[11] for it was the prophet Luther who *did* something about the evils, and whose escape from marytrdom was the merest accident. This helps to explan also why, in a later age, it was the churches of Germany more than its universities which gave effective resistance to Hitler. The feelings are bolder than the mind.

But it is not wholly through cowardice or dislike of action that the intellectual is so often found "sicklied o'er with the pale cast of thought." It is partly that he sees so many sides to a question that he recognizes the complexity of reality and how difficult it is to effect one good without at the same time perpetrating many evils. His training has taught him to suspend judgment and wait until all the evidence is in. The fact that it never is all in gives him on the one hand an excuse for a comfortable aloofness from the battle, and on the other hand a judicial function to which he would be untrue should he forsake it for precipitate action.

Furthermore, the intellectual is an explorer in the field of ideas. In this sense he is an individualist and a pioneer. He is responsible for

[10] Jeremiah 8:8–9.
[11] See his letter to Richard Pace, written July 5, 1521, in P. Smith's *Erasmus*, p. 243.

the soaring theological ideas of the ages. It is the destiny for which he is made, and in this field he is another expression of the life urge in the religious consciousness. It is as the thinker that he plays his part.

SUMMARY

Along with the mystic, important religious personality types include the prophet, priest, and religious intellectual. In actual practice religious people show characteristics of several if not all of these types, yet for theoretical purposes it is helpful to keep them separate. The prophet like the mystic typically has an immediate experience of encounter with God from which he derives a sense of mission. With this as the basis for his highly individualized intuitions, he is concerned with righteousness and the welfare of the group. Consequently he is more "of this world" than the mystic in his involvement with society and his sense of history. Among the ranks of the prophets men predominate to a greater degree than among the mystics.

The priest is like the prophet in that he ministers to society, but his concern is not so much the pronouncement of new truth as it is the preservation of tradition through the religious institution. He sometimes thinks of himself as a special agent or representative of a prophet who has gone before him. The prophet is the religious individualist and perhaps the radical; the priest is the religious conservative and defender of the institution.

The religious intellectual may not be a religious person at all though in practice he usually is. The desire to understand motivates him and it happens that it is the data and material of religion that he chooses to study and to put in order. The theologian is the most typical religious intellectual and his apprehension of God is through his mind. Because he appraises religion by his intellect he tends to be distrustful of the enthusiasm of the prophet and may be critical of the intuitions of the mystic. He is not a man of action, partly because action does not fit his temperament and partly because he sees reality as too complex for precipitate judgment. He is a religious adventurer in the domain of the mind.

Chapter 14

PRAYER

Prayer is the most spontaneous and the most personal expression of religion.

—Friedrich Heiler

When Captain Eddie Rickenbacker was thrown into the Pacific Ocean as the result of a plane crash and floated for days on a small raft under what seemed like hopeless conditions, he prayed for Divine assistance. This reaction was not unlike that to be expected of the average person under similar conditions. For whether under the stress of a desperate emergency or driven by milder impulsions, people all but universally exhibit what Heiler has called "the most spontaneous and the most personal expression of religion." [1]

This generalization has been sufficiently demonstrated by empirical study. In his inquiry into the religious beliefs of youth Ross found that, in his sample of nearly 2,000, less than 15 per cent never prayed at all.[2] Even among young intellectuals, whom one might expect to be as unlikely a group for praying as could be found, the great majority admit to a more or less regular use of prayer. Allport, Gillespie, and Young, in their study of Harvard and Radcliffe students, found that 65 per cent of the men and 75 per cent of the women reported that they had prayed at some time or other during the previous six months.[3] This even included some who said they felt no need of religion in their lives. Yet prayer, by its very form, which involves ad-

[1] *Prayer*, p. 119.
[2] *The Religious Beliefs of Youth*, p. 61.
[3] See "The Religion of the Post-War College Student," or Allport, *The Individual and His Religion*, p. 42.

307

dressing an outside force that is greater than oneself, is conducive to that "sense of a Higher Power," which we have defined as religion. Such an important and universal road to the heart of the religious life deserves the respectful attention of the psychologist.

But how is one to approach this area of prayer in order to probe it with any depth? The essential stimuli are inner stimuli and the essential responses inner responses. While the process may be initiated by features in the external environment, the effects of these dive beneath the surface of man's external behavior. This leaves the psychologist either to wring his hands over the paucity of observable behavior to study, or else resolutely to turn his back on the problem declaring, like the fox with the grapes, that the whole business is not worth the trouble anyway.

But the importance of the subject keeps us from either of these paths. Nevertheless we must content ourselves largely with description. In the effort to be scientific, one must leave out God as a source of stimuli or as an objective responding being. To the deeply religious mind this will seem an egregious omission which condemns us to shallow conclusions. But in attempting to be scientific we cannot assume the theologian's mantle; while, on the other hand, balked in our attempt to pierce the living mystery of prayer with complete scientific precision, we must be content to be *as scientific as we can.*

As illustrated in the two previous studies, the chief means at the disposal of the psychologist in studying prayer are the questionnaire and the interview. But immediately we run into the difficulty, usual with such instruments, that the individual cannot always accurately describe his "inner experience" because he is not aware of it all. And in studying prayer we have the additional difficulty of surveying an area of the inner life of which the average person is loath to speak. If one prays at all, the matter is apt to concern his very dearest wishes. On this principle someone has remarked that there is no better test of love than the capacity of two individuals naturally and easily to share their prayers, for few are willing to expose their intimate prayers on any basis less than that of complete mutual trust. Consequently, the psychologist who wishes to inquire about prayer must assure his informers of anonymity and make certain of his rapport.

At times it has been suggested that prayer, or at least its effects, might be made the subject of experiment. One such suggestion was that over a period of time the recovery of half the patients in a hospital could be prayed for without their knowledge. The recovery rate of these could be compared with that of the corresponding control group "unprayed for." The results might be expected to measure the efficacy of intercessory prayer. Most would agree, for different reasons, that such an experiment would be absurd. Some will be certain nothing would happen, while others may feel that an investigation into sacred matters is inappropriate and sacrilegious.[4] At any rate the presence of a widespread body of opinion supporting the latter point of view makes the attempt difficult if not hazardous for the psychologist. It would seem no more sacrilegious for the psychologist to try to test the efficacy or lack of efficacy of prayer than it is for the religious partisan to claim that prayer has concrete and miraculous results. If such people do not hesitate to recount instances of answers to prayer of a rather specific nature, it is hard to see how in logic there should be denied to the social scientist the attempt to demonstrate the truth or falsity of such claims by the methods that he chooses. Of course we should grant that our investigator must be sincere and show a proper respect for religious amenities and decorum. One may well hold, however, that the effects of prayer are too subtle for investigation. Even so, it would seem that reverently thoughtful and resourceful psychologists might set up experiments in this area which would help to tell us something more about the relationship between prayer and the human personality.

Prayer and poetry. It is to be noted that prayer in many cases runs parallel to poetry: many prayers are poetry as authentic as any that exists. This does not mean that *all* prayers are poetry nor that all poetry is prayer, but they have much in common. Wordsworth defined poetry as "the spontaneous overflow of powerful feeling," [5] and this definition would cover many prayers. "As the hart panteth after the waterbrooks," prayed the Psalmist, "so panteth my soul after thee, O God."

On the other hand, the use of apostrophe by many poets comes close to demonstrating the psychological attitudes of prayer. The poet

---

[4] For an example of such objection, perhaps partly for both these reasons as well as other more cogent ones, see Buttrick, *Prayer*, p. 105.

[5] See his Preface to *Lyrical Ballads*.

Shelley would have denied the description "religious." Yet it is doubtful whether many poets were more religious in essential spirit than he. Lines from his "Ode to the West Wind" will illustrate our point.

> . . . Be thou, spirit fierce,
> My spirit; be thou me, impetuous one!
>
> Drive my dead thoughts over the universe
> Like withered leaves to quicken a new birth!
> And, by the incantation of this verse,
>
> Scatter as from an unextinguished hearth
> Ashes and sparks, my words among mankind!
> Be through my lips to unawakened earth
>
> The trumpet of a prophecy!

His apostrophes are true prayers, and his sense of Higher Powers was no less religious for being described in a way that eschewed the conventional religious symbols of a society he knew to be in the main callous to essential religious values. All this is by way of enriching our psychological understanding of prayer by pointing out its relationship to poetry.

Motives of prayer. Why do people pray? This at least is one area of the subject where empirical data are reasonably plentiful. It is easy to ask people why they pray and to note their answers.[6] Of course whether they are fully aware of their motives is another matter, but we can gather some instruction from this type of study, especially if we realize its limitations.

Ross's study, cited above, is recent and will serve to provide the kind of information that such studies elicit. 1,720 answers to a question asking why people prayed gave the following results:

It is noteworthy that except possibly among the "other replies" nothing is said of the motive for coming into communion with God. On the contrary most of these responses suggest the magical attitude of trying to manipulate God or to get something out of the process of value for oneself. In other words, these replies do not very aptly fit

---

[6] Pratt's *Religious Consciousness*, Chap. 15, cites several studies.

Table 2 *

PERCENTAGE OF 1,720 YOUTH WHO GAVE CERTAIN ANSWERS
TO THE QUESTION "WHY DO YOU PRAY?"

	Per Cent
God listens to and answers your prayers	32.8
It helps you in time of stress and crisis	27.2
You feel relieved and better after prayer	18.1
Prayer reminds you of your obligations to man and society	10.7
It's a habit you have	4.0
All good people pray	0.9
One takes a chance if one doesn't pray	0.5
Other replies	5.8

* From Ross, *op. cit.*, p. 63.

our definition of religion as the "inner experience of a person when he senses a Beyond, particularly as evidenced by the effect of this experience on his behavior when he actively attempts to harmonize his life with that Beyond." Only the item, "Prayer reminds you of your obligations to man and society" suggests the use of prayer in harmonizing life with the will of God. Doubtless this is evidence of how widely essentially magical ideas are confused with religion in our society.

Pratt gives further evidence of this in listing published items showing "answers" to prayers including "a successful party," "cow recovered," "five deals made," "the healing of a sore finger," etc. He also relates the story reported by a Washington hostess who found herself coming down with a bad cold on the morning of an important reception. Having telephoned a "Kansas City prayer center" at 11:00 A.M., she found herself sufficiently recovered to greet the guests at 2:00 P.M.! [7]

Nevertheless it also is evidence of a limitation of this type of questionnaire. For the replies were in large part suggested by giving the respondents categories to check, while few seem to have taken advantage of the open-ended alternative where they could write their own replies. The motive of securing communion with God was much more prominent in some other studies, such as those reported or cited by Pratt.[8] Here as high as 65 to 70 per cent of those responding in some studies have testified to feeling the presence of a Higher Power

[7] *Ibid.*, pp. 322–323.
[8] *Ibid.*, p. 324.

in prayer. This presumably has acted as a motive of a considerably more religious nature.

Enough has been said to indicate that the motives for prayer are various and complex. Other motives will be suggested in our ensuing discussion. There is need for many and more thorough studies in this important area.

Some types of prayer. Like all complex phenomena, prayer may be classified in a number of different ways. In this analysis we will use several ways of classification that will help the reader to see prayer's psychological significance, but it must be realized that these are neither final nor exhaustive. They will serve to suggest certain relationships and provide a starting point for further study.

Pratt calls attention to two important aspects of religion, the *subjective* and *objective*.[9] Subjective religion focuses on the psychology and reaction of the person, while objective religion is directed at the consciousness and response of God. These two forms exhibit themselves, intermingled, in that entire inner experience that we have called "religion," and one place where they show themselves clearly is in prayer. Once the distinction between the two is pointed out, their psychological significance becomes apparent, for there is a world of difference between the attitude that sees the benefits of religion accruing to man and that which thinks of "God" as their recipient. But as with other areas of religion, these two concepts cannot be strictly separated. They interact and, as ideal constructs, help the student to get his psychological bearings.

Accordingly, prayers may be put into the subjective and objective categories depending on whether their main focus is on the individual who prays or on the object of his prayer. We will name certain types of prayer according to their function and at the same time try to subsume these types under the wider categories *subjective* and *objective*.

Under the *subjective* form of prayer the first and most obvious is the *prayer of petition*. The figures we have quoted above from Ross as to the motives for prayer will make it clear, if any proof is needed, that this is the most common of all forms of prayer. It further suggests that most prayer is egocentric, raising the question whether most

9 *Ibid.*, Chaps. 14–15.

praying is religious at all, if we think of religion as the attempt to harmonize one's life with God. Hence we are forced to note that many prayers of petition are mere *magic*, whereby it is supposed that the easy act of petition will secure some mundane advantage over one's neighbors or help one get ahead in the world on a kind of "something for nothing" principle. Such requests deserve the label *spell* rather than *prayer*.

But it by no means follows that simply by its form all petitionary prayer can be ruled out by the psychologist as magic. For the attitude of the one who is praying is more important than the method, which can often be nothing more than the vestigial remains of one's childish past. The intent of the petition may be nothing less than that God should reveal His will or do His will. And often a prayer that starts with petition may end in submission. So Jesus in the Garden of Gethsemane prayed, "O my Father, if it be possible, let this cup pass from me: nevertheless not as I will, but as thou wilt." [10] Thus in trying to classify prayers of petition as magical or truly religious we must take into consideration the attitude behind the words and the experience to which the prayer will lead. A prayer for rain or for the destruction of one's enemies is obviously in a psychologically different category from Solomon's prayer for wisdom.

And now, O Lord my God, thou hast made thy servant king instead of David my father: and I am but a little child: I know not how to go out or come in.
And thy servant is in the midst of thy people which thou hast chosen, a great people, that cannot be numbered nor counted for multitude.
Give therefore thy servant an understanding heart to judge thy people, that I may discern between good and bad: for who is able to judge this thy so great a people? [11]

Another form of prayer, chiefly subjective, is the *prayer of communion*. This may be in the form of petition, but the aim is to secure nothing but knowledge of God and communion with him. It is the mark of a more advanced stage of religious development. Thus St. Augustine prays, "Let me know Thee, O Thou who knowest me; let me know Thee, as I am known." [12] Closely connected with this form

[10] Matt. 26:39.
[11] I Kings 3:7–9.
[12] *Confessions*, p. 218.

is the *prayer of meditation*, which may, and often does, involve the subjective experience of communion. On the other hand it may chiefly concern the inner thoughts of the individual as he focuses his mind on certain problems or pious ideas. Richard Cabot says, "We often advise each other to 'think it over and see what on the whole seems best'; or we say, 'All things considered, I have decided to go.' Anyone who did this would be near to prayer." [13] What he had in mind seems to have been the prayer of meditation, which may be called a prayer when it has some measure of divine reference whether conscious or more covert.

Then there is the *prayer of confession* and repentance. When not merely ritualistic and formal this kind of prayer is apt to burst forth as the expression of an overwhelming sense of guilt. Because of the pent-up passion with which this type of prayer is charged, particularly when a sudden conviction of sin leads to its utterance, this form of prayer may become involuntary poetry. Consequently it may often find literary form. The General Confession in the *Book of Common Prayer* and some of the Psalms are examples of such poetry. "Who is he that hideth counsel without knowledge?" laments the convicted Job, "therefore have I uttered things that I understood not; things too wonderful for me, which I knew not. . . . Wherefore I abhor myself, and repent in dust and ashes." [14] Though directed to God and objective in some degree, the prayer of confession is commonly subjective in that the motive behind it, though eminently religious, is concerned with the relief of tensions in the suffering penitent.

Another subjective form of prayer, with nevertheless a large portion of the objective intention, is the *prayer of dedication* in which the praying person devotes himself to the service of the Divine. The objective part involves the concern for the affairs of God, but the intended result of the prayer is an influence on the life of him who prays. The prayer of Solomon quoted above, though petitionary in form, is dedicatory in spirit. The ejaculation of Isaiah at the end of his conversion experience is a brief prayer of dedication: "Here am I; send me." [15]

Two forms of prayer are essentially subjective but require almost a

---

[13] *What Men Live By*, p. 275.
[14] Job, 42:3–6.
[15] Isaiah, 6:8.

special category, *prayer of intercession* and *didactic prayer.* The former is a variation of the prayer of petition. It is objective in that it seeks no benefit for self, but is rather a prayer for another person or persons. A prayer for the innocent victims of a cruel war would be an instance, or a prayer for the recovery of a sick friend. Whether or not such prayers are effective is of course irrelevant to the definition of the type, which is concerned with inner experience and a state of mind. However, it is appropriate to point out that many such prayers, like other petitionary prayers, are psychologically another expression of magic; particularly when the prayer becomes an easy way of piously ridding oneself of a sense of obligation. As such the prayer is simply a convenient form of escape. But one easily senses that a prayer of intercession belongs psychologically in quite a different category when, for example, it is the last resort of one who has done or is doing all he can for those for whom he prays. It becomes then the spontaneous bringing of those whom one cares about most deeply and actively into relation with that which one conceives of supreme value, namely God.

The *didactic prayer* is also objective in that it is designed for others but, like intercessory prayer, subjective in that benefits are thought to accrue to man rather than to God. The didactic prayer is always a public or semi-public affair and is designed to give instruction. Such prayers may touch the depths of bathos and absurdity, as when, under the guise of prayer, the clergyman supplies God with information— facts which already might be supposed to be known to Him. The college president, in an often-reported incident, having forgotten to make an announcement and knowing the rush that would begin at the termination of the final prayer, called down a special blessing on "the class of Professor Owens, which will meet in Edwards 9 instead of Smith 18 at the termination of the chapel service." Many pastors perpetrate prayers only a little less obvious and crass. On the other hand, every public prayer is in some sense didactic in that the example of the form and spirit of the prayer cannot fail to have its effect on the hearers. It is this which lends to didactic prayer its dignity. Properly conceived it may be fully self-conscious and wholly appropriate. The Lord's Prayer, given to instruct the Disciples in the art of praying, is the most eminent example.

There are two prominent forms of prayer which are mainly *objec-*

tive in that God, rather than the individual and his concerns, constitutes the psychological center of attention. The first of these is the *prayer of adoration and praise*. This type of prayer is born from a sense of the greatness of the Creator and from a sense of wonder and awe at the marvels created by Him. Much less primitive than the prayer of petition it belongs to a more mature stage of religious development and is frequently utilized by mystics. Like the prayer of confession, the original prayers of adoration were spontaneous outpourings of the spirit so that this form also, possessed of the genius of poetry, has been crystallized in literary form. One of the great prayers of the Church, the *Te Deum Laudamus*, is typical:

> We praise thee, O God: we acknowledge thee to be the Lord;
> All the earth doth worship thee, the Father everlasting.
> To thee all Angels cry aloud; the Heavens and all the Powers therein;
> To thee all Cherubim and Seraphim continually do cry,
> Holy, Holy, Holy, Lord God of Sabaoth;
> Heaven and earth are full of the Majesty of thy glory. . . .

Closely related to the prayer of adoration and praise is the *prayer of thanksgiving*, likewise a spontaneous tribute to the Creator, but for blessings received rather than from a sense of wonder and awe. The prayer of thanksgiving is also closely related to petitionary prayer in that it is apt to follow any actual benefits conceived to have been bestowed as the result of petitionary prayer. Its counterpart in the ordinary commerce of living, thanking one's associates for favors received, is commonplace and self-conscious. Consequently because the giving of thanks is a habit, that variety of prayer is more common than other forms, such as those of adoration, confession, communion, or dedication. Children are enjoined to say thanks in their prayers almost as soon as they are taught to pray at all, while a prayer of thanks is as regularly a part of an extemporaneous pastoral prayer as it is of a ritualistic service.

It is obvious that there is something psychologically more wholesome about objective prayer than subjective prayer, generally speaking. Though directed toward God and designed to minister to His pleasure, objective prayer confers benefits upon the individual simply because it is a means of turning his attention toward something larger than himself. It makes no difference whether God is a reality or an idea. We find then another example of the paradox of personality so often illustrated by the religious life—that activity designed for the betterment of another confers its surest benefits on the individual who is outgiving. And so the petitionary form of *subjective* prayer, with its weakness for the circumscribed interests of the *me*, may actually diminish that which it is designed to benefit, while *objective* prayer, aimed at an idea or Person larger than self, expands that self and enlarges its vision.

Types of prayer in relation to personality types. Another way to classify prayer is to relate it to the four types of religious personality we have described in former chapters, the mystic, the religious intellectual, the prophet, and the priest.[16] According to their religious orientation and aim, each of these personalities tends to pray in his own characteristic way. We will allow ourselves a brief look at this kind of distinction in prayer.

The aim of the mystic is to cultivate the presence of God and finally to become one with him. Hence *mystical prayer* is such as to implement these strivings. Since the mystic tends to depreciate possessions and to mortify his desires, he seldom uses the crass forms of petitionary prayer. Indeed, if he uses petition at all, he asks for heavenly favors. "I call Thee into my soul," prayed St. Augustine, "which by the desire which Thou inspirest in it Thou preparest for Thy reception." [17]

When mystical prayer is subjective it is apt to take the form of the prayer of communion, meditation, and confession. But the mystic is found still more often using objective forms of prayer, especially that of adoration and praise. An example, touched with a note of thanksgiving, is from St. Teresa of Avila:

O Lord of the universe, all creatures would praise Thee! Who can proclaim loudly enough how faithful Thou are to Thy friends? Would that I had understanding and knowledge and words wholly new that I might glorify the wonders of Thy love as my soul feels it.[18]

---

[16] This classification has been suggested chiefly by Heiler's *Prayer*. Readers will find a full treatment of the subject from this point of view in that excellent work.

[17] *Confessions*, p. 340.

[18] Quoted in Heiler, *Prayer*, p. 187.

Intellectual prayer, or *philosophic prayer* as Heiler calls it, is domi-nated by thoughts arising from and concerned with the ethical ideal. Since the religious intellectual is sensitive to religious inconsistencies, he is apt to be particularly hostile to the naive forms of petitionary prayer. And because he has something of a reputation for logic, in-sight, and straight thinking to keep up in the world, he is apt to find himself so hedged about by theological inhibition that it becomes hard for him to pray with any spontaneity. He does not wish to get caught by his professional colleagues in the act of any sentimental outpouring that might not bear the scrutiny of a cold philosophical eye. This subjection of prayer by the intellectual to critical scrutiny cools its ardor and deprives it of passion.

But for the intellectual ethics are always a respectable concern; con-sequently a petition for moral good will frequently be found in this type of prayer. Submission to destiny, for which philosophers are famous, is another note that is often struck. Finally a sense of the vast cosmic plan and the greatness of its Creator is also found in philosophic prayer. We find this strain in the characteristic poem of Joseph Addison that has become a familiar hymn:

> The spacious firmament on high
> With all the blue ethereal sky
> And spangled heavens a shining frame,
> Their great original proclaim.

The other features of intellectual prayer may be found in one by that child of the Enlightenment, Benjamin Franklin. In his *Auto-biography* he tells of his attempts to achieve moral virtue, in pursuit of which he composed the following:

> O powerful goodness! bountiful father! merciful Guide!
> Increase in me that wisdom which discovers my truest interest.
> Strengthen my resolution to perform what that wisdom dictates.
> Accept my kind offices to thy other children as the only return
> in my power for thy continual favors to me.[19]

In short, intellectual prayer is instructed by reason rather than pas-sion. Its aims are lofty, its language dignified, and its ideals purified.

[19] P. 93.

But in its relative coldness it is not the kind that issues from or inspires the ordinary man. Heiler may be too hard on it when he concludes that "It possesses no constructive energy; it can produce only dissolving and destroying effects." [20] If thought and criticism have their place in religious experience, they certainly deserve to be represented in prayer as elsewhere. The prayers quoted reflect the wisdom of their composers, are not without a proper modicum of feeling, and are such that no worshiper need feel ashamed of them. But reason in prayer is such that those who need it do not utilize it, and those who use it have too much of it already.

In turning to *prophetic prayer*, we cannot say that it makes too much use of wisdom, though in common with intellectual prayer it is concerned with ethics or, as the Hebrew prophets would prefer to put it, righteousness. The prophet may be a person of great intellectual gifts, as in the case of Luther, but he is primarily a man of passion. Therefore in prophetic prayer, the intellectual element is apt to be submerged if it appears at all.

In a sense we can think of prophetic prayer even in its more magical aspects as an extension of personal prayer. Like personal prayer, it derives from a sense of need, and often conceives of God as a pretty direct ally in the struggle for the cause. "Let them be confounded that persecute me, but let not me be confounded" was one of Jeremiah's prayers; "let them be dismayed, but let not me be dismayed: bring upon them the day of evil, and destroy them with double destruction." [21] Or we have the primitive and prophetic song of praise following the Israelites' passage of the Red Sea, ascribed to the prophetess Miriam: "Sing ye to the Lord, for he hath triumphed gloriously; the horse and his rider hath he thrown into the sea." [22]

But when the prophet speaks for his personal needs it is not a circumscribed concern but a personal wish raised to a higher power. He wishes strength for his cause, and though on occasion he may be a prime fanatic and bigot, nevertheless his needs have become spiritualized, and the cause is not his but the Lord's. In a particularly gracious example of this type of prayer, Pascal prayed, "I ask Thee for neither health nor sickness, neither life nor death, but that Thou may dis-

[20] *Op. cit.*, p. 103.
[21] Jeremiah, 17:18.
[22] Exodus, 15:21.

pose of my health and sickness for Thy glory, for my salvation, and for the good of the Church, and of Thy saints." [23]

Prophetic prayer, then, is like intellectual prayer in its concern for ethical and moral good. It also has a certain kinship in the breadth of its scope, its vision being directed beyond the personal. It is like mystical prayer in that God is felt as personal and intimate. But it is unlike both of these in that it reflects the social activism that is so much a part of the prophet's religious orientation. And it is directly in contrast to intellectual prayer in its rejection of wisdom coldly conceived and in its passionate concern for the personal spiritualization of the prophet's life and the immediate promotion of a kingdom of righteousness.

Priestly prayer partakes of some characteristics of all of the three preceding types. The priest, as such, expresses a religion that is derivative, for he considers himself a representative in two ways. First of all he represents the people in an approach to God and, even more flattering to his ego, he represents God to the people, sometimes as an ambassador and spokesman, and sometimes as an agent with the power to bind and loose. Also, since it is his function to conserve, he echoes the accents of those who are more deeply religious than he. These may be the mystics, philosophers, or prophets of the ages, or the humble men and women in his congregation whose religious lives may be primitive and even magical in their essence.

Priestly prayer, as such, is always in some sense public, hence it is subject to the social-psychological pressures of the public context. This means that it is less apt to draw on the mystical tradition, which is peculiarly individual and private, than from the philosophical tradition, which is cold enough to be intellectually acceptable to more sophisticated congregations, or from the prophetic tradition, which involves larger issues of public concern. It also may perform a hortatory function. In this and other ways the prophetic and priestly traditions may mingle with one another through the instrumentality of public prayer.

This public feature of priestly prayer also exerts a strong influence in favor of emphasis on form. Mystical prayer may achieve its form as an expression of the gradualism of the mystic's progress toward unity; intellectual prayer naturally derives its form from the philo-

[23] Quoted in Heiler, *op. cit.*, p. 250.

sophic bent toward order and logic, while the prophet's passionate outpouring finds appropriate form the most effective vehicle for the deliverance of his spiritual impulses. The form of these and other more private types of prayer develops from the inner genius of the one who prays. Priestly prayer, on the other hand, finds its form largely dictated from without. The fashionable congregation struck with horror at an ungrammatical expression or a slurred syllable will naturally not fail to influence the pastor as he considers diction in his next Sunday's prayer. He who prays privately, on the other hand, is not likely to imagine a gasp of divine disapproval should his prayer be guilty of such horrendous lapses.

But this concern with form in priestly prayer has its more creative aspects in that it acts as a kind of screen to set apart the more digni- fied and effective prayers for public worship. Particularly in the litur- gical churches, most prayers are printed. These often first issued forth as private outpourings and then were chosen for priestly utterance. Since in the best prayers form and substance tend to be associated, the prayers on priestly lips not only tend to be graciously expressed but, when properly appreciated, representative of the sincere aspira- tions of the congregation. It is standards such as these that have pro- duced the beautiful and moving accents of *The Book of Common Prayer*. Witness for example the following prayer, ascribed to Car- dinal Newman:

O Lord, support us all the day long, until the shadows lengthen and the evening comes, and the busy world is hushed, and the fever of life is over, and our work is done. Then in thy mercy grant us a safe lodging, and a holy rest, and peace at the last.[24]

Such a prayer is eminently appropriate to public worship, illustrating as it does the deeply poetic and restrained quality of priestly prayer at its best.

For this same reason priestly prayer becomes ritualistic in nature. That is, it tends to repeat itself both in actuality and in form. The prayer that has demonstrated its effectiveness and offended no canon of good taste is apt to be utilized by the priest again and again as a formula tried, true, and safe. This means that ritualistic prayer easily may become simply verbiage, the *reductio ad absurdum* of which is

[24] P. 583.

the partly honest and partly laughable device of the Buddhist prayer wheel.

As representative of the people, the priestly prayer can often be spotted by its use of the first person plural. Also, since it is one of the vehicles in the functioning of the Church, it is often didactic as well as hortatory and intercessory in nature. All of these strains may be detected in this familiar supplication from the *Book of Common Prayer.*

O God, the Creator and Preserver of all mankind, we humbly beseech thee for all sorts and condtions of men; that thou wouldest be pleased to make thy ways known unto them, thy saving health unto all nations. More especially we pray for thy holy Church universal; that it may be so guided and governed by thy good spirit, that all who profess and call themselves Christians may be led into the way of truth, and hold the faith in the unity of spirit, in the bond of peace, and in righteousness of life. Finally we commend to thy fatherly goodness all those who are any ways afflicted or distressed in mind, body, or estate; that it may please thee to comfort and relieve them, according to their several necessities; giving them patience under their sufferings, and a happy issue out of all their afflictions. And this we beg for Jesus Christ's sake.[25]

To summarize this section, we may point out that we have characterized four types of prayer according as prayer tends to be expressed by four types of religious leadership, *mystical, intellectual, prophetic,* and *priestly.* The list is not comprehensive and might be extended. Certainly each one of these types stands in contrast to the ordinary prayer of the common man, which is personal, often magical, sincere, usually routine, but sometimes passionate, depending on the intensity of inner needs.

Prayer and personal life. It will be recalled that in an early chapter we distinguished what we call primary, secondary, and tertiary religious experience; primary religion being first-hand and lively religious experience, secondary being a faint echo of what was once primary, while tertiary religious experience is simply an imitation of the religion of someone else. These categories are well illustrated in the prayer life of individuals. One need only look within himself to realize that prayer occurs on all levels of intensity and with varying

[25] Pp. 18–19.

degrees of consciousness of reality. This occurs not only in the prayer life of the ordinary mortal, for even religious geniuses, like the great mystics, complain bitterly of their "periods of dryness," or the "dark night of the soul." These are the times when, woodenly and unresponsively, the individual goes through the motions of his prayers. Unhappily, there are many worshipers whose experience is always of this nature. Prayer usually *is* a routine affair, and since others superficially go through the same outward movements, these tertiary religious personalities suppose that their own prayers are representative of the best, and dutifully continue their uninspired chore in quest of religious respectability.

The chief difference between these and the secondary personality at prayer is that the latter has a standard of comparison. Looking back to glorious moments of inspiration, he knows how far short his prayers fall of being genuine and creative. The recollection of these moments may be all that keeps him faithful to his routine. But it also keeps him humble. If those who "hunger and thirst after righteousness" are to be filled, these are the people for whom the future offers substantial hope. St. John of the Cross found his "dark night of the soul" merely a gate to a more satisfying experience than he had ever known. This does not mean that every secondary prayer is bound to be followed sooner or later by the recapture of an original ecstasy. It depends on the single-mindedness of the worshipper and the intensity of his aim. The world's many interests are powerful to forestall the vision splendid despite sincere intentions. But this remembrance of things past is enough to put the secondary prayer in a very different category from the tertiary prayer, even though on occasion one may be as insipid and uncreative as the other. If nothing else, perspective tends to engender humility, a commodity very necessary if one is to achieve the highest reaches of primary prayer.

Another brief comment we may make concerning prayer and personality is that, while all prayer is conscious, it tends to be expressive of unconscious urges and the real "me." We can pretty much except from this statement priestly and public prayer, but it remains true of private prayer. In the solitudes of the soul and in the presence of what man thinks of as his understanding and forgiving Maker, he is less likely to play a part unless this role is very deeply ingrained. One wonders whether even Mr. Pecksniff's private prayers were quite as insufferable as his public utterances. But for the most part, the average person, if he were bent on analyzing himself, might look on his prayers as a kind of private Rorschach or Thematic Apperception test whereby his inner life might be assessed. It is not on record that psychoanalysts have shown a curiosity about their patient's prayers comparable to their interest in their dreams. Certainly it would be difficult for a clinician to probe this deeper significance of prayer. Yet it would seem that here is an area for investigation that might prove fruitful.

This last reflection on prayer as the expression of the deep urges of the individual suggests that it has creative value. If painting may be a release for the artist and music for the musician, why should not prayer serve this purpose for the average man? This is in fact one of the functions of prayer that keep it alive, and doubtless prayer has served to some degree as an inexpensive substitute for the psychiatrist's couch.

Still another benefit to be derived from prayer is its suggestive value in keeping before an individual his dearest aims and desires. This function is to some degree in opposition to that of which we have just been speaking. To the extent that prayer, as is often the case, helps to hold before the mind an unfulfilled ideal, it may increase rather than relieve tension. But we have seen that some measure of tension is necessary for creative growth, and while the individual at one moment may need release, at another he needs the orientation toward the good life that religion encourages. The performing of these functions is part of the value of prayer.

But it may be asked whether these and other subjective values are all there are to prayer. Are there not objective achievements for prayer far beyond the confines of the individual mind? May not God in some way benefit from our prayers too? These are questions that the psychologist is not equipped to answer. Certainly he cannot rule out objective benefits, but neither can he rule them in. Pratt discusses this problem at the end of his chapter on prayer in *The Religious Consciousness,* and we can do no better than quote his somewhat whimsical conclusion.

. . . it is interesting to note the fervor with which certain psychological writers extol the value of prayer and in the same breath either state or imply that its value is due entirely to subjective conditions. These writers seem to have forgotten what Dr. L. P. Jacks has well called the "alchemy of thought," "to interpret experience is to change it." For since the subjective value of prayer is chiefly due to the belief that prayer has values which are *not* subjective, it will with most persons evaporate altogether once they learn that it is all subjective. Hence if it be true both that the subjective value of prayer is very great and that it is the only value which prayer possesses, this latter fact should assiduously be kept secret. The psychologist who knows it and publishes it broadcast is like the physician who should disclose to his patient the great value and the true nature of bread pills. "Take these," the doctor may be conceived as saying: "take three of these after each meal and seven after Sunday dinner, and they will completely cure you. They contain nothing but bread and have no value in themselves, absolutely none; but since you don't know this fact and are unaware that you are being fooled, their subjective value upon you will be invaluable."

No, if the subjective value of prayer be all the value it has, we wise psychologists of religion had best keep the fact to ourselves; otherwise the game will soon be up and we shall have no religion left to psychologize about. We shall have killed the goose that laid our golden egg.[26]

SUMMARY

If prayer is "the most spontaneous and the most personal expression of religion," it is here that religion may best be tested and appraised. Hence it will be profitable to hark back to Chapter 11 and our ten criteria for mature religion. The individual may best determine the maturity of his religion by evaluating his prayer life.

Is it primary? Does prayer spring from a lively sense of need, or is it a dull chore performed from a sense of duty or in imitation of another person? *Is it fresh?* Does it contain some element of that cosmic wonder and awe which mystics seem to experience and which Rudolf Otto described in his *The Idea of the Holy?* "O what a friend we have in Jesus!" runs a sentimental hymn, and up to a certain point a sense of commonplace closeness to God may be a good thing. But a person whose prayer life is simply a commonplace extension of the social communication of everyday living, bringing no sense of mystery to enlarge his vision of reality, is one whose religion has been arrested at a very mundane level. *Is it self-critical?* Has he evaluated

[26] P. 336.

his prayers in some such manner as we are now suggesting? *Is it free from magic?* Does he look on his prayer life as a means of harmonizing his will with that of the Divine, or does he consider it a means of securing celestial favors and Divine help in getting ahead in life?

Is it dynamic? Does it give meaning to life and make a difference in attitudes and behavior? *Is it integrating* in that this difference operates in the direction of a firmer moral life consistent with worthy aims? *Is it socially effective?* Does it tend to strengthen one's sense of community with others and responsibility for society at large? *Is it growing?* Does prayer life lead toward progressively deeper spiritual insights, or does it become an increasingly static experience imperceptibly decaying as the years go on? One should be able to look back on his prayers of ten or twenty years before with an unmistakable sense of progress. *Does prayer make one humble* with a wholesome appreciation of his failings and a knowledge of the extent to which he has fallen short of ideals, or does he derive from it a pious sense of self-congratulation that he is not like other men? *Is one's prayer life creative?* Does it develop its own values underived from the religion of those around him? Few persons will find that their prayer life can pass this test and at the same time satisfy the other criteria. But a prayer life that does measure up to these standards is an indication of religion at its best and most mature.

Otherwise in this chapter we have described prayer in a variety of its forms according to several categories. We have indicated the subjective forms of the prayers of petition, communion, meditation, confession, and dedication, and didactic prayer. We have noted the objective prayers of adoration and praise, thanksgiving, and intercession. And we have also noted that prayer may be linked to personality types. Thus we have distinguished prayers characteristic of the mystic, the intellectual, the prophet, and the priest.

The individual concerned about prayer might well ask, "Which of these forms should one emphasize?" The answer must be determined by one's own needs and his own personality. The pattern of the prayer life of no two people will be exactly the same, particularly as prayer becomes less imitative and derived and grows toward the individuality of maturity. But if a generalization is desired, it might be said that all types have their place in the complete religious life.

Even some of the magical forms of prayer may have their value if they are looked upon as stages in the growth toward fuller maturity.

But there is need not only for a balance within the individual's prayer life among the different forms of prayer, but also for a more creative tension between prayer life and other expressions of the religious life. Without some kind of prayer it is hard to envisage religion as we have defined it. To quote Heiler once again, "Religious persons and students of religion agree in testifying that prayer is the centre of religion, the soul of all piety. . . . Without prayer faith remains a theoretical conviction; worship is only an external and formal act; moral action is without spiritual depth; man remains at a distance from God; an abyss yawns between the finite and the Infinite." [27]

[27] *Op. cit.*, p. 362.

Chapter 15

PSYCHOLOGICAL
CONSIDERATIONS
IN WORSHIP

So, unless we are blind to beauty, deaf to the call of righteous battle, incapable of prolonged reflection, a stranger to the poignancies of joy and sorrow, incapable of wonder, we are in perpetual danger of falling into worship. . . .

—Richard Cabot

Art, science, and religion all have this in common: at their best they involve values pursued for their own sake rather than for some utilitarian purpose. Most educated people are familiar with the distinction between the scientist and the technician. The pure scientist like Copernicus, Newton, or Einstein is spurred primarily by the motive of discovering scientific truth. The technician, who popularly passes for a scientist in our society, takes the truths discovered by the scientist and adapts them to some use. For the true scientist this is simply a fortunate by-product, the possibility of which never entered his consciousness when immersed in his studies.

A somewhat similar distinction may be made in religion. There is the person like the mystic for whom religious experience has value for its own sake. There is the religious technician who approves of religion because it is "good for you" or "good for the people." To illustrate this latter derivative aspect, ethics may be simply a by-product of religion; so may pastoral counseling that furthers mental health. They are the technologies of the religious life, not its essence.

328

THE ESSENCE OF WORSHIP

Prayer is often used as one of these religious techniques, and yet it is inseparably linked with its cognate, worship. But worship tends to fall into the category of pure religion. Though one can and should cultivate worship for the best results, one is apt to fall into it spontaneously as Richard Cabot reminds us. "So, unless we are blind to beauty, deaf to the call of righteous battle, incapable of prolonged reflection, a stranger to the poignancies of joy and sorrow, incapable of wonder, we are in perpetual danger of falling into worship as the tired mortal falls asleep." [1] We could add to this list the urge toward aspiration, praise, adoration, and thanksgiving, directed toward the "Beyond" at the same time that religious experience is stimulated by such attitudes.

Statements such as these may seem extravagant to those who have never experienced worship. But just as the lover longs to pour out praise to his beloved, or the mother delights to babble sweet nonsense to her child, so the worshiper, if he is a true worshiper and not just a play-acting one, burns with the desire to praise God, to know Him, and to do His will. These comparisons are not merely rhetorical, for all human experiences trace their origins to a common psychological matrix in such impulsions as the urge to self-expression, the desire for affection, and the need for an aim to give life meaning. To describe worship in this way the psychologist is not dependent on the objective existence of God any more than he is in describing prayer. For God *seems* real to the worshipper, and this is his reaction to the Reality that he senses. The description will seem strange to many "religious" persons because they have never experienced worship in its full intensity and know it only in its tertiary [2] form. They have so often participated in worship merely in a perfunctory way.

True worship is a state of being which envisages all of life and enables the individual, in part consciously and in part unconsciously, to bring all of his experience and concerns under survey and direct them toward an Object which integrates them and gives them meaning. This in turn yields perspective, the capacity to distinguish between

---

[1] *What Men Live By*, p. 271.
[2] For a distinction between primary, secondary, and tertiary religious behavior, see Chap. 2, pp. 23–28.

values, and a reduction of tensions. Most people think of worship in its self-conscious public form, which so often fails of its function because of its segmental, partial character. One participates in it because of its "beauty," or because it symbolizes the doctrines of the Church, or because the minister says that it is one's duty. It is obvious that none of these reasons, taken alone, could mediate the kind of worship experience of which we have been speaking. In its more spontaneous, comprehensive form it may become an antidote for the unwholesome tensions which plague modern life and constitute a poignant milestone in the ascent of creative growth. Let anyone who is puzzled about our reference here, or is disposed to self-congratulation over the general all-around satisfactoriness of the weekly Sabbath pilgrimage to his place of worship, compare his worship experiences to that of Job when he learns of the destruction of his children.

Then Job arose, and rent his mantle, and shaved his head, and fell down upon the ground and worshipped,

And said, Naked came I out of my mother's womb, and naked shall I return thither: the Lord gave, and the Lord hath taken away; blessed be the name of the Lord.[3]

PUBLIC WORSHIP

The study of worship. The foregoing has had particular reference to worship in its private, more essential form. It is difficult for the psychologist to acquire any scientific understanding of this aspect of it, and only slightly less difficult to study worship in its more concrete, public form. Nevertheless there have been a few attempts to gather empirical data in this area and study them in a systematic way.

An example of this is a study carried out by Professor J. Paul Williams of Mt. Holyoke College.[4] In this questionnaire the answers given were scaled to yield a "worship score." This had reference to the total impression made on the worshipper of a service of worship. Similar questions yielded indices covering various aspects of the service, such as the sermon, the music, and participation in prayer. These questionnaires then were administered following services to worship-

[3] Job, 1:20–21.

[4] "An Objective Approach to the Study of Worship."

pers at several different churches or chapels until seven or eight hundred measures were secured. These were then averaged and correlated in order to test hypotheses and to learn what the measures indicated about the worship services. In one case a worship service was deliberately altered for the purpose of comparing the effectiveness of different emphases within the service. In other words, an experiment in worship was set up and tested. The instruments developed in this study could be used or adapted by churches to evaluate the effectiveness of their worship services with some measure of scientific rigor.

Consequently, here and there we can make statements about public worship for which we can give empirical support. For the most part, however, even in this area our statements must be largely speculative and conjectural. Then we must remember that public worship is worship only in a very restricted sense inasmuch as it may be doubted that the experience is a very intense one and so primary to a very large proportion of the average congregation. It is true that Professor Williams' respondents frequently indicated that their worship experiences were very real. But he himself points out that there is some question of the validity of the measure, and doubtless there was considerable relativity and confusion about definitions in each individual's reply. For example, a good sermon tended to produce a "halo effect" which resulted in all other ratings being higher. Yet one would hesitate to state that all such sermons would result in true worship. Public worship represents all worship in the popular mind because it has the name of worship and is therefore concrete.[5]

Objective and subjective worship. In connection with prayer we called attention to Pratt's distinction between objective and subjective religion. This distinction has been developed by Pratt most notably in a chapter of *The Religious Consciousness* entitled "Objective and subjective worship." [6] The distinction is a useful one in considering worship, and has its roots in basic psychological orientation.

[5] Some of Prof. Williams' conclusions: Worship scores tend to rise with (a) increasing age, (b) lower level of education, (c) women as compared to men. Neither music nor agreement with the sermon will insure worship.

[6] Chap. 14.

In brief, objective worship conceives as its function the delight and edification of God. Appropriate to this function of worship are such features of a service as praise and thanksgiving. Pratt cites the Roman Catholic Mass as one primarily of this character. The priest will execute the service whether there are other worshippers present or not. For the most part he faces not the congregation but the altar, and addresses himself to God. Furthermore the parts of the service when he addresses the people are the less important parts, such as the sermon, which often is curtailed or even omitted.

Subjective worship, on the other hand, conceives as its main function that of edifying and inspiring the people. This is a predominant form in Protestant worship, where the sermon is the main feature of the service, the minister faces the congregation throughout the service, and the pulpit occupies the focus of interior architecture. The Protestant minister, if none or few are present, may pack up his Bible and dismiss the congregation, for they are the losers through their poor attendance and God does not require the ritual of praise in an empty church. When the church is full, the worship takes on warmth, for the service is for the people, and even the prayers are often homilies but thinly disguised as petitions to God. These usually exhort Him for help in making the people good, thank Him for their blessings, and supply Him with a quantity of information.

The distinction in practice is not quite so clear-cut as the theory suggests, particularly since Protestant services in recent times have become more liturgical and have appropriated more and more of the objective orientation. It may also be doubted that the edification of the worshipper has been quite so far from the minds of the fabricators of objective worship as this theory holds. As a matter of fact one of the chief justifications of objective worship is that in making God, and not the individual, the center of the worshipper's consciousness, the objective service directs the individual away from his selfish concerns to the contemplation of cosmic realities.

Doubtless the best wisdom lies in a judicious mingling of the two types, depending partly on the tradition of the worshippers and the situation. The criterion as to which is better involves going back to the essential definition of worship. Whatever stimulates the comprehensive bringing of one's total life experience into harmony with ultimate cosmic Reality deserves a place in the effective framework of worship.

A sermon, for example, may do this as well as a rendering of the *Te Deum*. This framework, whether objective or subjective in form, must never be confused with worship itself, which is a wholly inner experience and hidden from the eye of the prying psychologist. The latter can judge of the reality of this experience only by its fruits or by what the worshipper may be able and willing to tell him about it.

Liturgical vs. non-liturgical worship. Closely identified with objective and subjective worship are liturgical and non-liturgical worship, as has been hinted in the foregoing discussion. Liturgical worship tends to be objective and non-liturgical subjective, so that in large measure the discussion of this issue may be conceived as an extension of our remarks on objective and subjective worship. It may be further noted that liturgical and objective worship tend to be appropriated by the priestly type of mind, while the prophet, with his emphasis on preaching, will take more readily to the non-liturgical forms, if he can be confined by any forms at all.

Another difference is that the early stages of a religious movement are apt to stimulate services that are non-liturgical, while a liturgy crystallizes and hardens as time goes on. This was true of the Christian church in the development of the Lord's Supper, for example, which started as an ordinary meal and is now celebrated in a number of highly stylized liturgical forms. Enthusiasm and zeal characterize the beginnings of most religious movements, and these characteristics do not favor liturgy and ritual.[7] Furthermore, in the early stages a movement is more apt to emphasize the expression of its tenets in everyday life; its message is more prophetic, and a liturgy is felt as an artificial constraint. But as time goes on religion becomes more sophisticated and self-conscious. This toning down of unfashionable crudities and native vigor brings along with it the demand for decorous clothing and the amenities. The spontaneity of free worship tends to be replaced by a demand for a more ecclesiastically correct and ordered service. Just as the spectacle of an invited guest eating with his knife will threaten his fashionable hostess with apoplexy, so will a departure from the jot and tittle of liturgical punctilio

[7] See A. T. Boisen, *Religion in Crisis and Custom*, Chap. 2.

cause similar disturbances among the guardians of liturgical correctness.

Though of course each individual most often will prefer that type of worship in which he is brought up, in the main the pressure of change works in the direction of the more liturgical service. Many old-time Protestants have seen liturgical innovations in their services that a generation earlier would have been branded as positively pagan. Empirical studies have supported this drift. Liturgical services, for one thing, make much greater use of symbolism than do non-liturgical ones. Johnson cites a study in which two types of services were prepared, one with much use of symbols, such as a cross, religious pictures, and candles, and one without.[8] These were presented 28 times to seven groups of young people. The great majority of them, when questioned, indicated preference for the service with symbols, while their behavior and participation in the services seemed to bear this out.

Observations and studies such as these point to a kind of paradox, a problem with respect to worship which has yet to be studied adequately and to which one can only propose speculative solutions. This is that while objective, liturgical worship would seem the type most psychologically justified, and while actually this kind of service does seem to yield the best results and to be preferred by the greater number of cultivated people; nevertheless the early, more effective stages in a religious movement tend to be those associated with non-liturgical worship. Thus the glorious days of Methodism are not so much the present, when the spiritual heirs of John Wesley are counted in millions and the assets of the Methodist churches in hundreds of millions, when vested choirs are becoming the rule and a liturgy bids fair to smother the enthusiasm for which the old-time Methodists were famous. They were the early days of the movement in the eighteenth century when recent converts rose before the break of day to gather in each other's homes to sing and pray and read the Bible, and when Wesley traveled over the countryside of England to speak in the open air to the throngs of factory workers who came to hear him. It was through such irregular means of worship that the moral climate of England was transformed. If such results

[8] *The Psychology of Religion*, p. 165.

can accompany non-liturgical worship, how does it occur that people will consider anything else?

This cannot be answered with any precision, but certain theoretical considerations present themselves. First of all, the *form* of worship is more incidental to the worship experience than it is a cause. As is so often superficially assumed, it is not the worship service that mediates the experience so much as inner stimuli and preparation. This does not mean that the form of worship has no effect whatsoever on the experience, but that the form is not the essential element. A powerful and sincere religious personality, such as Wesley, together with a fellowship of many like-minded worshipers—in other words, the social element—would seem of all outward elements the most essentially influential. Since such individuals tend to feel constrained by ritual, the creativity of their natural religious genius seeks freer forms and expresses itself more powerfully in such ways. Hence the distaste for liturgy in the early stages of many religious movements.

But the non-liturgical form of service without sincerity, zeal, and the transparent religious power of the worshippers has little attraction for the casual observer. Its occupation is all too clearly gone, and its stark flatness or sentimentality makes the educated participant ashamed. Perhaps not the least influential of society's protections against nudism is the fact that so few of those who arbitrate fashion and the social mores possess figures that would look well undraped. In somewhat analogous fashion the liturgical churches may be unwilling to display the spare ribs of their spiritual poverty, while those who are traditionally non-liturgical hasten to assume a decorous ritual as fast as a decent respect for the ways of their spiritual forebears will allow them. At any rate, a liturgical service nearly always has the recommendation of some measure of beauty. At its best this latter may serve as a poignant and appropriate symbol of a deep experience of worship, enhancing it and conveying to it religious accents echoing down the centuries. At its worst it may be merely a superficial bit of esthetic indulgence that hides from the pseudo-worshiper the fact that spiritually speaking he is simply going through liturgical motions. In neither case does it offend the sensibility of the educated sophisticate who, while he may be superficial, will never be vulgar. Liturgy, then, may simply act as a façade to cover a lack of zeal.

  Still another reason for the development of liturgy is that liturgy is easier on the clergy than the non-liturgical requirement of extemporaneous prayer or emphasis on the carefully constructed sermon. Furthermore it is preferred by highly institutionalized churches as safer and more generalized. Strong and vivid religious personalities have ever been the bane of the institution. Preoccupation with liturgy naturally keeps them more confined to what is dogmatically proper and serves as insurance against those most dangerous threats to institutional equilibrium, spiritually sensitive ideas.

Another psychological support for liturgy, particularly in its sacramental aspect, derives from a peculiar but universal kind of magical or "labor-saving" urge to which human beings are subject. It may seem strange, not to say blasphemous, to liken a rite like Baptism or Holy Communion to a modern mechanical gadget. But honest observation testifies that many are "the faithful" for whom this mechanical function becomes a sacrament's chief meaning. This may not have been the intention of those with whom a rite originated, but it is quite obvious that if Baptism is to raise up the soul of one's infant out of limbo, or attendance at Holy Communion to lend a special grace unattainable in other ways, it would be only the foolish churchman who would neglect them. Furthermore, the feeling that spiritual events are really happening, that celestial work is being done, is psychologically not completely different from dropping a quarter into an insurance-vending machine before a journey knowing that if one is maimed he will be compensated, or if killed, his family will be provided for. What is required from one is so little; the possible rewards are so great! In either case the real work is done by someone other than the beneficiary, whether the agent by whom the work is done is spiritual or economic. For many people this may be a sacrament's chief appeal.

While this is a gross caricature of the presentation of conscientious priests, nevertheless those who measure their success in figures of church attendance and the annual balance sheet are not unwilling to promote this one-sided interpretation of the use of sacraments. A generation used to push-button manipulation of its physical environment will naturally be disposed to carry over such expectations to the spiritual realm, particularly when the hurry and stress of modern existence allows it little time to reflect on the cosmic issues of life and death together with their relationship to one's manner of worship. If participation in a sacramental ritual is exalted as the indispensable means of taking care of these issues through a few hours spent weekly in their punctual performance, who is so irresponsible as to stay away? Does not the average housewife put in ten to fourteen hours daily in attendance on the mundane and petty issues of home economy? Then why neglect the more important cosmic issues, the keys to which are in the hands of the church that, one's liturgical duties duly performed, is only too ready to handle the details?

This attitude in the layman, in turn, will contribute to a not disagreeable sense of power in the priest, who himself is capable of much satisfaction in the feeling that through his ordination ceremonies he has acquired a power not given to ordinary men. The wholly spiritual among the churches' servants will react to this sense of power with humility, but all priests have some admixture of the human. A fully honest one capable of introspection will detect, particularly in the first flush of post-ordination, a pride in this sense of power not unlike the glow that comes to most of us when we first sit behind the controls of a very powerful car. It is only natural that this same feeling is apt to return whenever ratified in sweeping processions of liturgical splendor, amid the dignity and pomp of a ritual designed indeed for the glory of God, but incidentally feeding the egos of those in the least disposed to spiritual pride. In the solitary silences of the unconscious, such priests may be willing to appropriate the service to psychological uses of their own.

Distressing though these considerations may be to adherents of the liturgical churches, they nevertheless must be faced if liturgical worship is to be psychologically understood. Furthermore they *must* be understood if people are to make alterations within themselves to bring their worship more in line with the profounder implications of the religious life, and not, in the words of Hocking, to have it "turned over chiefly to the student of abnormal psychology." [9] It was the preponderance in ritual of urges similar to those of which we have been speaking that led the prophet Amos to proclaim in behalf of the Lord,

[9] *The Meaning of God in Human Experience*, p. 345.

I hate, I despise your feast days, and I will not smell in your solemn as-
semblies.

Though ye offer me burnt offerings and your meat offerings, I will not
accept them: neither will I regard the peace offerings of your fat
beasts.[10]

But these considerations suggest that the liturgical forms of public
worship are little more than an escape, in one form or another, from
the rigorous demands of real life or the heroic requirements of a
vital religious faith. It hardly seems likely that, if this were all that
could be said about the liturgical tradition, it would remain as per-
sistent and as vigorous as it has throughout the centuries. It would
seem obvious that it does not tend to be the expression of religious
worship in the early, more spontaneous, and more creative stages
of any religious movement. It belongs rather to a religion's later
stages, when creativity has hardened into custom and spontaneity
has been confined by form. But this does not mean that it can serve
no legitimate purpose, nor that it may not stimulate the worshiper,
in the words of our definition, to "sense a Beyond." Religion, like
individuals, must learn to cope with age as well as with youth.
Liturgy is the accompaniment of religion's maturity and old age; as
such it performs positive functions.

In the first place a liturgical worship usually has beauty to commend it. There is indeed a distinction between a worship service
that is religious and one that is merely beautiful. The latter may be
moving in an esthetic sense, and this may be mistaken for religion.
But on the other hand, there is no virtue in ugliness when it serves
no purpose. When integrated into a religiously meaningful whole,
the esthetic element may enhance the religious experience already
stimulated by other elements of public worship. Furthermore, if
mature religion is to be comprehensive and integrated, as we have
pointed out in a previous chapter, it should include all legitimate
capacities of the human spirit, of which the capacity to be moved
by esthetic stimuli is one. It would seem that graceful and harmonious symbols of men's aspirations toward the Unseen would
better express the realities that they conceive to lie beyond their
grasps. And meaning itself carries a freight of esthetic appeal; the
profounder the meaning, the more moving the appeal.

[10] 5:21–22.

One of the instruments of non-liturgical worship in the Christian tradition that has redeemed many otherwise banal services is itself basically liturgical in this best sense. We are speaking of the King James translation of the Bible, which, even in places where it may be difficult for modern ears, nevertheless has the virtue of dignity and the *power to move*. This power is one of the hallmarks of language at its best. For the most part it is achieved both by the translation's profound expressions of religious truth and by its dignity. Witness the two familiar passages following:

Whither shall I go from thy spirit? or whither shall I flee from thy presence?
If I ascend up into heaven, thou art there: if I make my bed in hell, behold, thou art there.
If I take the wings of the morning, and dwell in the uttermost parts of the sea;
Even there shall thy hand lead me, and thy right hand shall hold me.[11]

Consider the lilies of the field, how they grow; they toil not, neither do they spin:
And yet I say unto you, That even Solomon in all his glory was not arrayed like one of these.
Wherefore, if God so clothe the grass of the field, which today is, and tomorrow is cast into the oven, shall he not much more clothe you, O ye of little faith? [12]

A second virtue of liturgical worship is that, paradoxically, at the same time that it is very public in its essential composition, it may be very private in its practice. On the other hand, the very hearty, unrestrained evangelistic worship may be, and usually is, quite coercive in its congregational effect. Whether the social pressures lean in the direction of a public profession of conversion or merely a vigorous participation in the singing of the hymns, the individual is under considerable constraint to join with his fellow worshippers in expressing whatever behavior seems to them appropriate.

In liturgical worship he retains much more privacy and anonymity. It is true that his observable behavior must follow very carefully prescribed patterns. But these have become so routine and stereotyped

[11] Psalm 139.
[12] Matthew 6:28–30.

from years of practice that they have lost any real significance as indicators of inner religious experience. The worshipper's inner thoughts and meditations may therefore follow patterns of their own. These of course are not necessarily religious. Galsworthy describes Soames Forsyte, the "man of property," as one who never went into a church except when he wished a quiet place to think over his business. But on the other hand, these inner thoughts not only may be, but frequently *are* religious. The Roman Catholic worshipper at Mass is not necessarily expected to follow the service at all points. For the most part he does not even understand the language nor is the priest always careful to speak in tones that can be heard even if they could be understood. This places on the worshippers the burden of praying their own prayers and approaching God, to a large degree, in their own ways. From the point of view of inner experience, which we have defined as the essence of the religious life, this can be highly individualistic.

To return to our paradox, non-liturgical worship, the expression of religion in its most spontaneous, original, and creative stage, may be exceedingly coercive for many worshippers. Liturgical worship, the expression of tradition and form, through its guarantee of religious privacy, may actually free the individual to follow his own creative impulses. But we must not be tempted by the fascination of paradox to push this difference too far. We have no very exact empirical estimate of the actual psychological effects of these two types of worship, while a casual survey of history suggests that the weight of religious creativity tends to associate itself with the freer forms of worship.

In addition to the facts that liturgical worship is beautiful and that it may be more private than one might expect, there is one more point that should be made with respect to it. This is that it is more apt to be suggestive of the mystical life. If the heart of religious experience is mystical, then worship should express this and suggest it. Consequently it would seem that services like the Roman Catholic Mass in an appropriate Gothic setting would be superior to most Protestant services of the freer sort in this respect. Yet at the same time we should note that the bare and stripped Quaker Meeting, with the well known Quaker emphasis on the Inner Light, is at the opposite pole from Catholic liturgy and has been more successful than many other Western traditions of worship in stimulating and expressing the mystic way. The importance of this aspect of worship of course will differ according to one's conception of the value of mysticism. Furthermore there is bound to be difference of opinion as to what type of service is best suited to the mystic life. Unfortunately there has not been much empirical investigation in this field, so that there are little more than opinions to guide us, informed sometimes by acute observation and at other times merely by prejudice.

However, this problem of the ages remains with us: how to combine the beauty of suggestive symbols that we find in liturgical worship with the vigor and sincerity of the non-liturgical forms. Here the psychologist of religion may make his contribution.

SUMMARY

Worship is the bringing together of one's experiences, especially the most poignant, and relating them to a transcendental Object of worship through praise, thanksgiving, or meditation. Through worship man may find his life's meaning by learning to know God and do His will. In its most essential aspect worship is individual and private rather than public.

Worship has not yet been adequately studied by the psychologist. But worship, like prayer, can be classified as *objective* or *subjective*, according to whether God or man is considered the focus of the worship experience. In its more spontaneous aspects worship is non-liturgical but, as tradition lengthens, the worship impulse tends to crystallize in liturgy. On the one hand, this may be the expression of the urges of the worshipper to deceive himself through show and the fantasy of magic; on the other, of the willingness of the priestly mind to exploit such weakness. But liturgy may also symbolize the religious experience of the great spirits of the ages and so, congealed in forms, suggest faint echoes of the mighty spiritual achievements of the past. Heard by those who have ears to hear, these echoes may serve as stimuli to awaken new experiences of worship and to bring alive the realities of the religious life.

Chapter 16

RELIGION AND
ABNORMAL PSYCHOLOGY

Even more, perhaps, than other kinds of genius, religious leaders have been subject to abnormal psychical visitations. . . . Often, moreover, these pathological features in their career have helped to give them their religious authority and influence. . . .

If there were such a thing as inspiration from a higher realm, it might well be that the neurotic temperament would furnish the chief condition of the requisite receptivity.

—Wm. James

. . . to whom is the arm of the Lord revealed? . . . He is despised and rejected of men; a man of sorrows and acquainted with grief.

—Book of Isaiah

According to popular folklore, genius and insanity are inseparable. This myth has been quite thoroughly discredited, notably by Lewis M. Terman in the investigations summarized in his *Genetic Studies of Genius,* where the very reverse seems indicated. Yet one can prove it either way, depending largely on how he defines that elusive term *genius,* which is not necessarily what Terman took it to be, simply a high IQ. If we think of the genius as one who has made an unusual contribution to society, we are struck by many instances of high achievement joined with a degree of individualism amounting to eccentricity at the very least.

There would seem to be some theoretical support for the associa-

342

tion of genius and pathology. He who brings into being some creative innovation must be sufficiently out of touch with convention
and what is commonly thought of as *reality* to be free to develop
things in his own way. And yet, if he is a true genius, on quite another level he must be in touch with a profounder and more subtle
reality than is seen by the ordinary observer. Therefore on one level
he is an eccentric, a misfit, even a psychotic. On the other level he
may be so completely in touch with reality that strangely even his
insights seem an expression of eccentricity to less discerning eyes.
This is the paradox of genius. It must be kept in mind as the back-
drop for our discussion of religion and the abnormal.

Theoretical considerations. If there is anything to our theory that
at least some relationship exists between genius and instability, it
would seem nowhere better illustrated than in the field of religion.
Jeremiah, Ezekiel, Paul, Fox, Luther, Bunyan, Carlyle and Dostoevsky are just a few religious geniuses who were clearly neurotic, if not
psychotic.[1] Even Jesus was thought by his friends to be "beside himself,"[2] while some scholars have been able to make out a case,
though not an entirely convincing one, that he was mentally sick.[3]

What is there about religion that should make religious genius
more subject to pathology? In the first place, involving as it does the
issues of life and death, religion is capable of arousing in exceptional
people the deepest of all human concern together with the passion
that accompanies it. This in itself can generate a kind of unbalance
not unlike the "madness of love," another great unsettling passion.

But society is more tolerant of the madness of love, since so many
have known it to some degree and can consequently be sympathetic.
However, fewer have experienced religious passion. This means that
the average person, who supposes himself deeply religious but actually is not, unconsciously substitutes another passion for authentic

[1] Most readers are familiar with the distinction between the two terms. A
neurotic illness is largely mental in its origin and its symptoms milder. The patient usually recognizes the fact that it is crippling his full efficiency. A psychotic
illness may be either mental or physiological in origin. It is more severe, often
involving serious delusions and little insight. Psychosis usually requires hospitali-
zation.

[2] Mark 3:21.

[3] See Albert Schweitzer's *The Psychiatric Study of Jesus* for a discussion.

religion, perhaps the making of money, or professional patriotism. He becomes very sensitive to any threat to his ego-involved pseudo-religious sentiments. The true religious prophet or saint constitutes at least a silent protest against a prostituted religious urge. Hence such nonconformists are most violently cast out by their self-righteous contemporaries. Thus the original tendencies toward self-direction and social isolation that facilitated their religious insights are accentuated and compounded by the rejection by their fellows. The schizophrenic symptom of withdrawal tends to appear. In a specialized sense and to a certain degree, the religious genius, and especially the prophet, tends to be a schizoid personality. In one sense this habit of mind is necessary for his religious insights; in another, the role is thrust upon him. This will be apparent in the subsequent case discussions.

Moreover, the extreme abstraction that characterizes certain types of psychosis, notably schizophrenia in its catatonic form, may actually favor the facing and thinking through of issues in a way that is impossible in normal living. This type of insanity involves withdrawal to the degree that often the catatonic seems oblivious of his surroundings, sometimes lacking the interest to dress himself or to eat. Yet we know, on the authority of those who have recovered from such episodes, that during them the inner life may be extremely active. We will consider the case of at least one such psychotic for whom a period of mental illness had lasting religious significance.

Another reason for the association of peculiarity and religious genius is that popular concepts of the supernatural tend to lead to an overvaluation of the strange. This means that simple eccentricity may be mistaken for religious genius, inspiration, or possession, particularly among the credulous. Ostow and Scharfstein [4] cite the case of a doctor who lived among Sadhus in India. He reported that, side by side with the most exalted searchers for religious truth, were those of degraded mentality expressing their religious urges in the most bizarre and repulsive manner. If strange religious behavior is rewarded by adulation, it is apt to be accentuated and confirmed. This suggests the reflection that most self-styled religious geniuses are in their own ways escaping from the harsh demands of outer reality and, far from being sublime, they succeed only in being peculiar.

[4] *The Need to Believe*, pp. 134–135.

For we must remember that "God" is an elusive concept. Since the reference of the term is a very intangible one, it follows that considerable subjectivity is involved.[5] For one person "God" will symbolize truths of profound reality, while for another, the grossest kinds of escapism and unreality. In still others the elements will be mixed, and it is inevitable that in at least some of these cases various mechanisms of escape will alloy great religious genius.

A fourth reason may be the most cogent of all. This is that essential religious ideas are so radical that only a person who in some sense is a social deviate can follow them. Jesus enjoined his Disciples to "take no thought for the morrow," and they went out preaching and living by faith. Yet few members of contemporary Christian churches want their sons or daughters to do likewise; while any radical religious group that decides to take some particular aspect of the Gospel literally is apt to be looked upon with extreme suspicion by the great body of Christian society. Yet part of the power of a religious genius is that he *does* take truth seriously and acts accordingly. The average man, no matter how sincerely religious, has too much regard for people's opinion. This facilitates those compromises between religious profession and expediency that are honored by the unreflecting man of "common sense," and prevent the radical action that is necessary for the creative moralist and prophet.

Anyone familiar with the behavior of the mentally ill knows that frequently a symptom of such illness is the perfect freedom and abandon with which the psychotic will act out his impulses. Since the ideas behind such impulses may be destructive and bizarre, the patient has to be segregated from society in a hospital. But the same freedom of impulse joined with superior insight may result in behavior which can revolutionize society. Contemporaries will rub their eyes in astonishment, some in admiration at the courage and boldness of utter devotion to an ideal, others in fright and horror, for they see a lunatic at large. This is one of the reasons why the religious genius tends to be controversial, and it also explains why the religious leader must not be classed too hastily with the perverted and the demented. Here is one of the areas in which the psychologist must beware of statistics and categories. For no one is more thor-

[5] See my article, "How Do Social Scientists Define Religion?" for documentation of this statement.

oughly individualized than the religious genius, and he must be appraised on the strength of his total contribution, not just that aspect of his personality which he may share with the inhabitants of mental wards. This will be well illustrated in our account of George Fox.

Perhaps we might reiterate our warning against the too ready use of statistics in studying such cases, and the reliance on mere numbers. For example, if a survey were made of the total population of our mental hospitals, while a large number of religious ideas would doubtless be found, few would be likely to qualify as socially useful. Furthermore, a survey of effective religious leadership would quite likely show at least average, and probably above average stability of mind. This does not mean that statistical studies have no place, for more and not fewer are needed in this important area. But the flower of creative religious leadership is a tiny élite. Its study requires that we begin at least with close scrutiny of the individual. It is for this reason that we have selected three figures, one contemporary and two from history, to illustrate our generalizations and to illuminate in their own right.

imp. contemporary - started training for Pastor

Anton T. Boisen. Our first case is not to be classed among the great historic prophets and discoverers of religious truth. And yet the contemporary Anton T. Boisen is certainly a creative religious spirit in that he has illuminated and enriched the thinking of psychologists by his insights into the character both of mental disease and of religious inspiration. Furthermore, as the result of a psychotic episode and its accompanying religious experience he became a pioneer and innovator in the ministry to the mentally ill. One of the remarkable documents of modern psychiatric science is his *The Exploration of the Inner World*, in part a development of his ideas concerning the relationship of religious experience and mental disease, and in part an account of his own experience.

To summarize briefly, in 1920 Boisen was a young minister who, as the result of moral conflict, some confusion as to his vocation, and a distressing love affair that seemed about to have a happy consummation, was suddenly seized with an acute form of catatonic schizophrenia. He was hospitalized, and his relatives were informed that there was little hope of his emerging from the psychosis. In delirium he was obsessed with the fear of an imminent world catastrophe, an obsession apparently brought on by absorption in the task of writing out a statement of his religious experience. During the delirium he was concerned not only about himself but also about those he loved. Thus his illness was not so wholly self-centered as psychoses are likely to be. A feature of his case was the fact that his illness cleared up almost as rapidly as it had come on. But having made the mistake of recovering when the doctors had pronounced his case hopeless, he had some difficulty in getting his release for several months after regaining his health.

Having an inquiring mind and being very curious about his own case, he spent the time talking with other patients and thinking about his own symptoms, his future, and his philosophy of life. The experience he had been through had jarred his previous preconceptions, imposed on his life a new framework, and led him to the insights that have since made him famous. Furthermore he interpreted the experience in religious terms, a point of view which the doctors were either unwilling to understand or incapable of understanding. He did much reading in psychiatric books, but for the most part the important first steps in insight he had to take alone. As a result of this activity he became aware of the spiritual longing that was a very genuine and hopeful factor in the consciousness of many a patient, and he saw how its therapeutic possibilities were wasted by unsympathetic doctors whose doctrinaire position led them to discount all religion as just another aberration. His conviction that there was great need for a ministry in hospitals led to his becoming, several years later, at the Worcester State Hospital in Massachusetts, the first Protestant chaplain in an institution of its kind. It also led to the institution of clinical training for young ministers at many theological schools and the founding of the Council for Clinical Pastoral Training.[6] Thus, for Boisen, the association of the pathological and the religious was creative.

The significance of Boisen's book for our purposes lies in his theory of schizophrenia, developed largely from his own experience, but also from study and close observation of other cases. In essence he

[6] For opportunities for study and training in this field, see the annual Directory number of *Pastoral Psychology*, published each January. The Institute for Pastoral Care parallels the function of the Institute.

holds that the catatonic especially is withdrawn from the world because he is wrestling with his own problems. When these involve the great issues of life this inner activity is essentially religious. A Messianic delusion accompanying this state may simply symbolize the acceptance of social responsibility by the patient and represent his attempt to define that responsibility. The inner panic that the process often entails is an overwhelming sense of the importance of the issues and a fear of not being equal to them. Thus it is seen that catatonic schizophrenia may be described in positive and profoundly religious terms.

But Boisen goes on to state that this pathological crisis may serve to "make or break" the patient. As long as his attitude toward the crisis is a responsible one, no matter how distorted some of his ideas, there is hope that he may get back in touch with reality and so recover. Indeed his stability may be firmer than before. But if the crisis breaks him and he gives up, he may become a "drifter," like the simple schizophrenic, or utilize a delusion of persecution to excuse himself, as in paranoid schizophrenia, or, worst of all, degenerate into the silliness and complete disorganization of hebephrenic schizophrenia.[7]

Through this theory of mental disease we see Boisen's conviction that the illness may possess saving elements. For him at least it was a defeat out of which he fashioned victory. The attack drove him into isolation and loneliness, while the failure of the doctors to understand what was going on within him accentuated his isolation and prolonged it. This recoiling upon himself, partly created by the stresses of his own inner nature and partly enforced by others, gave him a chance for the radical reorientation of his values and his vocation in life. Cut off through the seriousness of his symptoms both from the woman he loved and from an opportunity to procure a pastorate, he gained the freedom to take a new direction. Preoccupied with the idea of his responsibility for the coming crisis, he linked this with his concept of God, and so the experience became religious. The isolation enforced by his disease became an advantage to his religious concerns by enabling him to focus on them;

[7] Because of limitation of space, this is a gross oversimplification of Boisen's theories of the dynamics of mental disease. See his *The Exploration on the Inner World*, especially Chap. 5.

while his religious ideas, in their turn, enabled him to conquer the disease. Thus out of crisis and suffering this "sick soul" reached a new creative level, and so demonstrated this type of religious growth.

But Boisen also helps us understand the strange paradox that a very serious weakness, mental unbalance, may actually be an element of strength in the personal economy of a religious genius, given the right pattern of forces and circumstance. In this case part of the pattern was the right proportion between isolation and concern for others, between withdrawal and reality. This means neither that we are going to look to catatonic schizophrenics for our religious geniuses nor that we should cultivate such extreme forms of withdrawal in the interest of religious development. But it will serve as a clue and warn us against the too ready dismissal of a religious leader simply on the ground that some of his habits are peculiar.

George Fox. We started with the case of Anton T. Boisen because of the availability of data. We know the diagnosis. Furthermore we have the analysis written by the subject himself, a person not only religious but also conversant with modern psychiatric concepts.

With George Fox, founder of the Society of Friends, we are on less secure ground. While we are fortunate to have a documentary account of his life in his *Journal*, most of which was written about 1675 when he was a little over fifty years of age, we have no way of evaluating accurately the undoubtedly pathological side of his nature. He himself was little aware of this as a handicap. Since modern psychiatrists often disagree in their diagnosis even when the patient is in full view, it would be hopeless for us to pronounce on Fox's illness farther than to present some tentative speculations. But as a study of one of the great productive religious leaders of modern times, Fox's case should give us illumination and instruction.

He tells us that he was born in Leicestershire, England, in 1624, the son of a righteous weaver. Solemn from childhood, he never mingled readily with his peers. At the age of 19 he left his relations and "brake off all familiarity or fellowship with young or old." Along with this schizoid withdrawal, there came depressions as well as the indication of some possible hysterical symptoms, since he tells us of one occasion when attempted blood-letting could stimulate no blood flow,[8] and of another when he was struck with temporary blindness.[9] He was much concerned about the state of his soul and seems very largely to have confined his conversation to religious matters, strictly avoiding the "light and airy." He speaks of a kind of cataleptic visitation that stayed with him for 14 days and may possibly have been of a catatonic nature, perhaps to some degree parallel with Boisen's attack. Certainly at an early date he acquired a Messianic concept of his mission in life reinforced by frequent hallucinatory visions.[10] His behavior at times was extremely bizarre, as when he took off his shoes and walked the streets crying, "Woe to the bloody city of Lichfield!" without quite knowing why.[11]

At about this same time, and along with these other manifestations, he acquired certain insights, which he called "openings" and which he believed were sent by the Lord. One of the most important of these ideas was that it was not necessary for a person to study at Oxford or Cambridge in order to preach the Gospel. He believed in the equality of all men before the Lord to the radical extent that he taught the early Quakers to take off their hats to no one and eschew the use of all titles. Though honest to a fault, he followed literally the New Testament injunction and refused to swear an oath. This caused him and his movement no end of distress, for it enabled his enemies to subject Quakers to cruel imprisonment for refusal to swear the oath of allegiance. Though no stranger to verbal aggression, he nevertheless held strictly to the tenet of physical nonviolence and refused to bear arms. He was obsessed with the iniquity of what he called the "steeple-houses," and the early part of the journal contains a number of places where merely the sight of a steepled church or the sound of a church bell, as he puts it, "struck at my heart."

A reading of the entire journal also gives one the feeling that Fox's personality had at least some points of similarity to that of a paranoiac. True paranoia is a rather rare condition stemming chiefly from a fixed central delusion of persecution. However, aside

---

[8] *Journal*, p. 6.
[9] *Ibid.*, p. 26.
[10] *Ibid.*, pp. 20–21.
[11] *Ibid.*, p. 71.

from the central delusion, the individual is so much in touch with his environment, and his delusional system is so logically worked out, that only those who know the patient very well suspect any difficulty. The paranoiac is usually very intelligent and often extremely able. Some of Fox's beliefs and behavior suggest the litigious type of paranoia, which has frequent recourse to law to protect its rights; or the grandiose type, which sometimes conceives a divine mission and courts martyrdom. The paranoiac takes himself very seriously, is humorless, and has great difficulty in tolerating anyone who disagrees with him. Fox had all these traits to a considerable degree. One receives the impression of a man whose egotism was well-nigh insufferable. Any minister whose opinions ran counter to his own was likely to be put down as a "light, chaffy man," or a "high notionist." The expression of aggression which he denied himself at the physical level he sublimated on the verbal. To the polite greeting of an adversary, "Your servant, Sir," his forthright reply was, "Major Ceely, take heed of hypocrisy and a rotten heart!" [12] He took great satisfaction in noting the deaths of his enemies, especially when they were dramatically horrible, as when an adversary was gored by a bull.[13] He was several times accused of blasphemy in arrogating to himself divine powers, and indeed he seems to have skated close to the edge of delusion and a grandiose sense of mission, as when in a letter to Cromwell he calls himself the "son of God." [14]

Such traits are certainly not those of a common or normal individual. But to say that Fox had many of the characteristics of the paranoiac is not to say that he was a paranoiac, though we can easily imagine him to have been if some of his fixed ideas had been different. The saving consideration was the kind of response that his message brought forth in the hearts of others. It was a time of great political controversy concerning religion, but with little attention paid to its essentials except by words. Fox was one of those radicals, so troublesome to the comfortable professors of religion, who really *did* something about his convictions. If Jesus preached nonviolence, then he would not bear arms and would steadfastly suffer all manner of abuse from rowdies, refusing to lift a hand against them. If the

[12] *Ibid.*, p. 250.
[13] *Ibid.*, p. 363.
[14] *Ibid.*, p. 197.

Gospel forbade oaths, then this heroic witness to the truth, on whose slightest promise even his enemies could implicitly rely, would suffer the filth and the cold of a Doomsdale dungeon for months on end, and still not take the oath of allegiance. If the Bible said that honor was due only to God, then he would refuse to take his hat off before a Cromwell even though rude constables might be officious in showing him his duty. His insistence on honesty, his rejection of flattery and show, his belief in the dignity and religious competence of the common man: all these were not paranoid delusions but emphases that England needed and accepted. His ways of expressing these truths were often bizarre and certainly dramatic. Sometimes his beliefs were inconsistent. But he had made them his own, and his genius lay in the uncompromising way in which he demonstrated them and suffered for them. He illustrates the fact that religious ideals are essentially so radical that only a social deviate can live up to them. He must be notably self-directive. With pardonable pride Fox quotes the comment of some soldiers and officers who had had their share of troubles with him. "He is as stiff as a tree and as pure as a bell, for we could never stir him." [15]

We have mentioned the isolation and loneliness of Fox's earlier days. As with Boisen there was a long period of confusion as to his life purposes. A normal person, in a more healthy-minded way, would have found his vocation in something more ready at hand, perhaps in the trade of his father. Thus he might soon have followed a path that had been well beaten by others. But the very peculiarity that sent him out to walk "mournfully about" by himself at night and to sit "in hollow trees and lonesome places" seems to have facilitated the wrestling with considerably profounder issues. Thus we again have a case where pathological weakness plays into the hands of spiritual sensibility to produce a combination of strength and religious achievement.

Jeremiah. For our last case we will have to pierce even more deeply into the mists of history, and so the definition of what we see will be that much less distinct. But our other two cases will provide a background against which we may clarify our vision to some degree.

[15] *Ibid.*, p. 502.

We have selected the Hebrew prophet Jeremiah, not only because his writings give us definite indications of mental unbalance, but also because he is considered one of the greatest prophets of all times. Perhaps, as some scholars believe, he might be the greatest of that remarkable collection of religious seers whose writings compose the books of the Prophets in the Old Testament. Thus we are dealing with an acknowledged religious genius.

Jeremiah lived through the last days of the Israelite Kingdom of Judah, terminated by the fall of Jerusalem and the Exile of its people to Babylonia about the year 586 B.C. Sensitive and lonely in his early years, like Fox, his nature was retiring rather than active, and he never would have injected himself into the political and religious controversies of his day if his sense of religious mission had not amounted to a compulsion. While he had some followers and even supporters in high places, particularly under the strong King Josiah, for the most part he sensed the coming doom of Judah. The prophecy of such unwelcome events brought him for the most part opposition, and tribulation followed him during most of his ministry.[16]

Luckily for psychologists of religion, Jeremiah was not only introspective but took the trouble to write down his thoughts, or have a scribe do it for him. Thus we have in the Old Testament Book of Jeremiah not only a number of his prophecies but also sections that scholars have called "Confessions of Jeremiah." These, together with facts about his life that the book supplies, give us clues to the nature of his personality. Though, as in the case of Fox, we can only guess at the extent and specific nature of his mental disease, if there were any, there seems nevertheless little doubt of the fact that Jeremiah's social deviation was pronounced.

At the time when he lived, the independence of the Kingdom of Judah was steadily declining, and its only hope for political survival lay in allying itself with one of the three great powers contending: Egypt, Assyria, or Babylon. Contrary to the majority of political thinkers in Jerusalem, Jeremiah had no confidence in Egypt, and eventually saw that the fortunes of Judah lay in co-operation with the rising power of Babylon. His stand in these matters brought down on his head much political persecution. Further, he, like other Hebrew prophets, insisted that the sufferings of Israel were punish-

[16] For an available scholarly commentary, see E. A. Leslie, *Jeremiah*.

ment by God for departing from His ways. His emphasis on the importance of the inward religious life as against the outward aroused the wrath of the priests, who made their living through activities of outward observance. The crown of his misery was that so little heed was paid to his teaching.

Jeremiah also was visited by an awareness of crisis, in his case real enough politically, though he sensed the crisis more poignantly, more profoundly, and far in advance of others. Along with this he had a definite experience of call and a sense of mission, which at various times during his life operated as a compulsion. An indication that this urge was probably pathological lies in his extreme reluctance to prophesy, coupled with the feeling that he must do so. So severe was his conflict that God appeared to him almost as an enemy who was forcing upon him behavior which served no purpose other than mockery and derision.

O Lord, thou hast deceived me, and I was deceived: thou art stronger than I, and hast prevailed: I am in derision daily, every one mocketh me.

For since I speak, I cried out, I cried violence and spoil; because the word of the Lord was made a reproach unto me, and a derision daily.

Then I said, I will not make mention of him, nor speak any more in his name. But his word was in mine heart as a burning fire shut up in my bones, and I was weary with forbearing, and I could not stay.[17]

Whether it was the direct consequence of the unpopularity of his prophetic teachings, or the natural bent of his personality, there is no doubt of his social isolation nor that his sensitive spirit felt this isolation very keenly. "I sat not in the assembly of the mockers, nor rejoiced," says he; "I sat alone because of thy hand. . . ."[18] Furthermore, he feels that the Lord wishes him to remain celibate, and he ascribes this to the fact that the coming crisis will be so severe it will be a mercy that no children be born. We have no right to infer that this is necessarily another symptom of his schizoid tendency of withdrawal, for many have avoided marriage in deliberate pursuit of what to them are higher values. Yet it was another feature of his isolation and deviation from other people and raises the question whether some sexual abnormality were not present.

[17] 20:7–9.
[18] 15:17.

Like George Fox, he could be exceedingly aggressive with his tongue, and it would seem that he often went out of his way to say things that would offend people, as if he were courting martyrdom. He wishes evil on his enemies and asks the Lord to destroy them "with double destruction." [19] Even worse, he wishes God to "deliver up their children to famine, and pour out their blood by the force of the sword." [20] Surveying Jerusalem, he implies that he can find no man who "executeth judgment, that seeketh the truth," whether he seeks among the poor or among the rich. They "committed adultery, and assembled themselves by troops in the harlots' houses. They were as fed horses in the morning: everyone neighed after his neighbor's wife." [21] These are hardly words that seem appropriate to one who wishes to win friends and influence people.

Another questionable symptom was the depression that overtook him at intervals during his ministry. Since he lived in depressing days, we must ascribe some of this to outward events, which form no part of the pathology of the prophet. Yet the healthy-minded person has within him the means of maintaining a reasonable optimism even in the face of black misfortune. Jeremiah's fits of melancholy were chronic, and he has left us eloquent testimony of the depths of his despair.

Cursed be the day wherein I was born: let not the day wherein my mother bear me be blessed.

Cursed be the man who brought tidings to my father, saying a man child is born unto thee; making him very glad.

And let that man be as the cities which the Lord overthrew, and repented not: and let him hear the cry in the morning, and the shouting at noontide;

Because he slew me not from the womb; or that my mother might have been my grave, and her womb to be always great with me.

Wherefore came I forth out of the womb to see labour and sorrow, that my days should be consumed with shame.[22]

Finally there were instances when his behavior could be described as unusual at the very least, if not positively bizarre. On one occa-

[19] 17:18.
[20] 18:21.
[21] 5:7–8.
[22] 20:14–18.

sion, acting under the direction of his prophetic impulse, he made himself a yoke, such as was used with oxen. This he fitted upon his neck and went about the streets preaching that similarly Judah must undergo the yoke of the Babylonians. On one occasion he stood with it before the king.[23] On another occasion he bought a linen girdle and went on a journey of many days in order to bury it by the waters of the Euphrates. Then once again he was commanded by the Lord to take another long journey in order to dig it up and return the spoiled object to Jerusalem. This he used as a parable to indicate the decay of Israel.[24] While some scholars, noting how contrary to common sense such behavior would be, have attempted to explain away the fact of the journeys, the indication would nevertheless seem to be that the narrative is literally true. Furthermore it is not unlikely that an obsessive neurotic would go to extreme lengths to act out these strange compulsions. Yet, however strange such behavior, it evidently was effective in calling people's attention to Jeremiah and making his points vivid.

Though on the basis of the oddities of this peculiar fellow we might be disposed to discount him as a religious leader, yet the fact remains that so profound were many of his insights that his teachings are still regarded by religious people as having validity far beyond the confines of his own times. Some of the things they point to are Jeremiah's emphasis on inwardness, his sense of God as acting within history, his witness to the importance of the individual and the victory of conscience over inclination, his reliance on righteousness as man's ultimate hope, his prime valuation of all these things as against the secondary function of the religious institution. Furthermore the vigor and the fertile imagination of his speech mark Jeremiah as no mean poet, as even our scattered quotations have perhaps suggested. In such ways religious scholars justify the high contribution of Jeremiah to religious tradition.[25]

But one other contribution requires special mention, since its secret is puzzling and partly psychological. This is the demonstration of a profoundly religious nature in contention with God, a situation by

[23] See Chaps. 27–28.

[24] See Chap. 13.

[25] See Leslie, *op. cit.*, Chap. 10. for a discussion of abiding values in Jeremiah.

no means unusual in creative religious lives. To the ordinary, complacent religious participant, whose expression of religion is tertiary, or at best secondary, it seems improper and almost indecent that God should in this way be called in question. The desires of God are of course thought of as contained in the Bible, or the creed, or in the teachings of the Church. One does not live up to these desires—so the idea goes—but it is a good thing to know what one is expected to believe for reasons of personal satisfaction or in case one gets into a discussion with a member of another religious group. For religious experience at this superficial level, one's concepts of what God requires of him need only be respectable and as consistent as possible.

But for Jeremiah no such glib acceptance of the insights that came to him was possible. We have noted that one of the characteristics of the religious genius is that he *acts out* his convictions. Consequently when an idea entered Jeremiah's being with the authority of "Thus saith the Lord!" it might involve a matter of sore labor or the courting of unwelcome unpopularity or even death. From our vantage point in the twentieth century, we may object that Jeremiah was frequently benighted,, as when he calls down God's wrath on the heads of his personal enemies. But we cannot complain that he was superficial or insincere. And it is to be noted that it was out of this experience, psychologically presenting itself to his mind as a dispute with God, that his message was forged or the issue joined. Jeremiah's relationship with God was to him primary and real, even to the extent of quarreling with Him.

> Righteous art thou, O Lord, when I plead with thee: but let me dispute with thee of a matter of justice: Wherefore doth the way of the wicked prosper? wherefore are all they happy that deal very treacherously? [26]

The modern psychologist can easily explain these experiences of Jeremiah as the result of conflict within his own nature. While it is not possible, with the data that we have, to spell out the contending factors in detail; nevertheless it is clear from the record that Jeremiah's sensitive nature drove him to seek retirement, while the proclamation of his message from the Lord required the most extreme

[26] 12:1.

form of distasteful publicity. But to label this very human situation as conflict is not to discredit it. Evaluation must be done by the theologians and religious scholars, and we have already indicated that by their standards the religious achievement of Jeremiah was considerable. As psychologists we can simply emphasize what we have said before about the "sick soul" type of religious development, the function of doubt, and the place of suffering in religious development. Pathology simply sharpens the suffering, and in Jeremiah's case accentuated the development as well.

But in some ways it may have diminished his achievement. His ineffectiveness with his own generation may have been the result of his unbalance and social isolation. But, as with Fox, neurosis played into the hands of righteousness, which has seldom been proclaimed so clearly. In addition to this, the frustrations of Jeremiah's spoken message led to his putting his words on paper. This kind of message always looks better in writing after the exigencies of the contemporary situation have passed and its truth can be evaluated with more objectivity. We can attribute this necessity for the written word, at least in part, to the prophet's extravagance.

In these ways the case of Jeremiah helps our insight into the interaction of abnormal personality traits and the values of religious experience.

As we look back over our three cases of creative religious personalities, it would seem that the significant points we have made concerning them are (1) all of them experienced periods of isolation from their fellows which gave them an opportunity to think about their own problems and those of society, (2) they acted out their insights in radical form, and (3) their sensitivity to religious values has been acknowledged as superior.

It is the first two characteristics that the religious genius shares with the average psychotic, and it is so easy to cite examples from history that it seems likely that a statistical survey would support this generalization. Jesus, Socrates, Buddha, Moses, Paul, St. Francis, Mohammed, Loyola, Tolstoy, Gandhi, all had their periods of withdrawal, and all acted out their religious beliefs radically. But their religious insights were beyond those of common men, and it is this characteristic that accentuates their "abnormality" but with a difference, so that the essential connotation of the term "abnormal" does not really apply.

Boisen recognized the true abnormality of his own case but at the same time expressed his belief in the validity of it.[27] His own catatonic symptoms he looks at as a type of regression, or as the Freudians would term it, a return to the "intra-uterine mind." [28] He sees it in general as an opportunity for the individual to return to an earlier stage of development and so to assimilate masses of experience that were not properly organized before. It is in this way that the religious person prepares himself for his insights, or "openings," as George Fox put it; or the Hebrew prophet obtains those certainties that enable him to proclaim "Thus saith the Lord!" It would not seem that this regression would be made possible only by a catatonic attack, but perhaps this is what William James was trying to get at when he said, "Borderland insanity . . . has certain peculiarities and liabilities which, when combined with a superior quality of intellect in an individual, make it more probable that he will make his mark and affect his age than if his temperament were less neurotic." [29]

But the religious genius, especially as a prophet, runs great risks in his communion with God. His concentration and intensity are part of the secret of his profound insight. But the consequent social isolation may deprive him of the recognition and affection that are necessary for the normal development of personality. This psychological undernourishment may further accentuate any existing unbalance. Dependent on God to supply these deficiencies, the prophet may at one moment see into the heart of divine mystery or utter sublime truths; at the next, paranoid fantasy may represent God to him as a monster bloodthirsty for the life of his enemies. We have seen that this is the case with Jeremiah.

We find this dualism expressed particularly in the Old Testament, sometimes within the same passage. In I Samuel 15 the prophet speaks the splendid prophetic truth, "Hath the Lord as great delight in burnt offerings and sacrifices, as in obeying the voice of the Lord? Behold, to obey is better than sacrifice, and to hearken than the fat

[27] *Op. cit.*, p. 115.
[28] *Ibid.*, p. 111.
[29] *Varieties*, pp. 23–24.

of rams." In the next moment he savagely turns on Agag, the suppliant king of the Amalekites, with the words, "As thy sword hath made women childless, so shall thy mother be childless among women." Then Samuel "hewed Agag in pieces before the Lord!"

To return to our point that isolation is characteristic both of the prophet and the psychotic, we note that the religious genius has ever been, at least in some phase of his career, a solitary and lonely figure cast out by his fellows, laughed at, and set apart. He is indeed "despised and rejected of men; a man of sorrows and acquainted with grief." Yet we must repeat that this does not mean we are to comb the asylums for the voice of God, nor that religious education should be directed toward exaggerating peculiarity. So much is each prophet an individual that we can describe him by no universal formula but only note a few common characteristics.

The true prophet is one in ten thousand. Furthermore no society would last if it were made up wholly of strong-minded religious geniuses, any more than if it were composed wholly of paranoiacs and catatonics. It could not long endure without the social cement provided by the overwhelming majority of us who are passive, co-operative, and ordinary. This generalization applies equally to the world of religion where indeed we venerate the saint but interpose custom, sacrament, and myth between his conduct and our own to protect ourselves from the rigor and the harshness of religious reality, lest "seeing God we die" either to social integration or to reason.

Dostoevsky's Grand Inquisitor speaks for all ecclesiastical organizations when he tells the sorrowing Jesus that the Church has been wise enough to dilute and distort His Gospel in order to serve the many. Only a few own the heroic proportions to tread in the authentic steps of the true prophet and retain their sanity.

Abnormal psychology and the reality of God. We have noted that it is not the function of the psychologist to pronounce on the existence or non-existence of God. However, when psychology might have pertinence to a theological problem, the psychologist should point out the fact.

Consequently we would like to refer to a common observation made by psychiatrists with respect to sick people. When a person suffers from a delusion—that is, a serious misapprehension of his environment—he is said to be "out of touch with reality." This in turn will affect his adjustment in that his delusion will interfere with his life and tend to disorganize his personality. Often the observer cannot tell whether or not a fixed idea is false, and has to rely on its effect on the person's efficiency and adjustment to help him decide. An idea far out of touch with reality is not apt to be an aid in individual adjustment.

We have stated that the concept of "God" is a vague one and means different things to different people. For some the implications of a belief in God are unreal. They lead to escape, personality disorganization and bizarre behavior to no purpose, as when George Fox cried, "Woe to the bloody city of Lichfield!" Such results should make one question the reality behind the concept.

On the other hand the God concept may have a consequence which is the direct opposite. God may be a factor in morale and instead of disorganizing the personality may vitalize and stimulate it. Quite obviously this was the function that in the main was served by the idea of God in the cases of Boisen, Fox, and Jeremiah. Without their belief in God it is hard to imagine their achievement being what it was. At any rate, any one of them would have testified that he could not have accomplished what he did without the help of God. Doubtless they would have had difficulty conveying to a scientist's mind just what reality it was to which the word "God" corresponded. But unless there were some kind of reality behind it, we would have the psychiatric anomaly of a delusion pervasively facilitating achievement, stimulating morale, and helping adjustment. It would seem that the pragmatic test of whether the idea of God helped or hindered people's personal efficiency might be a helpful clue to the theologians in their search for the reality that lies beyond.

We can see that at least part of the morale-building factor inherent in the concept of God is that the truly religious person sees his God-given mission as the serving of the welfare of others in some way, not simply as a means of grandiose self-betterment or the fulfillment of some quixotic urge. There was evidence of this in all three of our cases of religious genius. Boisen felt he was to play a part in a coming world crisis; Fox walked the streets of Lichfield without his shoes; while Jeremiah journeyed to the waters of the Euphrates in order to bury a linen girdle. Had they continued to think of God as presiding over activities like these their careers and personalities would have ended in disorganization. But this was not the situation. Through God they saw themselves linked with others. Their God-given mandate was to serve others, and it was their contact with reality through this service that kept them sane. Boisen's mission grew to be the ministry to the mentally distressed; Fox's concern was the Quaker movement, and alleviation of the suffering of his supporters; while Jeremiah labored to turn his countrymen from rushing toward the doom they seemed determined to court.

Furthermore their contact with reality was enjoined not merely on the basis of their response from others. Had this been true, all three must have faltered long before their careers were ended. It was the fact that their relationship to others was not simply face to face but had a *cosmic* reference. It was not *just* their brotherly love that kept them going. This doubtless played its part; but fundamentally they saw their mission more profoundly as *part of the nature of things* and an expression of the very deepest relationship that they knew. They were convinced that their relationship with others was rooted in this deep cosmic relationship symbolized to them in the word "God." This psychological experience lay behind their words, as when Boisen speaks of his mission as having been given to him by an "Intelligence beyond my own," or George Fox cites his "openings," or when Jeremiah declares "Thus saith the Lord!" It was this kind of experience that was such a factor in their morale and upheld them in their wrestling with such stubborn realities.

Indeed it is a similar experience which helps us to understand why it is in the history of religion that we find more instances of heroic endurance and perseverance than anywhere else. We cannot say that the mere fact of belief in God will guarantee wholesome results, for events have shown that men of God can also be destructive, as in the case of Torquemada and the Spanish Inquisition. But it is a Gestalt of factors in which the idea of God is very basic that has served to create history's most effective personalities.

It would seem, then, that in their search for the reality behind the idea of "God" theologians would have to take into consideration the psychology of personality. The pragmatic test of whether this idea helped or hindered personal efficiency should be a helpful clue to the reality that lies beyond.

SUMMARY

It is claimed that genius is often linked with nervous instability. Though there is some evidence which tends to refute the idea, there would seem to be some support for it in a study of religious genius. Not all, but many religious leaders have been unstable, and our review of the lives of Boisen, Fox, and Jeremiah illustrates this. Theoretical speculation as well as these illustrations suggest that two characteristics religious genius shares with the psychotic are (1) a tendency to withdrawal and isolation from their fellows, and (2) a tendency to act out their central impulses with less than normal inhibition. What distinguishes the religious genius from the mental patient would be a superior religious sensitivity which seems to bring the individual in touch with a profounder reality than is sensed by the ordinary person, religious or non-religious. This sense of divine mission and cosmic relationship is a factor in his morale. Only if religious concepts correspond to some essential reality can we as psychologists explain the acknowledged achievements of the great religious personalities of the ages.

Chapter 17

RELIGION AND
PSYCHOTHERAPY

The physician's love heals the patient.
—Sandor Ferenczi

There is a sense in which religion as a *means* to health is not religious. The quest for knowledge of God and harmony with Him is an end in itself, and to degrade this quest to a search for health is to change it into something other than religion. God, not man, is the center of religiously oriented striving.

Yet among the great religious traditions, just as religion and ethics have always been associated, so have religion and the need for good health. Sickness has often provided the stimulus for the religious search. That the sick were healed and the lame walked were taken as indications of Jesus' authority. And as the centuries have succeeded one another, the miracles ascribed to God have less and less concerned outward circumstance, such as arresting the sun in its progress across the heavens, and more and more they have concerned changes within people of a physical or psychological nature. Also more and more it has been conceded that if God is concerned in the process of healing it is up to man to co-operate. In this way older magical presuppositions have given way to attitudes that approach those of the therapists at the same time that medical men in very recent years have become better disposed toward religion. They have begun to wonder whether there might not be more things in heaven and earth than have been dreamt of in their philosophies.

364

This has meant that, whereas about the turn of the century psychiatrists and religionists were regarding each other warily, they now have made more than tentative approaches toward one another, even if they are not yet quite ready to clasp one another in a firm embrace. Such indications as the popularity of books on religion and mental health, the foundation of the National Academy of Religion and Mental Health, the flowering of the pioneer work of A. T. Boisen in ministering to the mentally ill, and the success of the journal *Pastoral Psychology* are all concrete evidences of this approach. Perhaps it is best dramatized in the title of a new periodical sponsored by the Institute for Rankian Psychoanalysis, the *Journal of Psychotherapy as a Religious Process*.[1] It is psychotherapy as a religious process as well as religion as a psychotherapeutic process that we wish to examine in this chapter.

SIMILARITIES OF RELIGION AND PSYCHOTHERAPY

If one examines statements by those who have had what we have called a primary religious experience, particularly when this has involved conversion, one is struck by expressions that usually signify improvement in mental health. If the reader wishes corroboration for this statement he will find it in Part 3 of the author's *The Oxford Group*, which includes many case studies of religious conversion. The effects of conversion on mental health were studied, and though outcomes were various the majority of cases abound in indications that the conversion experience increased the individuals' energies, zest for living, and capacities to handle their own personal problems. One of these cases, fairly typical of those in which these results were marked, is reproduced in our chapter "Conversion" on pp. 199–200, as the case of Samuel Hoffman.

Also it will be remembered from our discussion that one of the prerequisites for a conversion experience is a sense of unrest or "conviction of sin." This is equivalent to the insight that is secured in the process of successful psychotherapy, while a change in behavior is one of the indications of effectiveness both of therapeutic treatment and conversion of any depth.

[1] See also the Religion and Psychiatry Number of *The Bulletin of the Menninger Clinic*, November, 1955.

When a conversion experience is acknowledged to be effective both by the individual himself and those who know him and have a chance to observe him, changes in his behavior are pretty apt to be identifiable as improvements in mental health. But that religious experience and psychotherapy are by no means interchangeable terms is indicated by the fact that successful psychotherapy is less apt to show features that are explicitly religious. The student, for example, who learns through therapy that his failures in college are simply the expression of revenge on the dominating parents who wish him to do well, and so is able to improve his grades, has achieved insight but not necessarily insight of a religious variety. It is true that religious experience may develop out of this, for any kind of improvement in self-insight has a potentially religious significance. But insight in itself is not religion, and most psychotherapeutic processes are carried on either in too limited an area of the personality to be called genuinely religious, or else the religious implications of the changes are un-recognized as such either by the patient or the therapist. In this connection one is reminded of the often quoted declaration of C. G. Jung to the effect that he had never encountered a neurosis in a person over 35 in which the problem was not basically religious. But we can conclude that, though psychotherapy is not identical with re-ligious experience, there is overlapping to the extent that a thorough conversion might almost be seen as a special case of psychothera-peutic growth.

We assume that the reader has referred to Chapter 9 to refresh his memory on the features of conversion and to read one or two of the case studies. These will illustrate religious experience serving also as psychotherapy. To illustrate the reverse situation, psychotherapy that developed religious significance, we will briefly summarize two cases already published elsewhere.

The case of Joe.   Joe was a young man of about 28 at the time of this experience. He was the son of well-to-do, sophisticated, upward mobile parents. Their religious interests were either nominal or negative, and they neglected their four children, of whom Joe was the third. A grand-mother was the only one in the family described by Joe to be religious; nevertheless he was sent to Sunday School until he was 13. Though fundamentally likable and able, he could never feel himself accepted in any society.

Partly as the result of this maladjustment, he developed homosexual and alcoholic problems. Also his lack of success in school and business brought more rejection from his socially ambitious family. All these things generated intense guilt in him. Beginning when he was about 20, the family secured for him therapeutic help in and out of sanitariums. From therapists he secured a variety of advice, one recommending to him promiscuity with women, another castration. Actually he did receive some treatment with electric shock and sex hormones. From none of these sources did he receive much help.

His fifth therapist reasoned that since all these measures had failed, he would try a warm relationship with him based on acceptance and simple understanding, according to the Carl Rogers' client-centered, non-directive technique. He was careful to help Joe formulate his own feelings but gave him no interpretation or advice. Joe brought up the problem of the meaning of life in his first interview but then dropped it for many months.

In the meantime he started to attend the Catholic Church with a friend. In part he considered this an act of rebellion against psychiatry, which he thought was anti-religious. Perhaps he also looked on it as a rejection of his family's standards. He went so far as to study Catholicism and discuss it with priests. At the same time that he was gaining an interest in religion he was increasing in his confidence in the therapist, who approved of his religious activity but without explicitly saying so. However, Joe was still not solving the problems of a job and independence from his parents.

This process went on for ten months and about 100 therapy sessions. One Sunday morning he was shaving when suddenly the idea came to him that he was expecting God to do things for him, but that he had acknowledged no obligations to God. With this his doubts about joining the church and accepting its discipline vanished. It was shortly after this that the therapy apparently came to an end. Three years later he reported himself a staunch member of the church. He had complete control over his drinking, while his sexual problems had considerably lessened. He was leading an independent, self-supporting life.[2]

The effective agent here, as far as the therapy was concerned, seemed to be the acceptance and sympathy, or love, which Joe received from his therapist. It supplied what he had never received from his family, and this acceptance gradually freed him to explore

[2] Summarized from P. Bergman, "A Religious Conversion in the Course of Psychotherapy."

more objectively the possibility that religion could fulfill his needs. Gradually he grew to the point where the passivity he had heretofore shown—expecting life, and then religion, to do something for him— yielded to the acceptance of responsibility for himself. It was at this point, when he was before the shaving mirror, that his therapy orientation might be said to have become basically religious. Before this time he was concerned with himself. Now God became the focus of his striving.

One can see shortcomings in his faith, as the account points out. For example, the choice of a church as a rebellion against his family and psychiatry is not the sign of a mature religion. But on the whole his new religion was integrated with his total personality. His church became the center of his social life. Through it he had conceived of a Power higher than himself, and this conception gave him the strength to deal with his problems. What began as therapy developed into a full-fledged religious experience "not of dull habit but an acute fever." It was a primary religious experience that made a difference in Joe's life.

Case of Mrs. Oak.[3] This is another case where therapy was carried on by the non-directive method, this time under the direction of Carl Rogers and analyzed by him. The religious aspects of the case were considerably more subtle than in the case of Joe, but one nevertheless receives the impression that the psychotherapeutic change is basically and authentically religious. This is implied by Mrs. Oak's therapist who states, "As is nearly always true with me, whenever a client goes deeply into himself in therapy, I find myself experiencing a profound respect, almost an awe—it is the closest I come to a feeling of worship. . . . I felt this with unusual strength in dealing with Mrs. Oak."[4]

The case was part of an extensive research project and so was very thoroughly studied and reported. By practically every research criteria Mrs. Oak had grown and changed during therapy. An extraordinary feature of the case was that the client seemed to have been exceptionally inarticulate and incoherent in her logical processes at the

---

[3] Summarized from Rogers and Dymond, *Psychotherapy and Personality Change*, Chap. 15.
[4] *Ibid.*, p. 264.

same time that she was often eloquent in conveying the essence of her inner emotional life. The therapist was able to reflect this and so to perform a valuable function in helping to bring about the resolution of her conflicts. Another feature of the case was that after the fifth interview Mrs. Oak spoke very little of the problems that initially brought her for therapy. She concentrated on her own inner life, and the ability to handle her problems seems to have come as a by-product of a process that was considerably more profound.

Because of these features it will be impossible to give either a full or very clear account of the case. In our summary we will concentrate on those features that suggest the religious aspects of Mrs. Oak's experience and make use of direct quotation from the recording of the interviews.

Mrs. Oak seemingly was an average, not very highly cultivated housewife of about 40. She was concerned about friction with her husband and very much concerned about her relations with her adolescent daughter. Also she felt that she would like to take a job but lacked the courage to do so. Before the termination of therapy she was given 48 interviews.

After the early interviews her immediate problems faded into the background of her therapy and gave way to a deep emotional facing of herself. So much strain and struggle does this entail that one has a feeling of observing one of Plato's prisoners in the Cave as he struggles and frees himself from illusion.[5] Mrs. Oak does not use the conventional symbolism of religion to describe this process but at one or two points makes clear that she considers it religious, as illustrated in the following bit of dialogue during the latter part of her therapy:

Client: Oh, another thing, I recognized that the—the therapeutic experience for me, in comparing others that I've known—and this'll be difficult, I think it will, oh, no I don't—has . . . has been somewhat akin to the . . . religious kind of experience, which last summer rather bothered me. And yet . . .

Therapist: That is, sort of mystical.

C.: Yes.[6]

She says in one place that what she has been saying seems more like poetry than prose and that it is a kind of song she has been singing.[7]

[5] See Book 7 of *The Republic*.
[6] Rogers and Dymond, *op. cit.*, p. 340.
[7] *Ibid.*, p. 313.

Furthermore the figures that she uses suggest mysticism, though her points seem very confused logically. She seems to sense a power that the mystics would have identified as God:

C.: It seems to me that what I'm saying is that somewhere (pause) very deep in self, is a kind of force, which—which apparently seems clearer to me in terms of a flame, a (pause) a flame which is, is cold, ah, so very, very, ah (pause) crystal, and that isn't the word, but so much generated, so much heat generated, ah, that it's cold, and—and, so bright that ah, it's almost, you can't, you can't look through it, it's a kind of blinding, then it seems to me that I said, that it is the individual, ah, who has somehow gotten there, has somehow made the journey. It begins to—to (pause) it somehow may be a terrible journey, I mean, there *is* something of that in it, and it seems to me that—that if I can just not be afraid of the word. Well anyway, ah, if once they've gotten there, a sort of having dared, and then begin to walk away, to walk back up the road, backward, facing this thing, and just—just, a very little way, they begin to feel the warmth, and see the color. I guess what I'm saying, I know I'm saying, is that it's kind of big. . . . And of course this ties up so completely with my conflict . . . the apparent rejection of a love philosophy. (Pause) I *know* what it is, it's a feeling that so much in this love philosophy . . . is too far off the road, a kind of thing that has turned its back on this flame of self.[8]

The impression that Mrs. Oak is trying to describe an experience of a mystical type is heightened by her sense of the very different quality of her everyday life experiences and the activities within herself. She is trying to grasp this so firmly that she can live by it rather than by the values that society imposes on her.

C.: That's exactly the point. My feeling is, if I can't get in and examine those things, and really pick them out and . . . things, they aren't things . . . really kind of harness it, put it into shape, then it's not going to work. And I think, I think I'll find my way back, or forward. Of course you see, and then, I ask myself when I go out into the sunlight and dodge a few cars . . . well, what in the world are you looking for, what in the world are you looking for?

T.: What are you chasing cobwebs for?

C.: That's right. What are you looking . . . maybe you're off on a wrong track.

T.: Seems awfully shadowy and sort of dubious when you get into the white light of day.

C.: M-hm. Sort of a sense of an embarrassment. Yeah. That's it, I

[8] *Ibid.*, pp. 333–334.

mean, sort of a "Come take your place in this gorgeous progressive twentieth century." I mean, "stop it."

T.: Almost "What are you doing out there in that other realm?" You ought to be a little ashamed of yourself somehow.

C.: M-hm, that's right. And yet, when I listen to myself, I know that's it. So, of course I mean, I just feel that if I could hold on to that I'll find it, that it's much more real.

T.: It may not seem like the twentieth century to you, but, when you get hold of it, you're pretty damn sure that it is something very real. The kind of thing, I take it, where you don't need someone else to tell you, "Yes, that's important"; you *know* that's important.

C.: Yeah, yeah. That's what I meant when I said that, when I, when I can just listen and sort of feel a push and that's it. (Long pause: 12 minutes.) I think this conflict of . . . what I feel should be genuine— the feeling of a sort of experiencing self and the adjustment to the world, has really always caused me trouble really.

T.: M-hm. You're saying there has always been kind of a rift between the real experiencing of yourself and the way you operate to get along in the world.

C.: Yeah. It's probably way, way back. I think . . . I think I can remember always . . . or very often having a definite feeling, a being certain that the—the values people seem to live by and uphold were kind of unreal things.

T.: All this structure that they live by is really sort of a shell, not really the real thing.[9]

Our final excerpt will show that the emotional relationship, or love of the therapist, is an important factor in the experience. The commentary of the therapist preceding the passage confirms that this is so.

C.: . . . Now isn't that true of therapy, am I wrong? See I found that here, somehow. Now isn't that true? . . . There might, there might be something I don't know what it is. I mean there might . . . there might be a communication . . . rather than "I love you" . . . now I'm thinking, I'm talking about a therapeutic situation, I don't know . . . There might be a recognition . . . a projection . . . of this, of this, of this bit of self-love that one has, . . . this secretness . . . so that rather not "I love" but that "You are my love." I think that there might be something to that. I don't quite know.[10]

Through such moving incoherencies the reader is privileged to follow the living record of a human spirit in search of itself and the

[9] *Ibid.*, pp. 317–318.
[10] *Ibid.*, p. 335.

meaning of life. Not well acquainted with the language of poetry or mysticism, Mrs. Oak is ill equipped to verbalize her struggles. The therapist has acted in part as her mouthpiece in helping her to express her thoughts and feelings. Even more importantly he has given her support and acceptance, which she reciprocates and verbalizes as love.

It is quite obvious that she has come in contact with a new level of being and a new set of values not clearly seen but vaguely felt. These shadowy apprehensions assume a growing reality as therapy proceeds. There are many parallels with the mystic's experience, particularly of the milder type. We find the same ineffability together with the recourse to figurative language as a means of conveying knowledge. The experience is noetic, for Mrs. Oak emerges with the sense of knowing truths she did not know before. There is the same sense of the reality of the inner life as opposed to everyday existence. Furthermore there has come an enhancement of life, an experience of awakening, with more than a little suggestion of purification and illumination. Could Mrs. Oak somehow be spirited out of "this gorgeous progressive twentieth century," we believe she would have found her heart speaking a common language with that of Thomas à Kempis, Madame Guyon, or Teresa of Avila.

Though by no means a religious genius and though she exhibits none of the symptoms of the psychotic, Mrs. Oak nevertheless reminds us of one or two of the points we have made in our chapter, "Religion and Abnormal Psychology." Certainly her problems have been worked out in isolation, apart from the press of everyday affairs. Then, while she would hardly qualify as a radical, the account suggests that she has shed many of her inhibitions and acted out impulses in a way that for her constituted considerable boldness. We are told that she effected a separation from her husband, though without bitterness, and resolutely went through with her desire to find a position. Her hope for better relations with her daughter was fulfilled. By reason of her withdrawal within herself to face her problems she came more fully into touch with reality. Not just the therapist but her friends also noticed the change.

Mrs. Oak's experience meets our definition of religion in that she senses a higher power, though very subjectively and from deep within herself. If one is disposed to quibble over whether this really constitutes religion, we might say that it is in the depths of her being that Mrs. Oak encounters this "thing," as she sometimes calls it. Certainly she herself does not make the point very explicit, for, on the whole, she subordinates religious terminology to her own highly original symbolism. Yet the therapist declares himself in awe of a power arising unbidden within her that he does not completely understand and cannot control, nor does he wish to. He leaves her free to fight her own battles but, like Good Works in *Everyman*, he will "go by her side." This power alternately attracts and frightens her with its requirement of loneliness and rejection of the standards of the world, but it enables her to build a more solid relationship with her daughter as well as to effect what she feels is the necessary separation from her husband. Psychologically the experience at many points closely parallels aspects of the religious consciousness that we have described. Certainly in this stirring of the depths of her being, Mrs. Oak has much more in common with the great religious spirits of the ages than does the average churchgoing citizen who passes for religious.[11]

THEORY OF RELIGIOUS PSYCHOTHERAPY

What difference does the concept of God make? There are bound to be those with a distaste for conventional religion who will raise the question whether or not God makes any difference in the process of psychotherapy. Does faith in God give the neurotic in search of mental health any advantage over those who do not have that faith? Does not the believer under therapy improve by the same process as the atheist or agnostic?

In this field there are no very well-controlled and definitive studies of which we are aware and which would enable us to answer these important questions. We can only speculate and make use of bits of empirical support here and there.

In general, our suspicion is that individual cases differ, so that the answer to the questions we have posed will vary slightly from case to case. But there should be some generalizations and hypotheses that we might put forward in a tentative way.

[11] If at all possible, the reader is advised to read the whole of Rogers' account of this remarkable case.

In the first place we might note that the answer to our question will differ as between the cases of Joe and of Mrs. Oak. With Joe, apparently the concept of God did make a difference, and explicit religious considerations seemed essential in this therapy, whether they were worked out in the therapy sessions or outside of them. Therapy without religion had repeatedly done him no good. On the other hand there was little or no mention of God in the account of Mrs. Oak, and while she recognized the religious implications of her therapy, this seemed to be more of an afterthought coming as the result of reflection on the process. The impression gained is that the outcome of therapy would have been much the same without this explicit recognition. Certainly we can conclude that the absence of a conventionalized and religious framework is no bar to deep emotional changes comparable in quality to religious conversion or mystical experience. Mrs. Oak's experience seems religious *in fact*.

But we also note that there are some cases where conceptualized religion does seem to constitute an essential element in the change. Once again it is pertinent to quote William James.

If asked just where the differences in fact which are due to God's existence come in, I should have to say that in general I have no hypothesis to offer beyond what the phenomenon of "prayerful communion," especially when certain kinds of incursion from the subconscious region take part in it, immediately suggests. The appearance is that in this phenomenon something ideal, which in one sense is part of ourselves and in another sense is not ourselves, actually exerts an influence, raises our centre of personal energy, and produces regenerative effects unattainable in other ways.[12]

Something like this seems to have been the process within Joe. Without his religion, a cure would have been improbable if not impossible, though we must not forget the role of his therapist. There is also the same story, over and over again, to be found among Alcoholics Anonymous where the second of the "Twelve Steps" is to come to believe that "a Power greater than ourselves could restore us to sanity."[13] For example, "Bill" had been in and out of hospitals many times and had been given up by the doctors. It was his realiza-

---

[12] *Varieties*, p. 513.
[13] *Alcoholics Anonymous*, p. 71.

tion that he could no longer help himself and his belief that God could that enabled him to get on his feet.[14] It is a matter of record that there are people who *do* gain therapeutic help with their problems from religion, help that can be duplicated from no other source.

It appears that what we have, at least in *some* cases of effective psychotherapy and in *some* cases of profound religious experience, is the occurrence of psychological changes which, if not identical, are certainly very similar. Doubtless there are some cases in which the religious significance is not even suspected; in other cases, like that of Mrs. Oak, the religious aspects are realized and expressed only after the process has continued for some time; while in still other cases a religious frame of reference is a *sine qua non* of emotional growth.

What is the function of the therapist? This has been the subject of much speculation and some pontificating among psychotherapists. Each school of psychotherapy has its own theories, in line with its own method and conception of the self, while many are the degrees of heightened blood pressure generated in the verbal battles carried on among the differing schools. However, it has been said that about the same amount of help is secured by clients regardless of the technique used. This is perhaps an oversimplification, yet it points to the therapist himself as more crucial than the method. Sigmund Freud is said to have been an extraordinarily skillful therapist, yet with all his brilliant theorizing he was not always able to impart his skill to his disciples. Apparently it is what the therapist *is* and the experience he has had that are more important than his technique.[15]

Then what are the qualities to be looked for in an effective therapist? Doubtless we cannot separate what the counselor *is* from what he *does*, for in large degree his method will be an expression of himself bound up closely with his basic attitudes toward those with whom he counsels. The good counselor must be *non-judgmental* and *accepting* with his client. Also he must be profoundly *understanding*, both in his capacity to conceptualize or help the client to con-

[14] See *ibid.*, Chap. 1; also the latter section of the book for many similar personal stories.
[15] For evidence, see Shaffer and Shoben, *The Psychology of Adjustment*, pp. 545, 526.

ceptualize his problems, and in his ability to empathize with the client. By the latter is meant that the therapist must to some degree be able to "feel with" the client. Any process of deep personality growth involves intense emotional surges within. These the therapist must recognize and accept, while the client must feel that this is so. Also the client must feel that the therapist is himself involved in the process of therapy in that he too *cares* for the client and is concerned about the outcome. This was crucial both in the case of Mrs. Oak and of Joe. In other words, an affectional bridge, not merely an intellectual one, must be built between therapist and client. The therapist must "love" the client and the client the therapist. The *understanding* of the client by the therapist must demonstrate that term in the fullest richness of its meaning. Indeed, "it is the physician's love" that "heals the patient." [16]

Just how this should occur is beyond the scope of the present discussion, even if we could go beyond speculation to conclusion, which we cannot. It will be sufficient to remark that the emotional sources of the need for affiliation are very deep. Consequently we would expect that these would be involved in any fundamental personality growth and change. It is when such depths are stirred that this kind of change can eventuate. The therapist, then, acts as a kind of catalyst, freeing forces within the individual for constructive work.

This suggests a parallel with religious change. Thoroughgoing religious conversion that affects behavior more than superficially is not brought about so often by the fast-talking, pulpit-thumping variety of evangelist. He may have the power to move thousands in the atmosphere of mass enthusiasm or mass fear. But it is doubtful whether the effect of this is very deep apart from the intimate relationship with an apostle who cares. One of the secrets of the success of the Moral Re-Armament movement is that its leader, Frank Buchman, had had a chance to work with the evangelist Billy Sunday and noted the futility of much of his spectacularly dynamic preaching. The result was that, while Buchmanism has never exactly been a movement to neglect the dramatic, nevertheless the core of its work is in inter-personal relationships in small groups. The convert who has been "changed" usually is the recipient of the support

[16] "Love" in this context must be clearly distinguished from erotic love.

of many individuals and the particular attention of one. Many of these converts testify to the quality of the fellowship in this movement, and there is no doubt that this is a prime factor in the character changes that often occur.[17]

Similarly the success of Alcoholics Anonymous, basically a religious movement, is largely due to the concern that members show for one another. No special training, as for psychoanalysts or psychiatrists, is required for these lay evangelist-therapists. Yet they frequently accomplish what no psychiatrist can in the curing of other alcoholics. This is due not only to the fact that the demands on the individual, being religious, are thoroughgoing, but also to the fact that he is supported by another who not only cares but understands. The latter has been through the hell of alcoholism himself and so has been trained in a school of understanding denied to the ordinary therapist. Of the man who helped to cure him, one member of Alcoholics Anonymous says, "He was the first human with whom I had ever talked, who knew what he was talking about in regard to alcoholism from actual experience." [18] "In our town," says another, "there are some 70 of us, ready and willing to spend our time to show the way to sobriety and sanity to men who are like what we used to be." [19]

We cannot say that it is *only* through the agency of an empathetic mediator that a deep psychotherapeutic change or religious conversion may take place. For example, in the previous chapter we pointed out the role of loneliness in the religious development of many notable religious personalities, like Boisen, Jeremiah, and George Fox. Actually the growth must take place through a kind of tension in the client between his wish and need for dependence and his urge for independence, between his death urge and his life urge. The therapist, or the pastor, presides over only one phase of the complete therapeutic process.

It is the existence of such psychological needs that has had its effect in shaping theological ideas, and it is notable that concepts of

[17] See for example cases of Susan Robertson (p. 168 ff) and Mrs. Ross Danforth (p. 208 ff) of my *The Oxford Group*. The latter will also be found abridged on pp. 206–207 above in the chapter on "Conversion."

[18] *Alcoholics Anonymous*, p. 192.

[19] *Ibid.*, p. 295.

God, even though not directly derived from psychotherapeutic experiences, nevertheless run parallel to them. If one to any degree subscribes to our theory that religious ideas are rooted in human psychological needs, then it is not surprising to find God conceived, now as a loving father who supports, sustains, and understands, now as the supreme Being who hides Himself in mystery that man may be thrown on his own resources to develop the spark of divine individualism that lies deep within him. It is noteworthy that, with varying degrees of emphasis in different psychotherapeutic systems, modern psychotherapy defines the role of the therapist in roughly similar terms. Through a measure of acceptance and understanding by the therapist the client finds himself and so is free to help himself. Perhaps this throws some light on the paradoxical fact that the Bible in one place encourages the individual to cast his burden on the Lord,[20] in another to bear his own burden,[21] and in still another to bear other people's burdens.[22] Thus the Lord may be seen as playing the role of the Good Counselor in approving all of these attitudes in their proper places.

Also from the vantage point of therapy, we can understand why partial or one-sided theological ideas may be harmful for an individual. The individual who emphasizes merely God's acceptance may become religiously dependent or escapist, while he who emphasizes mainly his responsibility for himself may become arrogant and self-centered. A fully developed concept of God includes the kind of therapy relationship of which we have been speaking and yet it is much richer in that it also symbolizes a source of power, vocational responsibility, service, and the meaning of life. It is the recognition of such implications that makes religion at its best so much more satisfying than a mere counseling experience. And yet good therapy may facilitate a religious attitude, as we saw in the case of Mrs. Oak.

Something of what we have been trying to say is implied in Ian D. Suttie's *The Origins of Love and Hate.* With a psychoanalytical background Suttie criticizes Freud's emphasis on sex and the Oedipus situation as fundamental in the psychological urges of the normal person. Suttie prefers the simple need of the infant for affection and

---

[20] Psalms 55:22.
[21] Gal. 6:5.
[22] Gal. 6:2.

the role of the mother in supplying this need as the basic psychological fact of life. In a chapter on healing cults [23] he examines homeopathy and Christian Science. In part this chapter supports our contention that there is similarity of technique in religious and non-religious forms of therapy. He points out that love, however disguised, is the effective agent of therapy in both of these forms. "Now making allowance for the fact that Homeopathy is an affair of 'Doctor and Patient,'" says Dr. Suttie, "while Christian Science works with the ideas of 'God and the fellowship' (i.e., a number of 'patients'), there is a most significant identity between the two systems of 'comfort'." [24] In Christian Science, then, we have a particularly concrete example of a case where God is cast in the role of a therapist.

To make our point with just one more illustration the reader is asked to turn back to the chapter on Conversion (pp. 196–198), and reread carefully the excerpts from Carlyle's *Sartor Resartus*. The first is from "The Everlasting No" and represents Carlyle's pre-conversion state, while the second records his conversion in "The Everlasting Yea." Both record his attitude toward the universe and God. In the first, God is represented in negative terms and the universe seems "one huge, dead, immeasurable steam-engine, rolling on, in its dead indifference to grind me limb from limb." Any psychiatrist would be alarmed to hear a patient speak in this way. But following his conversion, the world takes on purpose and becomes alive. It is not indifferent to him but benignant. The "Universe is not dead and demoniacal, a charnel-house with spectres; but godlike and my Father's. . . ."

Without the benefit of any obvious human agent, Carlyle had recast his philosophy of life—his theology. Out of a universe that had seemed indifferent to him Carlyle had fashioned a heavenly Therapist, a God who really cared for him. He who reads with attention the whole of that fine chapter, "The Everlasting Yea," will find what a psychiatrist might describe as wholesome therapeutic attitudes directed toward God. But he will also see what we mean when we speak of the psychological richness that a full conception of God may bring to an experience of what otherwise might have been a commendable but merely commonplace example of emotional growth.

[23] Chap. 10.
[24] *Ibid.*, pp. 168–169.

Who should preside over therapy? This is an issue that has recently occasioned much pulling and hauling between medicine and psychology on the one side and the Church on the other. During earlier times in the Judeo-Christian tradition the priest had such a monopoly on prestige that nearly anything on which he wished to pronounce was apt to be settled in his favor. If one wishes to thumb through the so-called Laws of Moses in the Books of Exodus, Numbers, Leviticus, and Deuteronomy, he will find numerous instances where rules about health are mingled with the ethical code. For example, it was up to the priests to declare whether or not a person had leprosy. Later, in the New Testament, mental illness was explained by the theory of demon possession, and the Gospels relate several instances where Jesus cured people by commanding the demons to leave. Even as late as the eighteenth century, particularly in New England, it was the clergy who spoke the most influential words respecting such matters as witchcraft, which was often more a matter of dementia than of active ill will.

In modern times the shoe has been shifted to the other foot, and it is when the medical man opes his mouth that no dog is supposed to bark. The poor clergyman, with his pitiful salary, must stand around with his hat in his hand for such wretched crumbs of encouragement as the psychiatrist may wish to throw his way. He can not even call the field of morals his own, for Freudians have arrogated to themselves the power to bind and loose in such situations as extramarital intercourse or divorce.[25]

But happily the pendulum has begun to swing back so that more and more psychiatrists are coming to the position that the clergy may be worth listening to after all. Many clergymen, on their part, have shown a desire approaching eagerness to read the works of Freud and other great mental healers and to co-operate with medicine in any way they can. The division of responsibility has not yet been made on terms entirely satisfactory to either. One can expect that concern for vested interests will always surround the situation with a certain amount of flying dust. But if both sides can make themselves heard in a climate of mutual respect we can expect progress.

In the meantime the logical and easy solution would seem to be

---

[25] The author knows of at least one case of a man who sought a mistress, then divorced his wife on the advice of his psychiatrist.

to divide the field so that to each will fall his own specialty. Let the trained therapist take care of mental disease, while the clergyman is allowed to reign supreme in the field of religion and morals. Make sure that each does not trespass on the domain of the other. This point of view has been expressed very clearly by Dr. Abraham N. Franzblau. In a paper given before a meeting of the Society for the Scientific Study of Religion in New York in 1955, he said:

> The importance of maintaining sharp demarcations between these two fields becomes particularly clear if it is borne in mind that the minister, in approaching the psychiatric function, must have, almost by definition, a number of conflict areas that will hamper his role. He is committed to a system of values, to a moral code. He cannot sit in an office with a patient, as psychiatrists can, and be non-judgmental, shuffling off, if I may be allowed the expression, his "moral coil," and then be judgmental again as soon as he steps into his pulpit. This must create a sort of schizophrenic fluctuation within him which very few men, it must be agreed, can handle.
>
> . . . There has to be a certain consistency in a man's orientation, and if one assumes that a person can shed his values in a moment, the basic integrity of our inner selves and of our calling is diminished, whether we be ministers or psychiatrists.[26]

There is no doubt but that it is the duty of both minister and psychotherapist to become aware of the role that his specialty imposes upon him. It is just as important that he understand the role of specialists whose specialties may be confused with his own. The first step in any approach between these two fields is that both priest and psychiatrist understand one another. Each should understand his own limitations as well as the part that the other may have in the healing of sick personalities. It would not seem too much to require that the psychiatrist become acquainted with the field of theology and religious experience, at least at second hand, as well as know something of the Church and its requirements. Such information will extend his knowledge of human nature, the "stuff" with which he has to deal.

As for the minister, he should have at least some elementary knowledge of the symptoms of mental disease. How is he to know when to refer a parishioner to a psychiatrist if he does not know when the

[26] Pp. 48–49 in Werner Wolff (Ed.), *Psychiatry and Religion.*

person is sick? Beyond this, it is well for him to have some measure of clinical training if that is at all available to him. His "feel" for mental disease will be immensely sharpened through first-hand contacts with mental patients under the direction of medical experts. This training should also include some experience with psychotherapists, their ideas, techniques, and special skills. All this will help him to understand what he can and what he cannot do.

But when this has been said there remains the practical problem of translating the theoretical clarity of the separation of roles into actual practice. It would seem that this might be somewhat easier for the psychiatrist, who deals with the special category of mental disease, than for the minister, who deals with all phases of life. Yet even the physician likes to think that he deals with the whole person, for often he must if the patient is to survive.

Case. A Jewish businessman was required to retire because he was suffering from heart trouble and hypertension which were partly psychosomatic in origin. Even after rest his condition did not improve much because of his conviction that he would be dead within six months. No purely medical treatment by his physician seemed to avail. Finally his physician gave up all talk of medicine and suggested a trip of piety to Palestine some five years hence. The hope of the trip kept up his morale and his health.

On another occasion the news of the sudden and tragic death of a son threatened shock that might have been fatal. By skillfully turning his attention to the effect the news would have on his wife and her need for his comfort, this crisis was also passed.[27]

In the above case we have an example of a physician stepping out of his role as a medical man to assume part of the role of the minister. This illustrates the fact that the psychiatrist will have times when the demands of healing in its broadest sense will require that he assume the mantle of the pastor.

With the pastor himself it will be even more difficult. There are bound to be borderline cases between mental health and disease where he will be at a loss whether or not to refer them to a psychotherapist. In the meantime they may require counseling from the

[27] Summarized from H. A. Savitz, "The Cultural Background of the Patient as Part of the Physician's Armamentarium." Three other similar cases are cited.

clergyman. This may be a decisive factor in turning the scales toward mental health, in which case the pastor has become a kind of psychotherapist. The following was related to the author.

Case. A theological student came to a clergyman for counseling about problems concerned with study and personal relations. He felt he had failed in a position he had held before coming to theological school and the sense of failure had a tendency to return. In the course of counseling he remarked that there had been times when he had the feeling that he was God. He realized it was a foolish thought. At the moment it had receded and he laughed about it.

The clergyman had a certain amount of psychological sophistication and recognized this as a potentially dangerous delusion. But he happened to be in a place where he knew of no one to whom to refer the student or to whom he might apply for advice. The student was impecunious and, besides, he seemed to have insight and a wholesome attitude toward his strange idea. The clergyman explained to him in a matter-of-fact way that he should let him know if the delusion had any tendency to grow. Otherwise he counseled with the student about his problems largely in a non-directive way.

Over the months the delusion continued to recede to the point where it seemed practically non-existent. The student married about a year later, was graduated, and, according to reports, has made a satisfactory adjustment to life and is successful in his calling.

There might be differences of opinion among psychiatrists as to whether the clergyman handled the case correctly. Certainly there was some risk that the delusion might grow compulsively within the student before proper steps of prevention could be taken. However, it illustrates the kind of borderline situation which may confront any minister, as well as the desirability of some psychiatric knowledge. On the whole it would seem that the clergyman acted sensibly considering all the circumstances. But it is certain that there was a measure of encroachment on psychiatric preserves.

In his *The Courage to Be*, Paul Tillich approaches the subject of the relation of religion and psychiatry from the point of view of a theologian. His attitude is quite similar to that of Dr. Franzblau up to a point, where he acknowledges that the two areas cannot be completely separated. He distinguishes between two kinds of anxiety, *existential* and *neurotic*. By existential anxiety he refers to the anxiety that will trouble any thoughtful person in the ordinary process of living. Chiefly this concerns problems of fate and death, guilt and condemnation of self, and finally doubt and meaninglessness of life. The wholesome man faces existential anxiety and accepts it realistically, which is what Tillich means by "the courage to be." Neurotic anxiety, on the other hand, avoids the issue through some partial or limited solution of the problem. Anxiety is displaced onto insufficient or inappropriate stimuli and magnified out of reasonable proportion. To allay pathological anxiety is the province of the psychotherapist; existential anxiety is the business of the priest. But, says Tillich:

> Neither the medical nor the priestly function is bound to its vocational representatives: the minister may be a healer and the psychotherapist a priest, and each human being may be both in relation to the "neighbor." But the functions should not be confused and the representatives should not try to replace each other. The goal of both of them is helping men to reach full self-affirmation, to attain the courage to be.[28]

It is clear that both psychiatrist and minister may "meddle." The psychiatrist should certainly be in a position to *understand* his client's religious views, but he should refrain from giving advice that will deeply offend these views. The minister should avoid treating psychotics and severe neurotics with the idea that primarily he is curing their illnesses, particularly if this involves diagnosis or attempts at psychological interpretation. This does not mean that he may not incidentally help or even cure psychosomatic troubles through spiritual direction. Furthermore there is no reason why he should not sympathetically listen to a recital of his parishioners' troubles. This in itself is likely to have psychotherapeutic value. He should be in touch with the physician if treatment is involved.

On the whole it strikes us that he may learn much through an acquaintance with, or some training in, the non-directive or "client-centered" approach to counseling, for even in his purely pastoral work it may be of considerable help. This technique involves chiefly the reflection and clarification of the counselee's problems and emotions, as we have already indicated.[29] The technique is not so easy

---

[28] *The Courage to Be*, pp. 77–78.
[29] The best exposition of this school with reference to the ministry may be found in Seward Hiltner's *Pastoral Counseling*.

for the average pastor to learn as would seem at first thought; but if faithfully followed at least it can be said that only a limited amount of harm may result, particularly if the seriously disturbed are not prevented thereby from receiving more expert help. On the other hand, enormous benefits may be conferred. The average minister, however, does not have the time to give one parishioner his undivided attention over an extended period, and he may have trouble in handling the difficult problem of the transference of the parishioner's affections to him.

On the relationship between psychotherapy and religion we have simply presented some tentative generalizations. Details need to be worked out through frequent and sympathetic contacts between the two.[30]

SUMMARY

There is a close relationship between psychotherapy and some aspects of the religious life, especially conversion, in that similar therapeutic results are often effected. Psychotherapy would seem to be particularly effective when it involves genuine religious elements, whether these are specifically recognized as religious or not. This is to be ascribed to the fact that mature religion is so much more comprehensive of positive elements than most psychotherapy is likely to be or should be.

The good psychotherapist is non-judgmental, accepting, and understanding. Through this attitude he helps the individual to help himself. Thus the relationship between the good counselor and his client is similar to the ideal relationship between people enjoined by the great religions. The physician cures his patient through love. Also it is through this relationship that the theologian may enrich his ideas about God, who may be thought of as the Good Counselor. The more wholesome attitudes toward God and the universe parallel the relationship in effective psychotherapy between client and counselor.

In an age of specialization it is logical that pastor and psychotherapist should understand one another but keep their functions separate. The priest should keep to moral teaching and theological

---

[30] For a recent study comparing cases of religious conversion and effective therapy see the doctoral dissertation of Joseph Havens listed in the bibliography.

exposition, the psychotherapist to the healing of mental disease. But in practice this is not possible, nor even always desirable. Yet in general it can be said that each should be aware of the other's role as well as of his own, and be careful not to interfere in areas where he has no competence.

But despite the fact that psychotherapy and religion have become much more understanding of one another in recent years, there is still need of more co-operation between the two and more study of relationships in this area.

Chapter 18

SOCIAL FACTORS IN RELIGION

A church which becomes so absorbed in discussing the problems of the day, or increasing the social welfare of its members, or developing the esthetic side of worship, or fighting to preserve certain rituals to which it is devoted, that it neglects the spiritual life and health of mankind is neglecting its chief duty. . . . A church which fulfills this duty by knowledge of the truth and faith in the good cannot but improve the community.

—E. L. Thorndike

Since they all have their impact on the behavior and attitudes of religious people, we will be speaking in this chapter not only of the influence of groups but of less definite social pressures, particularly the influences of class, economics, nationalism, and the church itself as an institution. Also, since benevolence, morality, and desirable behavior generally are considered socially valuable results of church activity, we will be particularly interested in how social pressures may affect these factors.

The influence of class. One of the pervasive influences on behavior is that of *class* and its more solidified and overt form, *caste*. People in general are pretty well aware of class, even though they are sure that they rise above it, while the average American is positive that such an anachronism as caste could never exist in so enlightened a society as his. At the same time Negroes, both in the North and particularly in the South, constitute as striking an example of a separate caste as a sociologist could desire.[1] But we will confine ourselves to a discussion of the influence of class. Much of what we say could apply to caste in more accentuated degree.

Like most motivation, the psychological roots of class are various and not always clear. Probably most fundamental is the need for affiliation that all people possess. Class status is a means of implementing and channeling this need, and so it acquires a high value among human beings. But though it starts as a mechanism and as a means, it degenerates into an end. Like other mechanisms that properly deserve to be means, it becomes contemptible as an end especially when it drains off energy from more wholesome pursuits. But no less contemptible is it when it operates as an inappropriate means, as an ego-inflating symbol of achievement, or as a lever to advance business designs. These reflections will help to explain why we intuitively reject class status as an associate of true religion with its emphasis on love for its own sake and its high valuation on the naked individual unclothed with the apparel of class distinction.

Yet so pervasive is the desire for lofty class status that none of us is completely free of it. We all long to be summoned to sit at the head of the table, and many are the works of the imagination that play on this theme. *Vanity Fair, The Late George Apley, Le Père Goriot, Pride and Prejudice, David Copperfield,* and *An American Tragedy* are just a few of the novels that in one way or another are concerned with the urge for social advancement. It would be strange if the religious life did not have in the desire for upward mobility a rival that frequently dominates it or, more often, leaves it far behind.

That this is indeed the case has been sufficiently demonstrated and ratified in many social-scientific studies, some of which we have already mentioned.[2] The Hartshorne and May study, one of the earliest and most extensive, has shown that honesty among children is much more closely associated with socio-economic status than with Sunday School attendance.[3] Havighurst and Taba showed that, with the exception of a group of Norwegian Lutherans, reputation for character among young people in a Mid-western community was closely asso-

---

[1] See Davis and Dollard's *Children of Bondage,* or the writings of W. Lloyd Warner.

[2] Particularly in the chapter on belief.

[3] Compare Chaps. 9 and 19 in *Studies in Deceit,* Book I.

ciated with social class and very feebly associated with church membership or non-membership.[4] The exception we will have occasion to discuss later.

A story illustrating this supremacy of social considerations over religious values is told in Hollingshead's *Elmtown's Youth*.[5] The Methodist Church in Elmtown had two reasonably active girls' clubs, one with girls from families of higher social status than the other. The new minister felt this was both unnecessary and un-Christian, and brought his influence to bear with the result that, by common consent, the two clubs merged. But attendance began to fall off, until a few months later only one lonely lower-class girl attended the weekly meeting. The upper-class girls had absented themselves as a means of protest, while the lower-class girls had apparently felt unwanted. The minister admitted defeat and the following year allowed the clubs to revert to their former status.

E. L. Thorndike underlines this same feebleness of moral influence by the church, though he implies rather than proves that this is due to the interest of church members in social respectability. In *Your City* he reports the results of an extensive factual survey of several hundred of the largest American communities. These he evaluated by 37 specific criteria of "goodness" covering the general fields of health, education, public recreational facilities, circulation figures of nationally known periodicals, wealth, and other areas in which most impartial observers would not be apt to disagree as to what constituted municipal goodness. A score for each city was compiled and compared with other factors to discover what features would be apt to correlate with the goodness of a city. A *priori* one might reasonably suppose that churches would foster civic virtue so that goodness would correlate positively with such measures as the proportional number of clergy in a community and the incidence of church membership. Thorndike did find that there was a positive correlation for the relative numbers of Unitarians, Universalists, and Christian Scientists in a community, but for the churches as a whole both of these measures were *negative*.[6]

[4] See *Adolescent Character and Personality*, Chap. 6.
[5] Pp. 253 ff.
[6] Pp. 83 and 96 ff. The findings were based on the figures of a generation ago. It is possible, though doubtful, that a more modern survey would show different results.

It would seem then that church activities are very pallid affairs for the average church member and that for the most part they represent religion in what we have called its secondary and tertiary forms. This generalization would seem to hold good for Catholic as well as Protestant churches. Father Joseph Fichter of Loyola University of the South found that in a large Southern urban parish about 30 per cent of those on the church rolls were completely inactive, while the activity of many of the others was of an exceedingly routine and lukewarm variety.[7]

But for the comfort of those clergymen who tend to preach zealous church attendance as the whole duty of man, it should be said that there are straws of empirical evidence in the winds that point in a somewhat different direction. A more intense degree of church attendance and participation seems to be associated with desirable moral qualities. In the Havighurst study of "Prairie City," as has been noted, class status rather than church membership was associated with a reputation for desirable character traits *except* in the case of the Norwegian Lutheran group, whose character reputation was higher than their class status would lead one to expect. The religious involvement of members of this church typically was intense. The discipline enforced by the pastor was very strict, and ostracism from the group was often the penalty for those who strayed too far from the path of churchly rectitude. This intensity of their involvement with the church seemed to be the significant causative factor here.

In another study previously mentioned [8] the author collaborated with Caroline M. Warner in a study of the relationship of reputations for honesty and kindness with church attendance in a rural, predominantly one-class community. This led to the encouraging conclusion that, with the influence of class status largely eliminated, the more regular the church attendance the higher the reputation for honesty and kindness. Since they were freer than most churchgoers from the pressures of class mobility, perhaps people in this community were subject to more essential motives. Certain features of the study suggested that this reputation was not mere "halo effect" from the fact of church attendance.

This suggests that the religious influence of the church is exerted

[7] "What Is a Parishioner?" See also his *Dynamics of a City Church.*
[8] See chapter on Faith, p. 227.

through a limited number of core members, who are to be distinguished in part by their zeal and participation in church activities. These people confirm the fact that their religion has made a difference to their manner of living outside the church, in that they are more reliable and kindly than those whose church attendance is less regular. But these persons must not be confused with the general mass of church members, for whom social status is such an absorbing quest. In many churches a hierarchy of influence may be discerned based on class membership and wealth. In Protestantism, particularly, socio-economic prestige may perform the suggestive function that authority and ecclesiastical paraphernalia supply in Catholicism. It is hard for the Catholic to withhold some kind of homage when he sees his bishop officiating with crosier and miter; similarly it is difficult for the Protestant to resist the impression that the ushers who march the collection to the sanctuary in such solemn file are invariably people to be admired and imitated, especially when he knows that some of them are leaders in their social set and have a great deal of money in the bank. It is such uncritical acceptance of church leadership and imitation of the wrong qualities that may keep the moral influence of the church at a low ebb.

The influence of economics. Very closely allied to the influence of class is the influence of economics on religion. In the 1920's the "economic interpretation of history" was very popular with historians. According to this view, those pioneer groups who colonized America and who were supposed to have emigrated from their homes for religious reasons were mainly activated by economic impulses. Though this motive was overemphasized—for religion was a very real factor at that time—economics did play its part. Economic considerations have always had their effect on religion ever since the days of the relations of Jacob with Laban, and of Joseph in Egypt. Furthermore the influence has usually been such as to alloy the purity of religious impulses and to distort their expression. Doubtless this was in the mind of the Apostle Paul when he stigmatized the love of money as the "root of all evil."

It would be very surprising if business interests did not cast their shadow over religious expression in our own day. Capitalism has played such a large part in forming our way of life and system of values that this is inevitable, whether the influence is direct or subtle. The Lynds pointed out that in Middletown one of the prevalent opinions about religion was "that preachers should stick to religion and not try to talk about business, public affairs, and other things 'they don't know anything about.' " [9] Such opinions reflect the suspicion that what ministers have to say about business, when they do talk about it, is not particularly flattering. Though there are notable exceptions, the average clergyman, dependent as his salary is on the contributions that come into his church, will think twice before he takes a stand critical of the ways of the parishioners who are best able to make those contributions. The dilemma is a real one. But there is no doubt that formal religion finds its lot much less complicated when it obeys the Biblical injunction "to speak evil of no one" where business interests are concerned.

A case in point is that of the professor at a theological school who tried to get the ministers of a Pennsylvania mining community to pass a resolution advocating the right of the miners to put in a check weighman of their own to see that they received honest wages. The ministers would have nothing to do with the resolution, though they did pass one denying the right of the miners to play baseball on Sunday.[10]

Similarly the dominance of business interests results in the application of commercial standards to churches. They are supposed to be run according to the strictest business principles. A minister's salary is not so much commensurate with the purity of his life and his approximation to Christ as it is to his success in attracting new members and improving the plant.[11] This cleavage between materialism and religious values is a perfectly natural one and causes poignant conflict, not only in the minds of many clergymen, but also in spiritually sensitive laymen. Lest we become overly cynical, we must remember that it is out of such conflicts that creative spiritual individualism often emerges.

We must remember too that religion may have direct influence on business for better or for worse. There is a certain dulling of the sharp

[9] As quoted in Britt, *op. cit.*, p. 455.
[10] Cited *ibid.*, p. 458, from Jerome Davis, *Capitalism and its Culture.*
[11] Cf. *ibid.*, p. 456.

edges of competition among church members, and doubtless the amenities of business life are promoted through the church, though often merely superficially. Then there are religious teachings that facilitate business dealings, such as a code of honesty. The Wall Street broker takes great pride in the fact that securities worth millions of dollars change hands by the unsupported agreement between two dealers; but without this convention the speed of security dealing would be considerably delayed and complicated. An unreliable broker would soon find no one to deal with him. He sees that his communication is "yea, yea" and "nay, nay," not so much because of the Gospel's admonition, but rather because of personal advantage.

Likewise, if we are to trust the theory of Max Weber, capitalism itself owes a debt to those forms of Protestantism which emphasized frugality and industry, for thereby a reserve of capital was gradually accumulated. The discarding of the medieval ban on usury made it possible for the laborer and merchant to add the earning power of their money to that of their labor. Thus the foundation of modern capitalism was laid.

But just as there are forms of institutional religious life that accommodate themselves to the middle classes and the rich, so there are churches and religious associations that recommend themselves to the poor and disinherited.[12] The lower-class person feels himself unwelcome and rejected in the average middle-class church. W. Lloyd Warner found that in Jonesville 77 per cent of the upper-class individuals studied belonged to a church, while only 28 per cent of the lower-lower class belonged.[13] The lower classes tend either not to go to church at all, or to get their religion from churches and sects which are apt to be very conservative and to rely on religious emotionalism rather than on reason. Such were the Jonesville Free Methodist Church and the Gospel Tabernacle, whose membership was recruited mostly from the lower classes.

It is clear that in one way or another economic considerations add themselves to the pressures of class to influence the attitudes and behavior of religious people.

[12] For a discussion, see H. Richard Niebuhr, *The Social Sources of Denominationalism*, Chap. 2.
[13] *Democracy in Jonesville*, p. 154.

Nationalism and the churches. Religion in countries other than the United States has for the most part traditionally been closely associated with the state, usually by means of the "establishment" of certain official churches. This has been true particularly in Europe, where some of the denominations now current in America enjoy official status and receive funds and special privileges from the government, as do the Roman Catholic Church in Spain, the Anglican Church in England, and the Lutheran Church in the Scandinavian countries. This practice is a relic of medieval and Reformation times, and though there may be some advantages in it, nevertheless there seem to be more disadvantages. The dangers far outweigh the benefits. On the whole it would seem that disestablishment has led to a more vigorous and healthy development of institutional religious life.

H. Richard Niebuhr notes that Europeans are amazed to find in the United States, where religion receives no official sanction, so high a proportion of church membership.[14] Competition for church members among the several hundred denominations and sects in America has its absurd aspects, but at least it has prevented the sects from dying out. Furthermore, not only in America but wherever it has had real competition, the Roman Catholic Church has developed its most vigorous and admirable branches. The Catholic Church in Germany or America, at least to the average American, would seem much more vigorous than the Church in Spain.

But even when there is no alliance between Church and State, nationalism and sectionalism tincture religious views and sometimes paint them with pretty strong colors. The Civil War caused strong differences of opinion with respect to the Negro, and the Gospel is still read very differently even by members of the same denomination, depending on which side of the Mason-Dixon line they stand. War invariably distorts what purport to be religious valuations, and the welfare of the nation in which one happens to reside is invariably identified with the will of God. Pacifism would seem to be the most logical position for a follower of Jesus, yet few American clergymen preached pacifism during the recent world wars. The same association of national interest and religion prevailed among the enemies of

[14] *Op. cit.,* p. 206. Chaps. 5 and 8 discuss the general topic of the denominations and nationalism.

America at these times. Shintoism in Japan, for example, was an exceptionally nationalistic and militaristic expression of religion.

Closely associated with nationalism is the expression of ethnic consciousness in denominations. Particularly in America, with its large and diverse immigrant group, churches have sometimes played as large a part in expressing the culture of the Old World as in expressing the characteristically religious urges. The German Baptist Dunkards, the Norwegian Lutheran Synod, the Polish National Catholic Church, as well as certain Roman Catholic congregations, are all examples of bodies which are or have been instrumental in preserving European languages and cultures. An effective means of preserving a culture within a culture is the use of the mother tongue in the services of the church, a practice to which especially the first generation tenaciously clings. Usually the custom begins to fade with the passing of this generation and the progressive Americanization of the second and third. Yet a certain pride in the traditions of the ethnic origins will still linger on long after the mother tongue has been forgotten, growing feebler with each successive generation.

Nevertheless the influence of once-cherished traditions will condition the customs and attitudes of those who care nothing for the country of their ancestors' origin. The average Episcopalian seldom thinks of himself as belonging to a church so English in origin that attendance at its services during the American Revolution was often considered tantamount to treason. He intones the words of his prayer book without the slightest notion that he is speaking in the stately accents of Archbishop Cranmer and echoing controversies current at the time of Henry the Eighth. Because his father taught him, the Pennsylvania German piously paints mystic symbols on the side of his barn, unaware that this strange expression had its origin among remote ancestors living in the mountains of far-off Germany.

The institution of the church.   Sensitive religious spirits have been more conscious than the social psychologist of the distortion of what may be called "true religion" by the demands and necessities of the religious institution. We have touched on this in Chapter 13, where we have spoken of the opposition of the Prophet to the Priest. Every individual pays some homage to those universal rules of conduct that are sometimes thought of as "ideals." And when individuals band together in a formal group, though the pursuit of ideals may be their collective aim, another psychological factor is added—the urge of every institution to preserve itself. This may lead to its forsaking the ideals it professes if to support them may weaken its own existence. We see this most clearly in the behavior of nations where preservation of the state is the first law of diplomacy. But almost equally obvious is this behavior among religious bodies, if one is discerning enough to observe it, even though the average man is apt to take for granted that whatever his church supports is pious and right. Consequently it is well that we consider a few of the ways in which the religious institution, chiefly in denominational form, conditions religious behavior.

Though denominationalism is not the only way in which the religious institution expresses itself, it is the most customary. For the sake of concreteness we will discuss the subject with denominations in mind. The causes of denominationalism are complex. We have already touched on some of them: social class, economic concerns, nationalism, and sectionalism. To these we can add another cultural factor, doctrinal considerations, commonly supposed to be the most cogent of all. It may be doubted, though, that this is a very strong psychological force for any but the most highly self-conscious proponents of any particular demonination. This factor acts on groups and can be thought of rather as a group influence.

Yet it has its individual significance as well. The individual, whether through cultural conditioning or group influence, prefers certain ways of expressing his religion. Furthermore his temperament may help to predispose him to certain forms rather than others. One person may worship best through the silences and simplicity of a Quaker meeting; another requires the whole paraphernalia of a sacramental system. In this way the diversity of denominations serves religious creativity, for they are not only the partial expressions of creativity themselves but stimulate it as well. A person at home in a religious group can feel much freer to express those original religious urges that are within him.

Thus it can be seen that denominationalism might be an unmitigated psychological blessing were it not for the institutional fly in the ointment. The urge of the institution to preserve itself fosters exclusiveness, narrowness of vision, an emphasis on the little things that maintain the denomination rather than on the big things that unite all religions. These, in their turn, foster intolerance, social punishment, and thought control, whether in the gross form of an Index of Forbidden Books or the more subtle but just as effective raising of a polite eyebrow when unorthodox religious ideas are expressed.

Perhaps the chief crime of the institution which the man of sensitive religious feelings would consider to be in opposition to the essential religious spirit is the distortion of values through emphasis on peripheral or nonessential matters. Nearly every denomination, sect, or religious grouping puts a disproportionate amount of time and emphasis on *something* of less than central importance. There is a good reason for this. In order to maintain its institutional *raison d'être*, it is forced to find a characteristic that distinguishes it from other similar organizations. Consequently no religious group would find it possible to require its adherents to love the Lord their God with heart and soul and mind and their neighbors as themselves, *providing* this was all that was to be required of them. There are too many people who agree with this, so that there would be little basis for the continuance of the denomination. There would always be the danger that this church's special purpose would no longer exist. Consequently most denominations find it necessary to raise up some article of faith so illogical, subordinate, peripheral, or strange that no one uncommitted to the denomination would be likely to believe in it. Anyone can demonstrate the truth of this by a simple exercise. Let him think of some denominations *other than his own* and the tenets that distinguish them. It will be clear that in nine cases out of ten these will fit our descriptions. Of course one will have more difficulty in identifying those of *his own* church that are similarly segmental, for these will tend to appear to him as marks of distinction of the "true church"—doctrines that should be patently clear to anyone with spiritual acumen comparable to his. But with only a modicum of objectivity he should see our point even with reference to his own beliefs.

Belief in such articles of faith is kept alive not only through the pulpit pounding and discipline enforced by church leaders. A far more potent weapon is the social punishment and threat of ostracism applied to those who stray too overtly from the denominational fold.

But that church members in general do not themselves believe quite so intensely in private what they profess in public is demonstrated in a study by R. L. Schanck.[15] In a poll of Baptists and Methodists regarding their attitude toward Baptism, *as church members* none of the Methodists and 67 per cent of the Baptists believed that immersion only was acceptable. *Privately*, however, six per cent of the Methodists and only 17 per cent of the Baptists supported the same article of faith.

But because of these distortions, can the psychologist cry "Anathema" on the religious institution? The situation is more complex than this point of view would suggest. The religious institution performs some legitimate functions that must be kept in mind to balance its shortcomings.

First of all, the church facilitates fellowship. To a certain degree it acts as a kind of community center requiring no entrance fee and at least theoretically open to all who share its aims and beliefs. Doubtless many churches develop this aspect of their function to the point where religion is obscured, and the church becomes hardly more than a respectable club. But though few churches attain the ideal, there is such a thing as fellowship in worship and the search for an experience of God. This search can be made more effective and the experience more vivid through the fellowship of the church.

In the second place the church implements the insights of the prophet and augments his influence. Most prophets do not intend to found a religious institution, but the rejection they are apt to experience from the institutions to which they have owed their allegiance often results in a separatist movement either within the larger institution or outside of it. This may occur on the initiative of disciples rather than the prophet himself. John Wesley did not wish to form a separate denomination outside Anglicanism, while the Christian church itself remained a movement within Judaism until a number of years after the Crucifixion. In this way the church first activates then conserves the experience and values of the past.

Finally, the church supplies discipline for the individual, and a concrete rallying point for his religious urges. Psychologically the need for discipline is a subtle one. But whether superficial or profound, religious thought and impulse require some expression if they are to

[15] Cited in Britt, *op. cit.*, p. 126.

be kept alive. Since only the exceptional individual can impose this discipline on himself without some outside support, he relies on the church to tell him what he should do. The requirements vary from attendance at church and obedience to a strict moral code to the swallowing of a belief that is distasteful and absurd. Such acts make him believe that he is sacrificing something to his church. It raises the level of his consciousness of membership and supports his morale. It feeds his self-regard and helps him to feel that his life is meaningful. Thus his whole personality may be toned up with results beneficial to areas outside of religion. The industry of the Calvinist is a case in point. Such benefits will react upon the church, enhancing its value for the individual.

This helps to explain why churches that are too liberal are less successful in enlisting members. They do not require enough of their parishioners. Or perhaps it is more accurate to say that they require so much that the implications of faith escape the imagination of the individual and lose all compulsion. To love God and neighbor is indeed a large order, the full implications of which are sufficient to discipline and revolutionize the life of any individual and to supply him with labor for all his days. But it is common for the adherent of a narrower faith to object to such liberal generalities. Drawing himself up to his full spiritual height, he will declare scornfully that he does not intend to "water down his faith," whatever the liberals may choose to do. Whereupon he will point proudly to the achievements of his denomination, and to the walls of his church bursting with the multitude of faithful worshipers.

What he *means* to say is that there is little discipline *unless the faith is watered down* for the average person. Unless faith is made concrete and specific, the average man cannot apply it at all. A liberal faith is a faith for spiritual giants whose combination of imagination and will helps them to see their duty and to fulfill it as well. Such a giant was Jesus, but to his contemporaries he seemed to be "watering down" the strictness of many Jewish rules. In liberalizing his interpretation of Jewish law he indeed loosened its compulsive hold on people, but at the same time made it more difficult for the average Jew. In our day, Albert Schweitzer is so much one of these giants that few people bother even to inform themselves about his denominational ties or what petty doctrines he may happen to profess. These factors are simply irrelevant. It is enough to know that his life demonstrates his clear and self-conscious Christian convictions.

But few individuals, including many whose perceptions of spiritual truth are keen and profound, can implement their perceptions. The trouble with the liberals and the unchurched is that few of them make good their lofty ideals. They prefer to sit around enjoying them, returning the scorn of the conservatives, at the same time that they solace themselves with the reflection that no one can live up to an ideal anyway. It is the function of the denomination to narrow the requirements for such people and to give these narrowed requirements the bite of some measure of compulsion. It is on some such basis that the psychologist may throw light on the appeal of neo-orthodoxy in these times. A more conservative theology enables the churches to make more concrete demands on their members and so to improve their morale. The effect of the institution is to make religion effective at the necessary price of distorting religious values. Here, as elsewhere, its value to society would seem ambiguous.

Religion and conformity.[16]   One of the generalized influences always at work in society is the desire for conformity. The individual feels more secure and comfortable when he is behaving like others than when initiating a new mode of behavior, and this urge plays its part in the formation of the church and other religious associations. As we have already indicated, church membership may derive simply from a desire for conformity rather than from an essentially religious impulse.[17]

Especially during times of stress and of danger, such as times of war and the threat of war, the need for conformity grows. The individual not only attempts to conform to the behavior of others but desires that others behave like him. He therefore is capable of becoming coercive and even persecutory. Since the church is such an eminently respectable institution, it is sought out by some people simply

[16] In this discussion I am indebted in part to "Some Socio-Psychological Sources of the Current Religious Revival," a paper given by Professor Milton J. Rosenberg of Yale University before the Society for the Scientific Study of Religion, at Harvard University, Nov. 5, 1955. See bibliography.

[17] A militant defense of that religious faith that is broad enough to accept religious pluralism will be found in Horace M. Kallen's *Secularism is the Will of God.*

as a means of expressing this conformity. Furthermore, for those attempting to escape the thrusts of demagogues who may be mounting attacks on political nonconformists, the church provides effective protective coloration. From the safety of a denomination, and particularly one of the more conservative ones, a man may criticize his country's political institutions with considerably more immunity than if he did so as a member, for example, of the Communist Party. This kind of church membership may help to give a spurious impression of the intensity of a nationwide religious revival.

The refuge of religion is not only sought by the timid social radical, but also by the successful businessman. He may feel somewhat dubious about his own success and about whether he deserves quite such a large share of this world's goods. Activity in his church and large gifts for religious purposes both ease his own conscience and are persuasive in convincing the general public that a heart of gold beats beneath his double-breasted business suit. Professor Rosenberg suggests that a manifestation of this tendency is the amount of free space and time given to religion in current publications and over the airwaves. The hucksters of commerce are frightened by their own success in purveying their wares to the public. But favors to organized religion help to insure that the average churchgoer will be on their side in accepting advertising uncritically as not only a necessary but a beneficent force in contemporary life.

To carry this a step further, if the poet Milton was concerned with "justifying the ways of God to Man," modern society is interested in justifying the ways of man to God. It is difficult for a mere single *individual* to recommend his unconventional behavior to the church. But if it suits the purposes of a large and powerful *group* in society to modify traditional teachings by enlisting the churches on its side, that is always possible—at least to a considerable degree. We have seen that the ancient ban on usury was abrogated following the Reformation. Mass murder is not only condoned but enjoined and blessed in every war for what is represented as a righteous cause, while the churches of each community tend to identify their particular mores with the will of God.

In addition to this more or less voluntary conformity, there is the involuntary type. Or rather, conformity comes about both through voluntary and involuntary means. Chief among the means of enforcing conformity is the practice of social punishment. Particularly in a well-knit and well-organized denomination, ecclesiastical and social pressure is brought to bear on nonconformists. We have seen that this was the case with the Norwegian Lutherans in Prairie City, studied by Havighurst and Taba. Deviation from strict moral standards and doctrinal purity was punished by ostracism, a powerful weapon when it is remembered that many of the members owed their closest social ties to the church. This kind of pressure is brought most powerfully and prominently into play when it involves marrying out of one's faith. It may mean rejection not only by one's friends but, more poignantly, by one's family.

Moral behavior secured by such means doubtless has its value to society, but whether it should be termed "religious" may be questioned. Furthermore, even when doctrinal beliefs are involved, the effect may be religiously and personally stultifying. The pressure exerted by social reward and punishment may have the value of limiting the restless, rootless, and pointless shifting from one denomination to another, in which some individuals indulge. But more often it stimulates a defensive kind of doctrinal loyalty which frustrates the honest and often painful self-examination so necessary to spiritual growth and that differentiated maturity of religious belief described in our chapter on mature religion. The person who wishes to achieve a consolidated doctrinal position, rather than merely the façade of such, must be willing to lose his faith, if need be, to gain it—or another more satisfying to him. The guardians of doctrinal vested interests are in league against this kind of self-examination and in nowise intend that the individual's self-examination be thorough if there is any danger that this might mean "leaving the faith." Their most effective tool in thwarting freedom for creative religious growth is social reward and punishment.

Thus we see that, in the interest of conformity, the church is at one time capable of imposing its will on its members, at another of accommodating its teaching to the requirements of popular social demand, and at all times of enlisting God on its side to ratify whatever it wishes to teach and to do. It is for this reason that occasionally individuals need to be raised up to oppose their creative religious insights to the communal forces of Church and Society. Thus are created tensions that discipline both the individual and the church to keep both morally wholesome and spiritually fresh.

How does the church affect community morality? As some of the figures that we have cited have suggested, there are many social scientists who feel the church has no influence whatsoever on community ethics and morality. As Thorndike has said, if communities where the church is strong are no better than those in which it is weak, why should public-spirited citizens spend either time or money on it? His point of view grew out of his objective investigation, and it is hard to see how any impartial person could come to any other conclusion if such figures tell us all there is to know.

We have already suggested some of our reasons for believing that these figures do not tell the whole story, mainly because they lump all church people into one large group and do not discriminate between the spiritually alive and merely nominal church members. Those who take their church obligations seriously are apt to be those for whom religion makes a difference in the larger sense, and we must not neglect, in our professional zeal for large statistical populations, the influence of this *élite*. Statistics are a great help to the social psychologist, but only when they are subtle enough to fit the problem being studied.

In the case of the religious *élite* of which we have spoken, it would seem that its influence on society would be both direct and indirect. Directly, the kind of intense spiritual experience that changes lives contributes to society the service that accrues to the community through these individuals. This does not mean that all of their ways are socially desirable. On occasion such people may become very troublesome and a social nuisance. But to the extent that they are made honest, industrious, and responsible citizens they do contribute positively. Most Americans, for example, are annoyed at the spectacle of Jehovah's Witnesses refusing to salute the flag. Yet the kind of integrity that refuses to act contrary to principle, no matter how bizarre that principle may seem to others, is an attitude which, if given a more general reference, may have tremendous social value.

In this connection it might be noted that in speaking of the church we are including the sect, for it is more apt to be adherents of sects who demonstrate the acute religious fervor that changes lives. While we will not have the space to distinguish fully between the two, it might be said that the church represents the more traditional, settled type of religious institution, with an educated and consecrated priesthood or ministry to pass on denominational tradition, perform certain well-defined pastoral duties, and administer sacraments. A sect is a movement within a church or, as Professor James Luther Adams of Harvard would put it, an *ecclesiola* within the *ecclesia*. Sometimes it is entirely separate from the church but involves those who feel themselves rejected by the church; yet even when not separate it has a tendency eventually to split off from the church and become an entity in itself. This was the development of the Christian Church, which started its history as a Jewish sect, while many of the branches of Protestantism, such as the Methodist Episcopal Church, have had a similar beginning. A sect is more likely to rely on a lay ministry, with the emphasis on spontaneous spiritual experience as the basis for membership. Members tend to be born into churches, but they join sects.

Scornful though the clergy of the traditional churches may be of the new-born sect, nevertheless it is the sect that is more likely to show the power to change lives and so build character and sustain individual morale. Usually the sect's appeal is emotional and more successful with the lower classes, who do not feel at home in the church; though here a hard and fast generalization cannot be made. The Moral Re-Armament movement, or Buchmanism, constitutes a modern sect whose appeal, atypically, has been mostly to the upper classes. The Norwegian Lutherans of Prairie City are a more typical group. Though each sect is peculiar to itself and may owe its start to a highly original prophet, yet its teaching is likely to be derived from the church, so that it can be considered a special aspect of the church. Had Thorndike sought out the sects in his study of cities, he might have come to a very different conclusion as to the effect of religion.[18]

Beside the influence of the church on society through its more dynamic members and especially through the sects, it has an effect that is more passive and indirect though at the same time more per-

[18] For a more extensive discussion of Church and Sect, see H. R. Niebuhr, *op. cit.*, p. 17 ff.

vasive. This is its influence on the customs and conventions of society, the attitudes and felt obligations of the ordinary citizen. By virtue of its respectability, the church sets standards that are bound to be marked by a considerable portion of those who are leaders in the community. Through them the attitudes become diffused throughout society, in that they are imitated, sometimes vividly but more often pallidly, by the rank and file. This influence must not be confused with religion, though its origins may be religious. Many people follow the lead of the church, not because they are religious, but simply because it happens to be "the thing to do." Often they are not aware of any influence of the church at all, and repel with scorn the idea that they are affected by it in the slightest degree. They behave like their neighbors but assume religious attitudes in the process of identifying themselves with their neighbors.

The dynamics of this assumption of attitudes are very different from those activating the person in whom the attitudes spring from a vital religious experience. In the latter case the drive is one that owes most of its force to an internally developed urge. In the former case it seems to owe its power, and certainly its form, to other people. Hence it is much less spontaneous. Since ordinary church members exhibit only secondary or tertiary religious behavior, they are not very different in their essential drives from their nonchurch neighbors. So whether they suppose they are pursuing pure religious objectives or what they may vaguely term "right living" makes little difference, for what both really desire is respectability. What they fear more than all ills is social punishment, such as being relegated to a lower social class or rejection from the charmed circle of a local exclusive club. This similarity of motive in the churched and the unchurched helps explain why so little difference in behavior is found, once difference in class is allowed for.

This can be illustrated in the usage of liquor. Though churches in general have disapproved of drinking, sociologists have pointed out that the use of liquor is class determined. In the lower classes it is used freely, particularly among men; in the middle classes, particularly the lower middle, total abstinence is the norm, while in the upper classes moderation is the rule. A person upward mobile from the middle class may hate liquor and disapprove its use because of the teaching of his church. But he will not refuse a glass at a social gathering because of his fear that his origins may be detected. Liquor companies are of course well aware of these distinctions. A study of liquor advertisements is enough to indicate how much money is spent to strengthen the idea that drinking is a "must" for the "best people." One will find many cases among sects like Moral Re-Armament and organizations like Alcoholics Anonymous, where primary religious experience has modified the drinking habits of upper-class people. However, there are very few cases where membership in a church has had the same effect apart from the desire for status.

This sort of thing can further be illustrated by the obligation that nearly every citizen feels to contribute to a community drive, like that of hospital support. He neither desires to part with his money in making his contribution, nor does he enjoy the thought of being asked to help with the collections. Yet reluctantly he will do both, partly out of a sense of duty and partly because of a desire to stand well in the eyes of his fellow citizens. Were it a truly religious impulse it would be done with joy and with little sense of effort. But it is the kind of obligation that the church has taught, and in this roundabout path of the concern to conform and the desire for status, the unwilling service of the average citizen becomes a means of social effectiveness.

Thus the fresh, creative insights of prophets and saints, preserved and mediated by the church, are transmitted to uninspired men. Under the illusion of righteousness, they pursue material goals clad in the drab uniforms of soldiers of the commonplace. But strange as most of them are to a lively experience of religion, they nevertheless act out the church's rules of righteousness and so provide that orderliness and co-operation without which our complex modern society would be impossible. But society is religious and moral, as expressed in the average man, only because he is afraid to behave otherwise in the face of convention. Underneath he knows this, which helps to explain why he so violently persecutes the prophet who tries to make him face his own hollowness.

What he really is after is conformity and respectability, which usually win him over through their immediacy and quickness of reward. But religion has its rewards, too, in durability and staying power. Its appeal is not immediate but to the depths. Your conventional, respectable, self-righteous average man never knows when he will be forced back on these depths. It is when this happens that primary religion is born. But such an individual finds himself leading a lonely existence in the typical church. It is then that he seeks a sect, or perhaps founds one himself. The sect influences its members creatively until it gradually congeals into a church and becomes itself respectable, whereupon it stimulates religious behavior of a secondary or tertiary nature and so makes its valuable though uninspired contribution to the cultural matrix. Such is the repeated cycle of influence from prophet to sect to church to society.

SUMMARY

This chapter concerns group expressions of religion and its modification by certain group forces. *Social class* is one of the forces which, studies suggest, is a more cogent determinant of behavior than religion for church members, barring a small, intensely religious minority. *Economics* is another influence which often blunts the application of religious teachings to life, especially for the average church, which in many ways is dependent on business for its fiscal existence. Yet just as there are churches for the wealthy and well-born, so there are churches and sects whose appeal is chiefly to the poor and disinherited. *Nationalism* also plays its part, for religion frequently expresses the culture and interests of national groups, even where the churches are not official arms of the state. God is usually conceived as marching with the national forces in battle.

Institutional factors condition the situation. The churches become more sensitive to social forces because of the tendency of every institution to perpetuate itself. Thus a variety of denominations is desirable, to meet a variety of religious needs, but each denomination is apt to exaggerate religious nonessentials in expressing its own uniqueness and justifying its existence. Yet the churches do perform valuable functions as means of facilitating religious fellowship and conserving values preached by religious prophets. Also they foster religious discipline and morale by defining sufficiently narrowly doctrine and practice to constitute concrete goals for the average church member.

The *desire for conformity* is another factor conditioning religious expression and the church. Some people join the church for reasons of prestige and as a defense against criticism for holding radical views; others as a means of expiating feelings of guilt over too-pronounced secular success and as a means of enlisting the church on their side. The church also may enforce conformity, though in our time more through various forms of *social rewards and punishment* than by overt compulsion. The church affects community morality both via the direct impact of its few members who are intensely religious—frequently members of sects—and more often indirectly through custom and the more or less ethical behavior demonstrated alike by uninspired church members and non-church members of the community.

Part 4

IN SUMMARY

Chapter 19

CONCLUSIONS

The kingdom of heaven is like unto leaven which a woman took, and hid in three measures of meal, till the whole was leavened.

— Jesus of Nazareth

We approach the end of our psychologist's attempt to describe and analyze the religious life, to explain what we can of this some-times strange, sometimes wonderful chemistry within the human heart. The picture is one of lights and shadows. Sometimes what is called religion is so superficial as to become laughable, and many are the religious disguises by which, usually unknown to himself, the churchgoer hides his more secular impulses. But at its most intense and in its most poignant forms, religion dives down among the deepest sources and springs of personality to carry on its work. It is for this reason that we have felt we should not turn aside from the difficult task of psychologically considering what seems to us personality's most important function.

And also, by way of calling attention to some of the threads of thought that have run through our chapters, we will set down a number of conclusions that might properly be drawn. Here, more than usually, we will be allowing ourselves the indulgence of value attitudes, in the interest of indicating ways in which our study may be of significance.

(1) *Like other expressions of life, religion requires a balance between activity and passivity, between the life urge and the death urge.* Though we derived these labels from Freud, it is doubtful that we

411

have used them in quite the way that he did, since he emphasized the actively destructive aspects of his "death instinct." At any rate it is clear that religion in some of its expressions is active, adventuresome, pioneering, and bold. In this respect it calls for courage, imagination, and creative spiritual insight, as in the case of the prophets. On the other hand, with equal propriety, it provides comfort, security, and the refreshment of relaxation. It is the religious radical and progressive who represents the life urge, while the conservative is more apt to express the death urge—the desire for rest that achieves its ultimate consummation only in death and disintegration.

We have pointed out that the religious institution, particularly as time passes on, tends more and more to express the death urge, just as the individual as he approaches old age is increasingly content with a vegetative existence. We also pointed out that perhaps this emphasis on the comfortable aspects of religion may help to explain why the average church seems to have more appeal to the old than to the young. However, since the human spirit expresses itself now in activity and now in passivity, one need alternating with the other, the rhythm between the life urge and the death urge must continue in the individual's religious life until the death urge triumphs in the ultimate mortal event.

(2) *It is important that we distinguish religion from magic.* We have defined religion in part as the attempt of man to harmonize his life with the Beyond, to do not his own will but the will of God. Magic is the self-centered attempt to coerce or influence supernatural beings or forces to serve man's own purposes. Magic and religion shade into one another so that in practice it may be difficult to separate them. But in theory it is easy, and the theory may help one criticize his religious life in such a way as to enable him to progress toward greater maturity. Furthermore the theory may help institutional religion to criticize itself from within and save it from that form of magical popularization which may rob the church of its real religious significance.

(3) *Conversion may be looked upon as parallel in some ways to psychotherapy, and in another way as a special case of religious growth.* The term is loosely used and may refer to an emotional epi-

sode at an evangelistic rally which upsets the individual temporarily but leaves him pretty much as he was before. On the other hand, conversion may refer to a person's drastic facing of himself in religious terms which stirs him to his depths, changing his fundamental attitudes and leading him to an integration of life that, without the experience, would have been impossible. It is this latter type of conversion that may be viewed in part as a successful piece of psychotherapy. Religious conversion as a substitute for psychotherapy, however, may be very dangerous in that it is so often manipulated by amateurs who believe their naive concepts of the Grace of God to be a sufficient resource. On the other hand, a changed life referred to a divine source with new relations to others, defined in religious terms, may add a dimension missing in the ordinary traffic of psychotherapy. This would help to explain why so frequently Alcoholics Anonymous is able to arrest alcoholism where ordinary forms of treatment have failed.

But conversion may also be looked upon as a special form of religious growth, not slow and gradual to the consciousness of the subject, but sudden and traumatic. Pressures may have been building up over a long period, and the soil usually has been prepared since childhood. But the very suddenness and force of the emotional discharge may enable the individual to abrogate habits that he has deplored over many years, and effect a change impossible with gradual attrition. There is need for more copious and precise studies in this area of personality change.

(4) *Vitality develops from the religion of healthy-mindedness, but depth and insight are more likely to spring from the religion of suffering.* Suffering indeed is a scourge and goad which may overcome and destroy the spirit of man. But more than any other human orientation the religious vision may give meaning to suffering, and so transform it and turn it to account. In other words, the religious person who endures suffering, through the meaning which he finds in it or imposes on it, may use his pain as a means to spiritual growth.

(5) *The significant forms of religious life are individual rather than social, personal rather than ecclesiastical.* At least that is the thesis of the present volume. It is in the fastnesses of the individual

soul and the uniqueness of each person's individual religious expression that one finds the creative sources of even the social forms of religious expression. This explains the loneliness that every great religious spirit experiences at some time or other in his religious career. Those who venture into the rarefied atmosphere of primary religious experience must be prepared for this. In our discussion of religious maturity we pointed out that such religion was creative. It follows that creative religion is also unique, and this uniqueness is bound up with the personal forms of the religious consciousness.

We cannot say that primary religious behavior is unique *in every respect*. There are many lively expressions of the religious life that are social in nature. The stimulating and suggestive character of group experience may engender an intensity both of inner and outer behavior that marks it as an "acute fever" rather than a dull habit. Furthermore, group influences are usually necessary in some degree for the implementation of religious impulses. But for our first views of religious truths and values, as they take form from the hidden resources of the cosmos, we must turn our gaze toward the unique and lonely soul of the religious individual.

(6) This brings us to the more general problem of the role of religion in creativity. *Not only may the religious life be creative in itself, but it often forms the background for other forms of creativity.* We have noted the heuristic quality in mature religion and the eternal incompleteness of the religious quest. Added to the uniqueness of the individual expression in religion, this quality of religion at its best helps to explain its fertilizing role in culture and civilization. But, as we have tried to point out, a paradox is involved. Often it is the interaction between religious faith and a certain degree of skepticism that results in insight. Through the paroxysmal conflict between faith and doubt the individual gains new vision, new truth, and new accomplishment.

But religion may stimulate fields other than its own, and it is often found associated with achievement and creativity. A generation ago the researches of S. S. Visher at Indiana University and Ellsworth Huntington at Yale showed that eminence was more apt to be found among children of clergymen and missionaries than in any other group. Particularly writers and statesmen are often found to have come from religious families, while Van Gogh is an especially good example of an artist whose origins and inspiration were essentially religious. But here again religion's influence is paradoxical, for often its role, wrongly directed, may be the exact reverse of creative. Its coercive hand may lie dead and stultifying on many a creative spirit.

(7) *Mystical experience constitutes an important, if not essential, element in the religious consciousness of most religious geniuses.* Obviously this element differs in intensity in different personalities, and it is very questionable whether it is wholesome in its most intense forms. Certainly in its inaccessibility to rational analysis and appraisal it provides a ready escape for the pseudo-religious spirit who wishes to avoid discipline and at the same time inflate his ego by congratulating himself on his reputation for piety. Furthermore, mysticism may lead to emotional excess. Yet it is doubtful whether religion would have survived the centuries without those immediate experiences of the presence of God that are to be marked not only among the great, but also in the ordinary believer during his moments of inspiration and uplift.

(8) *There are some ways in which religion and mental illness are allied.* That which deeply criticizes life, as true religion does, must to some degree stand apart from it. From the point of view of the mental hygienist, herein lies the danger of religion lived to its full intensity. We have seen this danger exhibited in lives such as those of George Fox, Anton Boisen, Jeremiah, and John Bunyan. Yet the man rejected by society may be in closest touch with its best interests. Like the pioneer who risks malnutrition to win a continent, so the prophet may risk social starvation in hewing a path through the trackless forest of spiritual doubt. He ventures to confirm the voice within that tells him there is something beyond. This social malnutrition may, and often does, result in unproductive madness. But in some cases it leads to a new vision that stamps the pioneer as a true prophet, a spiritual discoverer, a pioneer who has won through. The price of this victory may have been a deviation into madness—a sojourn among the lost.

(9) *Desire for success and social status plays a most important role in religion in its most visible forms.* Here the psychologist may

perform a service in helping to clarify the difference between the behavior of the churchgoer motivated by concern *for* his neighbor and of the one motivated by concern for *what his neighbor thinks*. The latter attitude aids in stimulating obedience to the *mores* and providing the social teamwork by which we live. Much of what we call common honesty, decency, charity, and good manners has its roots in this narrow form of ego-involvement rather than in a broader loyalty to basic religious truth. In this way we build our associations with a church, expressing in our religious behavior not our own individually developed convictions but the standards of our neighbors, the values of the world.

This is even to be seen—we might almost say especially to be seen —among the clergy, whom we might expect to demonstrate primary religion at its best. Yet often we find the clergyman vaunting himself, not so much because of the presence in his pews of publicans and sinners or the comfort given a woman taken in adultery, but because of the success of a building campaign, the numbers turned away at morning service, the leadership given a local charity drive, or the glitter of his ecclesiastical robes. Or, if he has achieved a position of sufficient eminence in his church, he glories that "thousands at his bidding speed and post o'er land and ocean without rest."

These reflections are wholesome not simply for a minister but for anyone who supposes himself religious and yet is caught up in the compulsive necessity of swimming with the tide of modern preconceptions and modern striving. But how else than by such swimming is the minister to stand before those shining demigods of our society, the bankers, captains of industry, engineers, people who manipulate metal and men, lawyers, doctors, and others whose income puts them at the top of the financial tree? They all may be members of his church, and he must meet them on their own ground and accept the things they value. But to what lengths of compromise should he go? Such is his dilemma.

This is not by way of deriding the clergy. It strikes us that there is no profession with a larger proportion of not other- but inner-directed individuals, a greater number of "holy and humble men of heart." All but a small minority of the worst offenders will recognize the point we are making. We are simply pointing out in psychological terms that pride is the deadliest of the Seven Deadly Sins, and the ego-involvement of many of the clergy concerns what they themselves call the "idols of the market place" and the cult of social status. What will hold true of even the most spiritually sensitive members of the church will certainly be true of the rank and file. And so it is basically the question of motivation and the problem of ego-involvement that helps us to understand why church members are usually no better than their neighbors. Few have passed through the trial of finding themselves and living, like Mrs. Oak, by that inner "thing" that they have discovered.[1] Religion, we are trying to say, if it is to be of the primary variety, involves in large degree the turning of one's back on the crowd and living by the motivation from within. This is a lesson we have learned from the convert, the prophet, the saint, and the mystic.

We may find the church ineffectual, and yet we cannot say that it is wrong in standing for the things that it does. If it backs truth-telling, the way to greater effectiveness does not lie in falsehood; the Commandment's "Thou shalt not steal" cannot be translated into a recommendation of embezzlement, nor should the traditional emphasis on sexual restraints be laid aside in favor of a crusade for adultery. It is not the wrongness of the church's teachings, but rather the superficiality of their influence on the worshiper that explains their ineffectiveness when we compare the churched with the unchurched. It is in his motives that the churchgoer falls short of religion. Even within the sanctuary his basic aims tend to be essentially secular—namely to comport himself decently, not before God but before his neighbor. Hence, in his weekday dealings his reasonable prejudice in favor of telling the truth is exercised more because it operates to maintain his business reputation; he realizes that embezzlement is hardly a royal road to respectability, while adultery is deemed permissible only if no one knows anything about it.

This superficiality of which we speak can be illustrated by the change in attitude toward drinking among American Protestant upper-middle class churchgoers since 1920. Thanks partly to the skillful advertising of the beverage alcohol industry, drinking has become respectable. While many still are not without their twinges of conscience while sipping a cocktail, and others deplore the nuisance

[1] See pp. 368–373.

of having to serve drinks, it has become accepted as bad manners even so much as to allude to what still is generally accepted as the church's traditional stand on drinking. It may be considered praiseworthy restraint to practice total abstinence, but how many upper-class church members are there who thereby would risk being relegated to the lower middle class? A symbol of upper-class status, upward mobility, and wealth, such as the "moderate" use of alcohol, just cannot be rejected by the average American still new to his money and insecure as to his social status. It is society and his class *mores*, not what he still vaguely considers the "will of God," that guide his actions.

And so church members may mouth such quaint phrases as those in which they acknowledge their sins and confess to being "miserable sinners" on Sunday. But the fact that they really believe no such thing is clearly to be seen on weekdays when they cannot be distinguished from those who do not go to church. So, except for sporadic outbursts of "revivals of religion" that do not last very long or go very deep, one is forced to turn to the sects for a demonstration of faith that really makes a difference in lives. But the psychologist dare not stop even there, for he is forced to look into the heart of man and seek out his motives. It is the individual, rather than social man, who best can be pronounced religious or irreligious.

(10) *The most essential and effective forms of religious behavior are demonstrated by only a tiny minority, a religious élite.* This is not to deny that genuine religion is widespread, nor that religion may be defined in such a way as to include nearly everyone. But what is called religion varies from the milk-and-watery gruel of conventional religious behavior, identified as tertiary or at best secondary religion, to the full-bodied and intense fever of mystics, saints, and prophets. It is these, whether prominent in the world's history or lost among the ranks of more commonplace people, who supply creative energy out of all proportion to their numbers. This influence is the "leaven in the loaf" of which Jesus spoke. It spreads out in concentric circles from its intense source in the individual, in some form or other, to touch even those who reject religion and would not recognize a saint if they saw one. It is this minority of

luminous individuals that is so influential in the complicated nexus which we call *culture*.

(11) *The most pervading reason for the eternal appeal of religion seems to be that religion more than any other human function satisfies the need for meaning in life.* Theoretical considerations point in this direction, and these are confirmed by empirical findings. Religion symbolizes the ultimate mystery of life and indicates a path without being able precisely to specify its end. The journey is unending, and the quest is capable of subordinating to itself all other human activities. At the end of the road lies God, the Beyond, the final essence of the Cosmos, yet so secretly hidden within the soul that no man is able to persuade another that he has fulfilled the quest. This cunning mystery that man pursues is partly a symbol of his own complexity as he looks within himself. What he finds seems partly nothing *but* himself, and partly resident in the farthest reaches *beyond* himself. He is baffled when he broods over that which may best explain his strange sojourn among the living, whence he has come, and whither he is so swifly hastening. But more often than any other explanation it is religion that seems to satisfy his restless spirit.

BIBLIOGRAPHY

BIBLIOGRAPHY

Allport, Floyd H. et al., "The Subject Matter and Methods of Social Psychology," Social Forces, 15 (1937), pp. 455–495.

Allport, Gordon W., Becoming: Basic Considerations for a Psychology of Personality. New Haven: Yale University Press, 1955.

———, The Individual and His Religion: A Psychological Interpretation. New York: The Macmillan Co., 1950.

———, The Nature of Prejudice. Cambridge, Mass.: Addison-Wesley Publishing Company, Inc., 1954.

———, Personality. New York: Henry Holt & Co., Inc., 1937.

———, The Use of Personal Documents in Psychological Science. New York: Social Science Research Council, 1942.

Allport, Gordon W., Gillespie, James M., and Young, Jacqueline, "The Religion of the Post-War College Student," Journal of Psychology, 25 (1948), pp. 3–33.

Allport, Gordon W., Vernon, P. E., and Lindzey, G., Study of Values. Boston: Houghton Mifflin Co., 1952.

Ames, Edward Scribner, The Psychology of Religious Experience. Boston: Houghton Mifflin Co., 1910.

Anonymous, Alcoholics Anonymous. New York: Works Publishing Co., 1941.

Anonymous, A Guide to the Twelve Steps of Alcoholics Anonymous. Pamphlet published by Alcoholics Anonymous of Akron, Ohio.

Anonymous, Basic Concepts of Alcoholics Anonymous. Pamphlet published by Alcoholics Anonymous.

Anonymous, Medicine Looks at Alcoholics Anonymous. Pamphlet published by The Alcoholic Foundation, New York.

Anonymous, "Psychiatry and Spiritual Healing," *The Atlantic Monthly*, 194:2 (August, 1954), pp. 39–43.

Augustine, Saint, *Confessions*; translated by J. G. Pilkington. New York: Boni and Liveright, 1927.

Barkley, K. L., "Development of the Moral Judgment of College Students," *Character and Personality*, 10 (1942), pp. 199–212.

Barnes, Harry Elmer, *Social Institutions*. New York: Prentice-Hall, Inc., 1942.

Barnett, Lincoln, "God and the American People," *Ladies' Home Journal*, September, 1948, pp. 37, 230–240.

Begbie, Harold, *More Twice-Born Men*. New York: G. P. Putnam's Sons, 1923.

———, *Twice-Born Men*. New York: Fleming H. Revell Co., 1909.

Bell, Howard Mitchell, *Youth Tell Their Story*. Washington, D. C.: American Council on Education, 1938.

Bell, John, *Projective Techniques*. New York: Longmans, Green & Co., Inc., 1948.

Benedict, Ruth, *Patterns of Culture*. Boston: Houghton Mifflin Co., 1934.

Bennett, John C., *Social Salvation*. New York: Charles Scribner's Sons, 1935.

Bergman, Paul, "A Religious Conversion in the Course of Psychotherapy," *American Journal of Psychotherapy*, 12 (January, 1953), pp. 41–58.

Boisen, Anton T., *The Exploration of the Inner World*. New York: Harper & Brothers, 1936.

———, The Genesis and Significance of Mystical Identification in Cases of Mental Disorder," *Psychiatry*, 15, 1952, pp. 287–296.

———, *Religion in Crisis and Custom: A Sociological and Psychological Study*. New York: Harper & Brothers, 1955.

———, "What Did Jesus Think of Himself?" *Journal of Bible and Religion*, 20 (1952), pp. 7–12.

Book of Common Prayer, According to the Use of the Protestant Episcopal Church in the U.S.A. New York: Oxford University Press, 1929.

Braden, C. S., "Why People Are Religious—a Study in Religious Motivation," *Journal of Bible and Religion*, 15 (1947), pp. 38–45.

Brand, H. (Ed.) *The Study of Personality: A Book of Readings*. New York: John Wiley & Sons, Inc., 1954.

Breckinridge, M. E. and Vincent, E. Lee, *Child Development*. Philadelphia: W. B. Saunders Co., 1943.

Britt, Steuart Henderson, *Social Psychology of Modern Life*. New York: Farrar & Rinehart, Inc., 1941; rev. ed., 1949.

Burnham, W. H., "The Study of Adolescence," *Pedagogical Seminary*, I (1891), p. 2 ff.

Bushnell, Horace, *Christian Nurture*. New York: Charles Scribner's Sons, 1861.

Buttrick, George A., *Prayer*. New York and Nashville: Abingdon-Cokesbury, 1942.

Cabot, Richard C., *What Men Live By: Work, Play, Love, Worship*. Boston: Houghton Mifflin Co., 1914.

Cabot, Richard C. and Dicks, R. L., *The Art of Ministering to the Sick*. New York: The Macmillan Co., 1934.

Callis, Robert, *A Casebook of Counseling*. New York: Appleton-Century-Crofts, Inc., 1955.

Carlyle, Thomas, *Sartor Resartus* and *On Heroes and Hero-Worship*; Everyman Edition. New York: E. P. Dutton & Co., Inc., 1908.

Cannon, W. B., *Bodily Changes in Pain, Hunger, Fear and Rage*. New York: Appleton-Century-Crofts, 1929.

Cattell, Raymond B., *Personality and Motivation Structure and Measurement*. Yonkers-on-Hudson: World Book Co., 1957.

Chave, E. J., "Measurement of Ideas of God," *Religious Education*, 27 (1932), pp. 252–254.

———, *Measure Religion: Fifty-two Experimental Forms*. Chicago: University of Chicago Book Store, 1939.

Chave, E. J. and Thurstone, L. L., *The Measurement of Social Attitudes: Attitude toward God*. Chicago: University of Chicago Press, 1931.

Clark, Elmer T., *The Psychology of Religious Awakening*. New York: The Macmillan Co., 1929.

Clark, Walter Houston, "How do Social Scientists Define Religion?" *Journal of Social Psychology*, 47 (February, 1958), pp. 143–147.

———, *The Oxford Group: Its History and Significance*. New York: Bookman Associates, Inc., 1951.

———, *The Oxford Group: Its Work in American Colleges and Its Effect on Participants*. Unpublished Ph.D. thesis: Harvard University, 1944.

———, "The Psychology of Religious Values," in *Personality*, Symposium No. 1. New York: Grune & Stratton, Inc., 1950.

———, "Sex Differences and Motivation in the Urge to Destroy," *Journal of Social Psychology*, 36 (1952), pp. 167–177.

Clark, Walter Houston, "A Study of Some of the Factors Leading to Achievement and Creativity, with Special Reference to Religious Skepticism and Belief," *Journal of Social Psychology*, 41 (1955), pp. 57–69.

Clark, Walter Houston and Warner, Caroline M., "The Relation of Church Attendance to Honesty and Kindness in a Small Community," *Religious Education*, 50 (September–October, 1955), pp. 340–342.

Coe, George Albert, *The Psychology of Religion*. Chicago: University of Chicago Press, 1916.

——, *The Spiritual Life: Studies in the Science of Religion*. New York: Eaton and Mains; Cincinnati: Jennings & Pye, 1900.

Cole, Luella, *Psychology of Adolescence*. New York: Rinehart & Co., 1954.

Cole, William G., *Sex in Christianity and Psychoanalysis*. New York: Oxford University Press, Inc., 1955.

Conklin, Edmund S., *The Psychology of Religious Adjustment*. New York: The Macmillan Co., 1929.

Curran, Charles A., *Counseling in Catholic Life and Education*. New York: The Macmillan Co., 1952.

Czatt, M. S., *The International Bible Students, Jehovah's Witnesses*; Yale Studies in Religion No. 4. Scottdale, Pennsylvania: Mennonite Press, 1933.

Daniels, A. H., "The New Life," *American Journal of Psychology*, VI (1893), pp. 61 ff.

Davis, Allison and Dollard, John, *Children of Bondage: The Personality Development of Negro Youth in the Urban South*. Washington, D. C.: American Council on Education, 1940.

Davis, Jerome, *Capitalism and its Culture*. New York: Farrar & Rinehart, Inc., 1935.

de Sanctis, Sante, *Religious Conversion*; translated by H. Augur. New York: Harcourt, Brace & Co., 1927.

Dollard, John, *Criteria for the Life History—With Analysis of Six Notable Documents*. New Haven: Yale University Press, 1935.

Dunlap, Knight, *Religion: Its Function in Human Life*. New York: McGraw-Hill Book Co., 1946.

Durkheim, Emile, "De la définition des phenomènes réligieux," *L'Année Sociologique*, 2, pp. 1–28.

——, *The Elementary Forms of the Religious Life*; translated by J. W. Swain. New York: The Macmillan Co., 1915.

Edwards, Jonathan, "A Treatise Concerning Religious Affections," Vol. III of Edwards' *Works*. New York: Leavitt & Trow, 1844.

Eister, Allan W., "Some Aspects of Institutional Behavior with Reference to Churches," *American Sociological Review*, 17 (1952), pp. 64–69.

English, Oliver Spurgeon and Pearson, Gerald H. J., *Emotional Problems of Living: Avoiding the Neurotic Pattern*. New York: W. W. Norton & Co., Inc., 1945.

Fagan, Gertrude, "Worship in a Young People's Group," *Religious Education*, 33 (1938), pp. 110–112.

Fallaw, Wesner, *Toward Spiritual Maturity*. Philadelphia: The Westminster Press, 1953.

Ferguson, L. W., *Personality Measurement*. New York: McGraw-Hill Book Co., 1952.

———, "The Evaluative Attitudes of Jonathan Swift," *Psychological Record*, 3 (1939), pp. 26–44.

Fichter, Joseph H., *Dynamics of a City Church*. Chicago: University of Chicago Press, 1951.

———, "The Profile of Catholic Religious Life," *American Journal of Sociology*, 58 (1952), pp. 145–149.

———, "What is a Parishioner?" *Theological Studies*, XIII, 2 (June, 1952).

Fox, George, *Journal*; Revised edition by J. L. Nickalls. Cambridge (Eng.): Cambridge University Press, 1952.

Franklin, Benjamin, *Autobiography*; Edited by F. W. Pine. New York: Henry Holt & Co., Inc., 1912.

Frazer, James George, *The Golden Bough*; 1 vol. abridged edition. New York: The Macmillan Co., 1922.

Freeman, Frank S., *Theory and Practice of Psychological Testing*. New York: Henry Holt & Co., Inc., 1950.

Freud, Sigmund, *The Basic Writings of Sigmund Freud*; translated and edited by A. A. Brill. New York: Modern Library, Inc., 1938.

———, *Beyond the Pleasure Principle*. London: Hogarth Press, Ltd., 1922.

———, *The Future of An Illusion*; translated by W. D. Robson-Scott. New York: Liveright Publishing Corp., 1949.

Fromm, Erich, *Man For Himself*. New York: Rinehart & Co., Inc., 1947.

———, *Psychoanalysis and Religion*. New Haven: Yale University Press, 1950.

Garrett, H. E., *Great Experiments in Psychology*. New York: D. Appleton-Century-Crofts, Inc., 1941.

Garrison, Karl C., *Psychology of Adolescence*; 4th edition. New York: Prentice-Hall, Inc., 1951.

Gee, Wilson, *Social Science Research Methods*. New York: Appleton-Century-Crofts, Inc., 1950.

Gibran, Kahlil, *The Prophet*. New York: Alfred A. Knopf, Inc., 1951.

Goode, William J. and Hatt, P. K., *Methods in Social Research*. New York: McGraw-Hill Book Co., 1952.

Gosse, Edmund, *Father and Son*. New York: Charles Scribner's Sons, 1908.

Gragg, Donald B., "Religious Attitudes of Denominational College Students," *Journal of Social Psychology*, 15 (1942), pp. 245–254.

Grensted, L. W., *The Psychology of Religion*. New York: Oxford University Press, Inc., 1952.

Hackman, G. G., Kegley, C. W., and Nikander, V. K., *Religion in Modern Life*. New York: The Macmillan Co., 1957.

Hall, G. Stanley, *Adolescence*; Vol. II. New York: Appleton-Century-Crofts, Inc., 1904.

Halliday, James L., *Mr. Carlyle—My Patient: A Psychosomatic Biography*. New York: Grune & Stratton, Inc., 1950.

Harding, Esther, *Adventure into Self*. New York: Longmans, Green & Co., 1956.

Harkness, Georgia, *The Dark Night of the Soul*. New York and Nashville: Abingdon-Cokesbury, 1945.

Harms, Ernest, "The Development of Religious Experience in Children," *American Journal of Sociology*, 50 (1944), pp. 112–122.

———, *Essentials of Abnormal Child Psychology*. New York: Julian Press, Inc., 1953.

Hartshorne, H. and May, M., *Studies in Deceit*. New York: The Macmillan Co., 1928.

———, *Studies in Service and Self-Control*. New York: The Macmillan Co., 1929.

Hartshorne, H., May, M., and Shuttleworth, F. K., *Studies in the Organization of Character*. New York: The Macmillan Co., 1930.

Havens, Joseph, *A Comparative Study of Self-Power and Other-Power in Religious Experience and in Client-Centered Therapy*. Ph.D. Dissertation, University of Chicago, 1956 (microfilm).

Havighurst, R. J. and Taba, H., *Adolescent Character and Personality*. New York: John Wiley & Sons, Inc., 1949.

Hegel, Georg Wilhelm Friedrich, *Lectures on the Philosophy of Religion*, Vol. I; translated by E. B. Speirs. London: Kegan Paul, Trench, Trübner & Co., 1895.

Heidbreder, Edna, *Seven Psychologies*. New York: Appleton-Century-Crofts, Inc., 1933.

Heiler, Friedrich, *Prayer: A Study in the History and the Psychology of Religion*; translated and edited by Samuel McComb. New York: Oxford University Press, Inc., 1932.

——, *The Spirit of Worship: Its Forms and Manifestations in the Christian Churches*; translated by W. Montgomery. New York: George H. Doran Co., 1926.

Helwig, Hjalmar, *Soul Sorrow: The Psychiatrist Speaks to the Minister*; translated from the Danish by Jeno Grano. New York: Pageant Press, 1955.

Herberg, Will, *Protestant-Catholic-Jew: An Essay in American Religious Sociology*. New York: Doubleday & Co., Inc., 1955.

Hilgard, E. R., *Theories of Learning*. New York: Appleton-Century-Crofts, Inc., 1956.

Hiltner, Seward, *The Counselor in Counseling*. New York and Nashville: Abingdon-Cokesbury, 1952.

——, *Pastoral Counseling*. New York and Nashville: Abingdon-Cokesbury, 1949.

——, *Religion and Health*. New York: The Macmillan Co., 1943.

Hocking, William Ernest, *The Meaning of God in Human Experience*. New Haven: Yale University Press, 1924.

Höffding, Harald, *The Philosophy of Religion*; translated by B. E. Meyer. New York: The Macmillan Co., 1906.

Hollingshead, A. B., *Elmtown's Youth*. New York: John Wiley & Sons, Inc., 1949.

Horrocks, John E., *The Psychology of Adolescence: Behavior and Development*. Boston: Houghton Mifflin Co., 1951.

Hunt, Chester L., "Religious Ideology as a Means of Social Control," *Sociology and Social Research*, 33 (1949), pp. 180–187.

Hurlock, Elizabeth B., *Adolescent Development*. New York: McGraw-Hill Book Co., 1949.

——, *Child Development*. New York: McGraw-Hill Book Co., 1942.

——, "The Value of Praise and Reproof as Incentives for Children," *Archives of Psychology*, No. 71 (1924).

Huxley, Aldous, *The Doors of Perception*. London: Chatto & Windus, 1954.

——, *Brave New World*. New York: Harper & Brothers, 1932.

James, William, *The Varieties of Religious Experience*; Modern Library Edition. New York: Random House, 1902.

——, *The Will to Believe*. New York, London and Bombay: Longmans, Green & Co., Inc., 1898.

Johnson, Paul E., *Christian Love*. New York and Nashville: Abingdon-Cokesbury, 1951.

———, *Personality and Religion*. New York and Nashville: Abingdon Press, 1957.

———, *Psychology of Religion*. New York and Nashville: Abingdon-Cokesbury, 1945.

Jones, Harold E., *Development in Adolescence*. New York: Appleton-Century-Crofts, Inc., 1943.

Jones, Rufus, *The Testimony of the Soul*. New York: The Macmillan Co., 1936.

Josey, C. C., *The Psychology of Religion*. New York: The Macmillan Co., 1927.

Jung, Carl G., *The Integration of Personality*. New York: Rinehart & Co., Inc., 1940.

———, *Modern Man in Search of a Soul*; translated by W. S. Dell and C. F. Barnes. New York: Harcourt, Brace & Co., Inc., 1933.

———, *Psychological Types*. New York: Harcourt, Brace & Co., Inc., 1923.

Kallen, Horace M., *Secularism is the Will of God*. New York: Twayne Publishers, Inc., 1954.

Kellogg, W. N. and Kellogg, L. A., *The Ape and the Child*. New York: McGraw-Hill Book Co., 1933.

Kempis, Thomas à, *The Imitation of Christ*. London: C. Kegan Paul, 1881.

Kierkegaard, Søren, *Fear and Trembling/The Sickness Unto Death*; translated and edited by W. Lowrie. Garden City, New York: Doubleday & Co., Inc., 1954.

———, *A Kierkegaard Anthology*; edited by R. Bretall. Princeton: Princeton University, Press, 1951.

Kinsey, Alfred C., *Sexual Behavior in the Human Female*. Philadelphia: W. B. Saunders Co., 1953.

———, *Sexual Behavior in the Human Male*. Philadelphia: W. B. Saunders Co., 1948.

Klein, David B., *Mental Hygiene: The Psychology of Personal Adjustment*. New York: Henry Holt & Co., Inc., 1944.

Kluckhohn, Florence. "The Participant Observer Technique in Small Communities," *American Journal of Sociology*, 46 (1940), pp. 331–343.

Kupky, Oskar, *The Religious Development of Adolescents*; translated by W. K. Trow. New York: The Macmillan Co., 1928.

Lake, Kirsopp, *Landmarks in the History of Early Christianity*. New York: The Macmillan Co., 1922.

Landis, Paul H., *Adolescence and Youth*. New York: McGraw-Hill Book Co., 1952.

Lantero, Erminie H., "The Problem of Suffering," *Pastoral Psychology*, 4 (1953), pp. 32–38.

Lee, R. S., *Freud and Christianity*. New York: A. A. Wyn, Inc., 1949.

Leonard, William Ellery, *The Locomotive God*. New York: Appleton-Century-Crofts, Inc., 1927.

Leslie, Elmer A., *Jeremiah*. Nashville: Abingdon Press, 1954.

Leuba, James H., *God or Man?* New York: Henry Holt & Co., Inc., 1933.

———, *A Psychological Study of Religion*. New York: The Macmillan Co., 1912.

———, *The Psychology of Religious Mysticism*. New York: Harcourt, Brace & Co., Inc., 1925.

———, "Religious Beliefs of American Scientists," *Harper's Magazine*, 169 (1934), pp. 291–300.

Liebman, Joshua L., *Peace of Mind*. New York: Simon and Schuster, Inc., 1946.

Ligon, Ernest M., *Dimensions of Character*. New York: The Macmillan Co., 1956.

———, *The Psychology of Christian Personality*. New York: The Macmillan Co., 1936.

Lipsky, Abram, *John Wesley, a Portrait*. New York: Simon and Schuster, Inc., 1928.

Lynd, R. S. and Lynd, H. M., *Middletown*. New York: Harcourt, Brace & Co., Inc., 1929.

———, *Middletown in Transition*. New York: Harcourt, Brace & Co., Inc., 1937.

McCann, Richard V., *Delinquency: Sickness or Sin*. New York: Harper & Brothers, 1957.

Maeder, Alphonse, *Ways to Psychic Health*, (trans. by T. Lit). New York: Charles Scribner's Sons, 1953.

McClelland, David C., *Personality*. New York: William Sloane Associates, Inc., 1951.

McConnell, Francis J., *The Prophetic Ministry*. New York and Cincinnati: Abingdon, 1930.

McDougall, William, *The Energies of Men*. New York: Charles Scribner's Sons, 1935.

———, *Outline of Psychology*. New York: Charles Scribner's Sons, 1923.

McGiffert, Arthur C., *Martin Luther: The Man and His Work*. New York: The Century Co., 1911.

McKenzie, John G., *Nervous Disorders and Religion; A Study of Souls in the Making*. London: Allen and Unwin, Ltd., 1951.

McNemar, Quinn, *Psychological Statistics*. New York: John Wiley & Sons, Inc., 1949.

MacLean, Angus H., *The Idea of God in Protestant Religious Education*, Contributions to Education, No. 410. New York: Teachers College, Columbia University, 1930.

Manwell, E. M. and Fahs, S. L., *Consider the Children, How They Grow*; revised edition. Boston: The Beacon Press, Inc., 1951.

Maritain, Jacques, *Three Reformers: Luther, Descartes, Rousseau*. New York: Charles Scribner's Sons, 1929.

Maslow, A. H. and Mittlemann, B., *Principles of Abnormal Psychology*; revised edition. New York: Harper & Brothers, 1951.

May, Rollo, *The Art of Counseling: How to Gain and Give Mental Health*. Nashville: Cokesbury, 1939.

————, *Man's Search for Himself*. New York: W. W. Norton & Co., Inc., 1953.

————, *The Meaning of Anxiety*. New York: The Ronald Press Company, 1950.

————, *The Springs of Creative Living; A Study of Human Nature and God*. New York and Nashville: Abingdon-Cokesbury, 1940.

Mead, Margaret, *Coming of Age in Samoa*. New York: William Morrow & Co., 1928.

Menninger, K. A., *The Human Mind*; 3rd edition. New York: Alfred A Knopf, Inc., 1945.

Mental Measurements Yearbooks, O. K. Buros, Ed., Highland Park, N. J. Gryphon Press.

Merry, F. K. and Merry R. V., *The First Two Decades of Life*. New York: Harper & Brothers, 1950.

Miller, N. E. and Dollard, John, *Social Learning and Imitation*. New Haven: Yale University Press, 1941.

Mottram, Vernon H., *The Physical Basis of Personality*. Baltimore: Penguin Books, Inc., 1944.

Munn, Norman L., *Psychology: the Fundamentals of Human Adjustment*; 2nd edition. Boston: Houghton Mifflin Co., 1951.

Murray, H. A. *et al.*, *Explorations in Personality: A Clinical and Experimental Study of Fifty Men of College Age*. New York: Oxford University Press, 1938.

Nelson, Erland N. P., "Religious Attitude Shifts and Overt Behavior,"

Mimeo obtainable from Prof. Nelson, Dept. of Psychology, University of South Carolina, Columbia, S. C.

Newman, Francis W., *The Soul, Its Sorrows and Aspirations*; 8th edition. London: Trübner & Co., 1868.

Niebuhr, H. Richard, *The Social Sources of Denominationalism*. New York: Henry Holt & Co., Inc., 1929.

Noble, Vernon, *The Man in Leather Breeches: The Life and Times of George Fox*. New York: Philosophical Library, Inc., 1953.

Nottingham, Elizabeth K., *Religion and Society*, Doubleday Short Studies in Sociology. Garden City, N. Y.: Doubleday & Co., Inc., 1954.

Oliver, John Rathbone, *Fear, the Autobiography of James Edwards*. New York: The Macmillan Co., 1934.

———, *Pastoral Psychiatry and Mental Health*. New York: Charles Scribner's Sons, 1932.

Ostow, M. and Scharfstein, B. A., *The Need to Believe: The Psychology of Religion*. New York: International Universities Press, Inc., 1954.

Otto, Rudolf, *The Idea of the Holy*; translated by J. W. Harvey. London: Oxford University Press, 1923.

Outler, Albert C., *Psychotherapy and the Christian Message*. New York: Harper & Brothers, 1954.

Page, James D., *Abnormal Psychology*. New York: McGraw-Hill Book Co., 1947.

Parker, W. R., and Dare, E. St. J., *Prayer Can Change Your Life: Experiments and Techniques in Prayer Therapy*. Englewood Cliffs, N. J.: Prentice-Hall, 1957.

Parsons, Talcott, *Religious Perspectives in College Teaching in Sociology and Social Psychology*. New Haven: The Hazen Foundation, no date.

———, *The Structure of Social Action*; 1st edition. New York: McGraw-Hill Book Co., 1937.

Pascal, Blaise, *Thoughts of Blaise Pascal*; translated by C. Kegan Paul. London: George Bell & Sons, 1889.

Pastoral Psychology, Special issue on Grief, Suicide and Bereavement, 4, (December, 1953).

Patterson, John, *Goodly Fellowship of the Prophets*. New York: Charles Scribner's Sons, 1948.

Perry, R. B., *The Thought and Character of William James*; briefer version. New York: George Braziller, Inc., 1954.

Phillips, D. B., Howes, E. B., and Nixon, L. M. (Eds.), *The Choice is Always Ours*. New York: Richard R. Smith, 1948.

Pierce, Elizabeth and Dillingham, Elizabeth, *Religious Doubts Among*

Middlebury Women. Unpublished term report, 1951. Copy in possession of the author.

Pratt, James B., *The Psychology of Religious Belief.* New York: The Macmillan Co., 1907.

———, *The Religious Consciousness: A Psychological Study.* New York: The Macmillan Co., 1920.

Prince, Morton, *The Dissociation of a Personality.* New York: Longmans, Green & Co., Inc., 1910.

Reichelt, Karl Ludvig, *Meditation and Piety in the Far East.* New York: Harper & Brothers, 1954.

Reik, Theodor, *Masochism in Modern Man.* New York: Farrar & Rinehart, 1941.

Ribble, Margaret A., *The Rights of Infants: Early Psychological Needs and Their Satisfaction.* New York: Columbia University Press, 1947.

Riesman, David *et al.*, *The Lonely Crowd.* Garden City, N. Y.: Doubleday Anchor Books, 1953.

Rhine, J. B., *The Reach of the Mind.* New York: William Sloane Associates, 1947.

Roberts, David E., *Psychotherapy and a Christian View of Man.* New York: Charles Scribner's Sons, 1950.

Rogers, Carl R., *Client-Centered Therapy.* Boston: Houghton Mifflin Co., 1951.

———, *Counseling and Psychotherapy.* Boston: Houghton Mifflin Co., 1942.

Rogers, Carl R. and Dymond, Rosalie F., *Psychotherapy and Personality Change.* Chicago: University of Chicago Press, 1954.

Rosenberg, Milton J., "The Social Sources of the Current Religious Revival." *Pastoral Psychology*, 8, 75, (June, 1957), pp. 31–40.

Ross, Murray G., *Religious Beliefs of Youth.* New York: Association Press, 1950.

Rousseau, Jean Jacques, *Émile; or, Education;* translated by B. Foxley (Everyman's Library edition). New York: E. P. Dutton & Co., Inc., 1911.

Salzman, Leon, "The Psychology of Religious and Ideological Conversion," *Psychiatry*, 16 (1953), pp. 177–187.

Savitz, H. A., "The Cultural Background of the Patient as Part of the Physician's Armamentarium," *Journal of Abnormal and Social Psychology*, 47 (April, 1952), pp. 245–254.

Schleiermacher, Friedrich, *On Religion* (trans. by J. Oman). London: Kegan Paul, Trench, Trübner & Co., 1893.

Schneider, Herbert W., *Religion in 20th Century America*. Cambridge, Mass.: Harvard University Press, 1952.

Schweitzer, Albert, *The Psychiatric Study of Jesus: Exposition and Criticism*. Boston: Beacon Press, Inc., 1948.

Sears, Robert R., *Survey of Objective Studies of Psychoanalytic Concepts*. New York: Social Science Research Council, 1943.

Shaffer, L. F. and Shoben, E. J., *The Psychology of Adjustment*. Boston: Houghton Mifflin Co., 1956.

Shand, J. Douglas, *A Factor-Analytic Study of Chicago Protestant Ministers' Conceptions of What it Means to be Religious*. Ph.D. dissertation, University of Chicago, 1953.

Schuster, George N. (Ed.), *The World's Great Catholic Literature*. New York: The Macmillan Co., 1944.

Skinner, B. F., *Science and Human Behavior*. New York: The Macmillan Co., 1953.

———, "Superstition in the Pigeon," *Journal of Experimental Psychology*, 38 (1948), pp. 168–172.

Smith, Preserved, *Erasmus*. New York: Harper & Brothers, 1923.

Snyder, William U., (Ed.), *Casebook of Non-Directive Counseling*. Boston: Houghton Mifflin Co., 1947.

Soper, D. W. (Ed.), *These Found the Way: Thirteen Converts to Protestant Christianity*. Philadelphia: The Westminster Press, 1951.

Sorokin, P. A., *The Crisis of Our Age*. New York: E. P. Dutton & Co., Inc., 1941.

———, *The Ways and Power of Love*. Boston: Beacon Press, Inc., 1954.

Sperry, Willard L., *Reality in Worship: a Study of Public Worship and Private Religion*. New York: The Macmillan Co., 1925.

Sprague, Theodore W., *Some Problems in the Integration of Social Groups with Special Reference to Jehovah's Witnesses*. Doctoral thesis, Division of Sociology, Harvard University, 1942.

Spranger, Eduard, *Lebensformen*. Halle: Max Niemeyer, 1924. *Types of Men*; authorized translation by P. J. W. Pigors, 1928.

Starbuck, Edwin Diller, *The Psychology of Religion*; 3rd edition. New York: Charles Scribner's Sons, 1912.

Stolz, Karl R., *Pastoral Psychology*. Nashville: Cokesbury Press, 1932.

———, *The Psychology of Prayer*. New York and Cincinnati: Abingdon Press, 1923.

———, *The Psychology of Religious Living*. Nashville: Cokesbury Press, 1937.

Stratton, George M., *Psychology of the Religious Life*. London: George Allen & Co., Ltd., 1911.

Strong, Anna Louise, *The Psychology of Prayer.* Chicago: University of Chicago Press, 1909.

Suttie, Ian D., *The Origins of Love and Hate.* New York: Julian Press, Inc., 1952.

Tawney, R. H., *Religion and the Rise of Capitalism.* New York: Harcourt, Brace & Co., Inc., 1926.

Taylor, W. S., *Dynamic and Abnormal Psychology.* New York: American Book Co., 1954.

Terman, Lewis M., *Genetic Studies of Genius*; 3 vols. Stanford: Stanford University Press, 1925, 1926, 1930.

Terman, L. M. and Merrill, M. A., *Measuring Intelligence.* Boston: Houghton Mifflin Co., 1937.

Thomas, W. I., *The Unadjusted Girl.* Boston: Little, Brown & Co., 1924.

Thomas, W. I. and Znaniecki, F., *The Polish Peasant in Europe and America*; 2 vols. New York: Alfred A. Knopf, Inc., 1927.

Thorndike, Edward L., *Your City.* New York: Harcourt, Brace & Co., Inc., 1939.

Thorold, Algar, *An Essay in Aid of the Better Appreciation of Catholic Mysticism Illustrated from the Writings of Blessed Angela of Foligno.* London: Kegan Paul, Trench, Trübner & Co., 1900.

Thouless, Robert H., *An Introduction to the Psychology of Religion.* Cambridge: Cambridge University Press, 1923.

Tiebout, Harry M., "Therapeutic Mechanism of Alcoholics Anonymous," in *Medicine Looks at Alcoholics Anonymous* reprinted from *The American Journal of Psychiatry,* January, 1944.

Tillich, Paul, *The Courage to Be.* New Haven: Yale University Press, 1952.

Toynbee, Arnold J., *A Study of History* (6 vols.). Oxford: Oxford University Press, Vols. 1–3, 1933; Vols. 4–6, 1939.

Underhill, Evelyn, *Mysticism: a Study in the Nature and Development of Man's Spiritual Consciousness.* New York: Meridian Books, Inc., 1955.

————, *Worship.* New York: Harper & Brothers, 1937.

Van Teslaar, J. S. (Ed.), *An Outline of Psychoanalysis.* New York: Modern Library, Inc., 1925.

Warner, William Lloyd, *Democracy in Jonesville: a Study in Quality and Inequality*; 1st edition. New York: Harper & Brothers, 1949.

Weatherhead, Leslie D., *Psychology, Religion, and Healing.* New York and Nashville: Abingdon-Cokesbury, 1951.

Wesley, John, *The Heart of Wesley's Journal*; P. L. Parker, ed. New York: Fleming H. Revell Co., no date.

White, R. K., "Black Boy: a Value Analysis," *Journal of Abnormal and Social Psychology*, 42 (1947), pp. 440–461.

——, "Value-Analysis: a Quantitative Method for Describing Qualitative Data," *Journal of Social Psychology*, 19 (1944), pp. 351–358.

White, Robert W., *The Abnormal Personality*. New York: The Ronald Press Co., 1948.

Wieman, H. N. and Wieman, R. W., *Normative Psychology of Religion*. New York: Thomas Y. Crowell Co., 1935.

Williams, Charles D., *The Prophetic Ministry for Today*. New York: The Macmillan Co., 1921.

Williams, J. Paul, "An Objective Approach to the Study of Worship," *Religious Education*, 40 (1945), pp. 218–227.

Wise, Carroll A., *Pastoral Counseling: Its Theory and Practice*. New York: Harper & Brothers, 1951.

Wolff, Werner (Ed.), *Psychiatry and Religion*. New York: MD Publications, Inc., 1956.

Wood, Ernest, *Great Systems of Yoga*. New York: Philosophical Library, Inc., 1954.

Woodworth, Robert S., *Contemporary Schools of Psychology*; revised edition. New York: The Ronald Press Co., 1949.

Woolman, John, *Journal and Essays of John Woolman*. London: The Macmillan Co., 1922.

Worcester, Elwood, *Religion and Medicine*. New York: Moffat, Yard & Co., 1908.

Worcester, Elwood and McComb, Samuel, *Body, Mind and Spirit*. Boston: Marshall Jones Co., 1931.

Yinger, J. Milton, *Religion, Society, and the Individual*. New York: The Macmillan Co., 1957.

Young, Kimball, "The Psychology of Hymns," *Journal of Abnormal and Social Psychology*, 20 (1926), pp. 391–406.

Young, Paul Thomas, *Emotion in Man and Animal*. New York: John Wiley & Sons, Inc., 1943.

Zaehner, R. C., *Mysticism*. Oxford: Oxford University Press, 1957.

STUDY AIDS

STUDY AIDS

These Aids, most of them tested in actual class use, have been prepared with many levels of academic competence in mind. The instructor or other leader must assist in adapting the material to the maturity of the readers.

Chapter 1 (Orientation)

SUGGESTIONS FOR FURTHER READING

The first or early chapters in any systematic book on the psychology of religion are apt to cover much the same ground that we have. Pratt's *The Religious Consciousness*, Chapter 1, has an excellent discussion of the definition and general nature of religion. Always stimulating, James treats the subject in Lecture 2 of *Varieties*. Chapter 1, sections 1, 2, and 15 of Johnson's *The Psychology of Religion* is clearer but not so thought-provoking as Pratt and James. In Stolz, *The Psychology of Religious Living*, the pertinent chapters are 1, 2, and 8. The first three chapters and bibliographical comment of Grensted's excellent little volume on *The Psychology of Religion* are worth noting. The first two chapters of Yinger's *Religion, Society and the Individual* discuss the definition and nature of religion.

Throughout his study the reader will find contemporary reading in articles from *The Journal of Pastoral Care, Religious Education,* and *Pastoral Psychology,* of which probably the last-named is the most popular and readable. Other religious and psychological journals will print an occasional article in the field. Probably the best way to locate articles on religion in psychological journals is to consult the yearly index number of *Psychological Abstracts*, while occasionally *Sociological Abstracts* and the *Education Index* will be helpful. The Society for the Scientific Study of Religion issues a bibliography twice a year. (Write the author for information.)

TOPICS FOR DISCUSSION

1. Do you think that the scientific approach to the study of religion is wholesome for religion? Support your ideas by concrete examples.

2. What is the reason for the recent publication of so many books on the subject of religion and mental health?

3. Most psychology books written more than 30 years ago are now out of date. Why do you think that this is not true of many works on the psychology of religion like those by James, Pratt, and Otto?

4. In what sense is religion too sacred or subtle to be studied?

5. Discuss the reasons for the backwardness of the psychology of religion, appraising the reasons given in the chapter and adding some of your own.

6. A philosophical issue of importance both to psychologists and religious thinkers is the following: Many psychologists are strict positivistic thinkers who hold that man is fundamentally a biological organism determined by his environment and operating by rigid laws of cause and effect. If we knew everything about man and his behavior so that we could control all life processes, at least theoretically, it would be possible to mold him as we choose. Dictators have taken a step in this direction by utilizing the familiar procedures of brain-washing. But the psychologist may use this knowledge for good also. Thus it would be theoretically possible by proper control of diet, heredity, and environment for the biologists and the psychologists to create a saint, a prophet, a mystic, or any type of religious personality that could be accurately described. (See Huxley's *Brave New World* or Orwell's *1984.*)

Discuss this proposition. This issue is of such fundamental importance for your basic attitude toward the psychology of religion that you may wish to return to it several times before you finish your study.

PROBLEMS FOR INVESTIGATION AND RESEARCH

1. Look up writings on the psychology of religion before 1900. Report on the ideas and characteristics you find.

2. Read and present a book review of one of the important works on the psychology of religion described in the chapter.

3. Interview several psychologists, philosophers, religious scholars, and ministers about their attitudes toward the psychology of religion in order to compare them. If you standardized the interview or devised a simple questionnaire, then collected enough cases, your results might be significant enough for publication.

4. Compare the number of items under "Religion" in the Index of *Psychological Abstracts* from year to year to see what this indicates as to the interest of psychologists in religion.

Chapter 2 (What is Religion?)

SUGGESTIONS FOR FURTHER READING

See these suggestions for Chapter 1.

TOPICS FOR DISCUSSION

1. Formulate and defend your own definition of religion.

2. Give examples from your own experience of what you would classify as *primary*, *secondary*, and *tertiary* religious experience. Can scientific principles be devised for telling them apart? If so, what are these principles?

3. Is anyone really incapable of a religious experience? Discuss.

4. Do you agree that the psychologist of religion must be neutral about the existence of God? Discuss.

5. Do you agree with William James, as quoted at the head of the chapter, that there is little profit in studying religion in people other than those in whom it is "an acute fever"?

PROBLEMS FOR INVESTIGATION AND RESEARCH

1. Collect as many definitions of religion as you can from printed sources. Classify these according to categories suggested in the chapter, or your own. Also note the disciplines or backgrounds of the authors. Do you find, for example, that definitions given by psychologists, or philosophers, or religious scholars, tend to have common characteristics? How do you explain the differences that you find?

2. Collect definitions of religion from various people. Classify and compare these as suggested in Problem 1 above. Try to secure interviews with your informants to discover what has influenced them in their definitions. Has it been personal experience, what they have been told, what

they have read, or has it been the requirements of their studies if they have been students of religion?

3. In your class, or in any other group, try to work out a group definition of religion. After this has been done, secure unsigned comments or criticisms from the group to find out to what extent the definition has really been accepted by all members. This may throw some light on the difficulties of agreement in studying religion.

4. Appraise the life of some well-known personage, where sufficient data exist, as to what extent his religious life falls into each of the three categories of *primary*, *secondary*, and *tertiary*.

Chapter 3 (Methods)

SUGGESTIONS FOR FURTHER READING

Johnson's *The Psychology of Religion*, Chapter 1, Secs. 2–3, treats methods very briefly. Pratt's *The Religious Consciousness* does not throw much light on specific methodology but treats rather thoroughly the philosophy of scientific psychology as it concerns religion. Munn's writing is always clear and thorough. Chapter 2 of his *Psychology* gives an excellent introduction to the scientific method in psychology. G. W. Allport's monograph, *The Use of Personal Documents in Psychological Science*, should be read by everyone intending to use personal documents for research in the field of personality and religion. Furthermore it is sufficiently well written to be stimulating to the psychologically sophisticated general reader. Chapter 9 in Stolz, *The Psychology of Religious Living*, deals with methods, while Chapter 10 discusses schools of psychological thought that impinge on the psychology of religion. The most extensive and up-to-date discussion of psychological methods applied to religion is to be found in Ligon's *Dimensions of Character*. However, it is diffuse and hardly adapted to a quick review. Brand's *The Study of Personality* is a generalized treatment of the subject for the advanced student, while Ferguson's *Personality Measurement* is another good reference. Cattell's *Personality and Motivation Structure and Measurement* is recent and very full. It features factor-analysis.

TOPICS FOR DISCUSSION

1. Make a list of the skills, background information, and specific qualifications with which the scholar must be equipped if he is (a) to study the subject profitably, or (b) to become an expert who will make creative contributions to the field.

2. What specific aspects of the religious life can usefully be studied by the psychologist and by what methods? What cannot or should not be? Give reasons for your conclusions.

3. Make a list of pieces of religious writing with which you are familiar that might be classified as "personal documents." How might they be scientifically studied so as to be useful to the psychologist?

4. Are there depths in, and insights into the religious life which have been sensed by religious people that no mere psychologist would ever discover? If you think there are, cite examples. Can the psychologist make any use of such insights or study them? If so by what methods? Compare the scientific and intuitive approach to religious truth. (In this connection you will find stimulating reading in Chapter 19, "Inference and Intuition," of Allport's *Personality*.)

5. Discuss the advantages and shortcomings of any of the psychological instruments described in the chapter as useful in studying religion, such as the questionnaire, the experiment, rating scales, etc.

PROBLEMS FOR INVESTIGATION AND RESEARCH

1. Design a projective test with generalized religious stimuli to distinguish between differing types of religious personalities, perhaps between a predominantly *primary* as opposed to a *secondary* or *tertiary* personality. This project would require considerable in the way of both psychological and religious background.

2. Devise an experiment to evaluate some aspect of a religious program; for example, the difference in instructional and emotional impact of the King James as compared with another version of the Bible, or the difference in effectiveness of two different types of worship.

Chapter 4 (Sources of Religion)

SUGGESTIONS FOR FURTHER READING

Probably the best brief up-to-date discussion of the psychological sources of religion is Chapter 1 of Allport's *The Individual and His Religion*. Lecture 1 in James' *Varieties* is interesting but rather narrowly confined to a discussion of sexual and pathological origins of religion and the significance of origins in general. The first part of A. T. Boisen's *The Exploration of the Inner World* makes a highly original and fascinating piece of documentation for James' thesis by a former mental patient who was also a deeply religious man. Chapter 3 of Pratt's *The*

Religious Consciousness, though somewhat out of date, is an interesting discussion of the unconscious as a source of religion. Chapters 2–4 in Stolz, *The Psychology of Religious Living,* touch on topics discussed in our chapter, while Chapter 15 approaches religion from the point of view of the three faculties. Chapter 2 in Johnson's *The Psychology of Religion* is pertinent but needs more illustration. An excellent source of the latter is Phillips' anthology of psychological and religious insight, *The Choice is Always Ours.* Selections related to our discussion will be found throughout the book, but perhaps one might start with Chapter 1. Those interested in magic as a source of religion will find a witty and beautifully written discussion in Chapter 4, "Magic and Religion," of Frazer's *The Golden Bough,* though it should be noted that not all scholars agree with Frazer's theories. Those with a background in Freud who are interested in his views of religion should consult the sources indicated in the notes. Those interested in a discussion of the relation of religion and anxiety should consult Tillich's *The Courage to Be.*

TOPICS FOR DISCUSSION

1. Mention and discuss some sources of religion not covered in the chapter.

2. When religion is derived from a sense of personal need, does this not mean that it is essentially selfish? Do you agree with James that it is the psychological results rather than the psychological origins that determine its value?

3. Do you think the religious urge is innate? What evidence can you cite to support or refute this view?

4. If you agree with the view that religious institutions cater too much to the death urge, what changes would you suggest so that they might better serve the life urge?

5. By what plan of attack or technique could the psychologist acquire a more exact idea of what the sources of religion are?

6. Discuss religion as that which gives meaning to life. What about other sources of meaning? Is religion pre-eminent here?

PROBLEMS FOR INVESTIGATION AND RESEARCH

1. Design and circulate a questionnaire designed to discover how many feel they have had a religious experience and what its sources were. You will find many who will be willing to co-operate, particularly if you pay them a personal call. Indeed, an interview would be the best way of collecting answers, which will give you a chance for follow-up,

and the interviewee a chance to expand points that seem of significance *to him*. But there should be some standardization of the interviews for best comparability.

2. Look up H. A. Murray's system of personal needs and show to what extent they may be sources of the religious life.

3. Investigate McClelland's "two-factor theory of motivation" and point out its implications for religion. Devise a way to separate those who have been *attracted* to religion from those who have been *driven* to it. Test their behavior and attitudes to discover whether there is any real difference.

4. Make a detailed study of the sources of religion as conceived by some prominent psychologist who has written on the subject, such as Freud or Jung. (Jung, particularly, should be tackled only by an advanced student.)

Chapter 5 (Childhood)

SUGGESTIONS FOR FURTHER READING

Chapter 5 of Pratt's *The Religious Consciousness* is a well-illustrated discussion of the child's religion. Manwell and Fahs' *Consider the Children—How They Grow*, especially Chapters 1, 6, 13, 14, and 15, is a very readable account by two women who have had much close contact with children. The approach is liberal, both educationally and theologically. Parts of Chapters 12 and 13 in Hurlock's well-documented *Child Development* are pertinent, while Chapter 12 of Merry and Merry's *The First Two Decades of Life* is equally well-documented and somewhat better written. Harms' "The Development of Religious Experience in Children" tells of his important study in an article that is both readable and stimulating, while MacLean's *The Idea of God in Protestant Education* is another account of research worth looking into. Allport's *The Individual and His Religion*, Chapter 2, and Johnson's *The Psychology of Religion*, Chapter 3, contain brief treatments of the subject. Chapter 2 of Book II of *Sartor Resartus* is a charming and poetic memoir of Carlyle's childhood and the place of religion in it. The personage Teufelsdröckh is essentially Carlyle himself.

TOPICS FOR DISCUSSION

1. Give examples from your own experience of the religious traits of the child mentioned in the chapter. Do you disagree with any of the

statements, and can you support your disagreement? Perhaps you can give examples of "childish" religious traits among adults.

2. Pratt says, "Theology has to be taught; religion cannot be." Is this wholly true?

3. Do you agree that the child will develop stronger feelings of conscience if unable to understand the implications of what he is taught? If so how should this influence the religious training of the child? Do you see any pertinence of Fromm's concepts of the "authoritarian" and "humanistic" conscience here?

4. Is Santa Claus a wholesome fiction for the child's mind? What should the parent or teacher do about the teaching of religious myths in which he does not believe?

5. What do you think are the most important factors in a child's religious development and what are the implications for religious education? What about rote learning?

6. Just what is meant by "treating a child with respect," and what is the significance of this for religious education?

PROBLEMS FOR INVESTIGATION AND RESEARCH

1. Try to work out a piece of research that will isolate the influence of fantasy in the young child to show that children who have been protected from fantasy develop superior or inferior religious concepts when they are older. Most important and difficult in such a study will be your provision for control that *association* and *cause* not be confused.

2. Devise an empirical method for testing the effectiveness of some procedure in religious education, such as teaching honesty, reverence, or sound intellectual concepts. Again be careful about control.

3. By proper stimulus, perhaps a variation of the techniques of Harms or MacLean, elicit the religious concepts of a large group of children. Analyze them for substantiation or refutation of ideas set forth in this chapter.

4. Review and evaluate from a scientific viewpoint (a) empirical studies of practices in religious education; or (b) the practices themselves in homes or in some particular religious denomination.

Chapter 6 (Adolescence and Youth)

SUGGESTIONS FOR FURTHER READING

Sources mentioned under "Suggestions" at the end of the previous chapter also appropriate to youth include the items under Allport, Harms,

Johnson, and Merry and Merry. Kupky's *The Religious Development of Adolescents* is a short book which analyzes the religious consciousness of adolescents through their literary productions. Chapter 6 of Pratt's *The Religious Consciousness* contains thoughtful observations. Chapter 9 in Garrison's *The Psychology of Adolescence*, 4th edition, is somewhat pedestrian yet full of pertinent factual information. Chapter 6 in Havighurst and Taba's excellent study, *Adolescent Character and Personality*, briefly treats the relation of the church to character formation, while a more sociological approach in a companion study will be found in Chapter 10 of *Elmtown's Youth* by Hollingshead. Both are well written. Chapter 10 of Hurlock's *Adolescent Development* mentions a number of empirical studies, while Landis' *Adolescence and Youth*, 2nd edition, Chapter 10, is another source with sociological emphasis. Ross' *The Religious Beliefs of Youth* is the most thorough study existent directed exclusively to examining the religion of youth. Its statistics are well digested and interpreted, and the book cannot be neglected by anyone with a scholar's interest in this field. Chapter 9 of Ross reviews other studies in the area. The Character Education Project at Union College, Schenectady, represents a unique attempt to apply scientific methods based on Christian assumptions to the development of character. It is described in E. M. Ligon's *Dimensions of Character*. A recent study of delinquency which considers religious factors among others is Richard V. McCann's *Delinquency: Sickness or Sin*, a readable and perceptive source.

TOPICS FOR DISCUSSION

1. Are girls more religious than boys? How does the religion of the sexes differ in adolescence? Can you account for this?

2. What characteristics distinguish the religion of adolescence from that of childhood?

3. How valuable in adolescence is an experience of doubt? To what extent are this and other forms of religious stress culturally determined? In this connection compare the experiences of typical Catholic, Protestant, and Jewish youth. (See Ross for some exact information here.)

4. How does social class affect the religion of youth? (See Hollingshead for information.) Are conditions here as they should be according to religious teachings? Could matters be improved, and if so, how?

5. From your observation do you agree that youth tends to neglect institutional religion? How would you suggest the churches solve the perennial "youth problem," of which they so often complain?

6. What does the average college student conceive as being "religious"? Psychologically how do you explain the attitude toward religion of college students you may know? Is religion a real "force" in their lives, and if not, should it be? Do you think that the college has any responsibility toward the religion of students; and if so, how should this be implemented?

PROBLEMS FOR INVESTIGATION AND RESEARCH

1. Devise a questionnaire and make a survey of a group of youth to which you have access. Focus on some aspect of their religious life which you feel significant, such as church attendance, the practice of prayer, doubt, or other questions raised in this chapter which you can test for yourself.

2. Review studies of the interaction of church membership and morals in the field of youth. Interpret these results for yourself, perhaps against a background of our concepts of *primary, secondary,* and *tertiary* religious behavior.

3. Make a survey of the "youth problem" in one or more churches. Since youth is not always aware of its own psychological urges, you may have to use a certain amount of subtlety in questioning and interpreting results. Remember that you must have the confidence of those whom you expect to co-operate. Mere written questionnaires should be followed up by case interviews whenever possible.

4. Make a thorough psychological case study of one individual adolescent in order to appraise his religious life. This should include home and family background, data from school and church, the peer-group, intelligence and other psychological test data, an autobiography, and a series of interviews. Though they are not particularly concerned with religion and are not comprehensive, *Development in Adolescence* by Harold E. Jones, and perhaps the excellent case studies of adolescents in Davis and Dollard's *Children of Bondage* will be instructive for you to read.

Chapter 7 (Doubt and Conflict)

SUGGESTIONS FOR FURTHER READING

Probably the best psychological analysis of doubt is to be found in Chapter 5 of G. W. Allport's *The Individual and His Religion.* However, Starbuck's *The Psychology of Religion,* Chapters 17–19, contains a very stimulating discussion of both doubt and conflict, supported by figures and case material. Pratt's chapter on "Adolescence" in his *The Religious Consciousness* is given over very largely to a discussion of doubt. Chapter 7 of Johnson's *The Psychology of Religion* on "Belief" contains a brief section on doubt. Chapter 23 of Wieman's *Normative Psychology of Religion* approaches the subject more philosophically.

On religious conflict James' chapter, "The Divided Self," in *Varieties* is characteristically well written, meaty, and supplied with copious case material. The reader will find a number of references to conflict if he consults the index to Wieman's book, before mentioned, though Wieman's discussions throughout his book tend to be general and without the wealth of illustration that makes James so much more lively and clear.

For the subject of psychological conflict in general, the thorough student will of course want to consult Freud. The concept is one of the cornerstones of psychoanalytical thinking of all shades. Good brief accounts will be found in Munn, Chapter 13; Klein's *Mental Hygiene*, Chapter 14; and Taylor's *Dynamic and Abnormal Psychology*, Chapter 9.

"The Everlasting No" chapter in *Sartor Resartus* is a vivid and classical introspective account of Carlyle's experience of doubt, while the reader will find additional documentary material if he follows up the citations from Augustine and Bunyan given in our chapter.

TOPICS FOR DISCUSSION

1. Give examples of the effect of doubt on religion. On the whole has it been a wholesome or unwholesome factor? Should it be encouraged in youth?

2. Think of examples of individual cases of doubt of which you may have knowledge and try to explain them in terms of the categories presented in the chapter. Can you add other categories?

3. If you were a religious educator, how would you handle particular cases of doubt; such as doubt of God, immortality, the Ten Commandments, the divinity of Christ, the Apostles' Creed, the Resurrection, etc.?

4. How important are religious origins as a means of determining religious truth? How is religious truth established?

5. Is the "religious agnostic" really religious?

6. Do you agree that the confusion of magic with religion is the source of much doubt among thoughtful people? Could you give concrete examples of magical presuppositions in organized religion or in personal religious practices and beliefs?

7. Supply concrete examples of religious conflicts and try to evaluate the effect on personality. Compare examples and try to explain why a certain conflict is severe with one person while a similar conflict seems to be of little importance to someone else. What forms do religious conflicts take, other than those described in the chapter? Distinguish doubt which brings conflict, from normal doubt.

8. The statement was made that it is possible that a tertiary religious personality may feel a conflict between love and religious loyalty even more keenly for the very reason that the loyalty is based on no essential religious experience. What do you think was meant by this statement, and do you agree with it?

PROBLEMS FOR INVESTIGATION AND RESEARCH

1. If religion is to be passed on from parent to child, it is important that at some point religious attitudes of the parent be "interiorized" or appropriated by the child as his own if they are to be accepted. Important in this process are good relations or *rapport*. Set up an empirical investigation to discover to what extent rejection and hostility of the parent toward the child may lead to religious doubt and conflict.

2. By means of questionnaire and interview make a study of religious doubt and conflicts of a certain group. Analyze these according to the categories suggested in the chapter.

3. Try to correlate actual cases of religious doubt or conflict with any factors that you think might be associated with them as causes, such as intelligence, educational level, religious tradition, etc., or as results, such as mental health, religious creativity or the lack of it, ethical behavior, etc.

4. Collect data on the prevalence of magic in contemporary religion and try to relate this to resulting doubt. For instance, one might mingle magical and religious statements on a check list and ascertain whether those who could best distinguish between them tended to be believers or doubters.

Chapter 8 (Healthy-Mindedness and Suffering)

SUGGESTIONS FOR FURTHER READING

All students should be familiar with the two sections in James' *Varieties* on which this chapter is based, "The Religion of Healthy-Mindedness" and "The Sick Soul." Some might like to follow up some of his cases and allusions, particularly *The Soul, Its Sorrows and Aspirations*, by Francis W. Newman, who first developed the concepts of the *once-born* and *twice-born*. Otherwise specific psychological discussion of these two types of religion is rare; of healthy-mindedness because this type is not interested in introspection so that documents are few, of the sick soul because psychologists have not given suffering the attention it deserves. Yet healthy-mindedness is approached to a certain extent in treatments of mental health and religion, and the student may find pertinent reading listed in the Suggestions for Chapter 16.

We know of no really competent psychological treatment of religious suffering, unless Boisen's *The Exploration of the Inner World* might qualify, though a good brief article on "The Problem of Suffering" by E. H. Lantero appeared in *Pastoral Psychology* for June, 1953. The December, 1953, issue of that periodical was devoted to Grief, Suicide, and Bereavement. By far the best reading on suffering is by a theologian with many psychological insights; Georgia Harkness' *Dark Night of the Soul*, particularly the first three chapters, is readable, well supplied with case material, and filled with both religious and psychological insight. Another good book dealing with modern anxiety against a background of the Christian existentialist position, is more difficult reading: Paul Tillich's *The Courage to Be*. Otherwise, suffering must be approached through intimate documents of a literary and personal nature, such as *The Book of Job*, Amiel's *Journal*, Tennyson's "In Memoriam," Bunyan's *Grace Abounding*, and the *Journal* of George Fox.

Browning's "Rabbi Ben Ezra" might be read as a typically healthy-minded approach to dark problems. Carlyle was never healthy-minded, but "The Everlasting Yea" chapter of *Sartor* may be contrasted with "The Everlasting No" as being the *more* healthy-minded. Both contain much matter on suffering. Chapter 5 of J. M. Yinger's *Religion, Society, and the Individual* discusses some contemporary expressions of religious healthy-mindedness and suffering.

TOPICS FOR DISCUSSION

1. Analyze different religious movements or well-known religious personalities in terms of the sick soul and the healthy-minded.

2. Do you agree that the healthy-minded believer tends to be superficial as compared to the sick soul? Illustrate. Need the person concerned about suffering and evil be a sick soul? To what extent is healthy-mindedness a blindness to evil? A matter of temperament? Psychologically valid and desirable? Less creative?

3. In religious teaching, how can allowance be made for growth through both healthy-mindedness and suffering? Be specific. How much can we control the religious development of another so that it will be healthy-minded or involve suffering? How would the philosophy of religious education typical of the two types differ? Support your statements by examples.

4. Do you agree that healthy-mindedness is losing ground in the world of today? Give examples pro and con. What is your estimate of the value of the two types to society?

5. In your opinion do the sick soul and healthy-mindedness express Freud's death instinct and life instinct respectively? Jung's introverted and extroverted types?

6. Do you agree with James that women are more apt to be healthy-minded than men?

PROBLEMS FOR INVESTIGATION AND RESEARCH

1. Make a thorough study to determine to what extent healthy-mindedness is manifested, and to what extent there is allowance for and emphasis on suffering in (a) Horace Bushnell's *Christian Nurture*, (b) any denomination's theory of religious education or its practice, or (c) the theology of a particular theologian or religious leader.

2. By use of a reliable adjustment scale or other measure of adjustment, try to correlate the mental health of a group of people brought up under a severe theology with an otherwise comparable one brought up in liberalism. Or by use of an introversion-extroversion scale make a similar correlation. Try to distinguish in your study between primary, secondary, and tertiary religious personalities. Why is this last caution necessary?

3. Devise some method to measure as accurately as you can the effect on healthy-mindedness of certain religious practices such as confession, worship, hymn singing, etc. Be careful to distinguish between cause and effect.

Chapter 9 (Conversion)

SUGGESTIONS FOR FURTHER READING

Nearly all systematic volumes on the psychology of religion have a section or a chapter on conversion. Lectures 8–10 in James' *Varieties* deal with it and contain a wealth of case material as well as theoretical discussion. The same is true of Chapters 7-9 in Pratt's *The Religious Consciousness*. More pedestrian treatments will be found in Johnson, 4, Stolz, 13, Wieman, 9, and Coe, 10. The two extensive empirical studies of conversion that should not be neglected by the thorough student are those found particularly in Part I and throughout Starbuck's *The Psychology of Religion* and E. T. Clark's *The Psychology of Religious Awakening*. Those interested in religious education will find Chapters 5 and 8 of the latter of particular value. A fascinating collection of first-hand accounts of modern conversions, though mostly of a more gradual nature, may be found in *These Found the Way*, edited by D. W. Soper.

It will also be very instructive to study evangelistic movements that feature conversion. One of the most famous and effective of these was the Methodist movement, credited with changing the religious climate of England within a generation through the spiritual power and organizing genius of John Wesley. The *Journal* of Wesley and nearly any biography will give an account of the movement, a particularly readable one being *John Wesley* by Lipsky, especially 12, 13, and 18. A vital modern movement is that of Moral Re-Armament, an account of which is to be found in the author's *The Oxford Group*. Part III contains a large number of case studies of conversion showing the varying effects of the movement on different people. The book *Alcoholics Anonymous* gives many accounts of conversion operating to cure alcoholism.

TOPICS FOR DISCUSSION

1. What are your opinions of the values of crisis conversion as compared with gradual awakening? Is conviction of sin necessary? What evidence do you have to support your views?

2. Do you agree that the psychologist should not concern himself with God? Where do you think God comes in or might come into the conversion process? How will one's theology affect it?

3. In what way does conversion support or weaken particular theories about the personality, such as the existence of the unconscious mind and the possibilities of changing personality through *catharsis* or emotional *trauma*? Compare examples of change through conversion and non-religious processes, such as psychotherapy.

4. Since conversion can be manipulated and suggested to some degree, are religious educators well advised to encourage it? What are its dangers as well as its advantages? Give evidence. How can we distinguish those for whom conversion might be possible and profitable from those for whom it would not?

5. William James says, "Converted men as a class are indistinguishable from natural men." How do you explain this statement, and do you agree with it?

6. What do you think of the theory of "conversion shock" and how helpful it is in explaining the personality changes that may accompany conversion? In what sense is conversion a "trauma"?

1. Define crisis conversion and gradual growth very carefully; then make a study of the proportions of certain religious groups or sections of the population who have experienced each. It will be well to check as many statements as possible by personal interview and the testimony of others. Test your own hypotheses or some proposed in this chapter such as: that more religious workers experience crisis conversion than non-religious workers; that conversion is preceded by unrest; that members of certain churches are more apt to be converted than members of others; that stern theology increases the likelihood of conversion.

2. Make a study of famous converts or of a particular revival movement to see how closely they confirm statements in our chapter. Contemporary movements making use of conversion include Moral Re-Armament, Alcoholics Anonymous, and Billy Graham's campaigns.

3. Make a thorough psychological study of some convert to whom you have ready access and who is willing to co-operate. It is possible that standard personality tests and surveys, such as the Allport-Vernon *Study of Values*, the Bernreuter *Personality Inventory*, the *Minnesota Multiphasic Personality Inventory*, or similar instruments may help you with this.

4. Compile a bibliography of contemporary studies of conversion. Organizations that might be of help in discovering such studies include the Society for the Scientific Study of Religion, W. H. Clark, Sec., Hartford Seminary Foundation, Hartford 5, Conn.; or the Research Society for Creative Altruism, P. A. Sorokin, Founder, 8 Cliff St., Winchester, Mass.

Chapter 10 (Faith)

The last chapter of Allport's *The Individual and His Religion*, "The Nature of Faith," contains an excellent summary of the way an individual validates his faith, and an original and suggestive section on the "religious intention." It is stimulating throughout. In James' *Varieties* material pertinent to belief will be found in Lectures 18 and 20, and also in the Postscript, though all of these tend to be more philosophical than psychological in nature. Pratt's *The Religious Consciousness* contains two good chapters on the belief in God and the belief in immortality, treated separately. Ross's *Religious Beliefs of Youth* is probably as good a source of empirical information about belief and its meaning as there is.

Freud's *The Future of an Illusion* gives his speculations as to why people believe, though this work is not one of his best. The psychoanalytical point of view is well summarized, more readably, in Ostow and Scharfstein's *The Need to Believe*, particularly in the last chapter.

Those who would like a generalized but simplified treatment of the subject will find Chapter 7, on the psychology of belief, in Johnson's *The Psychology of Religion* one of his best. He points out that atheists are subject to the same illusory urges that they sometimes ascribe to others. Appropriate sections on belief will be found in Stolz, Wieman, and nearly every volume that fully treats the psychology of religion.

TOPICS FOR DISCUSSION

1. Cite and discuss examples of (a) religion at each of the "four levels of belief"; (b) Sorokin's theory of polarity; (c) the author's theory of faith and skepticism as sources of creativity, as described in the chapter.

2. What influences in addition to those mentioned stimulate the transformation of belief into faith? Of all influences you can think of, which do you believe most potent? Support your ideas by illustration.

3. Can what we have described as "faith" exist apart from belief in God or at least a "higher power"? (Cf. Allport's discussion of "intention"; *The Individual and His Religion*, Chapter 6.) Why does faith, which involves at best only partial knowledge, result in the production of energy?

4. How necessary to religious experience are theological beliefs? Do you agree with James that the intellectual demonstration of religious truths is "absolutely hopeless"? (*Varieties*, p. 445.)

5. How does belief in God differ psychologically from a belief in immortality? Why do you suppose that Leuba found that more scientists believed in immortality than believed in God? Do you agree with Pratt (*The Religious Consciousness*, p. 249) that belief in immortality would be aided by more widespread practice of cremation?

PROBLEMS FOR INVESTIGATION AND RESEARCH

1. Make a systematic biographical study of a religious thinker and evaluate his psychology in the light of the principles described in this chapter.

2. Through your instructor obtain a copy of the Allport-Vernon-Lindzey *Study of Values*. This is a self-scoring questionnaire which will help you to analyze your own values according to Spranger's types. This instrument can also be used in more extensive surveys, though it is inappropriate for use with children or young adolescents. Use it to make a study of the values of some group.

3. Study and psychologically contrast a religious thinker in whom skepticism is prominent and one in whom it is slight, especially with reference to creativity. Can you discover a religious thinker in whom skepticism appears nonexistent?

4. Devise a questionnaire on belief and circulate it among differing groups that you may wish to study for comparative purposes. Calculate by proper statistical procedures the significance of the differences you may discover.

5. An advanced student might like to consult the study mentioned in the footnote at the end of the chapter and apply the same or a similar technique to a group of thinkers, artists, literary men, or other groups of creative persons to test the author's theory about faith, skepticism, and creativity. It would be wise to conduct the survey in whole or in part by interview if that is feasible. The theory might also be applied to an age or a movement, like the Renaissance, the New England period, the Victorian age, the Enlightenment, etc.

6. By methods somewhat similar to those suggested above, an empirical study might be made of psychological influences and processes which stimulate the development of faith from mere belief.

Chapter 11 (Mature Religion)

SUGGESTIONS FOR FURTHER READING

Probably the best brief discussion of the religion of maturity from a psychological viewpoint is to be found in Allport's *The Individual and His Religion*, Chapter 3. Lectures 11–13 in James' *Varieties* give his description of the characteristics of saintliness with the usual copious illustrations, while the following lectures constitute a brilliant essay on the value of saintliness. Chapter 19 of the Wiemans' *Normative Psychology of Religion* treats the appraisal of religious behavior and growth. Chapter 3 of Fromm's *Psychoanalysis and Religion* makes clear his distinction between *authoritarian* and *humanistic* religion, particularly from page 34 forward. The latter sections of Johnson's Chapter 3, "Religious Growth," in his *The Psychology of Religion* deal briefly with the subject of religious maturity, as does Chapter 20 in Stolz. Phillip's *The Choice is Always Ours* is an anthology of profound religious commentary by psychologists and great religious spirits which will supply many profound insights to supplement our chapter. Perhaps Part III, "Outcomes," is most pertinent here.

TOPICS FOR DISCUSSION

1. This chapter has been mainly theoretical, while theory takes on meaning only when applied to the concrete. Illustrate the ten points of mature religion by citing an example of each. Appraise your own religious life on this basis.

2. What characteristics of mature religion can you think of which have been left out of our discussion?

3. Do you think that religion ever really becomes functionally autonomous, or is it always dependent on some other need or drive? Give illustrations.

4. Are there dangers in being too critical in the mature religious life? In other words, is there danger that in certain respects the ripeness of maturity will give way to a less desirable stage? What are these respects and can you illustrate your points?

5. Do you prefer James' or Allport's concept of mature religion? Why? What is your own conception of its most important features?

PROBLEMS FOR INVESTIGATION AND RESEARCH

1. Devise, administer and evaluate a questionnaire or check list to appraise the maturity of religious lives based on our ten standards.

2. By means of the ten standards, evaluate the life of some great religious personality. As much as possible base your appraisal on his actual words or acts. Perhaps an instrument such as that suggested above might be adapted to help you in your study.

Chapter 12 (Mysticism)

SUGGESTIONS FOR FURTHER READING

One of the best comprehensive accounts of the mystics and their methods is Evelyn Underhill's classic, *Mysticism*. Though tending to be somewhat biased in favor of the mystics who were orthodox, Miss Underhill is nevertheless also very scholarly and catholic in her citations of mystics of all traditions. The edition which we have cited is paper-bound and inexpensive. Its bibliography is very full, and particularly valuable for one who wishes to do reading in the first-hand expressions of the mystics. Though not the most distinguished part of the work, another good readily available source is James' two lectures on mysticism in *Varieties*. The last five chapters of Pratt's *The Religious Consciousness* constitute an excellent brief treatise on the subject. A philosopher's approach to mysticism is to be found in Part V of Hocking's *The Meaning of God in Human Experience*. Of special psychological interest are Chapters 26–28. Leuba's *The Psychology of Religious Mysticism* is a full but very critical study of the mystical life. Chapters on mysticism will be found in the Wiemans' *Normative Psychology of Religion* and Stolz' *The Psychology of Religious Living*. Ostow and Scharfstein's *The Need to Believe*, Chapter 7, gives a psychoanalytic view of mysticism. Only the last of these titles is recent. Little work in the study of mysticism seems to have been done by psychologists of late. A reference on Eastern mysticism is Reichelt's *Meditation and Piety in the Far East*. Two opposed estimates of the value of drugs in the production of mystical states will be found in Aldous Huxley's *The Doors of Perception* (pro) and Zaehner's *Mysticism* (con).

TOPICS FOR DISCUSSION

1. How might his participation in a mystical experience affect the *reliability* of a psychologist's account of mysticism? Its *validity*? How could the study of mysticism be made more scientific?

2. Do you agree with the author on the importance of mysticism to religion? If not, why not? If so, how would you suggest that it be stimulated by the churches or otherwise?

3. Why does mysticism today tend to be depreciated and neglected?

4. Discuss further the values and dangers of the mystical life.

5. Since it is largely episodic, how does mysticism fit into a concept of religion as gradual growth? Religious education in general? Conversion?

6. How can we distinguish "true mysticism" from its sentimental counterpart? In religious education or church life, what practical steps can be taken to integrate mystical experience with the total life of the church or the individual?

7. Discuss the problem of whether mysticism is more of an individual or social phenomenon. What light does it throw on the problem of creativity?

PROBLEMS FOR INVESTIGATION AND RESEARCH

1. Where there is sufficient biographical material available and writings of the individual himself, make a thorough study of a particular mystic to discover how far his experience seems to support the generalizations of this chapter. Suitable selections would include Paul, Plotinus, Augustine, Suso, St. John of the Cross, Luther, Teresa, Loyola, Madame Guyon, and George Fox, as well as mystics where the experience was milder or less prominent, such as Pascal, Walt Whitman, John Woolman, Tennyson, Carlyle, Wordsworth, Amiel, Evelyn Underhill, or Rufus Jones.

2. Make a collection of expressions of the mystic consciousness from particular sources—among nature poets, in the Bible, among the New England Transcendentalists, philosophers, theologians, etc.

3. Make a study of the prevalence of mystical experience among ordinary people. While the data might be gathered through a questionnaire, this would be better done through a personal interview in view of the difficulty in making clear to people what a mystical experience is. Or, without labeling them, one might present a number of first-hand descriptions of mystical personal experience of differing types and orders of intensity; then ask people to check those they recognize as being similar to experiences of their own. If this could be carried out satisfactorily, participation in mystical experience might be correlated with other personality variables or measurements.

4. It might be instructive to try to compare the religious experience of presence or "oceanic feeling" with somewhat similar but non-religious states of consciousness in order to identify similarities and differences. Hypnosis and certain drug states are two that have been likened to mystical experience. Leuba reports an experiment where a sense of presence was stimulated through suggestion. (See his *The Psychology of Religious Mysticism*, p. 282 ff.)

Chapter 13 (Prophet, Priest, and Intellectual)

SUGGESTIONS FOR FURTHER READING

It is very difficult to find any up-to-date discussion of the prophet and the priest in current psychological literature. Howells' "A Comparative Study of Those Who Accept as Against Those Who Reject Religious Authority" has some pertinent ideas but the reference is hard to obtain. H. T. Moore's "Innate Factors in Radicalism and Conservatism" presents some general ideas that can be applied to religion. Also a few ideas dealing with radicalism, conservatism, and creativity that could be related to religion will be found in Britt's *Social Psychology of Modern Life*, the chapter "Psychology of Leadership and Invention." Probably the only discussion of prophet and priest by a psychologist is to be found under a 1916 copyright in G. A. Coe's *The Psychology of Religion*. An excellent comparison of the mystic and the prophet will be found in Chapter VI of Heiler's *Prayer*, while his Chapter IV hints at some of the characteristics of the intellectual. In Spranger's *Types of Men* his description of the "Theoretical Man," Part II, Chapter 1, describes the intellectual, though not with a religious reference.

From the point of view of the minister, two good sources, though not very systematic, both written by bishops, are *The Prophetic Ministry*, Chapter IV, by Francis J. McConnell, and *The Prophetic Ministry for Today*, Chapter VII, by C. D. Williams.

For the best insight into this subject the reader as usual is directed to primary sources, of which the Bible is the most available. A comparison of the Book of Leviticus with Amos, Isaiah or Jeremiah will throw light on the priestly as against the prophetic mind. Ecclesiastes is the typical intellectual. St. Paul's Epistles, on the other hand, bear the psychological marks of the prophet, priest, intellectual and mystic combined. Biographical and historical accounts will fill out background. The readable *Goodly Fellowship of the Prophets* by Patterson will do this for the prophet. While the book of Ezra gives the account of a typical priest, Erasmus of Rotterdam was a good example of the religious intellectual. The Gospels and other lives of Jesus show the prophet in conflict with the priest; while the classic struggle of modern times is that of Martin Luther against the Catholic Church. Two readable lives of Luther are those by McGiffert and Bainton, while a Catholic commentary on Luther will be found in Maritan's *Three Reformers*. In all cases historical accounts should be followed up by reading the works of the principals themselves as the essential psychological data.

TOPICS FOR DISCUSSION

1. Discuss some of the areas other than religion in which we find the equivalents of the prophet and the priest operating. What light does this throw on these religious types? What do you think are some of the psychological sources of the differences between the two?

2. Select examples, both from history and the contemporary scene, of individuals predominantly prophets, priests, and mystics, also some who show a combination of characteristics. Cite specific facts to support your choices.

3. Which of these types do you believe most important to the cause of religion in general? To religious institutions? Support your opinions.

4. Discuss several religious thinkers about whom you have enough information to indicate how nearly they approach the religious intellectual as we have described him, and to what degree they are more nearly purely religious. A few suggestions are Paul, Augustine, Aquinas, Calvin, Erasmus, Luther, Pascal, Jonathan Edwards, Jacques Maritain, Barth, Niebuhr, Tillich.

PROBLEMS FOR INVESTIGATION AND RESEARCH

1. Make a biographical study of a mystic, prophet, priest or intellectual, focussing on possible psychological sources of his religious turn of mind and its expression. Indicate from primary sources prophetic, priestly, intellectual or mystical elements.

2. Compare a group of each type for any patterns of sameness or difference between the groups.

3. An advanced student might develop a questionnaire or scale to identify and measure the priestly as opposed to the prophetic type of mind and attitude. One difficulty in constructing this would be that of validation because of stereotypes in people's minds. A man who supposed himself a prophet might really be a priest.

4. By adopting some masculinity-femininity scale, appraise, as objectively as possible, a group of typical prophets and mystics to test the statements in this chapter to the effect that the prophet is more masculine than the mystic.

Chapter 14 (Prayer)

SUGGESTIONS FOR FURTHER READING

Probably the best book on prayer from a descriptive point of view is Friedrich Heiler's copiously illustrated and perceptive *Prayer*. Not quite so scholarly, though often treating psychological issues of a dynamic nature, is *Prayer* by George A. Buttrick. However, neither of the foregoing deals with prayer in a thoroughgoing social-scientific sense. Though they are not particularly up-to-date, two small volumes, both bearing the title *The Psychology of Prayer*, one by Anna Louise Strong and the other by Karl Stolz, will supply the reader with much useful information.

Of chapters on prayer in full-length psychologies of religion, perhaps the best is "Prayer and Private Worship," to be found in Pratt's *The Religious Consciousness*. Chapter 5 in Johnson's *The Psychology of Religion*, "Prayer and Devotion," is worth reading. In his *An Introduction to the Psychology of Religion* Thouless makes an interesting attempt in Chapter 12 to explain the mechanisms of prayer in terms of suggestion. Parker and Dare's *Prayer Can Change Your Life* is an interesting book on prayer therapy of a healthy-minded, popular nature.

TOPICS FOR DISCUSSION

1. Suggest some appropriate problems for experiment in the area of prayer. How should these experiments be set up?

2. Identify and discuss some well-known prayers that are also poems, and some poems that in essential spirit are prayers. What information can you derive from this as to the psychological nature of prayer?

3. Analyze your own prayers for what they tell you of your interests and motives. Do public prayers have any comparable significance in this way? If so, how?

4. List the prayers utilized in 2 above under the classifications suggested in this chapter.

5. Since the petitionary form of prayer is so often magical and self-centered, do you think that some other form should be taught to children? Why or why not? If so, what other form?

6. Can prayer be taught? In what sense? Should its subjective or objective form be emphasized?

PROBLEMS FOR INVESTIGATION AND RESEARCH

1. Prepare and administer a questionnaire on prayer that will indicate what prayers disclose of people's motives and interests.

2. Devise an investigation to test whether prayer has any real therapeutic value, as suggested in this chapter. If it has, people who pray might be expected to be better adjusted than a control group who do not. However, it would be wise in such an investigation to try to differentiate prayers of a primary, secondary, and tertiary variety; also to consider the implications of the statement that the aim of the highest type of religion is not personality adjustment.

3. Compile a collection of the prayers of well-known historical personages. Evaluate these prayers for the light they throw on the personalities of their authors and the extent to which they meet the criteria for mature religion. If enough prayers of one person were available, this type of study might have biographical value.

Chapter 15 (Worship)

SUGGESTIONS FOR FURTHER READING

To our knowledge there has been little good empirical study of worship or psychological discussion based thereon. Most psychological accounts, like our own, tend to be descriptive and speculative. Among the best of these are chapters 12 to 15 in Pratt's *The Religious Consciousness*, especially the chapter "Objective and Subjective Worship." A similar chapter is to be found in W. I. Sperry's *Reality in Worship*, which also contains other thought-provoking matter on worship, though it is not closely organized. Heiler's *The Spirit of Worship* discusses the manifestation of worship in differing Christian traditions, while Evelyn Underhill's *Worship* is a discussion of the subject by a convinced and practicing mystic. Stolz in Chapter 17 of his book does this much more briefly. Part 4 of Richard Cabot's *What Men Live By* is a positive discussion of worship, while Chapter 12 of Thouless' *An Introduction to the Psychology of Religion* is more critical. P. E. Johnson makes use of concrete illustration in the chapter "Worship" in his *The Psychology of Religion*. Hocking is more difficult but also more profound in his discussion "Worship and the Mystics" in Part 5 of *The Meaning of God in Human Experience*.

TOPICS FOR DISCUSSION

1. There is much that we have omitted in our brief comments on worship. Discuss the pros and cons of objective vs. subjective worship; liturgical vs. non-liturgical worship; public vs. private worship.

2. What do you think is the most essential aspect of worship? How important is the mystical element? Is this best stimulated through liturgy, as in Catholic worship, or non-liturgy, as in the Quaker meeting?

3. Is worship possible without prayer? If so, give instances.

PROBLEMS FOR INVESTIGATION AND RESEARCH

1. Make a historical study of one or more religious movements to find support or refutation for the theses advanced in the chapter to the effect that ritual in public services of worship tend to increase as zeal and spontaneity decrease.

2. Through questionnaire or interview try to establish what motives people consider to be behind their acts of worship. You also might try to find what they consider their acts of worship, and under what conditions they feel they worship best. Categories established by such means, such as those preferring liturgy as opposed to those preferring non-liturgy, or those adhering to a young religious movement as opposed to those belonging to more established churches, might be compared as to the strength of their religious values as measured by an instrument such as the Allport-Vernon-Lindzey *Study of Values*. Also ratings, or other measures of behavior, might be correlated with motives or types of worship. In this way types of worship might be evaluated for their capacity to evoke mystical experience. On the other hand it may be that forms of worship are of little significance as indicators of mature religious living. Perhaps your study might seek to test this possibility and perhaps to establish what is *more* significant.

3. Construct a service of worship for a particular age group and justify each factor psychologically.

Chapter 16 (The Abnormal)

SUGGESTIONS FOR FURTHER READING

The first chapter of James' *Varieties* is a stimulating essay on the relationship of religion and the abnormal. No one interested in the subject should miss reading Boisen's *The Exploration of the Inner World*. The Introduction tells of Boisen's personal experience. Chapter 5 discusses the dynamics of mental disease and its relationship to religion, while Chapters 2 and 3 discuss various religious figures who suffered from nervous instability, with special attention to George Fox. The *Journal* of George Fox is an excellent case document preferably to be read in its entirety, or in an abridgement such as that edited by Rufus Jones. Since Carlyle was not primarily a religious genius, we have not discussed him in the chapter, yet in many ways his case will illustrate our generalizations. See Book II of *Sartor Resartus*.

Readers not familiar with the symptoms of mental disease should read the popular *The Human Mind* by Menninger, or one of the standard texts in abnormal psychology, such as those by Maslow and Mittlemann, R. W. White, Page, or Taylor.

TOPICS FOR DISCUSSION

1. Is it your observation that religious people tend to be unbalanced? Is there a distinction between the ordinary religious person and the religious genius? Discuss.

2. When is belief in God real, and when is it an illusion? Can you develop more precise psychological concepts than those suggested in the chapter for distinguishing between the two situations? From your knowledge of theology would you say that such a distinction would be of any help to a theologian?

3. What types of religious teachings would you expect to be helpful and what types harmful for the insane? How would you handle a person who claimed to be God or the Son of God? Under what conditions may harm be done by unbalanced religious leaders? Give concrete examples.

PROBLEMS FOR INVESTIGATION AND RESEARCH

1. By some objective method of selection—perhaps by taking all the religious teachers to whom a page or more is devoted in an encyclopedia —determine the proportion who show signs of mental unbalance.

2. With the generalizations of this chapter in mind, make a detailed case study of another religious genius, pointing out both similarities to, and differences from, the personalities we have discussed.

3. After reading Boisen's *The Exploration of the Inner World*, observe any insane people to whom you have access to find out whether his theories seem to be confirmed. Obviously this project would be only for advanced students under adequate guidance, and even then it would probably have to grow out of some regular work or study at a mental hospital.

Chapter 17 (Psychotherapy)

SUGGESTIONS FOR FURTHER READING

For reading in this general field, Allport's *The Individual and His Religion,* Chapter 4, is an intelligent discussion. Weatherhead's *Psychology, Religion and Healing* is a compendious work on the subject. Suttie's *The Origins of Love and Hate* is a good corrective to Freud's overemphases. Perhaps Chapters 10 and 12 are most pertinent to our present chapter if one does not have time to read the whole work. The papers edited by Werner Wolff under the title *Psychiatry and Religion* take up the subject and related fields from varying points of view.

Three books which approach psychotherapy from a theological standpoint are Paul Tillich's *The Courage to Be,* David Roberts' *Psychotherapy and a Christian View of Man,* and Albert Outler's *Psychotherapy and the Christian Message.* Those interested in the non-directive approach to counseling will find it discussed in Carl Rogers' *Client-Centered Therapy.* An excellent adaptation of this general technique to pastoral counseling will be found in Seward Hiltner's *Pastoral Counseling* and, more briefly, *The Counselor in Counseling.* Chapter 16 of Shaffer and Shoben's *The Psychology of Adjustment* is an excellent brief treatment of various schools of psychotherapy.

In order as much as possible to develop his own thinking about these problems as well as to become clearer on points made in the chapter, the reader should study as many case examples as he can lay his hands on. The chapter itself gives leads to follow up. In addition there is the abridged record of a series of interviews with a pastoral counselor involving religious commitment as related to certain emotional conflicts in Johnson's *The Psychology of Religion,* Chapter 5. Snyder's *Casebook of Non-Directive Counseling* presents very fully secular interviews that can be used for comparison. "The Case of Mrs. Madison" involves issues that might easily have been approached through religious counseling. Films depicting non-directive therapy may be secured through the Psychological Cinema Register, State College, Pa.

TOPICS FOR DISCUSSION

1. Discuss similarities and differences between psychotherapy and religion with respect to changing personality. Consider aims, methods, and relationship between individual and counselor.

2. Discuss the place and importance of the counselor in personality

change after reviewing some cases of religious growth (like Carlyle's or Boisen's) where no counselor or pastor seemed instrumental. How do you distinguish between the two types of cases psychologically?

3. Do you agree that concepts of proper relationship with a counselor help to form theological ideas? To what degree and in what way? Have your theological beliefs been modified at all as the result of this study?

4. What does the pastor need to know about psychotherapy, and what does the psychotherapist need to know about religion? Do you think the two functions can be kept separate? Explain.

PROBLEMS FOR INVESTIGATION AND RESEARCH

1. Study carefully the "Case of Mrs. Oak" in Rogers and Dymond's *Psychotherapy and Personality Change*. Then study the documents describing the mystical experience of one of the great mystics, preferably a woman, like Teresa or Madame Guyon. Note the similarities and differences. Then conclude whether or not what Mrs. Oak was talking about was a true mystical experience.

2. Read some cases of personality change such as are found in Snyder's book mentioned above, or *A Casebook of Counseling*, by Callis, Polmantier, and Roeber, to determine to what degree the different cases might be said to be religious, or to have religious implications. Similarly read some cases of religious conversion, as in my *The Oxford Group* or Carlyle's *Sartor Resartus* to see in what way the change could be said to be therapeutic. Also, read cases in *Alcoholics Anonymous* to determine whether you feel they should be termed primarily examples of religious conversion or psychotherapeutic change.

3. Interview several psychotherapists to discover what they feel about the place of religion in psychotherapy. Have ready specific questions that you would like to ask them. Similarly interview several pastors as to their views of psychotherapy. Write up your conclusions.

4. Advanced students may wish to set up a project for assessing personality change in pastoral counseling. Though it is unlikely that any such study could be as extensive, ideas can be secured by reading of the project for assessing cases of non-directive therapy carried through at the University of Chicago and reported in Rogers and Dymond, referred to above.

5. It has been said that because of their own experience with inner tensions there is higher than normal proportion of neurotics, those who have had actual breakdowns, and people with physical handicaps among the ranks of psychologists. This statement has also been made of religion on the ground that such people find comfort and support there. There

is little exact scientific information about this. Through a questionnaire offering appropriate anonymity sample a group of psychologists, such as members of the American Psychological Association, and a similar group from religion, for example, members of the National Association of Biblical Instructors, might be tested to see how much truth there is in these ideas. It would be well to have a control or comparison group to which such people would probably not be attracted.

Chapter 18 (Social Factors)

SUGGESTIONS FOR FURTHER READING

A good brief discussion of the social psychology of the church is to be found in Britt's *Social Psychology of Modern Life*, Chapter 18. H. R. Niebuhr's *The Social Sources of Denominationalism* is scholarly and interesting. *The Dynamics of a City Church*, by the distinguished Jesuit sociologist, J. H. Fichter, is a book that has caused controversy among Catholics. The following three titles are all very readable and report the results of some of the most thorough empirical studies in the combined fields of psychology and sociology of recent times. Chapters mentioned are the most pertinent to religion: Havighurst and Taba, *Adolescent Character and Personality*, Chapter 6; Hollingshead, *Elmtown's Youth*, Chapter 10; W. Lloyd Warner, *Democracy in Jonesville*, Chapters 10 and 11. The latter describes the Norwegian Lutherans as a sect and ethnic group. Chapter 6 of Grensted's *The Psychology of Religion* on "Corporate Religion" takes up some social-psychological ideas. Elizabeth K. Nottingham has written an excellent brief study for the paper-back Doubleday Short Studies in Sociology entitled *Religion and Society*. Chapters 6 and 7 are most pertinent to our discussion.

Students who wish to go more thoroughly into the sociology of religion should not neglect the foreign language works of Durkheim, Max Weber, and Troeltsch, the most important of which are available in translation. The Harvard sociologist, Talcott Parsons, has commented on these in *The Structure of Social Action*, as has Tawney in *Religion and the Rise of Capitalism*, where Weber's theories are criticized and elaborated. This distinguished essay has been reprinted as a Mentor Book. On a large canvas are P. A. Sorokin's stimulating *The Crisis of Our Age* and Arnold Toynbee's monumental *A Study of History*. Will Herberg's *Protestant-Catholic-Jew* is a stimulating essay on American religious sociology, while J. Milton Yinger's *Religion, Society, and the Individual* is a recent title. Chapter 3 of the latter would be pertinent to the present discussion.

Part 4 of Hackman, Kegley, and Nikander's *Religion in Modern Life* deals with the expression of religion in collective living.

TOPICS FOR DISCUSSION

1. Does your own experience support the statement that social class status plays a larger part in determining conduct than does the fact of church membership? With what facts or observations can you support your position? Can you also supply psychological reasoning to support your views?

2. Do you believe that money plays a part in influencing the attitudes of church people and church policies? What evidence do you have? Do you agree with the generalization that the wealthier members of a church tend to be more influential than poorer ones? If so, how do you explain this psychologically? Can you cite some ways in which the church or religion has had a desirable effect on business?

3. Discuss the pros and cons of denominationalism and competition among churches.

4. Give examples of churches that express ethnic or nationalistic interests. Show just how this is so by concrete illustration. Do national interests condition services or ideas in your own church in any way? Illustrate. To what extent do you think this distorts essential religious ideas?

5. Discuss the value of denominations and also that of the religious institution in general. Do you think that the need for conformity plays as large a part in religion as the chapter suggests? Think of examples to support your views.

6. Can you justify tax exemption for churches on the ground of their positive contribution to society? Can you think of ways in which religion influences social behavior other than those described in the chapter? Give examples of sects and their influences on their members' behavior.

7. Do you believe that conservatives "water down" their faith more than do liberals? Discuss.

8. Discuss once again Topic 6 under the Study Aids for Chapter 1 on page 438. Has your point of view changed at all since you started your reading?

PROBLEMS FOR INVESTIGATION AND RESEARCH

1. Make a study of empirical investigations of the social effects of religion. You can make a start by following up some of the references mentioned in this chapter. Also some of the notations in the Index of Harry

Elmer Barnes' *Social Institutions* under "religion" may be of help. Evaluate these and draw your own conclusions.

2. Check one of these investigations by devising an investigation of your own. For example, you might compare public and private beliefs of church members, or try to measure the behavior of individuals against their church activity.

3. Make a study of the social services offered by churches and try to determine to what extent these are the expression of the activity of sects.

NAME INDEX

Abraham, 268
Adam, 104
Adams, J. L., 404
Addison, J., 318
Aesop, 145
Agag, 360
Ahab, 296
Akiba, 224
Alacoque, M., 224, 285
Al-Ghazzali, 264
Allport, G. W., 11, 20, 21, 26, 31–34, 35, 50, 77, 78–79, 87, 88, 99, 101, 103, 114, 123, 137, 138, 140, 141–146, 189, 201, 219–220, 222, 225, 233, 244–247, 248, 249–251, 252, 253, 254, 271, 287, 304, 307, 440, 441, 443, 444, 446, 452, 453, 454, 455, 462, 464
Ames, E. S., 9, 20
Amiel, 449, 457
Amos, 101, 235, 295, 296, 298, 337–338, 458
Andrews, C., 265
Angela of Foligno, 280, 282, 287
Anonymous, 232
Aquinas, T., 58, 264, 303, 459
Ardigo, R., 201, 211
Aristotle, 63
Augustine, St., 6, 33, 46, 71, 80, 112, 148–149, 150, 151, 153, 177, 190, 194, 202, 204, 214, 217, 268, 271, 279, 303, 313, 317, 447, 457, 459

Bainton, R., 458
Barkley, K. L., 122
Barnes, H. E., 468
Barnett, L., 38, 220
Barth, K., 459
Begbie, H., 15, 199

Bell, H. M., 130
Bell, J., 48
Benedict, R., 91
Bennett, J. C., 168
Bergman, P., 367
Bernard, St., 264, 289
Bernreuter, 452
Binet, 113
Blake, W., 269, 279
Boehme, J., 264
Boisen, A. T., 13–14, 177–178, 182, 201, 333, 346–349, 350, 352, 359, 361, 362, 363, 365, 377, 415, 441, 449, 462, 463, 465, 466
Bourignan, A., 275, 279
Braden, C. S., 79, 83
Brand, H., 31, 440
Breckinridge, M. E., 90
Britt, S. H., 74, 392, 398, 458, 466
Browne, L., 220
Browning, R., 152, 155, 171, 449
Buchman, F. N. D., 161, 194, 206, 212, 231, 376
Buddha, 6, 214, 296, 358
Bunyan, J., 150–151, 153, 175, 201, 217, 276, 343, 415, 447, 449
Burnham, W. H., 7
Burns, 157
Buros, O., 40
Bushnell, H., 163–164, 172, 450
Buttrick, G. A., 309, 460
Byron, 157

Cabot, R. C., 15, 314, 328, 329, 461
Callis, R., 465
Calvin, J., 459
Cannon, W. B., 115

473

SUBJECT INDEX

479